WARD'S
SOCCERPEDIA

WARD'S
SOCCERPEDIA

ANDREW WARD

ROBSON
BOOKS

First published in the United Kingdom in 2006 by
Robson Books
151 Freston Road
London
W10 6TH

An imprint of Anova Books Company Ltd

ISBN 1 86105 983 3

A CIP catalogue record for this book is available from the British Library.

10 9 8 7 6 5 4 3 2 1

Typeset by SX Composing DTP, Rayleigh, Essex
Printed and bound by MPG Books Ltd, Bodmin, Cornwall

This book can be ordered direct from the publisher.
Contact the marketing department, but try your bookshop first.

www.anovabooks.com

In memory of Doris Walters (née Shenton) (1903–96)
A loyal football supporter from childhood to her late eighties

SOURCES AND ACKNOWLEDGMENTS

My first source was my father, Tim Ward, who managed four football clubs during my schooldays. He respected and befriended top-class referees, but he also had the manager's ability to blame. One time, after a 5–0 defeat at Bristol City, my father felt that the referee had erred in starting the game, because one of his players was still juggling a practice ball behind the goal when Bristol City scored after fifteen seconds. I often think about that story in those moments before a match starts; the players line up, the excitement is palpable, and the referee calmly counts the players and checks that the goalkeepers and assistant referees are ready.

As a teenage footballer I attracted a few strange stories in the 1960s. I played in a Sunday Cup semi-final that was abandoned when a dismissed opponent refused to leave the field. I was an early substitute in the Northern League, wondering if I could just run on the pitch when my team-mate was injured. And I once ran down the wing at Aspatria to find a Belted Galloway cow in my path.

When I trained as a referee in the 1970s, I realised how little I really knew of the laws. I had to learn quickly. In one game there were three dogs on the pitch, in another both teams wore white socks, and when writing reports I learned how to spell words like feud, gesticulation and infringement.

Later, as a writer, collecting stories for books like *Football's Strangest Matches,* I realised the need for a multi-purpose book on football's laws. I had been frustrated by the existing sources. Information was not easy to access, there were few stories from actual games, and there was no popular account of the evolution of the laws. I collected newspaper cuttings for twenty years and assigned material to an A to Z framework. It started as a small project but I had underestimated the game's legal sophistication.

Several sources helped me enormously. One was Peter Seddon's *A Football Compendium* (1995), which provided many more pathways. The writings of William Pickford, N L Jackson, E W Lovick, Jimmy Catton, and Geoffrey Green were important for the early years, while Sir Stanley Rous and Donald Ford's book, *A History of the Laws of Association Football* (1974), was seminal to my work, and Julian Carosi's refereeing website (www.corshamref.net) is an incredible resource. Also valuable were the autobiographies of referees, and books by refereeing technicians such as David Ager, John Baker, David

Elleray, Robert Evans & Edward Bellion, and Stanley Lover.

Special thanks go to a number of people who helped in major ways: David Barber, Julian Carosi, John Harding, Danny Hoyle, David Kynaston, Michael Morton, Anton Rippon, Rob Wilkinson, and John Williams. Thanks also to Philip Beetham, Claire Corbett, Simon Crompton, Rick Darlington, David Davies, Frank Garrick, Brian Gearing, Pam Geggus, Eric Hayes, Julie Highmore, Graham Kelly, Ann Lee, Brian Levison, Kevin McCarra, Callum May, Tim Newburn, Al Partington, Jill Peay, Philip Rhodes, Fran Shall, Dave Swanson, and Steve Way. I would also like to thank my previous co-authors – Ian Alister, Tim Newburn, Anton Rippon, Geron Swann, Rogan Taylor and John Williams – who have allowed me unlimited access to oral-history material we collected together, and Simone Hoogendoorn, who conducted the interview with Rene van der Kerkhof (in 1990). Finally, extra-special thanks to Alan Jenkins for his continuing interest in this project, and to Alan and his wife Barbara for their help, patience and support during and after my year in a wheelchair.

INTRODUCTION

It is five past ten on a Sunday morning. Church services have just begun, club cyclists are on the road, and the players of Brotherhood Works and Ebeneezars are five minutes into their cup tie. Three players converge on the ball and send it over the touchline.

'Our ball,' a dozen players shout simultaneously. They are the alternative Sunday choir.

One assistant referee is smoking a cigarette while jogging along the touchline and the other is a substitute. There are no fourth officials here, no marked technical areas, and no cameras. The 1998 FIFA World Cup™ Final may have been watched on television by two billion people, but in truth almost all football matches are as low-key as this one, where the players outnumber the witnesses.

The pitch is bordered by a mini-soccer field, disused tennis courts and two dilapidated cricket sightscreens, but the line markings are instantly recognisable. This universal layout of rectangles, circle, arcs and spots is an artwork of geometric beauty and intense personal meaning. Gavin, scorer of the first goal after fifteen minutes, could draw a diagram and mark the spot where he headed in a corner-kick to score for Ebeneezars.

'Ref, Ref, keep an eye on ten, please!' shouts one player.

'Thank you, player, get on with the game,' the referee replies.

Referees are a symbol of neutrality. They are protected in the laws by phrases explaining that they are the sole judge on matters of fact and opinion. Matches are replayed only in rare circumstances where a technical error (an error in law) can be proven. The players have to accept a referee's judgment.

By now this referee knows the players by name. They have been introduced to him by their team-mates.

'Well done, Gupper.'

'Unlucky, Ad.'

'Go, Wardy, go!'

The ball disappears over the touchline again.

'Our ball.'

The throw-in is taken, but the whistle goes.

'Both feet on the floor when you release the ball, please,' says the referee, the agent of the lawmakers.

Football has arguably the most pervasive and most used legal system in the world. The laws were first developed in Britain, and this is still recognised in the composition of the International Football Association Board (IFAB), the game's ultimate rule-making body. IFAB currently has eight representatives – one from each of the four United Kingdom countries and four from the Fédération Internationale de Football Association (FIFA), the organisation that oversees more than 200 national football associations. IFAB meets once a year to make subtle changes to the laws. These changes impact throughout the world.

The Brotherhood Works assistant referee holds up his flag and the referee blows for offside.

'Never, Ref, never!' shouts an Ebeneezars defender from fifty yards away.

'How can you see from there, Gobby?' an opponent shouts back.

Play restarts but soon stops again for a foul.

'I went for the ball, Ref,' pleads the offending player, as the referee comes over to talk to him.

The lawmakers of IFAB try to maximise players' safety while recognising the physical nature of the game. The safety-first principle is one of many themes underlying the laws. Goalposts must be safe, and footwear should conform to regulations. Free-kicks are given if a player challenges for the ball in a manner considered by the referee to be careless, reckless or with excessive force. Cautions are issued for reckless challenges, and players are sent off for using excessive force.

Grey-haired Eddie equalises for Brotherhood Works, following up when the goalkeeper drops the ball. The teams look well matched.

'Face up, Yellow, come on.'

'Step it up a bit.'

'Make these chances count.'

'Our ball.'

Both sides have appealed but the referee gives a corner-kick. Stewy takes it and then puts Brotherhood Works 2–1 up when the ball is headed back to him.

'Quality, Stewy.'

The referee gives two blasts of his whistle to signal half-time. Ebeneezars stay on the pitch, and Brotherhood Works go to the dressing-room. When play restarts, Ebeneezars equalise immediately. Then, while Brotherhood Works players wait to take the kick-off, an opponent stops to tie his bootlace at the edge of their penalty area.

'Player, do that in your own half, please,' says the referee.

'What if he trips up coming back?' yells a player, and everyone laughs.

The laws must make the game enjoyable for players (especially at the grass-roots level) and entertaining for spectators (particularly at professional matches). The game also needs to satisfy match officials and coaches. Football should be a fast and flowing game that commands attention. This is the spirit of the advantage clause, the backpass law, quick free-kicks, and an offside law that increasingly favours attackers. The amusement takes all forms. Football is a lifelong interest, a way to stay fit, a collection of anecdotes, a bunch of mates and characters, and a spirit of camaraderie and belonging.

An hour gone and two quick goals have put Ebeneezars 4–2 ahead. But now some frustration comes in. A late tackle is followed by a retaliatory foul. Now everybody is a commentator:

'Give one studs-up and you've got to give all studs-up.'

'Put your finger down, mate, get on with your football.'

'That was a hospital ball.'

A football match can be as raw and emotive as a contested divorce. In this volatile arena, where participants are preoccupied with victory and success, the game is held together by its laws. Referees can punish players whose emotional outbursts may threaten the equilibrium of the game.

'That ball's too soft, Ref,' shouts an Ebeneezars player. 'Use the other one.'

'The other one's too hard,' complains an opponent.

The lawgivers have anticipated possible events, and guidelines have been established. Everybody must be treated fairly. There are approved standards for equipment, and a set code for dealing with misconduct cases.

Brotherhood Works make a couple of substitutions, and Stewy hits the crossbar with a long-range shot. Three more excellent chances are missed. Ebeneezars bring on two fresh defenders.

'Keep going,' they tell each other. 'We've won nothing yet.'

An appeal for a penalty to Ebeneezars is turned down, and one of their players is cautioned for dissent. It is the first caution of the match, after seventy minutes.

One of football's inherent problems is that a match result can be swung by a penalty-kick, a sending-off, or a 'goal' disallowed. Tempers flare around these so-called 'big decisions'. In other games, like snooker and bowls, the referee is largely absent, called upon occasionally to spot a ball or make a measurement. At the other extreme from football, ultimate frisbee is a competitive sport which is self-refereed. The challenge for the lawmakers is to give referees enough power but not too much.

Ebeneezars score again, making the score 5–2, but Eddie (Brotherhood Works) heads against the crossbar from three yards out. The assistant referees have changed. One is a substituted player, the other is the Ebeneezars manager.

'Shall we go to four at the back?' the manager shouts, while trying to keep up with play. 'Well done, Jacko.'

'Well done, Jacko,' echoes a player. 'You're running midfield. You're like that Ukulele.'

'Who?' Jacko asks.

'Macca-ukulele.'

Ebeneezars score a late goal. The referee gives three long blasts of his whistle and it's all over at 6–2.

'Well played both teams,' says the referee.

'Thanks, Ref.'

'Thanks for the game.'

Yes, indeed. Association football is a *game*, and a game is defined by its rules. That is the focus of this book. While acknowledging that football has spawned businesses, provided careers, affected family lives, and dominated television screens, my subject matter here is *football the game*, more specifically the on-field activities of the eleven-a-side game. (I have excluded popular small-sided games such as futsal, mini-soccer, beach soccer, and disability football.) I have used many examples from the professional game, examples that may resonate with readers, but we must remember that football teams include the likes of Brotherhood Works and Ebeneezars from the Peterborough Sunday Morning League.

Football, like all games, has certain key components. Players try to bring about a specific outcome (such as a goal). They do this by complying with restrictive rules that prohibit more efficient means in favour of less efficient means. Football would not survive if a club's kit manager invented a smart boot that could electronically chip the ball past a goalkeeper at 200mph.

According to Bernard Suits, a Canadian philosopher, a game is the voluntary attempt to overcome unnecessary obstacles. Suits also invented the term 'lusory attitude' to refer to another essential component of a game – players' acceptance of the rules. This lusory attitude is part of the spirit of association football.

Each item in the laws has been etched out through precedent, incident and forethought. It is a journey that has lasted through 150 years of organised football. The spirit of the game is the preservation of past laws that work and the introduction of new laws that have looked good in experiments. The laws of soccer are constantly under review, so people need to be aware of changes. The only definitive source is *The Laws of Association Football*, published annually by FIFA. What follows in this book is my personal interpretation of the laws.

NOTE TO THE READER

The laws of association football have been developed by a number of key organisations, in particular the International Football Association Board (IFAB), the Fédération Internationale de Football Association (FIFA), and the four British national associations. Decisions by these organisations are often referred to in this Soccerpedia (see below).

Berkshire & Buckinghamshire FA referred the matter to a higher authority, and it was decided there was no objection providing the player with a wooden leg did not play in a manner dangerous to his opponents (FA 1907).

The British Football Associations have sometimes made key decisions, especially in the years before FIFA joined IFAB (1913).

Goalkeepers could handle headed backpasses and chested backpasses but players were not allowed to get around the new law by flicking the ball up with their feet and heading it back (1992), even if the goalkeeper didn't handle the ball (IFAB 1993). Initially, goalkeepers could handle a team-mate's throw-in, but this was later outlawed (1997).

An IFAB decision on how to interpret an existing written statement in the laws.

A change in the written statement of The Laws of Association Football, decided at the annual meeting of the International Football Association Board (IFAB).

The month and year of a pertinent incident. Competition details are omitted unless specifically relevant.

Thomas Grice of Cheshire was killed when he fell during a game and his belt buckle pierced his stomach (April 1897). Belts with heavy buckles were eventually outlawed (FIFA Referees' Committee 1934).

The FIFA Referees' Committee answers queries raised by individual national associations.

The second half of a Liverpool–Tottenham Hotspur game started short of one linesman (January 1954). This sort of embarrassment is why referees look towards both assistants before a place-kick.

Assistant referees were known as linesmen until 1996. The old term has been used to describe pre-1996 incidents.

Imperial measurements throughout the book have been retained as they form the basis for pitch measurements. Metric measurements were added later (1956).

Aa

ABANDONED MATCH *See* TERMINATING THE GAME

ABUSIVE LANGUAGE

A referee in the West Kent League once walked off the pitch in the middle of a match because he had had enough of players' moans, and a professional match in Holland was abandoned after eighty minutes because of abusive chanting by spectators (October 2004). There is a limit to what referees can take.

Abusive language is an appropriate first entry in this book because abuse is one of the major issues in football. There is a real problem retaining newly qualified referees, and one reason is that novices are constantly abused by players, coaches and spectators. As one administrator said, 'Who wants to get up early on a Sunday morning for ninety minutes of abuse?'

A sending-off offence for 'foul or abusive language' was introduced in 1927. In 1997, when the laws were rewritten into plain English with a clearer structure, the equivalent sending-off offence became 'offensive, insulting or abusive language'. Such gestures were also outlawed in 2000.

It is hard to set any fixed rules about specific phrases that will result in a sending-off. It is also difficult to distinguish between what is abusive, what is offensive, and what is insulting, but it doesn't really matter because any of these three is worthy of a sending-off.

Top-class referees are generally thick-skinned, confident and capable of handling abuse. They have heard it all before. They have been insulted about their sex life and often compared with Mr Segar Bastard, who refereed the 1878 FA Cup Final.

Inexperienced referees are more vulnerable to abuse, and consequently are more likely to take action, especially as a player's comment is more likely to be overheard on the sidelines and not lost in the roar of the crowd. One local football association found that nearly 16 per cent of sendings-off in the 2004–05 season were for abusing match officials. The percentage is lower in the professional game.

'Players who watch TV, and watch match officials have abuse hurled at them with very little action taken, are continuing this trend into local games, even parks pitches,' said one experienced referee, quoted in *The 'Lords of Truth'* by John Williams (1995). 'They do not understand why they are cautioned or dismissed on a Sunday morning when a player "got away with it" on a Saturday night.'

Abusive language is technically a sending-off offence regardless of who the victims are – referees, players, physiotherapists, officials, spectators, photographers, stewards, or nearby residents. Players invite trouble if they are abusive towards *anyone*. So do assistant referees and people in the technical area, who are also under the referee's control.

Abusive spectators can also be a problem. The Football Offences Act 1991 made indecent or racialist chanting an offence in England, but touchline parents can disrupt youth games. The Witney & District Youth League wanted to introduce a new rule to send off children if their parents were abusive on the sidelines (2005). This was rejected by the FA as impractical and contrary to the spirit of the game.

In a Staffordshire Senior Cup match in the 1930s, the referee stopped play while he had a word with a nearby abusive spectator.

'I've been watching you for some time,' the referee said.

'I can see you haven't been watching the game,' the spectator replied.

Abusive language became a separate sending-off offence in 1967, having first been classified under violent conduct (1927). In practice, all referees will have their own cut-off point. They will take into account a number of factors other than the actual words, for example whether they are sure about what has been said and who it has been said to, the context of the match, whether the player has been previously warned, whether spectators or children have heard, whether the abuser runs towards the person who is the object of the abuse, the tone and loudness of the abuser's voice, whether it is a racial or homophobic comment, and whether the facial expression conveys anger or threat rather than frustration or humour. When Rattin (Argentina) was sent off against England, it was said to be the look on the player's face that convinced the referee (July 1966). The louder, the angrier and the more repetitive, the more likely a sending-off will result.

Calling a referee a cheat will usually warrant a sending-off because referees value their neutrality above all except their physical safety. A player in the Notts Alliance Senior Division said, 'There's no need to cheat, lino,' and the referee produced the red card immediately. Calling a referee 'a coward' may provoke a referee into a brave sending-off decision, and another c-word is particularly likely to result in a dismissal.

Some top-level referees may be strong enough to let a 'cheat' reference pass if they are absolutely certain that it is not meant. When Tony Adams (Arsenal) said 'You cheat' to a referee at Millwall, the official thought seriously about sending him off, but settled for a lengthy conversation (February 1989). But only a confident and experienced referee can bypass such abuse.

So much depends on the circumstances. Let's start with a common insult: 'You must be blind, Referee.'

That is probably acceptable if it is muttered and the player immediately gets on with the game.

Now consider the same phrase with a swearword in front of 'blind' and 'referee' replaced with an insult: 'You must be f*****g blind, you b*****d.'

Now the player risks a sending-off. Add a loud voice, a red face, bulging eyes, and steps towards the referee, and now the player is demanding to be sent off.

Lee Todd (Cross Farm Park Celtic) was sent off after two seconds of a Taunton Sunday League game against East Reach Wanderers (2003–04). The referee blew his whistle to start the game, Todd said, 'F*** me, that was loud,' and off he went.

One top-class referee, Arthur Dimond, explained his criteria on swearing in an interview with the *Guardian* (November 1971):

> I work in a factory. How much bad language do you think I can take? They haven't invented the word that would shock me. Referees don't object to swearing. What they must clamp down on is direct face-to-face personal abuse, because then it is their authority that is being challenged. No referee worth tuppence ever gets upset over casual bad language. They simply try not to hear. But if the player runs to a referee and makes a showdown of it, well there can only be one winner, can't there? Anybody who gets sent off for swearing has asked for trouble. I sent one man off for swearing. In my first game in amateur football, I gave a bad decision and he called me a blanking idiot. I have never got caught like that again. If you give players a chance, more often than not they'll apologise for an outburst. I'd like a quid for every time a player shuffled up to me at half-time or at the end and muttered, 'Sorry for what I said, Ref.'

Referees have been known to swear back. Stuart Dougal was fined £200 and severely censured by the Scottish FA after BBC cameras caught him swearing at Christian Nerlinger (Rangers) during a match against Partick Thistle (March 2004).

Swearing comes naturally to many footballers but there are campaigns to reduce it. Some television viewers were shocked when Wayne Rooney (Manchester United) reportedly swore more than a hundred times at the referee during a match against Arsenal (February 2005), while Crawley Town manager Francis Vines was arrested and cautioned by the police for using threatening language at Woking (February 2005). If referees (or others) find the language offensive, then it is offensive.

In February 1998, parish councillors in Woodmancote, Gloucestershire, investigated residents' complaints about the swearing that came from a village football field. Residents could hear the language while working in their gardens or sitting in conservatories.

Sometimes the abuse infiltrates a referee's personal life. Urs Meier received more than 16,000 e-mails, including death threats, after handling a Portugal–England match (June 2004), and Anders Frisk received abusive e-mails after a Barcelona–Chelsea match (March 2005). Both men, at the very top of their profession, retired prematurely from refereeing. David Elleray installed a panic button at his home after receiving death threats and abusive phone calls from Manchester United supporters. He chose not to referee a game at Old Trafford for nearly two years.

Abuse has deep roots. It may stem from ignorance of the laws, lack of respect for authority, sheer frustration, a verbally toxic home life, or poor role models. If verbal abuse is tolerated in a coach or a captain, then others may think that abuse is acceptable and a sign of strength. Some youth-league referees say that parents and coaches are more abusive than players until the players turn fourteen or fifteen. The FA trains 9,000 new referees each year but about the same number leave the game. Traditionally about half of referees leave the game in the first couple of years.

The message to players and officials is that all abuse risks the possibility of a sending-off. The referee will log what is said, submit a report, and a disciplinary committee will almost always uphold the referee's stance. There are exceptions, of course. A referee once ordered off a dumb man for abusive language, and the decision was later reversed.

ADDED TIME *See* STOPPAGE-TIME

ADVANCING THE BALL

In 1998, the International Football Association Board (IFAB) introduced an experimental rule – advancing the position of the ball at a free-kick by ten yards directly towards goal if a defending player committed a cautionable offence, e.g. failing to retreat the necessary distance, delaying the restart by kicking (or taking) the ball away, showing dissent, or engaging in any other unsporting behaviour. The idea was eventually rejected by IFAB (2004), although it stayed in the English game for another season.

The concept had been around for some time – it was first mooted in the 1960s and a proposal was rejected by IFAB in 1983 – before a two-year experiment was conducted by the Jersey FA from 1998. The following season the test was extended to the Auto Windscreens Shield.

When Hull City won at York City, the referee cautioned a player for kicking away the ball but forgot to move the ball forward (December 1999). Referees already had a lot to consider when overseeing free-kicks. There were problems if a referee spent fifty seconds organising a wall only to be forced to caution an encroaching player, move the ball forward, and start over again. But some referees did feel that it had a beneficial effect on player behaviour.

The 2001 World Youth Championships were a further testing ground. At the start of the experiment, free-kicks could be moved into the penalty area – direct or indirect according to the offence – but from 2001 free-kicks could only be moved as far as the penalty-area line. Some players were not happy with this. They thought they had a better chance of scoring from a little bit further back, as it made it easier to get the ball over or around the wall.

ADVANTAGE CLAUSE

In a 1974 FA Cup semi-final, Malcolm Macdonald (Newcastle United) was pulled back by a Burnley defender on the edge of the penalty area. The linesman flagged for a foul but the referee allowed 'advantage' because he could sense that Macdonald was using his strength to ride the challenge. Macdonald's shot hit the goalkeeper but he scored from the rebound.

Referees were first given the power to refrain from awarding a penalty-kick if they thought the attacking side would benefit by play continuing (1903). This 'advantage clause' was later extended to all free-kicks (1938). When an *infringement* occurs – advantage cannot be applied when the ball goes out of play – the referee must quickly assess the situation: is it better for the non-offending team for play to continue? In 1956, Colin Grainger (England) put the ball in the Brazil net at the same time as the referee awarded a penalty. The penalty-kick was missed. This was obviously unjust.

The FIFA Referees' Committee clarified that a referee couldn't go back if no real advantage accrued (1934). This led to problems too. At Colchester United, in the 1950s, a Plymouth Argyle defender stopped a pass with his hands but the ball dropped kindly into the path of a Colchester forward. 'Play on,' shouted the referee, but the Colchester player, anticipating the free-kick, bent down and picked up the ball. The free-kick had to be given against the Colchester player instead.

When Watford played Blackburn, a player was brought down for an obvious free-kick (February 1973). The referee waved play on and the player was still shouting for the free-kick when his colleague rammed home the loose ball. The player was so busy complaining that he hadn't seen his team-mate score the goal.

Novice referees are usually advised to use the advantage clause sparingly, especially when the team deserving a free-kick is defending. Gordon Hill provided a salutary tale in his autobiography. He was refereeing a Bristol derby match when the linesman flagged a City player offside (1974–75). When Hill saw the ball dropping kindly for a Rovers defender he shouted, 'Play on.' Unfortunately the ball then bounced badly, the defender miskicked, and a City player scored.

One common use of 'advantage' comes when an assistant referee flags a player offside but the ball runs through to the opposing goalkeeper. A free-kick would slow down the game, and goalkeepers usually prefer to punt the ball rather than kick a stationary ball. 'Play on – advantage,' says the referee, signalling with arms raised to chest-level and palms up.

A problem arises if the three officials have not worked out how to handle advantage. For instance, the assistant flags for a free-kick twenty yards out, but the referee allows the advantage and then gives a penalty-kick for the next tackle, which is inside the penalty area. The defenders point out that the flag was raised for the original free-kick, so the referee goes over for a chat, and says that the advantage has been played. It can be confusing.

If the referee does allow play to proceed, the culprit is not pardoned from disciplinary action (IFAB 1960). In a 1996 play-off final, the referee allowed a flowing Crystal Palace move to continue despite a bad tackle by Izzet (Leicester City). When play next stopped, the referee cautioned Izzet. But advantage may not be prudent if the original foul is a sending-off offence, if there is a serious injury, or if it seems likely to provoke retaliation or a mêlée in the same passage of play.

From 1996, referees were officially allowed a few seconds to see whether a team gained an advantage before deciding whether to award a free-kick in the place where the offence happened (although top-class referees had been doing this anyway). The referee is now expected to assess the situation in, say, the first three seconds after the offence. If the anticipated advantage doesn't materialise, then the referee can penalise the original offence. But this is just a few seconds. It is not like rugby union, where the referee can allow play to proceed for thirty seconds.

Kings Lynn took the lead at Fisher Athletic with a disputed penalty (May 2004). A shot was handled on the goal-line. The referee waited a moment to see what happened when the ball rebounded to an attacker, but the attacker's shot was blocked on the line. The referee then gave a penalty and punished the offender. The defending team complained that advantage had been played. In contrast, a referee at Preston blew for a penalty-kick for the home team only for a Preston player to latch on to the loose ball and put it into the net (October 2004). That penalty was missed, but Preston still won 2–1. Similarly, Beardsley (Liverpool) put the ball in the net during the 1988 FA Cup Final only to discover that the referee had already punished a shirt-tug outside the penalty area by Thorn (Wimbledon). Nothing came of the free-kick, and within two minutes Wimbledon scored what would be the only goal of the game.

While some top-flight officials are confident enough to say 'advantage' a lot, other referees are more cautious. Playing advantage too many times may set a bad standard for the game as it could be misinterpreted as tolerating bad tackles. It is difficult to achieve a balance. Referees ask themselves, 'Should I let things go for the sake of a flowing game, or will I be running the risk of losing control if I don't use my whistle?'

When the advantage clause works well, it can be breathtakingly satisfying for the beneficiary and a peak experience for the referee. Consider the feelings of the referee at Bolton who allowed Barton (Manchester City) to score the only goal of the game rather than awarding City a penalty (December 2004). Or the one at Charlton who acknowledged his assistant's flag but let play continue and saw the ball passed upfield for a superb Charlton goal against Norwich (November 2004). Or the referee at Leigh RMI, who agreed with his assistant's flag-waving but allowed Bishop (York) to stumble back to his feet and continue forward before crossing for Nogan to score. You could sense the satisfaction of these referees: 'My two-handed signal had a hand in that goal.'

ADVERTISEMENTS

When the North American Soccer League started in 1967, one British referee complained that there was pressure on him to whistle for regular time-outs so that television advertisements could be shown. FIFA frowned on such stoppages.

Shirts bearing logos soon became commonplace in Britain – the pioneers were Kettering Town in 1975 – but clubs had to check the regulations for each competition. Liverpool had to have two separate kits for 1979–80, one of which had the sponsor's name in smaller letters for televised matches. UEFA banned commercial shirt logos in its European competitions until 1985–86, so clubs found they had to tape over the kit manufacturer's names on certain occasions. The *2004–05 FA Handbook* listed four pages of regulations for clothing advertisements.

In the early 2000s, IFAB continually reminded clubs that advertising was not allowed in certain areas: between the goal-line and the goal-nets; within the technical area; within one yard of the touchline; on goal-nets; on corner-flags; or on the pitch. In 2002 it was clarified that advertising was not permitted on shorts, stockings or footwear, and certainly not on undershirts that were being revealed during goal celebrations. Advertising on shirts was allowed.

Sponsorship continued to make inroads into the sport. In 2004–05, the Professional Game Match Officials Ltd (PGMOL) were sponsored by

Emirates Airline, a company that had previously been associated with Arsenal and Chelsea. Scottish referees had a more whimsical deal, being sponsored by Specsavers.

When referee Pierluigi Collina shared the same sponsor as AC Milan, it was deemed a conflict of interest by the Italian Football Federation (FIGC) and the Italian football referees' association (AIA) (August 2005). Collina resigned.

ALCOHOL

On match-days, in the 1950s, one professional player was known for varying his pre-match routine depending on whether or not he'd been drinking. If he was sober, he would walk straight up to his manager and say, 'Afternoon, Boss.' If he had been in the pub, he would creep around the side of the dressing-room. 'He scored five against Luton and he came into the dressing-room canned,' a team-mate recalled years later. 'He turned to speak to me, breathed, and I almost passed out.'

Many amateur team secretaries have tempted fate with instructions like 'Meet outside the Red Lion at two o'clock', with some players arriving early and conducting their warm-up in front of the pub fire. Contrary to popular belief, alcohol acts as a depressant rather than a stimulant.

On the pitch, referees who suspect a player of being under the influence of alcohol or drugs are advised to treat the matter sensitively at first – by talking to the captain or a team official. Referees do not carry breathalysers as part of their standard equipment.

Drink and football have been forever entwined. In the 1880s, when Aston Villa visited Scotland for the first time, they inspected a whisky distillery in the morning and lost their match in the afternoon. In 1898 Steve Bloomer (Derby County and England) was briefly suspended by the club's directors for 'attending the ground while under the influence of drink'. Three years later Bloomer received three more reprimands – for insobriety and inattention to training.

In the 1920s the Scotland team trainer gave each player 'a wee thimbleful of brandy and port just as we left the dressing-room', according to one player. Bottles of whisky have been left in dressing-rooms before professional matches, and professional players have been sighted in pubs before matches.

Grass-roots football has plenty of stories: the player who was stretchered off because he was too drunk to stand up; the winger who had to leave the field to pee every twenty minutes; the player who was so drunk that he tackled the corner-flag; the defender who pleaded with the referee to 'get that other ball off the pitch'; and the one who was so inebriated that he slurred his abuse at the referee.

The Sporting Events (Control of Alcohol Etc.) Act 1985 made it an offence for a person to be drunk inside a sports ground or when trying to enter a ground (any time up to two hours before the start and up to an hour after the finish).

ALL LEVELS OF SKILL

The laws of the game must cater for all levels of skill. Players are amateur and professional, male and female, handicapped and capped, young and old, small and large. Matches are occasionally played in front of crowds of over fifty thousand but more likely they will have less than ten spectators.

The English FA started the new millennium with about 43,000 clubs, but only twenty of these were Premiership members. The laws apply to all matches from international level downwards, but a better sample of the world game would be, say, Coquitlam City Xtreme against Chilliwack Impact in a girls under-sixteen game. Only a very small proportion of players are professional, and yet the media is dominated by the professional game.

IFAB has the challenge of drafting laws that are universally applicable. Certain laws already discriminate. Fourth officials and neutral assistants are required at professional grounds but are not essential when Folkestone Snooker Club Reserves play The York Arms. Technology has been used to determine misconduct in professional matches, but Victoria Stores Margate are more likely to install cameras to detect shoplifters. The technical area has a more sophisticated design at the Britannia Stadium than it does on Hackney Marshes. The question for the legislators is how much discrimination can be permitted without top-level football and parks football becoming different games. In 2001, the FA of Wales warned IFAB that it was greatly concerned about the prospect of a two-tier football system.

AMPUTEES

Although Wrexham are said to have fielded two one-armed players against Chester (1890), the real pioneer was a one-legged goalkeeper called Gyngell (Maidenhead Norfolkians) in the 1900s. Berkshire & Buckinghamshire FA referred the matter to a higher authority, and it was decided there was no objection providing the player with a wooden leg did not play in a manner dangerous to his opponents (FA, 1907). The following season, Hart (Folkestone) played with a wooden leg.

Fifty years later the FIFA judgment was different. The All-India Football Federation asked for a ruling on a goalkeeper who had played for four years with an artificial leg. Although the keeper had not caused injury to any other player, it could be argued that opponents were staying clear of him. FIFA ruled that an artificial leg was not part of standard equipment, so the player was banned.

More recently a dedicated form of amputee soccer has evolved. One account suggests that the game began in the late 1970s in El Salvador, where war victims were unable to get artificial legs. Using lightweight crutches to cover the ground, these disabled players found they were able to kick a football with their one good leg.

The professional eleven-a-side game has produced some excellent one-armed role models. Héctor Castro (Uruguay) played in the 1930 FIFA World Cup™ Final, Tony Ward (Arlesey Town) appeared as a substitute in the 1995 FA Vase Final, and Chris Perrior played for Walsall and Kidderminster Harriers in the late 1990s.

There have been a number of one-armed referees, including Alf Bond (Middlesex), who took charge of the 1956 FA Cup Final. In a North Regional League match in the 1960s, a player was sent off for abusing a one-armed linesman. 'You're badly handicapped,' the player said. 'Only one arm and can't see either.'

ANNOUNCEMENTS

On Boxing Day 1948 Linfield played Belfast Celtic at Windsor Park, Belfast. The teams were bitter rivals in the Irish League. Linfield was a Protestant club, and Belfast Celtic was Catholic. Halfway through the first half, Bryson (Linfield) was carried off after being injured in a tackle with Jimmy Jones (Belfast Celtic). At half-time the Linfield secretary announced that Bryson had been taken to hospital with a broken leg. This riled the Linfield fans. Immediately after the match, which ended 1–1, spectators rushed on to the field and attacked Jones, whose leg was broken in five places. Jones was in plaster for ten months. The Belfast Celtic directors responded to the incident by closing down the club.

The Windsor Park announcer's comment may, or may not, have been relevant, but announcers certainly have a part to play. A match between Reading and Bristol City was temporarily suspended when City fans invaded the pitch (April 1984). During the thirteen-minute stoppage, Bristol City manager Terry Cooper spoke to fans over the public-address system. He appealed for calm and threatened to concede the match if the fighting continued.

In the mid-1960s Coventry City began a new trend when their announcer passed on news to spectators during breaks in the game. But Coventry City were reprimanded for one incident. On the last day of the 1976–77 season, five minutes from the end of their vital clash with Bristol City, the Coventry announcer relayed the final result of an important match elsewhere. Both

Coventry City and Bristol City now needed a point for safety. The players passively fiddled with the ball for the last five minutes.

Other announcements include appeals for replacement officials – there was one at Charlton (versus Aston Villa) when the match referee was injured – but some announcers have been sacked for intimidating opposition fans or making derogatory comments. In 1995, the Swindon Town man was axed for offering his opinion about the referee's decision to send off a Swindon player. Stadium disc jockeys have also been in trouble for provocative behaviour. It pays not to dedicate Status Quo's 'Down Down' to visiting teams threatened with relegation.

APPEALING

In football's earliest days, a player had to claim an infringement or, indeed, a goal. The system was similar to cricket, where a batsman would not be given out without an 'Owzat?' except that in football the call needed to be more specific, for instance 'Hands?' 'Goal?' or 'Penalty-kick?' In the 1884 FA Cup Final, Blackburn Rovers beat Queen's Park 2–1, but Queen's Park would have been awarded another goal had they appealed.

Referees were eventually empowered to decide without appeal (1896). For the previous five years the only exception to this was dangerous play. By the 1950s refereeing instructions showed that players were forbidden to appeal. You've probably spotted the irony. In the days when players had to appeal they rarely did so; now that the referee decides without appeal the players never stop appealing.

'Our ball.'

'What about the push, Ref?'

'Ref-er-*ree!*'

ARMBANDS *See* CAPTAINS

ARTIFICIAL SURFACES

An international match was played on artificial turf in October 1976 – Canada versus USA in Vancouver, Canada – but it was only in 2004 that a paragraph permitting artificial surfaces was written into Law 1. Surfaces need to satisfy quality guidelines and competition rules.

Queen's Park Rangers played matches on an artificial surface in the 1980s. Opponents commented that the ball sometimes bounced very high or skidded awkwardly, and some players suffered grazes. The most memorable result there was probably the 5–5 draw with Newcastle United (September 1984).

An artificial pitch was laid at Feltham Sports Arena in 1984, and used by Feltham FC (known as Feltham & Hounslow Borough from 1990 to 1995). Other clubs followed suit – Luton Town, Preston North End, Oldham Athletic, Hyde United and Stirling Albion – but the pitches sometimes received a hostile reception. It was said that a Boeing 737 had a lot in common with a visiting manager – they both left Luton whining.

In June 1986 the FA banned cup ties on so-called 'plastic pitches'. The Football League also flagged a gradual wind-down. Luton Town and Oldham Athletic reverted to grass for the 1991–92 season, and other clubs did the same. They had been given advance warning that artificial pitches would not be allowed from 1994–95.

The design improved as manufacturers researched what would be the best surfaces for playing football. They settled upon grass-like fibres attached to a mix of sand and/or rubber. In 2001 IFAB recognised that artificial surfaces had improved, and that quality standards were available (e.g. the FIFA Concept for Artificial Turf and the International Turf Standard). Such surfaces were sanctioned for qualifying matches for the 2002 FIFA World Cup™ and the Olympic football tournaments. A two-year UEFA experiment at five clubs across Europe (2003 to 2005) monitored the bounce and roll of the ball, injuries, and ways of removing chewing gum and dog faeces. More and more clubs now train on artificial pitches and in some countries, such as Greenland, there are no viable alternatives.

ASSAULT

Trouble flared in the fortieth minute of a match in Oxford in February 2001 when Bobby Ahmed (Blackbird Leys) attacked goalkeeper Mark Rose (Great Milton). The referee showed Ahmed the red card. Then the player started hitting the referee before kicking the now-grounded goalie in the face. Rose spent three days in hospital with a broken jaw, eye socket and nose. He needed thirteen screws and three plates inserted, and his face was wired for seven weeks. When the case came to court, Ahmed was sentenced to thirty months in prison for causing grievous bodily harm and four months for common assault. He served fifteen months.

An assault is a sudden violent attack by one person on another. Football-related assaults are criminal offences and can result in police action: (i) common assault under the Criminal Justice Act 1991 (where there is no physical mark); (ii) assault occasioning actual bodily harm, contrary to the Offences Against Person Act 1861; and (iii) assault occasioning grievous bodily harm, also under the Offences Against Person Act 1861, an offence which carries a punishment of up to five years in prison.

The laws of football categorise an assault as a sending-off for either violent conduct (if it happens away from the ball) or serious foul play (if there is a putative challenge for the ball). Football-field assaults have involved almost every combination of people present at a match. To paraphrase a media warning, what follows involves scenes of violence.

When professional players are sent off for offences that cause injury, the police often ask victims if they would like to press charges. The players usually refuse. For instance, Derek McInnes (West Brom) declined to have charges brought against Patrick Suffo (Sheffield United), who was sent off for a head-butt that caused McInnes to have stitches (March 2002).

When Duncan Ferguson (Rangers) head-butted John McStay (Raith Rovers), the referee missed the incident, but the police compiled a case (April 1994). A year and a half later, Ferguson received a three-month prison sentence for assault. He served 44 days before being released.

Other landmark cases include that of Andrew Brannigan (Arbroath), who was sent off (December 1986) and convicted of assault (October 1987) for breaking the leg of Jim Deakin (Albion Rovers). In England, Chris Kamara (Swindon Town) was convicted and fined £1,200 (plus £250 compensation) in April 1988 for causing grievous bodily harm to Jim Melrose (Shrewsbury Town). Kamara had broken Melrose's cheekbone as the players left the pitch (January 1988).

Players have also been attacked by spectators. In September 1902, at a Birmingham court, Arthur Jackson was fined a shilling and costs for assaulting Robert Davidson (Manchester City) during a game at Small Heath. Davidson alleged that he was pushed against the railings, struck on the jaw and had his shirt torn. Davidson and his club asked for a lenient sentence because Jackson had apologised.

Robert Grant, an ex-soldier suffering from shellshock, was fined £1 at Brentford Police Court for assaulting Syd Puddefoot (West Ham) in a game (December 1918). When Hull City played Crystal Palace, 'a foul on Richardson [Hull] brought a spectator over the railings evidently to attempt to strike the aggressor, and for a minute or so play was suspended while order was restored' (1924–25). And Ron Patterson (Northampton) missed the second half at Leyton Orient after being struck by a spectator (January 1955). Referees would include details of such events in their post-match report.

Very occasionally players are at risk from referees. A referee was suspended for eighteen months because he retaliated after being punched by a player he had just red-carded at Rhuddlan (September 1981). A 43-year-old referee with seven years' experience punched a player in the face during a Norfolk Sunday League match after being taunted for not knowing the rules (February 1992). The referee walked straight off the pitch, and the match was abandoned.

A similar event occurred during an Andover & District Sunday League match between Southampton Arms and Hurstbourne Tarrant British Legion (March 1998). A referee lost his temper with a player who had allegedly pushed him. The referee punched the offending player several times and had to be dragged off by other players. The referee eventually walked off the pitch after producing a red card for himself and the match continued with a spectator refereeing.

Assault is both a crime and a civil wrong, and a number of civil actions have resulted in compensation payments. In all cases, the referee is a key neutral witness . . . unless he has been murdered. In Sabac, Serbia (then part of Yugoslavia), a player was sentenced to death for killing the referee, and seven other players were given sentences ranging from six months to twenty years (November 1952). The referee had disallowed a goal for offside.

Most referees have survived to write their reports. In an incident in Suffolk in 1966, the referee tried to caution a goalkeeper, but the player refused to give his name, brushed the referee aside and walked away. The referee's report contained these words: 'I asked him who he was pushing, and told him if there was any more of it I would send him off, whereupon he said, "If you are going to send me off I will give you something to send me off for." At the same time I was struck on the chin.'

In most cases of assaults on referees, the match is immediately abandoned. For example, a match in Sri Lanka was abandoned after eighty minutes when an experienced referee was assaulted by an Eastern Eagle SC player (2002). Having been shown a red card, the player snatched the card away, tore it into pieces and then kicked the referee. Other players joined in the mêlée, and the referee had to go to hospital for treatment.

The referee who sent off Lee Campbell (Leighton Town) was more stoical when Campbell knocked him over with a punch (November 1999). The official resumed the game after ten minutes of treatment but had to stay in hospital overnight with concussion.

Other sent-off players have sought retribution. In 1994 a referee sent off an Old Rose player during a Notts County Combination match, and the player got in his van and drove at the referee, who jumped to safety.

In the last minute of a Hull Sunday League match, a female referee awarded a free-kick after a reckless challenge (April 2003). A mass brawl broke out and spectators joined in. Goalkeeper Robert Bunn (Old Bottle) was later jailed for six months for common assault. He had head-butted the referee during the fracas.

Particularly worrying is the number of assaults on referees by young players: a thirteen-year-old player was banned from football for five years after he and his father assaulted a referee (1994); a fifteen-year-old was banned from playing competitive football for life after he had punched a referee twice at the end of a South Ceredigion Junior League match (2000); and police investigated when a referee was assaulted towards the end of an under-fifteen Cambridge & District Colts League game (2004).

Two players from Botafogo Youth (Brazil) were arrested by Stockholm police after an incident during a match in Sweden (July 1989). One allegedly kicked the referee to the ground and the other kicked him in the head. In the same month, the FA recommended automatic life bans for players or officials who seriously assaulted match officials.

Professional players can be far from exemplary. Juanito (Real Madrid) was so angry at losing a European Cup tie on away goals to Grasshoppers Zürich that he attacked the East German referee (November 1978). UEFA initially banned Juanito from all European competition for two years, later reducing the sentence to one year on appeal.

Other stars have been in trouble for a variety of aggressive acts towards referees – kicking (Maldonado of Venezia), clashing heads (Sinclair of West Brom), pushing (Hilaire of Crystal Palace), stamping on a referee's foot (Stoichkov of Barcelona), kicking down the door to the referee's room and strewing clothes (Wright of West Ham), barging (Mikoliunas of Hearts), and manhandling a referee (Gough of Fulham).

In a survey of referees in the West Midlands in 1995, John Williams (Leicester University) found that 24.5 per cent of referees saw assaults as the most serious problem they faced. Someone once estimated that referees could expect to be assaulted once every forty years, but such figures are not too heartening if you are a novice referee taking charge of the Dalton Gang against the James Gang in Dodge City. More referees may follow the lead of the Halifax referees who went on strike in 1996 as a protest against players' attitudes and behaviour, and the Bedfordshire referees who staged a strike after a member's jaw had been broken in two places by a Westfield player (February 2004).

The Bedfordshire incident came in the 85th minute of a local Cup semi-final. Duke Sports (Kempston) were awarded a penalty-kick. Before the referee could tell him to back away, a Westfield player launched an attack. The match was abandoned. In the changing-rooms, an assistant referee's clothes were burned, and his mobile phone and car keys stolen. Police later arrested the player and the Westfield club was suspended for ten months.

Early commentators on the game noted that the number of assaults on officials increased with the arrival of the penalty-kick law (1891). Referees are also vulnerable when issuing red cards. After an incident involving Paolo Di Canio (Sheffield Wednesday), who pushed over a referee after having been sent off, it was recommended that referees should be two arm-lengths away from a player when showing a card (September 1998). If a player comes closer, most referees will step back and hope that the player's team-mates will come in to restrain the offender. They watch the player rather than their notebook. Referees are not advised to slug it out, but there is a self-defence issue. Referees need to stay calm and think clearly. If they are assaulted, there is a protocol – getting medical treatment (and a record of it), calling the police, obtaining witnesses (spectators, assistant referees, etc.), writing a report of the incident while it is fresh in the mind, informing the relevant football authorities, and talking to a solicitor.

This also applies to attacks by spectators. Pitch invasions have resulted in numerous ground closures and competition expulsions over the years. There are legendary tales of referees being escorted from the ground by police (or escorted to the nearest duck pond by spectators). When referee Norman Burtenshaw was knocked out by pitch-invading spectators at Millwall, the incident almost provoked a strike by top-class referees (October 1967). 'I was escorted off the pitch by several police officers,' Burtenshaw wrote in his match report. 'We were jostled by spectators. I was then tripped from behind and whilst on the ground received blows, one of which was in the stomach.' There was more outrage when referee Roger Wiseman was assaulted at Birmingham (February 1992).

At the sound of the final whistle of a West Ham United v Stoke City match, Sheila West told her two sons that she would be back in a minute (May 1969). She ran on the field to attack the referee, hitting him repeatedly with her fists. Five policemen dragged her off. The Football Spectators Act 1989 made pitch invasion a criminal offence, but incidents still occurred at places like Blackburn Rovers (February 1995), Notts County (August 1997), and Barnsley (March 1998).

Assistant referees sometimes need eyes in their shoulder blades. One was punched unconscious by a Sheffield United supporter during a Portsmouth–Sheffield United match, delaying the start of the second half for fifteen minutes (January 1998). The fan was given a three-month prison sentence, banned from all football grounds for a year and banned from Bramall Lane, Sheffield United's home ground, for life.

A 21-year-old Middlesbrough fan threw a cup of boiling-hot Bovril over an assistant referee after an offside decision at Leicester City. The fan was convicted of assault and sentenced to two months in prison. And a Reading fan was banned from attending football matches for five years after he admitted throwing coins at an assistant referee at Cambridge (March 2002).

Assistants can be victimised by players and managers too. When Kirkup (Cambridge City) was sent off against Kings Lynn, he kicked the corner-flag in frustration, and the corner-flag hit the assistant referee in the face (November 1999). Millwall manager Dennis Wise reacted so strongly to late sendings-off at Cardiff that he threw a water bottle to the ground only for the bottle to bounce up and hit the nearby assistant (February 2005). Wise immediately became another sending-off statistic.

Other team officials have erred. The manager of FK Atlantas (Lithuania) attacked a Rhyl player at the end of a UEFA Cup tie (July 2005). In 1996 a Dynamo Moscow official was alleged to have pushed a referee into the Dynamo dressing-room after a match, knocking the referee unconscious.

Charlie Mitten played for Sante Fe (Colombia) in the 1950s and returned to England with plenty of tales. One concerned a local derby at Millonarios when the referee gave a disputed late goal to Santa Fe. Two local gendarmes, soldiers with rifles, escorted the referee off the pitch and then attacked him in the changing-room. The gendarmes were Millonarios fans.

Is there no one referees can completely trust? Not even assistants, apparently. A linesman attacked the referee at the end of a Sarmiento–Independiente match in Argentina (August 1982). The linesman was furious that his offside flag had been overruled.

The most highly publicised case of a player attacking a spectator was that of Eric Cantona (Manchester United) at Crystal Palace (January 1995). Cantona, sent off by the referee for kicking an opponent, was walking around the pitch on his way to the dressing-room. A spectator ran down the steps and abused Cantona, who launched a kung fu kick in retaliation. Cantona was given a two-week prison sentence (later reduced to 120 hours community service), banned from football for eight months, and fined heavily by the FA. The spectator was sentenced to seven days in jail after being found guilty of threatening language and behaviour.

In September 2003, El Hadji Diouf (Liverpool) was fined £5,000 at Glasgow Sheriff Court after he pleaded guilty to assault under provocation. Diouf had spat at a spectator during a match at Celtic (March 2003). The UEFA disciplinary committee fined Celtic £2,300 after deciding that Diouf had been incited by Celtic fans. Had the referee seen the incident, he would have sent off Diouf for violent conduct.

A Rhyl fan claimed that he was attacked by Gary Brabin (Total Network Solutions) after Rhyl's 3–2 win in Treflan, home of TNS, in November 2003. Brabin later received a police caution for common assault. Two Gillingham players, Ken Price and Dean White, were convicted of assaulting Ray McHale (Swindon Town) and Swindon trainer Wilf Tranter in the tunnel after a promotion battle (May 1979).

ASSESSORS

How do you referee the referees? In August 1963, a small item appeared in the Crystal Palace programme: 'For years the Scottish League has operated successfully an independent panel of impartial referee-assessors, and now the

Lancashire Combination is to do so. When will the Football League fall into line? The system of assessing referees by club reports has obvious flaws.'

Assessors first appeared in England in 1969–70, and their setup gradually became more and more sophisticated. Assessors help the development of referees at all levels by acting as observers and mentors. In 1972, they were briefed to comment on a number of issues: application of the laws and control; positioning and fitness; application of the advantage clause, stoppages and signals; and co-operation with linesmen (now known as assistant referees).

Top-level referees are very accountable. Indeed, some football-club personnel believe that they are too accountable, as they may try too hard to please their assessors.

ASSISTANT REFEREES

Until 1996 assistant referees were known as linesmen. The change of name was partly to cater for the increasing number of women coming into refereeing, and partly to acknowledge the key role played by those running the line. 'The linesman is, in reality, an assistant referee,' wrote W D Murdoch in the 1952–53 *FA Book for Boys*.

The term linesman came into being after 1891, when the referee moved from the sidelines to the field of play and the two umpires moved from the pitch to the surrounds. In the 1890s, Football League linesmen were club officials, and 'away linesmen' were subject to abuse from the home crowd. Derby County's Charlie Holloway ran the line in knickerbockers and Burnley fans used catapults to pelt his legs. The referee had to stop the game and rescue him.

Neutral linesmen were introduced around 1900. When Sheffield United and Sheffield Wednesday met in an FA Cup replay, two Wednesday players were sent off (February 1900). Referee John Lewis did not see the second offence but acted on information provided by a neutral linesman.

Clubs continued to provide linesmen in local games. Lovick gave the following advice to referees in his 1920s manual: 'During the first five or ten minutes take note of your respective linesmen and decide as to what extent they may be relied on for the remainder of the game.'

In park football the assistant is often a team official or a substitute. Most tackle the task conscientiously but occasionally one has a role conflict: 'Come on, lads, we're better than this. Stop wandering at the back, I'm having to watch the line.'

In professional football, neutral assistant referees have acquired more and more responsibility. They indicate whether the ball is in or out of play, and suggest which team is entitled to possession on the restart. They assess offsides, and look for offences and misconduct in areas of the field where they are better placed than the referee. They help with substitutions, take some responsibility at penalty-kicks (e.g. watching the goalkeeper's feet), and spot whether the ball goes over the line for a goal. These last three points were added to the laws in 2000, although many referees were already briefing their assistants accordingly. Also, since 2000, assistants can enter the field of play to help with encroachment issues.

The linesman's original duties were to point to the place where the ball went into touch, and then stand on one side to watch the throw-in. Pickford stated it clearly in his early book on refereeing:

> In practice the linesman is entrusted with the oversight of the touchline, the referee the goal-line and goal positions. This is a useful division of the work, but it is not a peremptory one – the linesman should keep an active watch on the ball crossing the goal-line so that he can if required help the referee either by signal or by consultation. The linesman should act as far as he can as a goal-judge. To achieve this, the suggestion is made that one linesman should work more along the touchline on one half of the field of play, and the other conversely.

There is a limit to what assistants can do. A Barnsley defender tackled Simon Sturridge (Stoke) near the touchline and accidentally tripped up the sprinting linesman (March 1996). Sturridge's cross resulted in a goal for Sheron (Stoke). Barnsley defenders claimed offside but the linesman was still getting to his feet.

Some referees argue that running the line is harder than refereeing, and the official report on the 2002 FIFA World Cup™ commented that assistant referees made more errors than referees. The basic challenge in the job is to keep one eye on the ball, one eye on the players to assess for fouls and off-the-ball incidents, and a third eye on the defensive line to check offside positions, all the while sprinting crab-like along a muddy or sanded touchline strip and holding the flag down with a straight arm. An assistant's sprint can be brought to a sudden halt by the sight of a player in an offside position. Then the assistant comes to attention and lifts the flag high (if the player is active in the play). Referees usually acknowledge signals from their assistants, even if they do not act upon them.

Running the line is now recognised as a specialist's job. It used to be that top referees would suddenly find themselves as a linesman for the first time in a year. FIFA referees would have to practise running the line in local matches to resurrect their skills before a major match. Then it was realised (after incidents like the Maradona 'hand of God' goal in 1986) that experienced, in-form assistants were needed for top matches.

Neutral assistants usually run the same defence in both halves, switching from one right wing to the other, and club linesmen are usually given their own defence to patrol. Neutral assistants will make a note of cautions, substitutions, sendings-off and goals. Before the advent of the fourth official, the senior linesman would take over if the match official was injured during the game. It is still the case in some competitions.

Neutral assistants will also carry the same equipment as referees. Linesmen's flags were traditionally supplied by the home club, but many referees now carry their own. An early FA instruction to club secretaries was for 'light-coloured flags' to be provided. Flags were smarter than handkerchiefs and enabled linesmen to give clearer signals. They have usually been about eighteen inches long (including the handle) and assistants know to keep them unfurled and ready, carrying them at the side of the body, below waist height, while they run. Never wrap a flag around the handle!

There are numerous examples of flags flying off the end of a linesman's stick and floating on to the pitch. A grinning player might return the flag with a choice one-liner: 'This your snot-rag, lino?'

Luminous flags were first tried at Villa Park in 1946, and there were experiments with luminous outfits in 1972 after complaints from referees about difficulty spotting linesmen during floodlit matches. A referee halted a game between Leyton Orient and Blackpool, and asked a spectator to move further back in the crowd because his shirt was clashing with the linesman's flag (August 1992). With the coming of replica shirts for fans, it became harder to find suitable flag colours, and a brightly coloured chequered flag became more popular.

Assistant referees are expected to give an opinion on incidents when asked by the referee. Assistants do not make decisions. That is solely the referee's job.

Assistant referees who interfere too much can be dismissed by the referee. Garry Parker (Leicester City) was fined £750 for using foul and abusive language to a referee while acting as an assistant referee during an Oxfordshire Sunday League match (February 1998).

Local clubs can be fined for failing to provide an assistant. Anyone is better than no one. At one Lewes & District Sunday League match, a club assistant referee hopped the line on crutches, somehow managing to raise his flag.

What if assistants are injured during matches? A local referee stepped in when a linesman pulled a muscle in the game between Liverpool and Wolves (October 1970), and Sheffield United substitute David Staniforth deputised for an injured linesman at Chelsea (February 1973).

A replacement was also needed when a linesman wrenched his knee after twelve minutes of a match between Arsenal and Liverpool (September 1972). A loudspeaker appeal brought three responses – an inexperienced referee, an ex-referee in his sixties, and television expert and former player Jimmy Hill, who had studied the laws of the game as a qualified FA coach. When the game resumed, after a fifteen-minute delay, Hill was running the line.

Despite a successful experiment with microphones and buzzers in 1999 and 2000, referees continue to rely on their assistants operating a system of flag signals. Assistants can show offside by holding their flag straight up in the air, in line with where the offence occurred, and they can indicate where the ball should be placed for the resulting indirect free-kick. They can also signal for an infringement (waving the flag and then pointing it in the direction of the offending team's goal), a corner-kick (pointing towards the nearest corner arc), a goal-kick (taking up a position six yards out and pointing across the pitch), a goal (running back towards the halfway-line with a thumbs-up or an arm pointing), a throw-in (waving the flag and signalling the direction of the throw-in), and a substitution (both arms raised with the flag gripped in two hands). Substitutions take place at the halfway-line. At a break in play, the assistant moves to the halfway-line and raises the flag. One player leaves the field, and the substitute enters on a signal from the referee. The assistant checks the substitute's footwear.

There is also a signal for penalty-kicks. It was used by an assistant at Crystal Palace when he saw a push on Wright-Phillips (Manchester City) in September 2004. The assistant, who was closer to the ball than the match referee, immediately waved his flag and then placed it across his chest.

At corner-kicks, linesmen in the early 1980s would stand on the goal-line, about fifteen yards from the corner-flag. In the 2000s it became more fashionable to stand by the corner-flag, a better position from which to judge whether the ball stays in play. Assistants have become much clearer about throw-in signals by switching hands (in the 1950s some linesmen were like contortionists with their efforts to put their flag over their head while holding on to it with their right hand).

Some referees have also used their assistants for emotional support. One time a referee gave an unpopular penalty decision and was surrounded by angry defenders.

'Talk to your linesman, Ref,' the defenders said.

The referee ran to the touchline.

'Do you have a watch?' the referee asked.

'Yes,' the linesman replied, nodding his head.

The referee ran back towards the penalty spot, pointing with complete conviction.

An assistant referee is a referee's best friend.

AWAY GOALS See DRAWN CUP TIES

Bb

BACKING INTO AN OPPONENT See PUSHING

BACKPASSES

In 1992, a distinctive change was made to the laws. Goalkeepers were no longer permitted to touch the ball with their hands when it was deliberately kicked to them by a team-mate. (The *backpass* terminology can be a bit confusing – the law applies to all passes to the goalkeeper, including square passes and forward passes.) Previously, passing to the goalkeeper had been resented, almost always booed, and referees had been loath to penalise goalkeepers who failed to release the ball quickly. A study of the 1990 FIFA World Cup™ showed that the ball was only in play for about 45 minutes per game. In some games the ball was with goalkeepers for as much as eight minutes.

A prototype was tested at the 1991 under-seventeen World Championship, and the law itself was introduced the following year. Goalkeepers could handle headed backpasses and chested backpasses but players were not allowed to get around the new law by flicking the ball up with their feet and heading it back (1992), even if the goalkeeper didn't handle the ball (IFAB 1993). Initially, goalkeepers could handle a team-mate's throw-in, but this was later outlawed (1997). All transgressions of the law were punishable by an indirect free-kick taken at the spot where the goalkeeper handled, or six yards out if the handling occurred inside the goal area.

Some people thought that the new law might induce lots of throw-ins if defenders opted to hoof the ball into the stand as a regular alternative to the old backpass. The main concern, however, was that goalkeepers would suffer injuries in tackles with forwards. This theory was stoked by an incident in July 1992, when Manchester City goalkeeper Andy Dibble broke a leg in a Dublin friendly when challenging an onrushing forward after a backpass.

Most people soon saw the entertainment benefits. The ball was in active play for longer and the weaker team put under more pressure. The early days brought several comic goals – goalkeeper Paul Crichton (Grimsby) completely missed a pass from team-mate Paul Futcher at Nottingham Forest (August 1993) – but goalkeepers quickly impressed with their standard of footwork. They began to be seen as footballers in their own right rather than crazy eccentrics.

The only tricky part of the law was distinguishing a deliberate backpass from a clearance that inadvertently went to the goalkeeper. When Brian Borrows (Coventry) miscued a clearance at Everton, the ball hit his other leg and bounced towards goalkeeper Ogrizovic, who picked up the ball (October 1992). The referee gave an indirect free-kick, having adjudged this deliberate.

Chelsea scored a disputed second goal against Wimbledon in a similar manner (March 1996) when the referee awarded a free-kick after goalkeeper Neil Sullivan picked up what was considered by the referee to be a deliberate backpass. Likewise in the Austria–England international (September 2004), the Austrian goalkeeper Manninger conceded an indirect free-kick, and England set up a goal for Lampard in the 2–2 draw. There is no refereeing signal for a backpass to guide the goalkeeper (and often there would not be time to give such a signal). Goalkeepers have to make up their own mind.

As more and more young players came into the game knowing not to pass back to the goalkeeper, free-kicks grew fewer and the game flowed. A new type of goal appeared, like the thirty-yard stunner from Gemmill (Nottingham Forest) when the Leicester goalkeeper hurried a clearance (February 1994).

BALL

A game needs a ball. This seems obvious but mistakes have been made. The 1887 London Cup Final was postponed because no one had brought a ball.

The ball's history shows a shift from a precious possession to a plentiful commodity. The original leather has been replaced by synthetic materials, an increasing range of colour options are available, and the old pig's bladder has been superseded by bladders of latex or butyl.

Yet certain things about the ball have stayed constant. Its circumference was fixed in 1872. It wasn't until 1938 that 'the ball shall be spherical' entered the laws, but that point had always been accepted.

Following the introduction of the FA Cup in 1871, ball conditions were standardised in line with the popular brown Lillywhite No. 5 ball. Average measurements were gathered and a ball circumference of 27 to 28 inches (68 to 70cm) was agreed upon (FA 1872, 1873).

A white ball was used in a floodlit game at Mansfield in February 1930, as explained by Jack Retter in *Mansfield Town*: 'So a young boy was employed, armed with a collection of balls and a bucket of whitewash – into which he dipped the balls and they were changed every few minutes (most likely every time the ball went out of play).' The white ball, legalised in 1951 and used in a cup tie at Hull City that year, later became popular for floodlit matches.

Television commentator Kenneth Wolstenholme found that the white ball was a godsend on smoggy winter days in the 1950s, when television 'wasn't black and white, it was grey and grey'. The introduction of a *grey* ball, in 2004, shows how far television technology has progressed. Modern balls are fashion statements. They provide marketing and purchasing opportunities.

In 1963, when snow and ice resulted in 261 FA Cup tie postponements, people argued for the use of orange, yellow or red balls. A standard orange Slazenger ball was chosen for the 1966 FIFA World Cup™ Final. A black-and-white patterned ball was used in most games during the 1970 FIFA World Cup™, but it was a brown ball that slipped past Peter Bonetti when England lost to West Germany in the quarter-final. In 1979, a white ball with red segments was considered very avant-garde when it was introduced for the League Cup Final.

Any colour is now acceptable, but the colour must suit the conditions. Obviously referees would not accept a white ball on a snowy pitch, nor a green ball on grass. An FA Cup tie between Nottingham Forest and Tottenham Hotspur began with a white ball, but a sudden snowstorm caused the referee to call for a brown one (February 1996). A fluorescent ball was used at Everton (April 1998). The referee is the sole judge of what should be the match-ball.

Referees are advised to check the state of the ball when it comes back from alien territory (e.g. brambles, a duck pond or horse stables). Players sometimes carefully toss the ball to the referee after it has landed in a cowpat: 'Better check this one, Ref. It feels a bit soft.'

Austrian team SC Wacker supplied the ball for a Festival of Britain game at West Brom, but the home team thought it was too small and light (May 1951). The referee asked for a tape measure and scales, and was satisfied by the measurements. Referees must report clubs failing to provide standard equipment (IFAB 1949).

Most referees can hold a ball and sense whether it is the correct weight. Some referees carry a piece of string, knotted at 27 and 28 inches so they can check the match-ball's circumference. Others carry a pump, just in case the ball is too soft. Referees like to make these checks well before the kick-off.

In 1889 the suggested weight of the ball at the start of the game was 12 to 15oz, but the standard later became 14 to 16oz at the commencement of the game (FIFA Referees' Committee 1937) with metric equivalents (396–453g) added in 1956. The air pressure was changed from 'atmospheric pressure' (1967) to a fixed one atmosphere ($1kg/cm^2$) (1972) and then to a range (600 to $1,100gr/cm^2$ at sea level) (1983). This last change merely reflected current practice. In the 1982 FIFA World Cup™, ball pressure had fluctuated between .9 and 1.1 atmospheres with no complaints. FIFA-approved ball standards, introduced in 1996, covered circumference, pressure, rebounding, retention of size and shape, water absorption and weight.

The ball's circumference used to have a particular significance at certain restarts – 'The ball must at least be rolled over before it shall be considered played' (1894) – but that was changed in 1997. The ball no longer had to travel its circumference, and play restarted when the ball *moved*.

Referees check the match-ball and try to ensure that suitable replacements are available. When Rochdale won 2–0 at Ilkeston Town, the match was halted for twenty minutes while officials used poles to retrieve the match-ball from a tree (November 1951).

Occasionally a ball is lost at sea. During a match at Fishguard in 1921 a ball was blown into Fishguard Bay and the players swam after it. Shrewsbury Town relied on a man with a coracle who recovered balls that dropped into the River Severn after clearing the ground's stand. But a 21-year-old man was swept away and drowned after wading into the River Wharfe (North Yorkshire) to retrieve a ball (April 1995).

When a ball becomes defective (burst, soft or misshapen) during the course of a match, play is stopped and then restarted with a replacement ball, dropped where the original became defective. (The only exception is at a penalty-kick when the kick is retaken with the replacement ball.) During the 1946 FA Cup Final, Stamps (Derby County) hit a shot at the Charlton goal. As the ball sped towards goal, Charlton's goalkeeper, Bartram, recognised the hissing sound of a burst ball. Aware of the law on restarting the game, Bartram caught the ball and immediately threw it out to the wing. In the 1947 FA Cup Final, between Charlton Athletic and Burnley, the ball burst near the touchline. A reserve ball was on the pitch and back in play within moments. By this time players and referees were accustomed to balls bursting as the manufacturing standard had fallen during the wartime period.

On occasions a match has been terminated because there was no replacement ball. The result of such an abandoned match is determined by competition organisers, but the home club is usually held responsible. Competition organisers also decide the time allowed for the home club to find a replacement (IFAB 1947).

If a ball bursts from a goal-kick, the referee has to ascertain whether or not the ball burst inside or outside the penalty area. The game is restarted with a retaken goal-kick (if it bursts inside the area) or a dropped ball (if it bursts outside). A similar decision (goal-kick or dropped ball) was necessary when Gerry Clarke (Chesterfield) burst the ball with a shot at Barrow (March 1967). If a burst ball crosses the goal-line into the net, the goal shouldn't count. If a ball bursts on hitting the crossbar, the game is restarted with a dropped ball on the six-yard line, level with where the ball hit the bar.

A defective ball is much rarer in modern football, but a match between Rangers and Dundee United was unusual, as documented by Mike Aitken in the *Scotsman* (March 1989): 'In front of a full house on a mild evening, conditions for football were hampered only by a flinty surface and the insistence of players to operate at a ferocious pace. The speed of play was so hectic that no fewer than three balls were commissioned in the opening twenty minutes.'

Unless the multi-ball system is operable, the ball should not be changed during the game unless authorised by the referee (1954). After thirty minutes of a Derby County–Northampton Town match, the referee asked for a replacement ball after testing the one in use (January 1967). There is still a protocol to go through, ensuring that one ball leaves the field before the replacement comes on.

The material of the ball's outer casing was stipulated as leather (1905), and leather alone (IFAB 1956) but other approved materials were eventually allowed (IFAB 1965). There is an apocryphal story of a vegetarian player walking off the pitch when he found out he was playing with a leather ball. Another version of the tale says that he was playing in Portugal with Celta Vigo, which of course made him a Celta Vegan.

The best early balls were made of specially prepared hide, with the bladder of high-quality vulcanised India rubber. Their laces very occasionally caused eye injuries that ended playing careers. Players used to ask for crosses to be 'hard and low and lace away', and they usually placed the lace away at free-kicks so that the ball would hit defenders lace-first. An innovative laceless ball was used in a Portsmouth–Newcastle cup tie (1924), and valve balls replaced laced balls more widely in the 1950s.

The ball used in League matches is the property of the home club (IFAB 1913), and it should be returned to the referee at the end of a match (IFAB 1956). Peter Knowles (Wolves) scored at Portsmouth and promptly kicked the ball out of the ground in celebration (February 1967). Portsmouth Football Club sent Knowles a bill for a new ball, and Knowles settled his debt. Presenting the match-ball to the scorer of a hat-trick is at the discretion of the club owning the ball.

Similarly, balls used in international matches belong to the national association hosting the game. A Scotsman, Willie Bell, refereed the famous 1928 international when Scotland's team of Wembley Wizards beat England 5–1. The referee deliberately blew the full-time whistle when Scottish goalkeeper Jack Harkness was holding the ball. Harkness stuffed the ball up his jersey and set off for the dressing-room. Years later Harkness handed the ball over to the Scottish Football Association.

Referees are the guardians of the ball during the match. They usually try to collect it at the end of each half. The best way to do this is to blow for half-time and full-time when close to the ball. This makes it easier to grab the ball and return it to the home club.

BALL BOYS *See* MULTI-BALL SYSTEM, OUTSIDE AGENTS

BANTER

Two players challenge for the ball in the first thirty seconds of the game. It is a fair tackle and the ball pops out for a throw-in.

'Any more f*****g tackles like that and you're in for it,' one says, while a team-mate fetches the ball.

'You'd better f*****g stay clear of me,' says the opponent.

'How've you been keepin', Fred?'

'Not so bad.'

They both laugh and get on with the game.

Footballers need to enjoy 'the verbals' but there are boundaries. It is a criminal offence (and a sending-off offence) to insult another person on the grounds of race or skin colour, and it is a sending-off offence to use offensive, insulting or abusive language. Any banter must be acceptable to all.

Banter is a conversation culture that accepts some aggressive wind-ups. Newcomers can feel at sea until they spot the hidden meanings, and sensitive people can be easily hurt. In football, banter is the mental equivalent of physical sharpness. The verbal one-two accompanies the physical one-two, the poking of fun goes with push-and-run, the antics work alongside the tactics. Banter is often what players miss the most when they retire.

All footballers have to create something from nothing. Matches are exciting but players spend a lot of time in situations that could be boring – changing, training, showering, travelling, hanging around hotel rooms, etc. They find weaknesses that produce in-jokes. They toughen each other up.

Occasionally the banter goes too far. Footballers often feel that it has to be the receiver's problem ('He can't take it') rather than the giver's ('He shouldn't say that'). If a player genuinely feels that the banter is offensive then it is offensive.

Referees have to use humour very carefully. 'I've got my cards ready for you,' a referee joked, when he saw the home-team captain in the car park before the game. An hour later the referee regretted his remark as he had cause to caution the same player.

'You'd decided to book me before the game started,' the player screamed. 'You'd decided in the car park.'

That referee curbed his pre-match banter after that.

BEFORE THE MATCH

Before a big match, the officials will meet for up to an hour to synchronise their watches and discuss a number of issues: which side of the field the assistants will patrol in each half; duties for inspecting the pitch and equipment; which assistant is the senior in case the match referee is injured or unwell; where they each stand at restarts; special communicative signals (e.g. a sign that the referee has seen the flag but has chosen to overrule it, or a code for misconduct if they do not share the same language); what each official will look for at restarts and in offside situations; the duties of the fourth official; how substitutions should be made, and so on. In 1973–74 and 1974–75, Football League referees were regularly teamed with pairs of linesmen.

For a short time (1969 to 1972), Football League referees visited dressing-rooms before kick-off to explain their interpretation of the laws. After one pre-match talk, to Oxford United players, a referee asked if there were any questions.

'Can we swear, Ref?' asked Ron Atkinson.

'Yes, I'll turn a deaf ear to any swearing,' the referee replied.

'Which is your deaf ear, Ref?' asked Oxford's Ken Skeen.

Most competitions will have a rule stipulating when the referee must receive a copy of the team-sheet (the full list of names and numbers of all the players and substitutes to be used in the match). When the Football League launched a rule in 1968 demanding presentation of the team-sheet at least thirty minutes before kick-off, Southport were soon fined £100. Their team list for the League Cup game against Barrow was delayed until ten minutes before the start. In 2002 two League of Wales clubs were each fined £200 for late submission of a team-sheet.

Team-sheet rules may be anything from two minutes before kick-off (a junior league) to an hour (the Premier League). In lower leagues, referees commonly receive team-sheets after the game, but substitutes must be named beforehand. In 2003–04, the team-sheets for Premiership clubs had to include shirt numbers and names of players (including substitutes), team colours (including goalkeeper's colours), and the names and job titles of a maximum of six officials who would occupy the trainer's bench. Most competition rules allow for a team change if a player is injured during the warm-up (i.e. it would not count as one of the team's substitutions).

Premier League matches begin with what the organisers call a 'processual entry'; the teams come out together five minutes before kick-off, led by the match officials. As soon as the referee steps on to the pitch, the players and team officials are under the referee's authority and can be reported for misconduct.

At big matches, a number of rituals may follow – presentations to dignitaries, a minute's tribute, anthems, photographs, handshakes with opponents – and the teams take up suitable positions. Steve Perryman, the official guest at the 2005 FA Vase Final, found he had to meet 22 players, 22 mascots, 10 substitutes and a bunch of club officials. It took some time to clear the pitch.

Of course, national anthems and presentations are the stuff of fantasy for most teams. Some local players are still putting up nets as kick-off approaches. They arrive on the pitch in dribs and drabs, and the referee has to be sure to count them all before the first place-kick is taken. The match may start a few minutes late, especially if someone has left the match-ball in the dressing-room or a pump has to be borrowed from the next pitch. Whatever the level, referees will check pitches and equipment to make sure everything is safe and in order. Before the match, local referees need to test the match-ball, receive their fees (to save going into an abusive post-match dressing-room), check team colours and (on big parks) find out the pitch number.

BIAS See NEUTRALITY

BLEEDING See INJURY

BOMB ALERTS

In the 62nd minute of Birmingham City's home game with Watford in December 1985, a policeman marched on to the pitch and took the referee by the arm. When the bomb alert was announced, everybody left the ground immediately. The game was temporarily suspended and resumed more than an hour later.

There is a story about a game at an RAF camp. A player took a corner-kick and the ball was in the air when bomb-disposal experts blew up a bomb in the next field. The footballers threw themselves to the ground and the ball sailed into the net. The referee had the courtesy to ask for the corner to be retaken.

Bomb alerts are occasions where the referee cedes authority, as safety and security are paramount. Matches at Derby (Easter Monday 1992) and Cheltenham (February 1998) were delayed, but two home-made bombs exploded on the terraces during the half-time interval of an Ajax–Feyenoord match (October 1989). Nineteen people were injured, but the second half was not disrupted.

A match at Everton was threatened with postponement because a World War II bomb had been found near the Goodison Park ground (February 1990). An England–Poland under-21 international kicked off at 10 p.m. after 'a suspicious package' was discovered at Wolverhampton Wanderers' Molineux ground (October 1996). The Worksop Town–Great Harwood Town match was postponed after a package was discovered in the club's car park (September 1997). The bomb squad set up a controlled explosion but the package proved to be harmless.

BOOKING See CARDS, CAUTION

BOOTS See FOOTWEAR

BOUNCE-UP See DROPPED BALL

BRIBERY

Nothing rankles more with football people than the thought that you can't trust a particular referee. Sadly, match-fixing has happened in many countries, and sometimes whole leagues have been suspended. There are normally one of two motivations – a club may approach a referee or opponents to secure a favourable result in a critical match, or a syndicate may try to set up a betting coup. Also, sent-off players sometimes try to bribe a referee into not sending in a report.

British referees have set a high standard for impartiality, and there is no major betting scandal associated with the country. (The scandals of the 1960s and 1990s involved players.) Referees know to report any approach to the appropriate authorities, and club officials should do likewise. When Groningen (Holland) beat Juventus in the first leg of a 1983 UEFA Cup match, the Groningen manager claimed that he was offered money and a plum job in Italy if his team lost the second leg. The manager reported the incident.

Referees have to be very careful about accepting gifts. That brought trouble for three Scottish referees involved in AC Milan bribery allegations (December 1978), and Dynamo Kiev were punished for allegedly offering fur coats to a Spanish referee before one European match (September 1995). In the early 1960s, Grimsby Town were stopped from giving parcels of fish to referees and linesmen. The Swedish referee chosen for a Real Betis–Chelsea match was replaced after he and his assistants were seen in the directors' box watching a Spanish League game involving Real Betis.

One referee, Arthur Ellis, received an offer of £35 if he let Preston North End beat Stoke City (January 1960). The first approach came by letter, the second by telephone, and Ellis reported the matter to the FA. The match ended in a draw and Preston won the replay.

A Premier League referee was in trouble in 2004–05 for not declaring his connection to a horse-racing syndicate. He was supposed to declare all outside interests and business concerns to Professional Game Match Officials Ltd. The FA Council banned betting by players in 1902, and the ban later included officials.

The lure of bribery is because football is full of 1–0 and 2–1 scores. This makes the game exciting, but it also offers plenty of room for 'what if?' questions. Referees really can affect the outcome with one or two key decisions.

There is evidence that a Spanish referee, Guruceto Muro, was bribed before the second leg of the 1984 UEFA Cup semi-final between Anderlecht and Nottingham Forest. Anderlecht won the game 3–0 after losing the first leg 2–0. The referee gave the home team a dubious penalty-kick, and in the dying seconds he ruled out a header from Paul Hart that would have sent Forest through on the away-goals rule. The probable bribery was not revealed until 1997, when new owners took over at Anderlecht. The incomers spotted the 'loan' to the referee, and also learned that money had regularly been paid out to a blackmailer who had threatened to reveal the story to the press. The referee couldn't answer accusations because he had died in a car crash two years after the game.

Brian Clough was the Nottingham Forest manager at the time, and he was also manager of Derby County for a 1973 European Cup semi-final against Juventus. A *Sunday Times* investigation revealed that Dezso Solti, a Hungarian with Italian links, had offered money to Francisco Marques Lobo, the Portuguese referee for the second leg. Lobo, who refused the bribe, was above suspicion – he never met football people without a witness, he reported Solti's $5,000 approach to his Referees Association, and he taped Solti's follow-up phone call confirming the offer – but the West German referee for the first leg at Juventus was widely condemned. Two Derby County players were cautioned for very little in the opening minutes, causing them to miss the second leg.

Bribery is an ongoing concern. It was present in the early 1900s – Billy Meredith (Manchester City) was suspended for a year for allegedly offering Leake (Aston Villa) ten pounds to throw a game in 1905 – and it is still present in the early 2000s. In 2004–05, a top referee in the Czech Republic was arrested, referees in China were charged with accepting bribes, 33 referees and officials were arrested in South Africa for alleged match-fixing, a number of top Polish referees were charged with corruption, and a German referee, Robert Hoyzer, admitted to fixing at least eight matches in conjunction with a Croatian gambling syndicate. Hoyzer, banned for life by the German FA, was arrested by police and sentenced in November 2005 to 29 months' imprisonment for fraud (pending appeal).

If a referee has been bribed, the national FA should expel the referee from football and replay the game (FIFA Referees' Committee 1930). Three matches in Brazil were replayed after a referee admitted that he had received money from an illegal betting ring (October 2005).

As Paul Hart has said about the Anderlecht game, it is sometimes better not to know that your best chance of a European medal has been scuppered by a bent referee. Feeling you were cheated is very hard to resolve. These issues threaten the whole moral and competitive basis of football.

BURST BALL *See* **BALL**

BY-LINE *See* **GOAL-LINE**

CALLING A NAME

If there is any possibility of ambiguity, players should call a name when shouting for the ball.

'Mine, Razor' – 'Chopper's' – 'Goalkeeper'.

Although opponents regularly claim free-kicks ('No name, Ref'), referees will generally only punish a nameless call (e.g. 'Leave it') if it tricks an opponent. There will also be a caution for unsporting behaviour.

The Portsmouth club programme once took up this issue (September 1949): 'In practice, clubs teach their players to shout to a colleague, and, also in practice, it is not for referees to make their own rules governing the game. Agreed, it is for the referee to decide in his own mind the possible effect upon an opponent and if in his opinion it was meant to deceive an opponent and not an instruction to a colleague, he is perfectly justified in awarding a free-kick against the offender.'

In a game shortly after World War II, a Sheffield Wednesday forward shouted 'Right' and a Fulham defender let the ball through to him. The Wednesday player put the ball in the net, but the referee awarded an indirect free-kick to Fulham. The Wednesday player was not called Wright.

CAMERAS See PHOTOGRAPHY

CAPS

In the 1870s players were identified by their individual caps. George Ramsay (Aston Villa) wore 'a round polo cap of the type popular among schoolboys at the time when Osman Pasha's name was on everyone's tongue'. When players started heading the ball, caps were jettisoned by all except goalkeepers.

There is nothing specific in the laws about caps, but if a goalkeeper took off his cap and threw it at the ball to save a goal it would be a caution and an indirect free-kick. Referees are allowed to wear black caps in extreme heat, though they run the risk of being tagged 'executioners'.

CAPTAINS

Captains have no special rights, but their role involves taking some responsibility for team-mates' behaviour. Captains may be asked for help identifying team-mates, or help in calming down particular players. On occasion referees have called together – and talked to – the two captains as a more preferable option to calling together all 22 players. Examples include the 1960 all-Sheffield FA Cup quarter-final, and an Oldham–Reading match (December 1966).

Modern captains identify themselves by armbands. The Russian captain wore a white armband in the 1952 Olympic Games, but a new era for armbands was heralded when Billy Bremner (Leeds United) wore one for the first time (December 1972).

CARDS

One day in July 1966, Ken Aston was driving through London while thinking about how referees could communicate better with spectators. Aston, FIFA's chief refereeing instructor, had spotted problems in recent matches. Journalists had been confused about whether the Charlton brothers had both been booked during the England–Argentina match (they had), and three players had taken an age to leave the field after being sent off. As Aston drove down Wrights Lane and stopped at the Kensington High Street traffic lights, he had the idea of red and yellow cards. He recognised the worldwide understanding of yellow lights (caution) and red lights (stop). Here was how a referee could make cautions and dismissals clear to all concerned.

The idea of the referee holding up a yellow card (to signify a caution) or a red card (to signify a sending-off) was tested at the 1968 Olympic Games. A Mexican referee used his red card three times to Bulgaria players in the final, won 4–1 by Hungary. Cards seemed a good way to overcome language problems. After cards were used in the 1970 FIFA World Cup™, the system was soon accepted as standard practice for international matches.

Before October 1976, when cards were first used in English domestic football, a referee's decision could be unclear. In March 1974, Doyle (City) and Macari (United) were sent off in a Manchester derby. They refused to leave the field, and there was much confusion. Referee Clive Thomas picked up the ball and took the players off the pitch. He went into his dressing-room, threw the ball down and watched it bounce, as he would recall, 'thirty-six times'. When he'd calmed down, he went into each dressing-room and explained that two players had been sent off and would not be returning. Then he restarted the match.

While the card system was beneficial in international football, there were doubts about its relevance to domestic football. English referees were taken aback when Tom Reynolds, a FIFA referee, received a short ban for failing to hold up a yellow card, and there were other teething problems. In his autobiography, Sir Stanley Rous wrote about a referee who cautioned six players for encroaching at a free-kick. The referee actually tore up a yellow card into six pieces, instead of correctly showing each player the yellow card in turn.

There was also clarification that the referee was to show both the yellow and the red card in turn when a player was sent off for a second cautionable offence (1993). A second yellow card is an automatic sending-off. People have often disputed whether this should be the case. In the 1970s, the idea of a super-caution was mooted whereby the player would remain on the pitch. However, the inherent nature of the caution is that it is a *warning* to a player.

In November 1980, the Referees' Association Council passed a resolution that red and yellow cards should be abolished at every level of the game in England. They felt that cards could provoke and humiliate players, thus sparking them into further bad behaviour. English football thus took a six-year break from the card system (from 17 January 1981). They were reintroduced because television viewers throughout the world saw no cards being used in England, and national associations started to query whether the English League used different laws. Red and yellow cards became obligatory in top-level football (IFAB 1987) and then mandatory at all levels (1992).

So red and yellow cards returned to English football in 1987. A referee's 'pack of cards' will usually contain different-shaped cards to ensure that red cards can be distinguished from yellow ones (e.g. round-edged red and oblong yellow) as there are occasions where referees have pulled out the wrong colour by mistake. Most referees carry their red and yellow cards in separate pockets as a safety mechanism.

If a player from each team is sent off, most referees would choose to send them off one at a time. Some referees think that it is best to send off the home player first so that the sending off of the away-team player is a finale that the crowd enjoy. Other referees think that sending off the visiting player first gets the crowd on their side (and the home fans might not even notice their player leaving). In all circumstances it pays to be two arm-lengths away from the player when showing a card. Otherwise the player might see red in more ways than one.

Some players have been shown the red card on more than one occasion in the same match. Goalkeeper Duncan McMillan (Brora Rangers) received three red cards in a Highland League match against Inverness Clachnacuddin (1999). The first was for violent conduct, the second for throwing his gloves at the referee, and the third for tossing his jersey at the referee. And Dean Windass (Aberdeen) was suspended for seven weeks after receiving three red cards at Dundee United – one for two cautions, another for abusive language, and a third for throwing the corner-flag to the floor (November 1997). Some people still believe that red cards are a real trigger for assault, abuse and wild behaviour. Fernando d'Ercoli (Pianti) ate one when the referee showed it to him (1989). Other sent-off players have grabbed the red card and run off with it.

Red and yellow cards are to be shown only to players, substitutes or substituted players, not team officials or other spectators (2001). Team officials can be dismissed from the immediate area (including the technical area) and any such incident should be reported as misconduct to the appropriate authority. A physiotherapist or medical assistant guilty of misconduct may remain in the technical area (at the referee's discretion) but the misconduct should be reported.

Cards of other colours have no official place in the laws of football but there have been experiments. After the 2003 Helsinki Cup matches, referees handed out green cards for fair play. In France, the green card has been used to show that medical attention is required. And an American experiment involved issuing green cards to unruly spectators at matches involving children. But the most commonly used card is yellow for caution.

CAUTION

A caution is an official warning. In the event of any further cautionable offence, the player will be sent from the field.

Despite the introduction of yellow cards, the procedure of cautioning a player has not changed much over the years. The referee notes the player's name and number, the minute of the match and brief details of the offence. The referee clearly uses the word 'caution' to warn the player. Only then will a yellow card be shown. Yellow cards are often shown to a player's back because the necessary business has already been done and the player is getting back into position. The yellow card is simply confirmation.

Referees ask for a player's name even if they already know it. They would normally check team-sheet spellings later, to see if the names match those in their notebooks. The names of cautioned players must be reported to the relevant football association. Referees are not allowed to retract a caution before it is reported. The caution can mean a fine to cover administration costs.

Sometimes an unregistered player will turn to his captain and say, 'What's my name today?' Referees report the name given to them, but they can note their suspicions. Giving the wrong name may lead to additional punishment. Charles Chaplin, who kept goal in the Northern League either side of World War II, had trouble convincing referees that he really was Charlie Chaplin, while a Castlebar Celtic goalkeeper called Pat Jennings suffered similarly when he was cautioned for time-wasting. Gordon Hill once cautioned a player during a game in Iran and it took him two or three minutes to copy the Arabic number from the player's back.

John Sleeuwenhoek (Aston Villa and Birmingham City) was a tough central defender who was surprisingly only cautioned once during his long career (and that was for time-wasting as a deputy goalkeeper). Sleeuwenhoek seriously wondered if it was because referees had trouble spelling his name. He knew that to be true on at least one occasion. The book came out, Sleeuwenhoek repeated his name twice, and the referee said, 'Forget it.'

The caution was first mentioned in 1880 as part of the referee's power to caution players for ungentlemanly conduct. When Rotherham County beat Gresley Rovers 3–2 in 1896, the referee took nearly every player's name and sent off Ward (Gresley), but it was rare for a player to be cautioned in the game's early days. Even in the 1960s a caution could bring a real stigma. When a Newcastle United player was cautioned on a close-season tour, he was sent home on the next plane.

Gradually the number of cautions per match increased. When Tongham Youth Club (Surrey) played Hawley (Hants), 22 players and a linesman were cautioned (November 1969). Notts County had nine cautioned against Manchester United, and their manager, Larry Lloyd, questioned why the other two weren't more committed (December 1983). A referee registered thirteen cautions and three sendings-off in a match between Burton Albion and Telford United (January 1996).

A caution brings no immediate punishment – temporary expulsions (sin-bins) have been rejected by IFAB – but there are totting-up procedures whereby a player will be suspended for continually offending. Clubs can be punished if their aggregate number of cautions exceed FA standards.

There are a number of cautionable offences: unsporting behaviour (previously ungentlemanly behaviour); entering the field without permission (1904); persistently infringing the laws (IFAB 1907); encroachment (FA 1910), showing dissent at a referee's decision (IFAB 1924); leaving the field without permission (1939); and delaying the restart of play. (For a fuller discussion of each offence, see under the relevant headings.)

There is no mention of *booking* a player in the laws. Referees may note names on cards rather than in books, and the names of sent-off players are noted too. As the referee Pat Partridge once said, 'Referees caution players, show-business agents book them.'

In August 1972, the FA made it clear that a player could be cautioned only once during a game. A second caution in the same game is a sending-off offence. When Chile played Australia, the referee cautioned Ray Richards (Australia) without realising that it was the player's second caution (June

1974). An off-the-field official pointed out the mistake to the referee, who sent off the offender. But the referee at Liverpool failed to send off Aufhauser (Graz AK) after cautioning him twice inside ten minutes (August 2004) and a referee failed to send off Croatia's number three (Simunic) because he mistakenly noted the name of Australia's number three (Moore) when cautioning Simunic for the second time (June 2006).

Referees don't need to stop play specifically to deliver a caution – they may wait until the ball is next out of play. If advantage is allowed, however, the same player may commit a second cautionable offence during the same passage of play. This is still a sending-off offence (IFAB 1972). John Moncur (West Ham) committed two cautionable offences within ten seconds in a cup tie at Macclesfield (January 2002).

Players have been known to be cautioned before the match has kicked off (for instance, a goalkeeper for marking a line in the centre of his goal) and players have cautioned during penalty shoot-outs. Edinho (Brazil) was cautioned during a shoot-out between France and Brazil (July 1986).

CELEBRATION OF GOALS

Dixie Dean scored 100 goals in 1927–28 (in all competitions), and afterwards it was 'never more than hitching up his pants and back to centre-circle, and maybe a handshake'. In the mid-1960s there was a trend towards players punching the air after a goal, and then Mick Channon (Southampton and Manchester City) began twirling his right arm in an impersonation of a windmill. Celebrations then became more demonstrative. In the late 1960s, Tony Coleman (Manchester City) told his manager that he didn't score many goals because he wanted to avoid all the kissing and hugging afterwards. The FA started talking about punishing excessive celebrations in February 1976.

Brian Fidler was an outrageous showman who played for Heanor Town, Macclesfield and Burton Albion in the 1960s and 1970s. After scoring one goal, during a Cheshire League match, Fidler taunted Altrincham officials until Altrincham manager Freddie Pye responded by throwing a bucketful of water at him. After scoring for Macclesfield in the 1970 FA Trophy Final, Fidler lapped Wembley before jumping the fence and hugging fans.

Sometimes players need protecting from themselves. Paulo Diego (Servette) had to have a finger amputated after catching his ring in a fence while celebrating a goal (December 2004), substitute Perry Groves (Arsenal) once knocked himself out on the dugout roof, and Celestine Babayaro (Chelsea) broke his leg while performing a backward somersault after a team-mate's goal. Children have suffered severe injuries when caught at the bottom of celebratory pyramids, Patrick Vieira (Arsenal) injured a knee with a post-goal slide against Manchester United (November 1997), and Roger Osborne

(Ipswich) was so overcome with emotion after his 1978 FA Cup Final winner and enduring the suffocating congratulations of his team-mates that he had to be substituted. After scoring in the 2006 FA Vase Final, Andy Kinsey (Nantwich Town) threw his shirt into the crowd and dislocated his shoulder.

Time-wasting is a critical issue. Some scoring teams sprint back into kick-off positions inside twenty seconds, particularly if they are still behind or are desperate for a winner. In contrast, it took 65 seconds to kick-off after Iliev (Lokomotiv Plovdiv) scored against Bolton (September 2005). This is one reason why FIFA instructed that a player should be cautioned for removing a jersey while celebrating a goal (January 1996). Faustino Asprilla (Newcastle United) was cautioned for taking off his shirt and hoisting it on a corner-flag after scoring. The shirt-removal rule stayed on the books until 2001, and then returned in 2004. The design of certain shirts, particularly those with built-in undershirts, meant that a player took several minutes to replace his shirt after a goal during the 2003 Confederations Cup. Some cultures found the exposure of the male chest offensive, but it was still a caution if a player took off a shirt and revealed an exact replica underneath.

Time-wasting takes other forms. Friio (Peterborough) scored an excellent goal at Port Vale in October 2003. He walked slowly and calmly back towards the centre-circle, and then decided to run past his own supporters doing an impersonation of an aeroplane. The referee cautioned him. Celebrations could still be innovative, but synchronised celebrations are not to be encouraged if they waste time.

The biggest concern for the police is excessive or provocative celebration in front of opposition fans. When West Ham United played Manchester United in a match that was televised live, Ray Wilkins (Manchester United) and Dave Swindlehurst (West Ham) were warned not to go to the crowd in their jubilation (November 1983). Referees were encouraged to report anything that might wind up the crowd. The FA found Gary Neville (Manchester United) guilty of improper conduct and fined him £5,000 after his wild celebrations of the winner against Liverpool, an action that would have warranted a caution had the referee seen it (January 2006).

Other bad-taste celebrations have included getting down on all fours and sniffing the goal-line to simulate cocaine use (Robbie Fowler), a Nazi-style salute (Mark Bosnich) and symbolising Protestantism by pretending to play the flute to fans of the notoriously Catholic Glasgow Celtic (Paul Gascoigne). Finidi George (Nigeria) once crawled to the corner-flag and raised his hind leg like a dog using a lamppost. After scoring against Chester, Liam Daish (Birmingham) picked up a toy trumpet tossed by a spectator, only to receive a caution for acting the musician (December 1994).

When Foresters scored their High Wycombe Sunday Cup Final winner against FC Beaconsfield, ten players formed the usual celebratory pyramid

(May 2005). The only absentee was the goalkeeper, who sprinted to the touchline and kissed a woman on the lips. Was that provocative behaviour? Only if it was someone else's wife.

In March 1997 Robbie Fowler (Liverpool) scored a goal against Brann Bergen and then lifted his jersey to reveal a 'SUPPORT THE SACKED 500 DOCKERS' T-shirt. Fowler was fined £900 as he was considered to be in breach of a UEFA regulation banning the use of sporting events for manifestation of non-sporting issues (in this case the dockers' bitter two-year dispute). Players must not reveal undershirts with advertising or slogans (IFAB 2002). Naturally that did not stop players. Roscoe D'Sane (Aldershot) revealed 'R U WATCHIN CPFC' after scoring against Accrington Stanley (August 2003), Jermain Defoe (Tottenham) unveiled 'HAPPY BIRTHDAY BABY' against Middlesbrough (November 2004), and Fulham's Collins John scored 'FOR MY MUM' at Derby (January 2005). All were cautioned.

A new wave of shirt-removal punishments began in June 2004, when Ronaldo (Portugal) was cautioned after his goal against Holland. Shirt-removal was an easy offence for a referee to detect, and referees are deemed to have failed in their duty if they do not issue a caution.

Tim Cahill (Everton) received a yellow card for lifting his shirt up and covering his head after scoring the winning goal at Manchester City (September 2004). Cahill was sent off, as it was his second caution of the match. There was confusion at the time. Partial removal of the shirt was not subject to a caution, but there was some doubt about whether the Ravanelli-style head-covering technique was cautionable or not. It was.

In September 2004 David Healy (Northern Ireland) scored against Wales and then managed to get himself cautioned twice (and therefore sent off) before play restarted. First he kicked the corner-flag out of the ground, then he made a provocative gesture in front of Welsh fans.

Kamara (Portsmouth) was cautioned twice in two days for removing his shirt in celebration of goals against Middlesbrough and Leeds United (October 2004). Pompey assistant manager Jim Smith considered sticking Kamara's shirt to his shorts with superglue.

Even though leaving the field of play without permission is a cautionable offence, the new law on celebrating a goal made it clear that players were allowed to leave the field to celebrate as long as they returned as soon as possible. When Lee Hendrie (Aston Villa) scored against Crystal Palace, he jumped over the advertising hoardings and made contact with the crowd. This was considered to be 'excessive celebrations' as it could easily have encouraged spectators to surge forward dangerously. Perhaps the weirdest-ever caution for excessive celebrating was that of Patrick Kisnorbo (Hearts) whose 'goal' against Hibs was disallowed (November 2003).

In contrast to players, referees remain impassive in the aftermath of a goal.

They are usually busy managing celebrations, dealing with disputes, making a note of the goal, and trying to resume the game as quickly as possible. However, referee Mike Reed was 'rested' for a match after he celebrated a well-judged 'advantage' which allowed Patrik Berger (Liverpool) to score against Leeds (February 2000).

Goals are potential flashpoints. Sometimes players run into the net and fight over the ball. When Damien Spencer (Cheltenham Town) scored against Swansea City, reducing his team's deficit to 2–1, Cheltenham players tried to retrieve the ball quickly and Swansea players tried to stop them. The result was a brawl involving most of the players. Trundle (Swansea) was cautioned.

Players *can* learn. One Ryman League goalscorer was cautioned for removing his shirt. Two minutes later the same player scored again. His hands grabbed his shirt and then his brain remembered. He fiddled a while and then just put his hands up in the air.

When Andrew Johnson (Crystal Palace) scored against his former club (Birmingham City), he was a model of restraint and responsibility (October 2004). Johnson simply turned around and ran back to the centre-circle. He had earned his place in history alongside Dixie Dean.

CELEBRITY KICK-OFFS

A rare 'celebrity kick-off' took place before a France–Switzerland international in March 2005. A small boy kicked off the match to draw attention to a children's charity. The boy was then led off the field and the match started in the customary way.

Local dignitaries often started matches in the early days of soccer. For instance, Captain Ratcliff kicked off the Burton-upon-Trent local derby between Swifts and Wanderers (April 1898), and Lord Beresford, Admiral of the Fleet, started a Newcastle–Sunderland friendly (September 1904). When Notts County played Coventry City in a charity match, Sir Oswald Mosley 'kicked off in favour of Coventry at 3.40 before about 2,000 spectators in bright and warm weather' (May 1919).

In March 1907, the FA Council decided that 'the practice of kicking-off by persons other than the players competing in a match is prohibited, except in charity matches'. When it was allowed, the correct procedure was for the referee to allow the celebrity to kick-off as a separate pre-match act. The players then resume their positions and start the game correctly.

Most referees would object to a celebrity kick-off, unless the celebrity was a film star of their dreams. Unsurprisingly, the referee allowed Marilyn Monroe to kick off a game between American and Israeli teams in New York (1957).

CENTRE-CIRCLE

The ten-yard encroachment distance for kick-offs existed in the original 1863 FA laws, but it was not until 1891 that a centre-circle, with a radius of ten yards, was added to the field markings. The circle was once known as 'the Smith circle' as it had been suggested by Robert J Smith, an FA Council member who had been an umpire for the 1890 FA Cup Final.

The circle has three purposes in modern football: it helps the referee ensure that opponents are at least ten yards from the ball at a kick-off or place-kick; (ii) it is where all the players (except the two goalkeepers and the kicker) have to stand during a penalty shoot-out; and (iii) it should impress on players 'from the very commencement that they must be ten yards off whenever any kind of free-kick is taken by their opponents' (1913).

CENTRE LINE See HALFWAY-LINE

CENTRE MARK

An appropriate mark in the centre of the field was added to the field markings in 1891. This assists the referee with place-kicks and kick-offs.

CEREMONIAL FREE-KICKS See FREE-KICK

CHANGING DECISIONS

Referees can change their decision as long as the game has not restarted (IFAB 1956) and the final whistle hasn't sounded (IFAB 2005), but referees bear in mind that this may detract from the respect shown them. Players get upset if they jump a fence and fetch the ball from an allotment only to find out that it isn't their throw-in after all.

Stanley Rous once blew for a penalty-kick in a match between Millwall and Charlton, but he immediately realised that it was the goalkeeper who had handled the ball and not a defender (as he had first thought). Rous walked past the penalty spot, past the goalposts, and called out to the crowd, 'If the man with the whistle blows it again I will have him removed.' Then Rous restarted the game by dropping the ball.

This is not the recommended action. Most referees would simply own up to their mistake. Their innate sense of fairness means they will want to correct a decision even if it might spark further wrath. In the 1960 FA Cup semi-final, Sheffield Wednesday seemed to have equalised against Blackburn Rovers.

The referee pointed to the centre to signal a goal, but then he changed his mind when he saw the linesman flagging.

Punishments can also be changed. In a Rangers–Celtic derby, the referee showed Tony Shepherd (Celtic) a red card but then changed his mind before play had restarted and allowed Shepherd to play on (October 1986). Lee Hendrie (Aston Villa) received a second yellow card in the 65th minute of a match against Arsenal (October 2000). At first the referee did not send off Hendrie but he was able to rectify his error before play had restarted. Another referee cautioned Davenport (Norwich) for simulation against Reading, but changed his mind after talking to an assistant, and awarded Norwich a penalty-kick (September 2005).

Penalty-kicks are sometimes given on second thoughts. Kember (Chelsea) brought down Armstrong (Arsenal) in a 1973 FA Cup tie. The referee initially gave a free-kick outside the penalty area, and Arsenal players protested. The referee spoke with the linesman and gave a penalty. Then the Chelsea players protested. A controversial penalty-kick also settled a EURO 2000™ semi-final. The referee had given a corner-kick to France when he noticed his assistant's raised flag. Xavier (Portugal) was penalised for handling, and Zidane (France) converted the penalty for a golden-goal winner.

Penalty-kick awards have also been changed. Harrison (Alfreton Town) was already moving forward to take a penalty at Ilkeston when the referee saw the linesman's flag, blew his whistle and eventually gave a free-kick to Ilkeston (January 1966). In February 2004 a referee at Portsmouth talked to his assistant for nearly a minute before retracting his decision to award Liverpool a penalty.

During a game at Fulham, the referee seemed to give a penalty-kick to Fulham when Ashley Cole (Arsenal) tackled Andy Cole (September 2004). The referee immediately realised that he might have made an error. He went across to his assistant, who explained that the Arsenal player had got the ball. The referee changed his mind and restarted play with a dropped ball. When questioned later, the referee said that the players' reactions had helped him to change his mind. Most pundits seemed to think this meant the referee had been influenced by dissenting players, but in fact the referee meant his immediate evaluation of the scene after the tackle. Referees see a tableau, like a camera image, which either looks right or doesn't. They take in the picture – where the ball is, how the players are lying, their body language, etc. – and sometimes they have second thoughts. Referees do not change decisions because they are shouted at and abused. They do so either because they sense they are wrong or because they receive more information (e.g. an assistant's flag). Sometimes they have anticipated something would happen and it hasn't. Everybody in football does that occasionally. Changing a decision is the refereeing equivalent of a mistimed tackle.

CHANGING ENDS

Until 1875, teams changed ends after every goal (or at half-time if neither side had scored). This could be a real disadvantage. A team could kick against the wind for 45 minutes, change round, score a goal, and find themselves kicking against the wind for another 35 minutes. Then they might concede a late equaliser and be too exhausted to stand up. From 1875, teams changed ends only at half-time.

Teams can also change ends before the first place-kick if the team winning the toss chooses to do that. Occasionally referees have resolved a crowd problem by asking the teams to play the same way as in the first half. This needs general agreement, and should not be considered if the weather or pitch conditions give any favour.

CHARGING OPPONENTS See SHOULDER-CHARGING

CHILDREN'S MATCHES See MODIFICATIONS TO THE LAWS

CIGARETTES

There are legendary tales of star players stubbing out their last pre-match cigarette in the tunnel as they go on to the pitch. And there are stories of amateur goalkeepers borrowing a cigarette from a spectator behind the goal.

The authorities are always worried about what might happen next. Where will it all lead? Allow a player to smoke and they might be stubbing them out on an opponent's arm as a corner-kick is taken.

Smoking a cigarette while the ball is in play is a cautionable offence (unsporting behaviour), but a player has a right to a half-time interval for the purpose of smoking.

CIRCUMFERENCE OF THE BALL See BALL

COACHES See TECHNICAL AREA

COLLUSION

In 1878–79, Trent Rovers needed to beat Newhall St John 49–0 in order to win a local Staffordshire amateur league. Guess what happened? Yes, Trent

Rovers won 49–0. Guess what happened next? Yes, league officials suspended both teams.

There is nothing in the laws to stop a team, or a player, from scoring deliberate own-goals, but the competition's authorities and the national association will certainly take action. It is a sure way to bring football into disrepute.

The most extreme case happened in Toamasina, Madagascar, when Stade Olympique l'Emryne (SOE) scored 149 own-goals and lost 149–0 to AS Adema (October 2002). The SOE players were protesting about a refereeing decision in their previous match, when they had conceded a last-kick equaliser to a disputed penalty. The Stade Olympique coach was suspended for three years, and four players received one-year bans.

Certain ill-conceived competition rules have provoked players into planning own-goals. One example was the 1998 Tiger Cup. Thailand and Indonesia both wished to finished second to avoid favourites Vietnam in the next round. With a few minutes left and the score at 2–2, Indonesia attacked their own goal. Despite fervent 'defence' by Thailand, Indonesia's goalkeeper got hold of the ball and threw it into his own net. The authorities punished the teams involved.

An even stranger example occurred in the 1994 Shell Caribbean Cup. The rules stipulated that drawn group matches would be decided by golden goals. More interestingly, the golden goal would count double in the for-and-against columns. When Barbados needed to beat Grenada by two goals to qualify for the next round, they realised that a 2–1 win was not good enough, so they deliberately scored an own-goal to take the game into extra-time. Then a golden goal gave Barbados a 4–2 win. (After scoring the own-goal, they had an awkward few minutes while defending at both ends of the pitch. A goal at either end would have taken Grenada through.)

Boxing rules stipulate that a boxer can be cautioned, warned or disqualified for 'hiding behind his gloves to avoid boxing' but football has nothing similar in its laws. In April 1898, Stoke City played Burnley in what was then called a Test match (similar to today's play-offs) to decide promotion and relegation. The players were aware that a draw would ensure higher-class football for both teams and there was hardly a shot at goal. Frustrated supporters did their best to stop the game by refusing to return the ball when it came their way. They even tried kicking the ball over the stand into the River Trent, but it was to no avail. The referee used five balls and the result was a 0–0 draw.

Bristol City players kept possession of the ball in their own half for the last five minutes at Coventry, whose players stood back because a 2–2 draw suited both teams (May 1977), and a match between West Germany and Austria sparked much controversy at the 1982 FIFA World Cup™. The Germans scored in the tenth minute and very little action followed. As Algeria had already completed all their matches, both sets of players knew that a 1–0 result would enable both West Germany and Austria to progress to the next stage at their expense. It later became common practice to synchronise the starts of matches where the outcomes had wider consequences.

Other league results suiting both teams include Holland and Ireland's 1–1 draw (June 1990), the 2–2 draw between Bayer Leverkusen and AS Monaco (December 1997), Swindon Town's 1–1 home draw with Hartlepool United (May 2004), a 1–1 draw between Uruguay and Argentina (November 2001) and Denmark's 2–2 draw with Sweden (June 2004). There was no evidence of any collusion in these matches – quite the opposite – but that did not stop accusations.

COLOUR BLINDNESS See EYESIGHT

COLOUR CLASH

The 1882 FA Cup Final was between Blackburn Rovers (blue and white quarters) and Old Etonians (light blue and white harlequin shirts). Rovers had to buy a new set of shirts when they arrived in London. In those days, two local teams would go on the pitch wearing the same colour strip, and the referee would toss a coin to decide which team would wear waistcoats or pullovers.

The most common colour clash in the early days was between a goalkeeper and his team-mates. Until 1909 goalkeepers wore the same colour shirts as the rest of the team. When Clapton Orient played Leeds City, the goalkeeper had to change his shirt to a more distinctive colour (March 1914).

After a shirt clash between two Football League teams, it was decreed that all clubs should register their colours at the start of the season, and that home teams should keep a spare set of shirts (1890). In the early 1920s, however, the Football League deemed it the visitors' responsibility to change shirts and socks in the event of a colour clash. Competition rules vary. The Bedford Sunday League requires the home team to change, while the Rochdale & County Sunday League puts the onus on the away team (2004–05).

Football League regulations stated that colour clashes only applied to shirts and stockings. One referee was mildly rebuked by the League when he allowed a team to change blue shorts, which clashed with the opposition's blue shorts (Bury v Mansfield Town, February 1968).

A clash of sock colours can be more confusing for players and officials than a clash of shirts. When Chelsea and Everton both wore white socks, the game was held up for eight minutes while Everton players went off to change to mustard-coloured socks (December 1966). A similar thing happened in Stranraer versus St Johnstone (November 1999), and Luton Town versus Sheffield Wednesday (September 2004).

As part of their pre-match routine, referees check that their own kit does not clash. The referee failed to do that when Sheffield met Glasgow at Hampden Park (September 1930). He wore a white shirt without a jacket, and Sheffield played in white shirts and black shorts. After several good passes to the referee, Sheffield captain Jimmy Seed asked the official to stop the game and put on a jacket. The referee obliged. Soon afterwards, an IFAB decision stated that the referee in international matches should wear a jacket or blazer 'in a distinctive colour' (June 1932).

Millwall, who played in royal blue, used to provide grey alpaca blazers for officials who arrived with a blue or black blazer. Referee Peter Rhodes wore a maroon sweater at Notts County to avoid clashing with Brentford's navy-blue change strip (November 1966), and Arthur Dimond wore a brown outfit for a match between Derby County and Bury (March 1967). After seven minutes of a match at Leeds United, referee David Elleray borrowed a training top because his kit clashed with Newcastle's away strip (October 1997).

For ordinary league games, the message to club secretaries is clear: check the opposition's colours in a current league handbook. When Coventry City met Southend United, both teams took to the field in variations of blue and white (January 1962). The referee stopped the match after three minutes and Coventry changed into red shirts on the field. A match at Walsall started late because the referee ordered Darlington to change shirts before the match (February 1967).

In April 1969, Derby County travelled to Millwall intending to play in an all-white kit. When they arrived they discovered that Millwall had changed their shirts from blue to white at the start of that season. Millwall loaned Derby a set of red shirts and black shorts.

Before the start of Middlesbrough versus Crystal Palace, Middlesbrough players protested that the Palace strip clashed with their colours and the players were told to return to the dressing-room for a quick change (August 1968).

Sometimes there is just too much of one or two colours. A referee ordered a change at half-time when Swindon Town (white shirts and red shorts) played at Rotherham United (red shirts and white shorts) in February 1979, and journalists complained of difficulties when Cambridge United (yellow shirts, black shorts and yellow socks) played Oxford United (black shirts, yellow shorts and black socks) in February 2005.

A new reason for a colour change arrived during the 1978 FIFA World Cup™. Hungary (red shirts) met France (blue shirts) in a group game, and television companies wanted viewers with black-and-white sets to be able to distinguish between the teams. The kick-off was delayed by forty minutes while a set of green-and-white shirts were borrowed from a local club. The delay disrupted television's tight schedule.

Shirts have become more stylish and colourful, and professional teams redesign their kit more frequently than in the past. In the 1990s, colour clashes became more of a problem. Michael Gibson, writing in the non-League magazine *Team Talk* (February 1994), stated his views on a Barrow–Emley match which saw both teams wearing blue and white: '. . . not only were the spectators confused, but it was obvious that the match officials could not always see who was playing for which side. On many occasions offside decisions were given, when in fact nobody was anywhere near offside, and free-kicks were awarded against the wrong team.'

When Manchester United wore two-tone grey at Southampton, the clash was with the background; United players complained that they couldn't see their team-mates (April 1996). In one parks match, the referee was confused because the two teams on the next pitch had exactly the same colours as the ones he was refereeing.

It is not considered to be too serious a problem if the referee's kit is the same as that of a goalkeeper, but it should be avoided if possible. At Old Trafford, the Real Madrid goalkeeper (Casillas) and the referee (Collina) both wore yellow shirts, black shorts and black socks (April 2003), while Robinson (England) matched the referee's all-black kit against Northern Ireland (March 2005), and goalkeeper Peruzzi (Italy) looked to be on the same team as the referee against Scotland (September 2005).

Technically, the two goalkeepers should wear distinctive jerseys in case one goalkeeper goes up for a corner-kick. Most referees would not see this as a major problem – it only affects the last minute of very few games – but there have been cases where two indistinguishable goalkeepers have jumped for the same ball.

Players' colours can also clash with spectators or stewards. The Queen's Park Rangers' mascot was despatched for confusing the referee in the game against Preston (February 2005), and Norwich City players complained that Lofty the Lion looked like a Bolton Wanderers player (March 2005). At top-class stadia, kit can clash with thousands of replica shirts in the crowd.

COMMON SENSE

Some people think that common sense is so rare that it should be called uncommon sense. Referees, however, value it highly. Their eighteenth (unwritten) law of soccer is the law of common sense – if the laws provide no obvious answer, find a sensible solution that is fair, safe, and in keeping with the game's spirit.

Common sense helps the game to go ahead when the markings aren't as clear as everyone would like. Common sense might lead to a team turning jerseys inside out to prevent a certain colour clash. Common sense is stopping the game for a dropped ball when the ball is trapped under a fallen player and an opponent is sorely tempted to hack at it. And so on. Common sense is taking the situation into account.

COMPENSATION

James Condon (Whittle Wanderers) was awarded damages of £4,900 (plus interest and costs) after he suffered a broken right leg as a result of a reckless and dangerous challenge by Gurdever Basi (Khalsa). Basi had been sent off by the referee for serious foul play, and Condon was off work for nine months. The match was played in January 1980, and the legal journey ended with an unsuccessful appeal in May 1985. As in all compensation cases, the referee was an important neutral witness.

In professional football, Brian McCord was awarded more than £250,000 in damages when he sued Swansea City and John Cornforth in a case that ended up in court (1997). Cornforth had gone 'over the top' to McCord (Stockport) in a game in March 1993. But the big landmark case came when Gordon Watson (Bradford City) was awarded over £900,000 in damages (to cover loss of earnings and medical care costs) after he suffered a double fracture of the leg following a challenge by Huddersfield's Kevin Gray (February 1997). The injury required six operations. Watson, 25, was in the fourth minute of his third game for Bradford City after a £550,000 move from Southampton.

George Shepherd (Macclesfield) successfully sued Bishop Auckland for £30,000 after having his leg broken in an FA Trophy tie. Other settled cases include those brought by Jim Brown (Dunfermline), John O'Neill (Norwich), Ian Durrant (Rangers), Danny Thomas (Tottenham Hotspur), Matthew Holmes (Charlton), Ian Nolan (Sheffield Wednesday) and Chris Casper (Reading). Footballers can expect a certain amount of physical contact, but all participants have a duty of care towards others.

Sometimes, however, legal actions are costly and they may not succeed. It cost John O'Neill (Norwich) £150,000 in legal fees to win an estimated £70,000 compensation, and cases brought by Darren Pitcher (Crystal Palace) and Paul Elliott (Chelsea) were lost in court.

COMPETITION RULES

One of the confusing things about football's rules is that they emanate from a myriad of sources – the written laws, IFAB decisions on the laws, FIFA

Referees' Committee decisions, FIFA experiments, directives from national football associations, UEFA rules, company or club statutes, police rulings, the laws of the land, and competition rules. The last of these (competition rules) applies to specific league and cup tournaments.

Competition rules will cover the likes of colour changes, submission of team-sheets, the number of substitutes, the number of match officials, the procedure for deciding drawn cup ties, the eligibility of players, disciplinary procedures, floodlight standards, duration of the half-time interval, pitch watering, referees' fees, and submission of the referee's report.

Referees need to understand competition rules, but sometimes they make mistakes. In a 1971 European Cup Winners' Cup tie, Glasgow Rangers beat Sporting Lisbon 3–2 in Glasgow, and Sporting won 3–2 in Lisbon. Both teams scored another goal in extra-time, so Sporting won 4–3 on the night. This meant that Rangers had won the tie – away goals counted double and the extra-time away goal gave Rangers victory – but the referee incorrectly ordered a shoot-out, which Sporting won 3–0. Rangers were reinstated as winners a day later.

CONSISTENCY OF DECISIONS

Coaches frequently complain that referees are inconsistent. On the other hand, referees have long debated about where the balance should lie between individual discretion (common sense or personal style) and standardised check lists (consistency). The authorities have worked very hard to promote clear criteria (e.g. what constitutes 'denying a clear goalscoring opportunity') at the risk of alienating those who favour flexibility. In the mid-1990s, one top Scottish referee resigned because he was unwilling to be a 'robot with a whistle'.

Consistency has many forms – consistency from one referee to another, consistency within the same referee from week to week, consistency in the referee's decisions from minute to minute in the same match. The consistency that most referees would love to see is a consistency in how players, managers and spectators behave towards referees. They would like their decisions to be accepted . . . consistently.

Consistency is absent in most realms of human activity, and referees probably fare well on the consistency scale when compared with jurors, teachers, judges, social workers, lawyers and doctors. Referees are certainly as consistent as players.

CONTACT LENS See EYESIGHT

CONTROL

As referee Jack Taylor wrote in 1975, 'The operative word for today's referee is control, a word that does not appear in the rules.'

'Get a grip, Ref.'

'You're losing it.'

'You couldn't control your own urine.'

Referees have to control a match without disturbing the players' momentum and concentration. This problem is not dissimilar to that faced by teachers, police officers, youth leaders, parents of teenagers, and chief executives – how do you retain overall control while allowing individuals to express themselves and perform to the best of their abilities?

In the early days, it was fairly straightforward, according to Pickford: 'The rules we played under were few and not too definite, but certain things were not done. We were rough and banged each other about like skittles. Occasionally human nature flared up and there was an angry moment, but on the whole the game controlled itself.'

Modern football is very complex. It is almost impossible for referees to be consistent in match control. They may treat players inconsistently, and they may have good reason. There may be different ways of dealing with different players. One referee swore a lot at players, until a player asked him not to speak like that, and the referee felt he had to apologise.

Referees may also have different styles of control. At one extreme, according to traditional wisdom, there is the sergeant-major type, the headteacher on the field, who exudes authority and calls players to order, lecturing them in front of the class. This headteacher-type is more heavy-handed and is highly visible to spectators and players. John Colquhoun (Hearts) noticed this when he was writing for *Scotland on Sunday*: 'There are certain styles which players hate. A referee who insists on imposing authority by standing ten yards away, eyes bulging, demanding that the player eats a large slice of humble pie and walks likes a naughty schoolboy to him, preferably with head down, to receive a dressing-down, is unlikely to be treated with any degree of respect by players.'

At the other extreme is the referee who is 'one of the lads', a background character who tries to take the heat out of situations and prefers to have a quiet word with miscreants. Ideally, these referees are horse-whisperers who rely on subtle body language to deal with bullying. They are butlers of the calibre of Jeeves, background servants whose job is to fuel the skills of their masters. The butlers are the real bosses but they don't let it show.

In practice, all referees will be a mix of these styles, choosing an approach that works for the situation, experimenting with methods along the way until they are confident they can handle most things. Most referees are firm but friendly, and know not to argue with an angry, abusive player. Like teachers, they may start out being stern, and then lighten up a little along the way. Most will maintain control with a range of techniques – a disapproving look, a quiet word, a public warning, a caution or a sending-off. As Evans and Bellion stress in *The Art of Refereeing*, referees should do the least that is necessary to control the situation.

CORNER ARCS

In 1875 it was stated that a corner-kick had to be taken 'within one yard' of the corner-flag, and that the corner-flag mustn't be moved for the purpose of taking the kick. The notion of a quarter-circle, marked at each corner of the field, inside the pitch with a one-yard radius, was first generally accepted (1877), then made compulsory (1887), and eventually logged in the laws (1938).

Disputes about the exact placing of the ball at a corner-kick are commonplace. Occasionally referees crack down on ensuring that the ball is inside the quadrant. Some players try to take liberties, especially if the assistant is on the far side of the pitch.

Matthew Etherington (West Ham) was cautioned for time-wasting at Norwich when he failed to place the ball in the quadrant when taking a corner-kick (February 2004). The referee had warned him twice. Etherington was sent off as it was his second caution of the game. Players have also been cautioned for lying down and rolling the ball slightly towards the flag, in the manner of snooker players spotting the ball.

CORNER-FLAGS

Corner-flags entered the game early in history, but were not mentioned formally in the laws until the mid-1890s: 'A flag with a staff not less than five feet high shall be placed at each corner.' A round-topped flag was advised.

If there are no corner-flags, the referee should make every effort to get them. If it proves impossible, then the game should probably continue but the club should be reported to the appropriate association.

Players should be cautioned if they wilfully displace a flag, and flags should not be bent or removed for a corner-kick to be taken (1895). Young players unfamiliar with taking corner-kicks sometimes get in a muddle by placing the ball on the far side of the quadrant and then finding the corner-flag in the middle of their run-up. Very occasionally a fledgling player will miss the ball and accidentally kick the corner-flag up in the air. The referee then replaces the flag, ensuring it is not dangerous, and the kick can be taken again (preferably by someone who knows how to do it). No caution for this one.

When Jack Taylor refereed the 1974 FIFA World Cup™ Final, he took his usual look around the pitch before starting the game and was astonished to see there were no corner-flags. He hastily organised them.

If the ball hits the corner-flag and bounces back on to the pitch, the ball is still in play. Corner-flags are part of the field. Pickford, the hero of Jimmy Baker's fictional fantasy *The Goal Maker*, conjured an improbable goal out of this knowledge: 'All the way down the line the Goal Maker was shadowed by the two Southboro' players and he did not appear to have the faintest chance of getting away from them. Then he gave the ball a prod with his toe. I saw it strike the bottom of the corner-flag and flash off it between Eskbank and Saxby. A terrific roar broke from the crowd as they saw Pickford dart between them and run along the by-line.'

In a 1978 FA Cup tie, Wrexham were a goal behind to Blyth Spartans when they were awarded a corner-kick in the last minute. The referee ordered a retake when he noticed that the corner-flag had blown over just before the kick had been taken. Wrexham scored from the retaken corner and won the replay.

The 1997 Auto Windscreen Final was held up for several minutes after a corner-flag snapped. Referees can move one of the optional halfway-line flags to the corner, where the flag is compulsory.

CORNER-KICK

It's a corner-kick. The referee has blown and pointed to the corner, a player is running to collect the match-ball, the referee is cautioning a defender, and the defenders are talking to each other.

'Get back in here quick, Joe.'

'Make it count.'

'I've got two 'ere.'

There are not many players in the goal area but the place looks crowded. An attacker backs into the goalkeeper, reaches behind his back and squeezes the goalkeeper's testicles.

'Ref,' the goalkeeper shouts.

'I'm watching,' the referee replies, looking across.

Then comes the excitement as the corner-kicker sends the ball across, and the referee blows as the attacker in the goal area impedes the goalkeeper.

The corner-kick was included in Sheffield rules from 1868 as a substitute for the rouge. It was adopted by the FA in 1872 or 1873. Corner-kicks had to be taken within one yard of the nearest corner-flag (1875) and the corner-flag could not be moved before taking the kick (1895). In the early days, kicks were usually taken by wing-halves. Not until the late 1890s did wing-forwards take kicks.

The laws make no arrangements for a minimum run-up for the kicker. On some grounds there is hardly a couple of steps, on others there is a sudden step down as the turf drops away to a cinder surround.

Taking a Saturday of the professional season at random, the average number of corner-kicks was twelve, but the range was large (five to twenty-eight). Corner-kicks are given when the whole of the ball goes over the goal-line (but not between the goalposts) and was last touched by a defending player. If necessary, the assistant referee will flag to indicate the ball is out of play, and will point to the nearest corner-flag arc. The referee will point to the appropriate corner. Unlike goal-kicks, which may be taken from either side (after 1992), a corner-kick must be taken from the side of the field nearest to where the ball went out of play.

A corner can be awarded for other reasons – if defenders 'score' directly into their own goal from a free-kick (indirect or direct), if players take a throw-in and throw the ball directly into their own net, or if a goal-kick is taken and the ball is blown back into goal after it has left the penalty area (without any other player touching it).

Once a corner-kick has been signalled, the ball must be placed inside the corner arc. If it is taken from outside the arc, it should be retaken. Scottish football had a rule where referees would award an indirect free-kick when a corner-kick was taken outside the quarter arc. IFAB rejected this idea and politely asked the Scottish FA to conform (1972).

Referees can stop a corner-kick being taken while they sort out any pushing and shoving. The Portuguese referee did exactly that when England played Azerbaijan (March 2005). He stopped Beckham from taking a corner-kick, and then cautioned Vujar Guliyer (Azerbaijan) for tussling with Lampard (England).

Originally, opposition players couldn't come within six yards of the corner-kick taker. In 1913 this distance was extended to ten yards. Attacking players can go closer to the kicker. Hence the advantage of the short corner-kick – it keeps defenders away. In the late 1930s, Preston North End catered for their small forwards by introducing the short-corner tactic. One of their players, Bill Shankly, later said, 'I remember how annoyed a referee was when we were taking a short corner. We objected to the fact that defenders were standing less than ten yards from the kicker. He tried to force us to take the kick anyway. He even threatened to send us off the field. Until then nobody had noticed that ten yards.'

Referees pointed out that an eleven-yard arc from the corner-flag would help them spot whether defenders were respecting the correct distance from the ball. Instead an optional marking was sanctioned – a short line off the pitch eleven yards from the corner-flag (1990). This followed a suggestion by Nottingham Forest (1973), support from the Netherlands FA (1977) and successful experiments (1981).

For decades, goals have been allowed if the ball goes straight into the goal from a corner-kick, but corners were indirect until 1924. Billy Alston (St Bernards) probably scored the first legal goal direct from a corner-kick (August 1924), and Willie Davies (Cardiff City) curled one into the net for a last-minute FA Cup winner against Leicester City (March 1925).

'An example of how minutely the changes in the law were examined and how quick players were to take advantage of such change became apparent about this time [1924],' said Rous and Ford in *A History of the Laws of Association Football*. 'It had always been understood that the corner-kick was a type of free-kick and that the player taking it could not play the ball a second time until it had been played by some other player. In 1923 this condition was made specific, but by some mischance the words "and corner-kick" were omitted from Law 10 in 1924. At once past practice was forgotten, despite the fact that it had been operative for many years. Some players dribbled the ball from the corner-kick, contending that the laws did not *forbid* them to do so.'

Legend suggests that Ernest Edwards, sports editor of the *Liverpool Echo*, spotted this oversight and dared Sam Chedgzoy (Everton) to dribble in a corner. The problem was soon rectified. A corner-kick taker could not play the ball twice (without a second player touching it) without being penalised by an indirect free-kick. Many years later, in a match at Anfield, Baros (Liverpool) ran over and placed the ball for a corner-kick (2004–05). Then he ran back to the penalty area while Luis Garcia ran to the corner and started dribbling the ball in. The Liverpool players claimed that Baros had kicked and moved the ball slightly, acting the deception so well that the referee hadn't realised (because the kick was retaken). But Michael Herbert and Darren Ritchie (Henley Town Reserves) succeeded with this ploy at Marston Saints, having warned the referee in advance (February 2006).

If the ball hits the referee, a goalpost or a crossbar, this does not count as a second player. A corner-kick plagued by this issue caused Huddersfield Town to be relegated (April 1952). Bill Carter described the game against Spurs in Huddersfield Town's annual yearbook:

> Town were beaten in the last minute by a goal that will go down in the game's history. Len Duquemin, the Channel islander, diverted the ball into the visitors' net after Eddie Baily had, in the opinion of players of both sides and of the overwhelming majority of the crowd, taken a corner which rebounded to him off the referee. Baily played the ball a second time before it had been touched by another player. The referee, Mr W Barnes, of Birmingham, told the Huddersfield chairman afterwards that he thought a player other than Baily had taken the second kick. But Baily himself admitted that the facts as outlined by Town were

> correct. Town's protest, embodied in their routine report on the
> control of the game, was sent by registered letter to Glasgow,
> where Football League officials were gathered for the Hampden
> Park international. The League Management Committee later
> received a full report from the referee – but Town had no
> consolation. Tottenham retained the points – and Town had to
> ruminate upon the indirect free-kick that might have been!

Apparently the referee was five yards from the corner-flag when he was hit in the back by Baily's corner-kick, and another Spurs player was near Baily. This incident is also interesting for another reason: the only reason a club can challenge a match result is if referees have made a technical error *in their knowledge of the laws*. In this case it was a matter of the referee's opinion, so the result stood.

CORNER-KICK ARC *See* CORNER ARCS

CORNER POSTS *See* CORNER-FLAGS

CROSSBAR

In the beginning goalposts had no crossbar or tape to connect them. A goal would be scored when the ball passed between the posts at any height. Then came an incident at Reigate when the ball was kicked thirty yards in the air and spectators had to vote on whether or not the ball had gone between the posts.

Tape was introduced to London rules in 1865, extending from one goalpost to the other at a height of eight feet. The ball had to be kicked under the tape to score a goal.

Sheffield rules stipulated a nine-foot crossbar in 1870, and in 1875 the crossbar became obligatory in London rules. When the two associations amalgamated their rules in 1877, they allowed for a 'tape or bar across them, eight feet from the ground'. In 1882, tape was outlawed (for all except friendly matches) and the crossbar made compulsory.

There is one quiz question that stumps referees: what would it be if the ball lands on the crossbar and stays there?

Answer: A miracle.

The most serious issue regarding crossbars is safety. From 1967, the laws stated that crossbars must be made of wood, metal, or other approved material. Nothing else was allowed. In 1956, an IFAB decision stated that the crossbar may be square, rectangular, round, half-round or elliptical in shape. The 'half-round' was later dropped, and an important phrase about crossbars was added – *they must not be dangerous to players*. It is this latter point that bears close scrutiny, because children have been killed by falling goalposts and crossbars. For instance, a ten-year-old boy died in Limerick, Ireland, when a crossbar fell on his head during a penalty shoot-out competition (August 2004).

National associations have recommended safety criteria for goal-frames, and a further change was made to the law in 1994: 'for safety reasons, the goals, including those which are portable, must be anchored securely to the ground'. This was reworded three years later: 'Goals must be anchored securely to the ground. Portable goals may only be used if they satisfy this requirement.' It was also clarified that a broken crossbar had to be *properly replaced* (1996).

Crossbars have been broken, or dislodged, in a number of professional matches. When Sunderland played Bolton Wanderers, the game was suspended for twenty minutes (1892–93), and a Barnsley–Crewe game was held up for fifteen minutes (1966). In a game in the 1950s, goalkeeper Albert Uytenbogaardt (Charlton Athletic Reserves) cleared the ball with a long kick from his hands. The ball picked up speed from a following wind and bounced over the head of the opposing goalkeeper and into the net. Eddie Firmani (Charlton) followed the ball in, jumped to avoid the fallen goalkeeper, tripped, fell into the netting and brought down the crossbar.

A replacement crossbar should be found (not a rope) and it should be fitted in accordance with safety guidelines. A friendly match can continue with tape or with the referee exercising judgment about what is a goal or not, but the broken crossbar must be properly removed so that it doesn't constitute any danger. If the match is competitive, and no safe replacement is available, the game should be abandoned (IFAB 1949). If the crossbar can be safely replaced, the match should be restarted via a dropped ball (if it had been in play at the time of the incident).

Keith Hackett, officiating in a Sheffield & District Sunday League game early in his career, saw the goalkeeper push the ball on to the crossbar, dislodging the bar in the process. The bar fell on three defenders on the line as a forward followed up to ram the ball into the falling crossbar. Dropped ball was the correct decision (IFAB 1966).

In the 1890s, the referee was given the power to award a goal if the ball passed, or would have passed, under the bar when the bar had been displaced, but this was only in that brief moment between the crossbar being displaced and the referee immediately blowing his whistle. In such an incident, in those early days, the referee had to assess whether the defenders were put off by the bar breaking (unless the goalkeeper had caused the bar to break). Referees can caution goalkeepers who pull down the crossbar because such an action might break it and this could lead to the game's termination. In a game in Ireland, a goalkeeper was sent off for two cautions. The second one was for pulling down the crossbar.

The crossbar's maximum depth was fixed at five inches (1895), and it is the lower edge of the bar that should be eight feet from the ground (1939). In December 1887, Crewe Alexandra and the Swifts replayed their FA Cup tie on the new Queen's Ground in West Kensington. The Swifts won 3–2, but Crewe protested that the crossbars were at different heights. 'The height of the goalposts formed the basis of an appeal against the result,' wrote the *Crewe and Nantwich Chronicle*. 'A measurement revealed that they were within a few inches of the specified height.' The appeal was upheld. The teams had to replay again on a neutral ground, and Crewe beat the Swifts 2–1 at Derby. After this controversy, the FA ruled that protests about the ground, markings and goals must be made *before* the kick-off, not at the end of the game.

Mistakes have been made more recently. Portsmouth officials were embarrassed when a Danish referee discovered that one Fratton Park crossbar was an inch too low when he made his check before an England–Czechoslovakia youth international (November 1989), there was a fuss at the Memorial Ground when Bristol Rovers returned to Bristol (August 1996), and officials surveying the Lausanne stadium before a Switzerland–Italy international found that the goals were not the correct height (June 1999). These problems were quickly rectified.

CROWD DISORDER See GRAVE DISORDER

Dd

DANGEROUS PLAY

In the 1880s a player called Dave Russell was so acrobatic that he would bring 'high balls down to the grass with a foot in the vicinity of an opponent's ear'. As one player said about Russell, 'He was a high kicker, as I have special reason to remember, for twice in one match his boot got so uncomfortably near to my forehead that for several days it only required a look in the glass to remind me of a somewhat unpleasant time with Russell.'

In Russell's day, players were allowed to raise their feet. After 1891 it was considered to be dangerous play if a player raised a foot above hip height and threatened to injure an opponent's upper body, or if an opponent had to withdraw from that type of challenge to save being injured. Dangerous play also includes occasions when players stoop too low to head the ball, thus causing opponents to withdraw their feet instead of risking injury to the person heading the ball (IFAB 1954).

The punishment is an indirect free-kick. Referee Mike Riley awarded one in the Bulgaria penalty area when a defender raised his foot high as Ibrahimovic (Sweden) went to head the ball. Riley cautioned the offender (June 2004).

A scissors-kick (or bicycle-kick) is permissible providing it is not dangerous to an opponent. A spectacular example was a goal kicked over his own head by Trevor Sinclair (QPR), with both feet in the air, over twenty yards from the Barnsley goal (January 1997). If the kick impedes an opponent's challenge for the ball, then the referee should award an indirect free-kick for dangerous play.

DEAD BALL See OUT OF PLAY

DEAFNESS

Teams of deaf players have occupied a special place in British football since the earliest days. Glasgow Deaf FC was formed in 1871, and 'deaf and dumb' internationals were played in 1892.

When England Deaf & Dumb beat Wales Deaf & Dumb 3–0 at Southampton, it was described as 'the quietest international ever' (September 1925). The 500 spectators handclapped at times but refrained from cheering.

The referee used a flag instead of a whistle. In matches involving deaf and hearing players, referees have used a whistle *and* a flag.

When Stockport County centre-forward Ray Drake lined up to kick off in the 1950s, he had to rely on a colleague tugging his shorts at the sound of the referee's whistle. Drake was deaf. This, and other stories, are documented in a book by Martin Atherton et al. called *Deaf United: A History of Football in the British Deaf Community* (2000).

Jimmy Case (Brighton), who had a hearing deficiency, was sent off for a second caution (for time-wasting) when his team led Leicester 1–0 in the final minute of a cup tie (September 1994). Case claimed that he hadn't heard the whistle to restart the game. It is the player's responsibility to inform the referee of any hearing impairment, and the team's responsibility to facilitate smooth communication between the referee and a hearing-impaired player.

While deaf players like Case and Drake have appeared in teams of hearing players, other deaf players have their own version of the sport, with special FIFA tournaments. Interpretation of the rules may be slightly different. The deaf player's equivalent of the professional foul is to stop momentarily as if seeing a flag and then continue playing.

There have been a number of deaf referees. Some say that it's an asset.

DEATH

Football is a physically demanding sport played outdoors in all kinds of conditions, so it is not surprising that there have been fatalities. After the death of William Walker (Leith) in February 1907, a jury recommended that rough play should be sternly suppressed. Walker had been kicked in the stomach by a Vale of Leven player, who was subsequently exonerated of culpable homicide.

A number of players have died from complications after head injuries or internal injuries. Goalkeeper Joshua Wilkinson (Dumbarton) died from peritonitis after receiving 'a heavy knock' in a match at Rangers (November 1921), goalkeeper Larcombe (Salisbury Corinthians) died after being accidentally kicked on the head by a Portland United player (1923–24), and Sam Raleigh (Gillingham) died of a brain haemorrhage after a clash of heads during the first half of a match with Brighton (December 1934). Thomas Grice of Cheshire was killed when he fell during a game and his belt buckle pierced his stomach (April 1897). Belts with heavy buckles were eventually outlawed (FIFA Referees' Committee 1934).

In some cases weather conditions may have played a part. Extreme temperatures can be particularly dangerous, and some authorities suggest a safety range for children. Twenty-year-old Duncan Gilchrist (Portsmouth Reserves) died during a friendly game at Gosport that was played through a blinding snowstorm (April 1924). Gilchrist collapsed after ten minutes and was dead on arrival in the dressing-room (despite artificial respiration). Sam Wynne (Bury) collapsed while about to take a free-kick at Sheffield United and died in the dressing-room (April 1927). The match was abandoned.

Terminating the match is the most humane option. That happened when Paul Sykes (Folkestone Invicta) died during a Kent County Cup semi-final with Margate (April 2005). The 28-year-old suddenly fell backwards as he ran out of the penalty area unchallenged. In some cases, where matches have continued, it has proved very traumatic for the participants. All home clubs, at all levels, should have a system in place to deal with medical emergencies. National football associations provide training in such matters.

Marc-Vivien Foé (Cameroon) collapsed and died in the 72nd minute of a FIFA Confederations Cup match against Colombia in France (June 2003). The cause of death was hypertrophic cardiomyopathy, one of a number of heart defects responsible for Sudden Adult Death Syndrome (SADS). Another SADS victim was 25-year-old David Longhurst (York City), who collapsed and died shortly before half-time in the match with Lincoln City (September 1990). Andy Scott (Leyton Orient) retired early when an electro-cardiogram (ECG) test showed he was at serious risk from hypertrophic cardiomyopathy (April 2005). There are now cardiological screening regulations for young players in academies.

Particularly vulnerable are older players who haven't played for a while. There have been an abnormal number of deaths in charity matches. Players need to either keep playing regularly or work up to a one-off match via a sensible fitness programme. One 48-year-old ex-pro played a full charity match and then died in the dressing-room after coming out of a post-match bath and saying, 'I don't feel very well.' Trevor Hockey (Wales) was 43 when he collapsed and died shortly after playing in a five-a-side tournament (April 1987).

In local football, one shocking story concerned 39-year-old Tommy Slattery (St Joseph's), who died after being attacked at the end of a North Birmingham Sunday League match against Lozells GMA (April 2005). Three men were later charged. In this case, as with all serious incidents, the referee's report was a key document.

Football grounds have also claimed the lives of referees. A referee in Montpellier, France, was shot dead during a local league match in October 1989. Harry Husband died at a Leicester–West Brom cup tie when he collapsed in the dressing-room and hit his head on a wall (February 1960). A linesman replaced him. Referees who have died during professional matches include Roy Harper (at York in May 1969), Jim Finn (at Exeter in September 1972), and Mike North (at Southend United in April 2001).

DELAYED START

FIFA secretary Sir Stanley Rous was once asked why the opening match of the 1950 FIFA World Cup™ finals had not been delayed by five minutes so that the Brazilian President could be in his seat. Rous explained that referees had instructions to start punctually because so many other people depended on it – the public, the transport services, journalists with deadlines, and the broadcasters with fixed programmes. In recent years, matches have been synchronised on the final day of major league programmes; it is essential that no team gains an unfair advantage by starting late.

Referees are required to report any delayed starts, and some of their reports must have been interesting: Sheffield United against Barnsley kicked off five minutes behind schedule after a dog had chased one of the practice-balls (February 1959); a cup tie at Aston Villa was delayed by eighty minutes while tickets were distributed (December 2002); a power failure caused turnstile problems and set back Celtic and Barcelona by thirty minutes (September 2004); the kick-off at Queen's Park Rangers was delayed for nineteen minutes by a demonstration on the pitch by fans (February 1987); a match between Egaleo and Middlesbrough was delayed by five minutes while goal-nets were repaired (October 2004); a cup tie at Abingdon Town started twenty minutes late so the ground staff could mop up gallons of water (November 2000); the Cheltenham Town ground was evacuated after a bomb threat, and the match against Stevenage Borough started an hour late as a result (February 1998); and a match between Cambridge City and Stafford Rangers was delayed by fifteen minutes while a replacement assistant referee was found (December 2002).

The most common reason for a delay is the late arrival of one team. Referees do not wait until *all* the players are present. The match will start as long as each team has at least seven. There are legendary tales of teams changing on the bus and finding themselves two goals down before they've got their land-legs. Newcastle United kicked off 25 minutes late at Huddersfield after their train broke down and they had to travel the last 57 miles by coach (March 1954). And motorway delays meant that Tottenham Hotspur arrived only five minutes before kick-off at Birmingham (October 1983). There are usually stiff fines for clubs causing a delay.

Barrow and Gillingham agreed a late start and no half-time interval with the Football League before their match in October 1961. Gillingham initiated these changes when they ran into problems on their journey to Barrow. They missed their train at London Euston after being stuck in heavy traffic, so chartered a plane and flew to Squire's Gate, Blackpool, before being driven seventy miles along winding roads to Barrow. Despite the teams changing straight round at half-time, the light failed at seven o'clock, and the match was abandoned after 76 minutes, with Barrow leading 7–0. Gillingham were fined and the score stood.

The most important aspect for gauging the starting time is crowd safety. The 1947 Burnley–Middlesbrough FA Cup tie was delayed by forty minutes while fans entered the ground. This was the season after the Burnden Park disaster, in which 33 were killed and about 500 injured.

When Chelsea met Manchester United, there were 53,000 people inside the ground and 10,000 locked out (March 1966). Thousands of youngsters invaded the greyhound track around the pitch, and the match started twelve minutes late.

After the 1989 Hillsborough disaster, which resulted in the deaths of 96 spectators, the Taylor Report recommended that kick-offs should be delayed if fans were waiting outside. This was effected immediately. Manchester United fans were catered for with 25-minute delays at both Derby County (August 1989) and Aston Villa (December 1989). In each case the police ordered the referee to wait. The same happened at the 1993 FA Cup Final replay, which was delayed by thirty minutes when bad weather brought traffic problems on the M1.

DELAYING A RESTART

Professional players have developed all sorts of tricks to prevent a quick free-kick being taken. They may stand near the ball, kick the ball away, or protest the placing of the kick. Sometimes defenders take turns to interfere to avoid being cautioned for persistent infringement. One player will stall the first free-kick, another will do the next one. Or sometimes three players will be involved with the same free-kick. One will protest, one will stand in front of the ball until the referee spots him, and then another player will come round and take over.

Technically all these actions are cautionable offences. A player who kicks the ball away after the whistle has gone is almost certain to be cautioned for delaying a restart. Otherwise it may depend on the state of the game – who is winning? – and the referee's boundaries. It can take up to a minute to set up a ceremonial free-kick while a referee paces out ten yards, gets the wall set correctly, takes up a position, and blows the whistle. Anything that causes further delay is outlawed. For a short time (1998 to 2004) FIFA experimented with a method of advancing the ball ten yards if a player was cautioned for delaying the restart. FIFA have also experimented in youth tournaments with cautions for any defending player who touches the ball after a free-kick, throw-in or corner-kick has been awarded (2005). Deco (Portugal) was cautioned for holding on to the ball and provoking a confrontation with Coch (Holland), who wanted to take a quick free-kick (June 2006).

DEMONSTRATIONS

Oxford United fans staged a pitch sit-in to protest against Robert Maxwell's proposed merger of Reading and Oxford into a new club called Thames Valley Royals (April 1983), the start of the second half was delayed by protestors at Fulham (February 1987), and the Northern Ireland–England international was the scene of demonstrations against the new Public Order Act (April 1987). If demonstrators enter the pitch during play, they are treated as outside agents (see separate entry).

The Football Spectators Act 1989 made pitch invasion a criminal offence, but demonstrations continued. Brighton fans occupied the Goldstone Ground fifteen minutes into a game with York, causing the match to be abandoned (May 1996). A few days before Airdrie went bankrupt, about 100 Airdrie fans invaded Ayr United's ground and broke a crossbar, causing that match to be terminated after 21 minutes (April 2002). Three people carrying a Palestinian flag were arrested when Leyton Orient entertained Israeli team Maccabi Tel Aviv (July 2002). Their protest – 'End Israeli occupation of Palestine' – resulted in charges being brought.

About thirty Manchester United supporters took to the field wearing black balaclavas during a reserve-team match at Altrincham (October 2004). They unfurled a 'Not for $al£' banner and tried to burn an American flag as a protest against a possible takeover of the club by Malcolm Glazer.

DENYING AN OBVIOUS GOALSCORING OPPORTUNITY

In 1990, in an attempt to counter the professional foul, the authorities created a new sending-off offence – denying an obvious goalscoring opportunity (known to referees as DOGSO). The offence had two categories – denying a goal or obvious goalscoring opportunity by handling the ball, and denying an obvious goalscoring opportunity by some other offence.

The first of these is often clear-cut. When Lundekvan (Norway) headed goalwards and McFadden (Scotland) handled the ball on the goal-line, the referee gave a penalty-kick and the sending-off was inevitable (October 2004).

In other cases, the adjudication of 'denying an obvious goalscoring opportunity' is complex. There is even an argument to say that a player should not be sent off for an offence in the penalty area because the 'obvious goalscoring opportunity' has not been denied – it is still there with the penalty-kick. If the offence is outside the area, a sending-off is a worthy punishment, as the chances of scoring from the free-kick may have been reduced to as little as one in ten.

Another argument says that the real target should be the person committing a cynical, deliberate foul, rather than the person who accidentally prevents a goalscoring opportunity. But how can you tell?

In practice, a sending-off is required if the referee answers 'Yes' to all the questions on a check list:

Is the attacker moving directly towards the goal?

Are there fewer than two defenders (including the goalkeeper) between the offender and the goal?

Is the ball close to, and in possession of, the attacker?

Does the attacker have a reasonable shooting opportunity?

Is the foul committed near enough to the goal to ensure a goalscoring opportunity?

Was the attacker onside?

Sometimes the check list doesn't help. Goalkeeper Lee Camp (Derby County) was only cautioned after fouling Marlon Harewood (West Ham) on the edge of the penalty area (January 2005). Most observers felt that Harewood would have gone on to score, but Harewood had played the ball to his right, to get past the goalkeeper, so the ball was technically going away from goal.

These can be critical decisions. When Peter Swan (Port Vale) was sent off at Wembley for fouling Bob Taylor (West Brom), the 0–0 scoreline soon changed into 3–0 for West Brom (May 1993). Henning Berg (Blackburn) was harshly sent off for a foul on Lee Sharpe (Manchester United) when his team led 1–0 (October 1994). The final result was 4–2 to Manchester United. People debated whether that decision might decide the championship, but Blackburn went on to win the title by one point.

An early sending-off can unsettle the expectations of the crowd and the players. When goalkeeper Ross Flitney (Barnet) was wrongly sent off for handling outside the penalty area after ninety seconds at Old Trafford, not only did Flitney lose his chance of an appearance against Manchester United but his team-mate Louie Soares had to be substituted to allow a replacement goalkeeper to come on (October 2005). Similarly, the spirit of the game seemed to be breached when goalkeeper Boaz Myhill (Hull City) was dismissed at Queen's Park Rangers (November 2005). Myhill slipped and handled the ball fractionally outside the area with no other player nearby (November 2005).

DIAGONAL SYSTEM OF CONTROL

Almost all referees run a wide diagonal from the top corner of one penalty area to the opposite top corner of the other penalty area, staying clear of the muddy central area as much as possible. Their assistants run the two halves of the touchline furthest from the referee's diagonal. Top referees stay clear of penalty areas and touchlines as much as they can, usually only going into those areas to issue cautions or sendings-off.

The diagonal system of control enables referees to stay up with play with minimum effort while making maximum use of their assistants. The idea is for the referee to be able to see at least one assistant at all times. In the old days, a referee was considered a good referee if he had a muddy mark on his kit (because he must have been up with play). Lately, a muddy mark has been seen as the hallmark of a bad referee (because it means he or she hasn't read the game very well).

The diagonal system was first proposed to English referees in 1936. It curbed some of the criticism that had led to experiments with two referees. The diagonal system was a contrast to the Russian linear system where the linesmen were both on the same side of the pitch, and the referee was on the other side. In the linear system, the referee took control of both penalty areas.

The diagonal system means that the referee will be closer to certain players during the match. This means that it is easier to have a quiet word with, say, a midfield player, than a goalkeeper. Referee Gordon Hill remembered covering the same patch in the middle of the park as Bobby Charlton, who was always shouting for Hill to get out of the way. But the referee has to run somewhere. One team practised a complicated free-kick that involved duping the opposition into thinking the ball was going in a different direction. They practised it to perfection in training, but when they came to use it in a match the referee ran across the key player. The referee had been duped too.

Referees may vary their positioning. One player once complained to a referee that he didn't know where the referee was going to stand at a corner. The referee told him that was exactly how he wanted it.

Referees will brief assistants on exactly what is needed. It is fairly common to see assistants staying with the same set of forwards for each half, with club assistants in minor games usually being given the task of patrolling the opposition's forwards. Assistant referees usually run right wings – it suits right-handed assistants – but sometimes the right-wing touchlines are worn down and boggy from persistent use.

DIRECT FREE-KICK See FREE-KICK

DISABILITIES See AMPUTEES, DEAFNESS, EYESIGHT, MODIFICATIONS TO THE LAWS

DISASTERS

Thirty-nine people died and 580 were injured in the Heysel Stadium disaster (May 1985). During the two hours between the height of the disaster and the delayed start of the match (Juventus–Liverpool), there were discussions about whether the match should take place. The chief of police decided the match should be played as a way of controlling an angry crowd. Given police reinforcements he felt it was safer to play than to evacuate the stadium. The players went through the game as if in a daze.

At other disasters – the Hillsborough crush (1989) and the Bradford fire (1985) – it became clear that the game must be abandoned, but the argument for continuing prevailed during the 1902 Scotland–England international. Twenty-six people were killed and hundreds injured when a section of Ibrox Park terracing collapsed. The game continued after an 18-minute delay. Said J J Bentley, writing in *CB Fry's Magazine* (April 1904):

> It was asking a great deal, for the injured were groaning in the very dressing-rooms, and not only this, but in order to reach the field of play, the men had to step over dead bodies with the groans and yells of the injured ringing in their ears, and then play football amid the cheering of tens of thousands who were absolutely ignorant of the terrible accident. This may seem strange, but out of the sixty thousand present, I make bold to say that not more than a thousand were aware of the fact that there had been a serious accident until they reached Glasgow. The ground was empty in twenty minutes. But had play been stopped, and the true state of affairs thereby become known, the dead would not have been numbered by twenties, but by hundreds. At the time it seemed a cruel, almost heartless thing to play on, but it was best.

The other big issue is whether a refereeing decision can trigger a major disaster. The example often cited is an Olympic qualifier between Peru and Argentina, when a possible Peru goal was ruled out two minutes from time (May 1964). In fact, only a handful of people came on the pitch. The disaster was caused by the police firing tear-gas into the stands and spectators responding by rushing towards locked exit gates. At least 318 people were killed in the crush and more than 500 injured.

DISCIPLINE See MISCONDUCT

DISMISSAL See SENDING-OFF

DISSENT

A player must not show any dissent through word or action (IFAB 1924). Initially players were allowed to make polite inquiries about referees' decisions, but that was quickly withdrawn (IFAB 1930). Dissent is a cautionable offence. It is not a sending-off offence unless a player continues to dissent after being cautioned.

Dissent includes *gestures* of contempt. Lauren (Arsenal) was cautioned against PSV Eindhoven for waving an imaginary card at the referee as if to admonish the referee for not cautioning an opponent (November 2004), and Rooney (Manchester United) was cautioned for sarcastically applauding the referee in Villareal (September 2005).

Players commonly appeal for a decision to go their way, but appealing is not to be confused with dissent. Dissent occurs after a decision has been made. It is when a player, or manager, openly questions a referee's decision, demonstrating disgust and perhaps even involving team-mates in the argument.

DIVING See SIMULATION

DRAWN CUP TIES

In 2004, FIFA made it clear that there was only one permitted format for settling a drawn cup tie needing a definite outcome: play thirty minutes of extra-time; then, if the scores are still level, stage a shoot-out with kicks from the penalty mark; and, if the match had to be abandoned, toss a coin to decide the victor. But away goals can still count double in two-legged ties in the event of an aggregate draw if competition organisers so wish.

This ruling came after years of studying the effect of many other methods. The system of using an infinite number of replays eventually became impossible in England because police forces needed ten days' notice to prepare, and replays had to be limited to none or one. Ties going to several replays had caused fixture congestion and player exhaustion, making a mockery of expressions like 'cup ties are one-off occasions'.

In the 1873–74 FA Cup competition, Sheffield and Shropshire Wanderers played two draws and then tossed a coin to decide which team would progress to the second round. A fixed period of extra-time (usually thirty minutes) was incorporated into competition rules as early as the 1860s, but sometimes there has been confusion about other competitions' rules. Romford walked off the pitch after ninety minutes of an Essex County Cup tie, whereas opponents Chelmsford City expected extra-time (September 1973).

In 1908–09 Broxburn and Beith met five times in a first-round Scottish Cup tie. The last three games were played on consecutive days. Beith finally won 4–2 on a Friday and met St Mirren in the next round on the following day.

A two-legged 1950 Mitropa Cup tie between Sparta Prague and Budapest Hungaria went to six games. The teams drew on aggregate and the replay consisted of two more legs. A dispute over an ineligible player led to two further legs being played. Another draw on aggregate meant the match was decided by a coin-toss anyway. In the early days of European competition, a third-game play-off was the normal method used to decide drawn ties. The third game would be played on a neutral ground, or the two teams would toss a coin to decide which of them would be the host.

In 1955, Stoke City and Bury played a total of 562 minutes at five different venues, and Doncaster Rovers and Aston Villa met five times in eighteen days. The record for replays belongs to Alvechurch and Oxford City, who took six games and 660 playing minutes to settle their FA Cup tie in November 1971. 'We didn't know the Oxford players at the start,' recalled Graham Allner (Alvechurch), 'but we were on first-name terms at the end. We were turning up as if long-lost mates. It was almost like going to work every day – the same teams, the same players, the same result. Tactics went out of the window. We didn't change anything. We just carried on playing the same way. Before every game, Rhys Davies used to say, "Go out and give it some tonk and bottle." That was his favourite phrase at the time!'

At the other end of the energy spectrum is the simple mechanism of tossing a coin. England Youth lost four tosses in four years – against Northern Ireland (3–3 in 1949), Belgium (1–1 in 1951), Austria (5–5 in 1952) and Yugoslavia (1–1 in 1953).

The first European tie decided by a toss-up was Wismut Karl-Marx-Stadt versus Gwardia Warsaw (1957–58). The normal procedure was for the two captains to join the referee in the centre-circle or the dressing-rooms. The visiting captain chose heads or tails, or if a neutral venue the referee allocated the choice (FIFA Referees' Committee 1966). Yugoslavia won a 1960 Olympic Games soccer semi-final on the toss of a coin after drawing 1–1 with Italy, and Celtic tossed out Benfica after winning 3–0 at home and losing 3–0 away (1969–70). But Tunisia complained after their third coin-toss loss to Morocco (1969).

Corner-kicks have been used as a tie-breaker. Hibernian won 6–5 on corner-kicks after a drawn Scottish League Cup tie against Rangers (May 1944). The 1930 Glasgow Charity Cup Final between Rangers and Celtic ended 2–2 but on that occasion the number of corner-kicks was also tied on 4–4, so the Cup was decided on a toss of a coin. Rangers won.

The golden goal had its roots in the 'first to score if it's a draw' method of settling cup ties during World War II. Cardiff beat Bristol City 3–2 with a goal in the 202nd minute (April 1945), while the Stockport–Doncaster match was abandoned after 203 minutes and still had to be replayed (March 1946). When Wolves played Aberdeen in a United Soccer Championship decider, they won 6–5 with a goal in the 126th minute, the sixth minute of sudden-death overtime (July 1967). The pitfalls of this method are evident. Players were exhausted at the end, and no one knew when they would be home for their tea.

The golden-goal method was used in a variety of competitions for a ten-year period until it was outlawed in 2004. The first goal scored in extra-time decided the tie. The 1995 Auto Windscreens Shield was won by Paul Tait's golden goal for Birmingham City. Had the scores been level after 120 minutes, the match would have gone to a penalty shoot-out. Eventually, however, people saw that there were problems with the suddenness of the match ending.

The silver goal was used for a short period in the early 2000s to try to rectify this. Having drawn the match after ninety minutes, the two teams played a full fifteen-minute first half of extra-time. If one team led at half-time of extra-time, they would be declared the winning team. If the match was still drawn, the two teams would play the second half of extra-time in full.

The most significant method for deciding drawn cup ties that are unresolved after 120 minutes is the 'penalty shoot-out' method. Settling ties by kicks from the penalty mark, to apply the true title, is great drama and tense entertainment. It is a mini-game that everybody can understand. In 1991 the FA ruled that all drawn FA Cup replays (in the competition proper) would be decided by penalty-kicks. The Scottish Cup had adopted a similar system (1989–90). In Bulgaria, cup ties were being decided by 'penalties' as early as 1967, and an innovative shoot-out system in Czechoslovakia stipulated that one player should take all five penalties.

Other forms of shoot-out have been used. The original American idea gave players five seconds to run with the ball from 35 yards and attempt to score against a goalkeeper. Similarly, Peñarol won the 1996 Copa Uruguay with an American-style shoot-out whereby players started from the centre-circle and had eight seconds to score. Peñarol won the contest 1–0 after five National players had failed in their attempts.

Many alternative suggestions to the penalty shoot-out have been put forward by the general public. One is removing players who have been cautioned before the start of extra-time. Another is removing a player from each team every five minutes of extra-time. A third is widening the goals during extra-time. A fourth is to give the tie to the team with the fewer sendings-off and cautions.

Other suggestions have included nine-a-side (with no offsides), penalty shoot-outs before the game (so one team won't play for penalties – but that still leaves one that will be happy to play for a draw), two goals clear on penalties (to save focusing the blame on any one player), penalties from greater distances (to give a fifty-fifty chance of scoring), shoot-outs before extra-time, withdrawing the two goalkeepers before extra-time, points awarded for corner-kicks, near misses, the amount of possession and/or the fewest fouls, a unified team for next tie, points awarded by judges for backheels, overhead kicks and 'nutmegging', number of shots on target, points for achievements in previous rounds, previous penalty shoot-out record compared with opponent, and so on.

Whatever the system, the most important factor is that the referee is sure about the competition rules, especially when it comes to away goals counting double in the event of a draw. Most referees would explain the regulations to the two captains when they meet at the start of the match.

DRINKS See ALCOHOL, LIQUID INTAKE

DROPPED BALL

A dropped ball is the way to restart play when no other possible restart is appropriate – after a serious injury, interference from outside agents, a burst ball, when the ball is trapped dangerously between a player's legs, after a referee has changed a penalty-kick or free-kick decision, after the ball hits a pre-existing condition (an overhead wire or a tree branch), etc. There is no ruling on the number of players to be present at a dropped ball – it could be as few as none – though it is common practice to have one from each side. Increasingly, from the 1990s, one player would stand back and allow the other to do something in keeping with what had happened to cause the stoppage, for instance to punt the ball back to the opposing goalkeeper, or kick it out for a throw-in.

The original equivalent was a throw-up. This was followed by the bounce-up, whereby the referee threw the ball down from shoulder-height, using no more force than to make it rebound to the same height if untouched (1905). Finally, the familiar dropped ball was introduced (1914).

When the referee drops the ball, players mustn't play the ball until it has touched the ground. At one time, players conceded an indirect free-kick if they played the ball before it touched the ground, and a direct free-kick if the ball was handled before it hit the ground (1924 to 1937). From 1937 the ball was dropped again. If a player repeats the offence, it would mean a caution for persistently infringing the laws of the game.

Referees should *drop* the ball, not bounce it on the ground. The correct technique is for referees to let the ball go from waist height and then escape quickly before players start kicking them rather than the ball. In 1984, dropped balls inside the goal area were outlawed. They had to be moved to the six-yard line. The following year various laws were reworded so that the goal-area circumstance was applied to every eventuality needing a dropped ball.

A goal can be scored from a dropped ball. In a Wrexham–Preston match, the Preston goalkeeper kicked the ball out to allow a Wrexham player treatment for a facial injury (January 1999). The referee blew his whistle to stop play before the ball went out, so he restarted play with a dropped ball about thirty yards from the Preston goal. The Preston players stepped aside, so that Jeff Whitley (Wrexham) could return the ball to the Preston goalkeeper. Unfortunately, Whitley clipped a superb half-volley over the goalkeeper's head and into the net. The referee disallowed the 'goal' and awarded Preston an indirect free-kick for unsporting behaviour.

A dropped ball is the only restart where there is no penalty for a player touching the ball for a second time before it is played by another player.

DROPPED SHORTS

Dave Gaskell (Manchester United) and Jimmy Dunne (Fulham) were summoned to court in the 1960s for taking their shorts down on the pitch. Sammy Nelson (Arsenal) lowered his shorts to the Arsenal crowd after equalising against Coventry (April 1979). Nelson's club immediately suspended him for two weeks and fined him two weeks' wages.

The biggest furore, however, came when eight Wimbledon players dropped their shorts to the crowd at half-time during a testimonial match (May 1988). Wimbledon were fined heavily by the Football Association, and the players concerned were each fined £750.

DRUGS

Many people are familiar with high-profile cases in the British professional game – Johnston (Scotland), Bosnich (Chelsea), Ferdinand (Manchester United), Mutu (Chelsea), Moran (Rhyl), Abel Xavier (Middlesbrough), etc. – but the greatest concern is at the grass-roots level. How does a referee recognise a player who is under the influence of drugs? How do team-mates deal with the issue?

These sorts of questions go far beyond the pitch. There are questions about legal and illegal drugs, and issues to do with the definition of banned drugs. Football associations and competition authorities have clear guidelines in place for what could happen, and players and clubs should be aware of the procedures. The *2004-05 FA Handbook* had 21 pages dealing with issues of doping control.

Football authorities initially followed the guidelines of the International Olympic Committee. The first official testing was at the 1966 FIFA World Cup™ finals when testers were supplied with a list of drugs from an internationally agreed list. After the final, the drug-test doctors presented Jack Charlton (England) with the Jimmy Riddle Trophy. Charlton had been the one England player randomly selected for testing after four of their six games in the tournament.

Drugs testing was first noticed in the 1978 FIFA World Cup™ finals when two players from each team were tested after every match and Willie Johnston (Scotland) tested positive. Johnston admitted taking Reactivan tablets. He was sent home immediately, and his international career was over. The next player to fail a major-tournament drug test was Diego Maradona (Argentina, 1994). Blood-testing was introduced in 2002.

Britain had a spate of cases in the early 2000s. Mark Bosnich (Chelsea) was banned for nine months after testing positive for cocaine, and Adrian Mutu (Chelsea) was suspended for seven months and fined £20,000 for similarly failing a test. Mutu had been dismissed by Chelsea shortly before the FA's decision (November 2004).

In the 2003–04 season, however, two cases showed the complexities faced by the authorities. The first was that of Rio Ferdinand (Manchester United), who failed to attend a routine drugs test on 23 September 2003, an offence considered as serious as testing positive. Ferdinand was allowed to continue playing for his club, pending his hearing, but he was left out of the England squad for a crucial EURO 2004™ qualifier in Turkey. This caused a real crisis when the England players insisted that Ferdinand be restored to the squad. Twelve weeks after the offence, Ferdinand was banned for eight months at a hearing.

The second case was that of Andy Moran (Rhyl), who tested positive for nandrolone after a Welsh Premier League match against Afan Lido (13 March 2004). This information was kept from the public until a second test had been conducted – in line with international guidelines – so Moran was allowed to continue playing until his FA of Wales hearing (12 July 2004). The player was suspended for seven months at the hearing, but there was outrage because Rhyl had won four trophies during the last month of the season and Moran had taken his season's tally to 47 goals. He won the League's Player of the Season Award, and the Golden Boot for 27 Welsh Premier League goals, although both awards were stripped from him after the hearing. Rhyl kept their team trophies, which left a sour taste with fans of Total Network Solutions (TNS), the League and Cup runners-up. As the Sky Sports News presenter Jeff Stelling was fond of saying, 'They'll be weeping and wailing in the streets of Total Network Solutions.'

Of course, the biggest drug of all is football itself. It provides players and fans with a buzz that can rival banned substances. It punctuates the routine periods of players' and fans' lives with short units of intense activity and adrenaline highs. 'The sheer excitement and intensity can lift players out of the everyday world into a kind of high octane, intoxicating existence,' wrote Brian Gearing in his analysis of what retired players missed the most (*Journal of Ageing Studies*, 1999).

DURATION OF THE GAME

Soccer is a ninety-minute game, and has been since 1877. The only permitted exceptions are matches involving children, youths, veterans, women and players with disabilities. Otherwise, referees are duty-bound to play for ninety minutes, adding on time for stoppages.

In 1908–09, a referee blew for full-time five minutes early when Norwich City played Northampton Town. Later, when he realised his mistake, he called the players out of the bath to play the last five minutes. The match must also be *of equal halves*, so the referee at Norwich was correcting two errors.

In the 1860s and 1870s, the duration of play was decided either by discussion among the teams or the park closing time. When The Wanderers played Civil Service, the score was 4–0 to Wanderers at full-time, but the teams played an extra half-hour, presumably because everyone was enjoying it so much (February 1872). The first rules for the FA Challenge Cup, in 1871–72, stipulated that games should last for an hour and a half.

In December 1886 Newcastle West End agreed to play fifteen minutes each way after the away team, Bishop Auckland Church Institute, were delayed on their journey. But this sort of thing was quickly outlawed, unless agreed with the competition organisers well in advance. A better model would be the cup tie between Fulham and Doncaster Rovers in October 1983. The match kicked off over an hour late because of floodlight problems, but the duration of the match was still ninety minutes.

Alterations were made to FA Cup rules so that the referee could stop the watch for time 'wasted either owing to an accident or other cause' and there were arrangements for a half-time interval. In 1897, IFAB accepted these rules into the laws of the game. In 1987 the law was altered to clearly state that the referee has discretion to add time lost through substitution, the transport from the field of injured players, cautioning and sending-off players, and time-wasting. Time can be extended to allow the taking of a penalty-kick, but only until there is a definite outcome to the kick.

Competition organisers have occasionally bypassed FIFA. The 1904 Olympic tournament had two periods of thirty minutes. In the 1960s, they played 35 minutes each way in Burma and thirty minutes each way in India, while the USA played four 22½-minute quarters in some games.

Ee

EARLY HISTORY OF THE LAWS *See* ORIGINS OF THE LAWS

ELBOWS

T E Andersen et al. found that elbow-to-head contact was the most frequent cause of head injuries in top-class Scandinavian football, followed by head-to-head contact in heading duels (*British Journal of Sports Medicine*, 2004). The main problem comes when the elbow is used actively at or above shoulder level.

John Uzzell (Torquay United) suffered a shattered cheekbone when hit by an elbow from Gary Blissett (Brentford) in an aerial collision (December 1991). Blissett was sent off but found not guilty of causing grievous bodily harm when the case went to court in 1993. A later compensation case was settled out of court.

Gary Mabbutt (Tottenham Hotspur) was badly injured by an elbow in an aerial challenge with John Fashanu (Wimbledon) in November 1993. Mabbutt suffered multiple cheekbone fractures and damage to the eye socket and was out of action for three months.

Referees became more vigilant about elbow offences from the late 1980s. Leading with the arm or elbow was deemed to be a cautionable offence, and using the arm or elbow as a weapon was a sending-off offence. Van den Hauwe (Millwall) had the ball at his own feet when he elbowed Oldfield (Leicester) to earn a straight red card (March 1994). An elbow by Leonardo (Brazil) floored Tab Ramos (USA) in July 1994. Leonardo was sent off and suspended for four matches.

Sendings-off for use of the elbow became more commonplace – Roy Keane (Manchester United), Mark Viduka (Leeds United) and Sol Campbell (Arsenal) in 2002–03 for instance – but it is difficult to spot the offence and even more difficult to judge it (especially when a player's running action involves an elbow catching an opponent behind him). Bergkamp (Arsenal) escaped unpunished when his elbow injured Bowyer (West Ham), and Arsenal scored in the same passage of play (January 2003). Giggs (Manchester United) suffered a fractured cheekbone, but no action was taken against Lille's Bodmer (October 2005). Professional players probably use elbows more than amateurs. They are sometimes coached to use their arms as leverage towards extra height or for holding off opponents.

ELIGIBILITY

All competitions have rules for player eligibility. These rules may cover transfer deadlines (which first appeared in 1911), restrictions on cup games (e.g. only one club per season), procedures for informing competition organisers about new players, suspensions, restrictions on foreign players or loan players, age limitations, and disability categories. Until 1974 amateurs were distinguished from professionals; after 1974 all footballers were called *players*.

Some referees ask, 'All players registered properly?' when receiving the team-sheet. The referee at Northwich Victoria had good cause when three local Sunday League players responded to a public announcement to make up the team against Maidstone in the Vauxhall Conference (November 1986). In those days Conference rules permitted registrations up to the kick-off, providing the forms were completed correctly and a Telemessage received first thing Monday morning.

Punishments for cup-tie rule infractions have varied over the years. Kettering and Tilbury replayed because one team had an ineligible player (November 1977), Leeds United were awarded a 3–0 win in a two-legged European Cup tie against Stuttgart (1992–93), and Leigh RMI were eliminated from the 2003–04 FA Trophy after drawing 1–1 with Stalybridge Celtic with the aid of an ineligible player. Sutton Coldfield fielded an ineligible player in *two* rounds of the 2004–05 FA Cup competition, and the second losers were reinstated. Italy's under-21s were awarded a 3–0 win after drawing 2–2 with Scotland, who had fielded Steven Whittaker when he should have been suspended for having received two yellow cards in the tournament (September 2005).

West Ham and Aston Villa were ordered to replay their Worthington Cup quarter-final (December 1999). On that occasion Manny Omoyimni (West Ham) came on for the last eight minutes of extra-time. West Ham won the match after a penalty shoot-out, but Omoyimni had already played for Gillingham in that season's Worthington Cup. Villa won the rematch.

Mixenden '76 were forced to turn out with ten players for the 1982 Halifax & District FA Dunkley Cup Final against Golden Fleece. The rules prevented them from including two players who had not taken part in earlier rounds. Mixenden lost 1–0.

Ensuring that players conform to age criteria is the duty of competition organisers and clubs rather than referees. In March 2003, Kenya received a two-year ban from all Confederation of African Football competitions after three under-seventeen players had been discovered to be overage. When Saudi Arabia beat Scotland in the 1989 World under-sixteen tournament, Scotland complained that the young Saudis looked so post-pubescent that they would be taking their medals home to their children.

Fielding an ineligible player in a league match led to one-point deductions for Preston North End (November 1973) and Halifax Town (August 1987), while Birmingham (September 1991) and Swansea (May 1992) were heavily fined. Point deductions rarely make a big difference to league tables – Ely City's three-point penalty dropped them from tenth to eleventh (2003–04) – but can affect player morale. In 2003–04, however, Maltby Main lost the Northern Counties East Division One title through a three-point deduction and two late defeats. Similarly, Didcot Town's one-point deduction cost them the Hellenic Premier League title (2004–05). And Altrincham were relegated from the Nationwide Conference after an eighteen-point deduction, losing all the points gained during games when they fielded the ineligible James Robinson (2005–06).

Some registration bizarreries are perfectly within the rules. On Boxing Day 1932 Jimmy Oakes played for Port Vale at Charlton Athletic when the match was abandoned with Vale leading 4–1. Three weeks later, Oakes was transferred from Port Vale to Charlton. When the match was replayed in April 1933, Oakes was in Charlton's team against his old club. Charlton won the rematch 2–1.

ENCROACHMENT

In the 1974 FIFA World Cup™ finals Brazil won a free-kick just outside the penalty area, and Zaire players lined up their wall. As the Brazilians prepared for their rehearsed free-kick, one Zaire player broke from the wall and ran towards the ball. He kept going, reaching the ball before the Brazilian free-kick taker and booting the ball upfield. He was cautioned for failing to respect the required distance at a restart. He had encroached and poached.

Players must keep their distance *until the ball has been kicked and moved* (rather than until the sound of the whistle).

To encroach is to intrude on boundaries. In football, the magical boundary is ten yards, but there are exceptions. Players only have to be two yards away from a player taking a throw-in providing they are stationary (one yard before June 2005); opponents must be outside the penalty area for goal-kicks and free-kicks (and at least ten yards away); and, for indirect free-kicks less than ten yards from the goal-line, defenders can stand on their own goal-line between the goalposts.

The earliest rules stipulated that defenders must be at least six yards from goal-kicks when the ball was kicked. Later, when free-kicks, corner-kicks and penalty-kicks were introduced, the same six-yard encroachment rule applied. The main exception was at the place-kick or kick-offs, where a special circle of ten yards was marked.

According to an FA Council minute (December 1910), 'Players who do not retire to the proper distance when a free-kick is taken must be cautioned, and on any repetition be ordered off. It is particularly requested of referees that attempts to delay the taking of a free-kick by encroaching should be treated as serious misconduct.' This has remained a cautionable offence. In 1997 Law 14 changed so that it was no longer a compulsory caution if players entered the penalty area before a penalty-kick, only when the player actively engaged in the play.

The encroachment distance for free-kicks was increased from six to ten yards in 1913, and the same regulation was soon extended to corner-kicks and goal-kicks, but only in 1948 did the law require opponents also to stay outside the penalty area for goal-kicks. However, the six-yard measurement continued to haunt pitch-markings. The placings of goal area, the penalty mark and the penalty area are all products of the outdated encroachment distance.

ENTERING THE FIELD

During a 1904 FA Cup replay, Rushton (Hull City) dashed back on to the field after receiving treatment for an injury. This action caught opponents Leeds City by surprise. The law was changed so that players returning to the pitch had to get 'permission from the referee' (1904).

It was later confirmed that permission was required not only after treatment to injury, but after changing equipment (1929), arriving late (1934), and by people other than players, referees and linesmen (1939). When returning after changing equipment a player needs to enter at the halfway-line so that the equipment can be checked. Substitutes also enter at the halfway-line, waiting for a stoppage in the game and a signal from the referee.

It is a cautionable offence to enter or re-enter the field of play without permission. But it is quite acceptable to leave the field briefly when celebrating a goal (providing there's no time-wasting) and it is acceptable to return without permission when your momentum takes you over the perimeter. During an FA Cup replay, Carr (Newport County) took the ball up the left touchline and crossed from near the Reading goal-line (December 1938). He fell beyond the goal-line and stayed there during a goalmouth scramble. A Newport forward shot, and the Reading goalkeeper fisted the ball out to the wing, near where Carr was standing. He stepped on to the field, collected the ball, crossed and Wood scored for Newport. The referee gave the goal.

An incident in an Arsenal–Chelsea match provoked similar discussion (October 2003). Crespo (Chelsea) strayed behind the goal-line during a Chelsea attack. He came back on to the field after the ball had been cleared.

The Arsenal defenders did not notice Crespo's return until he suddenly appeared in front of them to take a pass, turn and score from distance. The goal counted, the referee deciding that Crespo had not left the field intentionally in the first place.

Sent-off players cannot return to the field. Players cannot return to the field after being substituted, although certain countries may permit on-off-on substitutions in games involving under-16s or over-35s.

EQUAL HALVES

Halves must be of equal length. The referee of a Sunderland–Nottingham Forest match ended the first half two minutes early (September 1908). During the half-time interval he realised his mistake. After the interval he played the additional two minutes without the teams changing ends. Then he asked the players to switch ends and play the second half.

The referee of a Scotland–Canada international faced a similar problem when he whistled for half-time four minutes early (June 1983). The interval provides thinking time for referees as well as for managers and players. It must have been what the linesman said to them at half-time.

EQUIPMENT

There are five compulsory equipment requirements for players: a jersey (or shirt), shorts, socks, footwear and shinguards (1990). These and other equipment issues (colour clash, gloves, protectors, etc.) are dealt with under separate headings as they must be separate items (2006).

EXPERIMENTS WITH THE LAWS

The authorities have occasionally conducted experiments to see how a law change may affect the game. Examples include two referees, substitutes, the backpass law, kick-ins rather than throw-ins, advancing the ball, and various alternatives to the offside law. A 1978 youth tournament in Morocco tested the abolition of indirect free-kicks, temporary expulsions and kick-ins.

In 1972 IFAB decided that experiments would not be permitted unless sanctioned. In 1976 the sanctioning responsibility was handed over to FIFA.

EX-PLAYERS AS REFEREES

In six years as a professional (1947 to 1953), Bob Matthewson played six first-team matches for Bolton Wanderers. He later refereed the 1974 Charity

Shield match and the 1977 FA Cup Final. But Matthewson was an exception. There has always been a dearth of former professionals among high-level referees, whereas top-level cricket umpires are predominantly ex-players.

The culture of professional players does not convert easily to that of referees. Footballers are essentially biased and competitive (they want *their* team to win); referees must be neutral. Footballers are team-oriented and club-based; referees are loners (in their early careers) or part of a three- or four-person team. Footballers can have the vociferous support of a crowd; referees have little vocal support (except ironic cheers). Footballers have to cope with fame and celebrity; referees learn how to be unrecognised and unnoticed.

On the other hand, ex-players would have a better feel for the playing culture. They might be more liable to punish injury-causing challenges, and less likely to apply the laws mechanically. Some of the most injurious tackles in history have gone virtually unpunished on the pitch – Harald Schumacher (West Germany) on Patrick Battiston (France) (July 1982), John Cornforth (Swansea City) on Brian McCord (Stockport County) (March 1993), Ioan Ganea (Romania) on John Kennedy (Scotland) (March 2004), and so on.

One difficult issue is that professional players would normally need to be fast-tracked to reach the top level of refereeing – top-class players often do not retire until they are past thirty – and other referees may be opposed to this. In 1995, a new scheme trained 22 ex-players as referees. Nine years later none of them were refereeing. But a new initiative was launched in 2006.

Steve Baines came through the refereeing system just before that first scheme. After a career as a central defender at seven League clubs, he reached the League list in six years. But eyebrows were raised when he took a match between Bradford City and Oxford United in March 1996, because Baines had played for Bradford City for three seasons (1978–81). Bradford officials later complained that Baines went overboard not to favour them, while Oxford fans were sure Baines was biased towards his old team.

EXTRA-TIME

The idea of continuing a drawn game in order to find a definite winner is almost as old as football. It was formalised in the early FA Cup rules, and the 1875 FA Cup Final included extra-time.

Cup-competition authorities soon learned the importance of stating clear contingencies for a drawn game. After ninety minutes of the first Sheffield Challenge Cup Final, in 1877, Heeley and The Wednesday were level at 3–3. The players stood around in the centre-circle while officials decided what to do. The outcome was an extra thirty minutes, for the simple reason that arrangements had been made to present the trophy that day. Wednesday won 4–3.

Sometimes, in those early days, it was left to the two teams to agree. In an 1879 FA Cup tie, Old Etonians drew 5–5 with Darwen after ninety minutes. Old Etonians declined to play an extra half-hour, and this caused a fuss as Darwen had to pay to travel to London for a replay. In the 1883 Cup Final, however, Old Etonians kindly agreed to extra-time, even though they were down to ten men. They lost 2–1 to Blackburn Olympic.

Crewe Alexandra drew 2–2 with Swifts in an FA Cup tie at Crewe (December 1887). According to the *Crewe and Nantwich Guardian*, 'Conde, the Crewe captain, offered to play extra-time, but the visitors objected, and therefore the Alexandra have to renew hostilities upon the new Queen's Ground at Kensington, London.'

A Bass Cup tie between Burton Wanderers and Stoke City ended in confusion (April 1894). Burton claimed extra-time but Stoke refused, and Burton stayed out for ten minutes before going in.

Sometimes referees forget the competition rules. Liverpool won 2–1 after extra-time at Barnsley (February 1895). Unfortunately, the referee had made a mistake in playing extra-time when the score was 1–1 after ninety minutes. FA Cup rules deemed extra-time playable only in replays. The FA later ordered the teams to replay at Anfield, where Liverpool won easily.

The confusion of rules in the early days before substitutes was such that there were occasional debates about whether a team reduced to ten men could make it up to eleven at the start of extra-time. Orrell (Preston North End) left the field injured after six minutes of a second replay against Manchester City (February 1902). Could Orrell be replaced before extra-time? The answer (then and now) was, 'No, a player cannot be replaced.' Extra-time is not a new game; it is part of the same game.

The 1906 *Referees' Chart* clarified the extra-time procedure – captains toss again for choice of ends, and then the teams play two periods of fifteen minutes, changing straight round in between. This procedure was disrupted by experiments with golden goals (1993 to 2004) and silver goals (1998 to 2004), but then returned to favour. Extra-time is not to be confused with stoppage-time, which is added on for stoppages such as injuries, cautions, sendings-off and substitutions.

After ninety minutes there is usually an announcement: 'Ladies and gentlemen, there will now be thirty minutes of extra-time. If the teams are still level there will be a penalty shoot-out.' The two teams form groups *on the pitch* and three or four minutes will pass before the referee blows. The two captains will meet for another coin-toss – it may be two different captains if substitutes have replaced the originals – and the game restarts after a break of about five minutes.

At half-time in extra-time the referee shouts something like 'Straight round then, lads, straight round,' and the interval is as long as it takes two tired goalkeepers to travel the length of the pitch (about ninety seconds).

Nearly half of games going to extra-time produce a winner after 120 minutes.

EYESIGHT

Eddie Bannister (Barnsley) was one of the first players to wear contact lenses, but he had difficulty if a lens fell out. On one dark and muddy day in the late 1940s, Bannister inadvertently tackled the referee as he sprinted past. The referee, a railway clerk, was incensed until somebody explained.

Lots of players have forged professional careers with less than perfect eyesight. Nobby Stiles (England) used to tell team-mates to stay close because he could only see about fifteen yards. Alan Peacock was so colour-blind that he had trouble distinguishing Middlesbrough team-mates (red shirts) from Plymouth Argyle players (green shirts). Dean Shiels (Northern Ireland) lost the sight in his right eye after a domestic accident when he was eight. And the eyesight of Jack Howe (England) deteriorated so much that he had to leave the field at Huddersfield (December 1947). Howe's problem was remedied by contact lenses.

A few professionals appeared in spectacles in the early 1900s, including H S Bourne (West Ham), Alex Raisbeck (Liverpool) and the amateur goalkeeper Jim Mitchell (Preston and Manchester City). For many years, players were allowed to wear spectacles but they had to accept that they were playing at their own risk, and the spectacles had to have plastic lenses and safe frames.

Then contact lenses took over. Pat Partridge was refereeing at Stoke City one day when a home player lost a contact lens. Partridge threw a coin down to mark the place. After the game the groundsman looked for the coin, found it, looked for the contact lens and found that too.

Goalkeeper Jim Leighton (Scotland) had to be substituted at half-time against Wales (September 1985). Leighton had lost a contact lens on the pitch during the first half, and had forgotten to pack a spare pair. Iain Dowie (Crystal Palace) lost a lens during an FA Cup semi-final replay, and Manchester United scored while Dowie was getting a spare lens from the physiotherapist (April 1995).

Spectacles came back in fashion towards the end of the twentieth century. Edgar Davids (Holland) first wore special glasses in a friendly against Belgium (September 1999). Davids had been suffering from glaucoma in his right eye and his flexible, shatterproof glasses were apparently not dangerous to himself or others. In 2001 it was noted in the laws that new technology had made spectacles safer, but the final decision rests with the referee.

A more common eyesight problem is colour blindness. Hereditary defective colour vision is more common in men (7 per cent) than women (0.5 per cent). Given these figures, we would expect one or two players in a men's game to be affected by colour blindness, although not necessarily of a type to influence their sense of recognition.

Referees are tested for colour blindness as part of their qualifying examination. They are also tested for general vision. Here are the 1952 regulations:

> The initial examination shall be oral and written and shall include an eyesight and colour test by the card issued by the Football Association. Referees and linesmen who of necessity are compelled to wear glasses during the course of a match shall not be registered except to officiate in youth football at the discretion of a county association, such referees to be classified III. A person who has lost the sight of an eye shall not be registered.

That does not prevent insinuations about referees' eyesight.

'You're blind, Ref,' Aston Villa's Jimmy Dugdale said, during a match around 1960.

'What did you say?' the referee responded.

'Deaf, too, eh?' Dugdale added.

Referees are not blind but they have blind spots. Their viewing angle is about 45 degrees. One of the oldest expressions known to referees is 'You can only give what you see.' Near the end of a CIS Cup semi-final, Hibernian had a strong claim for a penalty-kick turned down after Ross (Rangers) had allegedly pushed O'Connor (Hibs) as the two players ran to meet a right-wing cross (February 2004). Television replays showed that the referee's view of the incident was blocked by players.

Sometimes referees just do not see things. In February 1973, at Highbury, a shot from Francis Lee (Manchester City) beat goalkeeper Geoff Barnett (Arsenal) and was entering the net when Jeff Blockley (Arsenal) punched the ball out. The referee, standing only three or four yards away, thought Blockley had headed the ball over the crossbar. He gave a corner-kick and was immediately surrounded by angry City players. The referee consulted the nearest linesman, who had not seen what had happened, and stuck to his original decision. Television later showed the handling incident clearly. The most likely explanation was that the referee was standing too close to the incident and at the wrong angle. Strangely, the linesman in the other half of the field saw it clearly but did not interfere.

Another astonishing episode came during a match between Partick Thistle and Dundee United (February 1993). Paddy Connolly (Dundee United) seemed to have scored when his shot went between the posts, hit a stanchion and rebounded to the edge of the goal area. A Partick defender picked up the ball and threw it to his goalkeeper. Dundee United players began to celebrate, the Partick goalkeeper kicked the ball downfield for the kick-off, and the referee waved play on. He had somehow missed the original goal *and* the handball incident. That referee, Les Mottram, went to the 1994 FIFA World Cup™ finals. It can happen to the best.

Ff

FAILURE TO TURN UP

Clubs usually forfeit games and face fines if they fail to turn up, but sometimes the circumstances are not straightforward. Dartford were en route to Leatherhead when they phoned ahead to check that the game was on (February 1978). Told that the match had been postponed, they returned to Dartford, but they had been hoaxed.

The Soviet Union refused to play a 1974 FIFA World Cup™ qualifier against Chile. The match was scheduled for 21 November 1973, less than nine weeks after a US-backed military coup had overthrown Salvatore Allende's elected socialist government. Furthermore, the scheduled venue for the Russia game was the notorious National Stadium, where hundreds of innocent people had been killed by the new Pinochet regime. Chile turned up, took to the field, and walked over to the finals. They actually kicked off with no opposition, stringing together several passes before a player shot into the empty net.

Estonia were scheduled to play Scotland in Tallinn (October 1996). The match had a 6.45 p.m. kick-off but, after hearing complaints from the Scots about the floodlights, FIFA switched the time of the match to 3 p.m. (with only a few hours' notice). Estonia complained about this new arrangement because it played havoc with security arrangements, television contracts, the players' preparation, and ticket-holders ability to attend (especially if they were at work during the day). When 3 p.m. arrived, only the Scotland players were present on the pitch. The referee started the game and abandoned it after the first kick. The match was later played at a neutral venue.

FAIR CATCH

The original 1863 FA laws allowed 'a fair catch'. If the ball hit any part of an opponent (or the opponent's clothing), it was considered a fair catch if the ball was then caught before it hit the ground. If the ball was kicked behind the goal-line, a fair catch could not be made. This law was the last remnant of the handling game. It was omitted from the 1866 FA laws, but it continued to be part of the Sheffield rules until the early 1870s.

FAIR PLAY

Certain acts of sportsmanship are common – kicking the ball out of play for the sake of an injured player – but others can take the football world by surprise. Steve Kember (Crystal Palace) told a referee that his shot had sent the ball through the side-netting and therefore it shouldn't be a goal (1971), Frank Ordenewitz (Werder Bremen) owned up to handling the ball in his own penalty area during a crucial league defeat (1988–89), and Paolo Di Canio (West Ham) caught the ball rather than try to head a stoppage-time winner because Everton goalkeeper Paul Gerrard was incapacitated with a bad knee injury (December 2000).

In a Carlsberg Cup match, Denmark were awarded a penalty-kick when an Iran defender handled the ball thinking the whistle had gone (February 2003). On instructions from his coach, Morten Wieghorst (Denmark) deliberately shot wide from the penalty mark.

Yeovil Town manager Gary Johnson told his side to concede a goal to Plymouth after a Yeovil player (ironically, Johnson's son) had accidentally scored when trying to return the ball to the Plymouth goalkeeper (August 2004). Crawford (Plymouth Argyle) was permitted to walk the ball through straight from the kick-off.

An American coach once offered to replay a match between two college teams when he realised that the opposition should have had a late equaliser because the ball had gone between the goalposts and through a hole in the goal-net. The opposition accepted the offer, and that 'probably did more to cement good relations between the schools than any other event in our history'.

The game of football continues because of a shared ethic. The ideal of fair play is to respect the laws, respect opponents, and respect officials and their decisions. By all means play to win, but play fair, learn and observe the laws, accept defeat with dignity, never argue with the referee or assistants, retire ten yards when a free-kick is given against you, keep your self-control at all times, do not retaliate, put the sport of football before yourself (or your team), reject drugs and other addictions, fight racism, and honour good sportspeople. As it said in the English Schools code of the 1970s, 'Accept victory modestly and defeat cheerfully.'

Sportsmanship was common in the game's early days. Indeed, it was even present in wars. J F C Fuller described the Boer War (1899–1902) as 'the last of the gentleman's wars', regretting the disappearance of the time when sportsmanship was the essence of soldiering. This attitude was known as the Corinthian spirit.

In the 1950s, it was common for players to carry the ball back when they were caught offside, and this would generate a round of applause from the crowd. It saved the goalkeeper fetching the ball, but it also gave the attacker and his colleagues time to regroup. Gradually the professional world began to frown on sportsmanship. Winning was what really mattered. John Giles was a professional for twenty years (1957 to 1977): 'When you're playing for your living the sportsmanship goes out of it very, very quickly, and you do what you can to win. And in the 1960s there was a shift towards that.'

Nobby Stiles, a World Cup winner, later looked back on a key incident in England's 4–3 win over Scotland (April 1966): 'There was a foul on the halfway-line and the ball had gone on to the track at Hampden Park. And Alf Ramsey, in a team-talk, said, "Can you remember what happened?" Well, from the free-kick Scotland scored. He said, "I'll tell you what happened. John Connelly went on to the track to pick the ball up and bring it back and give it to the Scotsman. Let *them* go and get it. You go and get organised."'

Since 1987, FIFA have presented Fair Play awards for services to football on and off the field. Gary Lineker (England), winner in 1990, was a model of integrity on the field. George Weah (Liberia), honoured in 1996, had helped former child soldiers and worked on AIDS and HIV awareness schemes. Julie Foudy, a Fair Play award winner in 1997, not only won 271 international caps for the USA women's team but she fought child-labour abuses and promoted causes for disabled children and female athletes.

Certain competitions are designed to reward fair play. The Neidersachsen Fair Play Cup is an annual children's tournament where points for fair play are awarded to players, coaches and opponents. Some major tournaments use fair play as a criterion if two teams finish level on points and are equal in other respects (e.g. goal difference and goals scored). Since 1999 UEFA Cup places have been made available for countries whose teams have good fair play records. Teams were marked according to the number of cards received, positive play, behaviour towards officials and opponents, and behaviour of team officials.

In England, in 1970–71, the Ford Sporting League gave two points for an away goal, one point for a home goal, and deducted five points for each caution and ten points for each sending-off. The winners, Oldham Athletic, received substantial prize money (for a new grandstand).

FÉDÉRATION INTERNATIONALE DE FOOTBALL ASSOCIATION (FIFA)

The Fédération Internationale de Football Association (FIFA) was formed in Paris on 21 May 1904. Representatives of seven countries – France, Belgium, Denmark, Netherlands, Spain, Sweden and Switzerland – met to establish an ultimate authority for association football. FIFA has since developed into the guardian of the world game. Its membership consists of over 200 national football associations.

The FIFA Referees' Committee, formed in 1923, oversees the development of refereeing throughout the world. This includes fielding questions about the laws, and their interpretation, from national FAs. The aim is for *unité de doctrine*.

FIFA representatives comprise half of the International Football Association Board (IFAB), which meets annually to make changes to the laws. FIFA is also in charge of establishing experiments that may lead to a change in the laws.

The history of the organisation is documented in *100 Years of Football: The FIFA Centennial Book* (2004) by Christiane Eisenberg, Pierre Lanfranchi, Tony Mason and Alfred Wahl.

FEIGNING INJURY *See* SIMULATION

FEUDS

Should a referee take note of a person's previous reputation or should each game start with a clean slate? Players like Alan Ball, Vinnie Jones and Robbie Savage have complained that their reputation went before them, suggesting that referees were watching them too closely. Sometimes it is not an individual's past but a relationship's history. Football has its feuds.

'If people kick me they're going to get a kick back,' said Dave Mackay (Scotland). 'I'm not going to get sent off for it, so I've got to do it in my own time. It might not be that game, but I'll get them the next time, and they would know that.'

Roy Keane (Manchester United) waited over three years to exact revenge on Alfe Inge Haaland. When Keane damaged his own cruciate ligament in September 1997, making a foul tackle on Haaland (Leeds United) for which he was cautioned, he resented a comment Haaland allegedly made. In April 2001, Keane was sent off for a wild lunge on Haaland (by now playing for Manchester City). The first edition of Keane's autobiography, *Roy Keane*, included a passage implying a revenge element behind the challenge on Haaland, as a result of which Keane received a five-match ban and a £150,000 fine for bringing the game into disrepute (October 2002).

George Santos (Sheffield United) was also sent off for taking retribution – an over-the-top tackle on West Brom's Andy Johnson (March 2002). Santos had suffered a broken jaw and fractured cheekbone after an incident involving Johnson's elbow the previous season, when Johnson was at Nottingham Forest (March 2001).

Feuds can be between clubs. A match in Ontario, Canada, between Olympic and Croatia was abandoned when kicking and fighting broke out among the players (July 1974). At that time, about eighty nationalities were represented in the soccer leagues of Toronto alone. Australia had such problems that ethnic team-names were banned in the 1990s.

Feuds can also involve team-mates. In one local game, players of a team leading 3–0 fell out with each other over misplaced passes, mistimed tackles, and missed chances. There was something approaching team rage, with players squaring up to each other, until one of them shouted, 'Come on, lads, if we were any good we wouldn't be here.'

FIELD OF PLAY See PITCH DIMENSIONS

FIFA See FÉDÉRATION INTERNATIONALE DE FOOTBALL ASSOCIATION

FIGHTING See MÊLÉE, STRIKING A PERSON

FINAL DECISION

Unless there is a matter that requires intervention from safety officers, police or medical services, the referee's decision on the field is final. And that's final.

Strangely, this can work two ways. In golf players can call penalties on themselves. In football it is usurping the referee's authority to call a foul on yourself. An interesting discussion followed an incident at Old Trafford when a fifty-yard shot by Mendes (Tottenham Hotspur) was fumbled over the line by goalkeeper Roy Carroll (Manchester United), who hastily retrieved the ball and played on (January 2005). Some people thought that Carroll should have owned up that the ball was over the line for a goal. Others pointed out that Carroll was just accepting that the referee's decision was final.

FINAL WHISTLE See FULL-TIME WHISTLE

FIRE

Any sign of fire means that referees must immediately apply safety principles and operate emergency procedure. At big grounds, police and the safety officers will take charge until emergency services arrive.

Small-scale incidents include one at Notts County, when smoke from a nearby chimney fire obscured the view of the game against Chester and thereby caused a delay (November 1964), and a fire in a wooden stand at Grantham, which was quickly put out by firemen (January 1967).

A match between Nottingham Forest and Leeds United was abandoned at half-time when a fire broke out in the Centre Stand at Forest's City Ground (August 1968). A few spectators fainted, but there were no serious casualties, partly because a favourable wind blew the fire away from the crowd. Leeds players vacated the ground immediately, leaving their possessions in the dressing-rooms. They walked to the Bridgford Hotel, left Nottingham in five taxis and reached Leeds around 7 p.m., still in their playing kit.

After forty minutes of the match between Bradford City and Lincoln City, a fire broke out in G Block of the wooden main stand at Valley Parade (11 May 1985). A policeman approached Bradford City manager Terry Yorath to ask the location of the nearest tap, spectators spilled on to the pitch, and the referee stopped the match. Fifty-six people were killed and more than 250 injured. Some crucial regulations laid out in *Guide to Safety at Sports Grounds* were found not to have been in place at Bradford. There was no dedicated person in charge, exit gates were closed, and building materials could have been safer. The fire was believed to have been caused by a lighted cigarette being dropped through a gap in the wooden floorboards and falling on debris that had collected beneath the stand. The 0–0 scoreline stood as a result.

FIREWORKS

The Sporting Events (Control of Alcohol) Act 1985 and the Football Disorder Act 2000 made it illegal to take fireworks or flares to a football game. There are good reasons. Roma goalkeeper Franco Tancredi (Roma) was hit by two firecrackers during a match in Milan (1987–88), a spectator was killed by a firework when Wales met Romania (November 1993), and Nelly Viennot, an assistant referee, was hit by a flare during a Strasbourg–Metz cup tie (April 2001). French referees boycotted the replay, which was played behind closed doors with a Bulgarian in charge.

A spectator at Wolverhampton Wanderers was hit by a firework during a pre-match display (November 2003). The woman spent two nights in hospital with a cheek injury. Seven other fans needed medical treatment.

FLAG-POST *See* CORNER-FLAGS, HALFWAY-LINE FLAGS

FLOODLIGHTS

Experiments with floodlit football began in the 1870s. Floodlights have never been mentioned in the laws, but most competitions will have rules and standards. The main issues over the years have been ensuring a visible ball and making provisions for floodlight failure. In the pioneering days, players and referees commented on dark patches, shadows or blind spots. When Wolves played Honved, they wore fluorescent shirts that glowed in the dark (December 1954).

The authorities gradually integrated floodlights into the fixture-planning during the 1950s, and the Football League eventually gave their blessing to all floodlit matches (1958). In the early days the referee would signal to the bench for the floodlights to be switched on.

The first big problem came when the lights went out halfway through the second half of a Watford–Shrewsbury match (April 1959). Three fuses had disappeared from the fuse-box. The pitch was virtually in darkness but the referee continued play until the 76th minute, when the match was abandoned. Fortunately, Shrewsbury, 5–2 ahead in the abandoned match, won the replay 4–1.

Other problems came with power cuts, equipment failure and sabotage. A match between Southampton and Leeds United lasted 158 minutes when the floodlights failed twice (December 1960). After several power cuts in the mid-1960s – a Crewe–Lincoln City match was abandoned after 36 minutes – it became commonplace for clubs to have a standby generator system, especially during periods of industrial action. A crowd of 13,000 people waited patiently in freezing conditions for an hour at Queen's Park Rangers, but electrical engineers were unable to restore power to two pylons and the match against Nottingham Forest was postponed (November 1985).

Certain matches ended in suspicious circumstances. A spate of floodlight failures in the late 1990s eventually led to four men being jailed for plotting to black-out floodlit football games as part of a betting coup (1999). The criminals were finally caught tampering with lights during a Charlton Athletic–Liverpool match. When the referee terminated a match between West Ham and Crystal Palace, he was asked by police to delay the announcement so that transport arrangements could be brought forward (November 1997).

FOG *See* WEATHER

FOOD INTAKE

When Rio Ferdinand (Manchester United) played his first Premiership match for eight months after serving a suspension, his physiotherapist gave him energy-bars towards the end of the match, which Ferdinand ate on the field (September 2004).

This was a poser for referees as the laws did not mention food intake. There were guidelines for liquid intake, injury treatment and cigarette smoking, but this was different. Chewing gum is not formally outlawed but it can be dangerous if it obstructs the trachea and oesophagus.

The authorities always worry that boundaries will be pushed further back. Would Ferdinand's energy-bars and Gascoigne's Mars bars open up a whole new can of worms, or perhaps a new can of beans? Was this acceptable, or will players soon be pulling out a two-leaf table to the centre-circle and expecting a four-course meal?

In practice, common sense will dictate that eating on the pitch should be at the referee's discretion. Diabetics, for instance, may need sustenance to keep their blood-sugar levels high enough.

FOOTWEAR

In the 80th minute, shortly after Miller (Middlesbrough) had been cut on the arm, Arthur Childs (Hull City) was ordered off the Middlesbrough pitch because a nail in his boot was projecting (September 1928). Childs was not allowed back on the field, even after changing his boot, because the law of the day stated that a player should be sent from the field 'not to return'. That law was soon changed – players sent off with inadequate footwear could return to the pitch, but only when the ball was out of play and the referee had given permission (having first checked that the boots were now satisfactory) (1929).

It is the player's responsibility to satisfy the law, not the manufacturer's. In 2004, *The Non-League Paper* ran a campaign against 'dangerous bladed football boots'. The newspaper argued that such boots were easily damaged by players running or walking across concrete. There had been a number of serious gash injuries, including those to Andy Hessenthaler (Gillingham), Neil Mellor (West Ham) and Gareth Risbridger (Staines Town). In 2005, referees were instructed to inspect footwear before every match.

Boot specifications were given attention in the earliest laws, and nail-heads had to be 'driven in flush with the leather, iron plates, or gutta-percha on the soles or heels of his boots'. Scotland was blessed with the famous 'crow's beaks' game, when Queen's Park objected to marks on the pitch at Vale of Leven because spikes were illegal (December 1876). Vale of Leven fans said that the marks were caused by crows plunging their beaks into the ground.

By 1891 the law was very detailed: 'Any nails should be driven in flush with the leather. Bars and studs should project no more than half an inch. Fastenings should be driven in flush with the leather. Bars shall be transverse and flat, not less than one-and-a-half inches in length and half an inch in width. Studs shall be round in plan, not less than half an inch in diameter, and in no case conical or pointed.'

A clause was introduced to prohibit a player with offending footwear from taking part in the rest of the match (1891), referees were given permission to examine boots before the match (1897), bars were lengthened so that they had to extend all the way across the width of the boots (1900), and referees could examine boots during the half-time interval (1910). Metal clips for lace-holds were later considered illegal, as were buckles on boots and shinguards. Much later, the law was changed to deal with combined studs and bars (1937).

To buy boots in the early 1900s a player could send a piece of paper cut to the exact outline of his foot. It would take players about three months to break in the boots. Some of them were so unreliable that the ball would fly into one corner of the goal while a boot-sole rippled the netting nearby.

On 23 June 1934, the FA Council ruled sensationally on what should happen if a player refuses to leave the pitch when told to change boots: 'If a player wears anything that the referee considers liable to cause injury to another player he must require the player to remove it, failing which the referee must order the player off the field, and such player shall not play thereafter without the consent of the Football Association.' Most players went meekly. In a match at Charlton, the referee sent Massie (Aston Villa) to the dressing-room to have a protruding nail removed from one boot (April 1939). At half-time in a Stoke City–Blackpool FA Cup tie, when players complained of scratches on the legs, the referee checked the studs of players of both sides and found nails protruding (1949). And the boots of Docherty (Preston) were examined after Quixall (Sheffield Wednesday) had been injured during the 1954 FA Cup semi-final.

From 1951, players were allowed to wear boots with studs shaped as truncated cones, provided that the diameter of the smallest circle was not less than half an inch and that they did not project more than three-quarters of an inch (an increase from half an inch). The invention of screw-in studs and the use of rubber-moulded soles revolutionised the design. Later, in the 1970s, players like Alan Ball, Terry Cooper, Peter Taylor and Alan Hinton wore white boots. In 1999 IFAB rejected the idea of team-mates having to wear boots of the same colour.

In 1972–73 referees and linesmen in the professional game were issued with gauges to measure studs, but manufacturers hadn't been consulted so a lot of illegal studs were identified. Before a Poland–Argentina match, a linesman inspected the players' footwear and expressed concern (June 1974), and as a result the referee asked two Argentina players to change their boots. After 1975, the laws referred to footwear rather than boots.

There have been times when players have played without footwear. In the 1930s, Celtic fielded Abdul Salim, who played with bandages around his feet. In the 1920s, Tewfik 'Toothpick' Abdallah preferred to play in bare feet but Derby County officials convinced him to wear boots.

Leonidas (Brazil) scored four in the 6–5 win against Poland (June 1938). At one point, feeling constricted by the mud, Leonidas took off his boots and tossed them away over the touchline. At once the referee ordered him to put them on again or go off himself as he was in breach of the rules. It was considered acceptable for the whole team to be barefoot but not one individual player (IFAB 1956). Indeed, a barefoot Nigerian XI played at South Liverpool (1949), and the Mohun Bagan team (playing barefoot) defeated an East Yorkshire regiment to win the India FA Shield (1911). In the 1960s there were instances of referees stopping players from playing if they wore trainers, plimsolls or winkle-pickers.

In 1989, the wording on Law 4 was altered to make it clear that suitable footwear *had* to be worn. Players without boots should be ordered from the field and not allowed to return until they have replaced them (1992). Players losing a boot are not allowed to play on in stockinged feet, but they may be allowed some leeway if they shoot and score in the very next stride. Against Holland, Milan Baros (Czech Republic) lost a boot in a challenge, then continued his dribble and took a shot at goal as a defender held back from damaging Baros's metatarsal (September 2004). The referee awarded an indirect free-kick against Baros and cautioned him for unsporting behaviour. A similar caution was issued to Beckham (England) against Azerbaijan (March 2005). Having lost a boot, Beckham needed to concentrate on replacing it. Instead he got up off his knees when the ball came his way and played a pass with his sock.

FOUL

A foul is a generic term. It applies to a whole catalogue of offences, most of which are dealt with under specific headings.

Some fouls are insignificant to the action, especially if the referee uses the advantage clause, but others can have a direct bearing on the outcome of a match. The most significant are fouls that result in penalty-kicks or direct free-kicks near goal, fouls inducing sendings-off, and fouls causing injuries.

Certain fouls are strategic – to slow down the game, to allow defenders to regroup, to get a substitute on – and many professionals accept them as part of the game. Coaches sometimes advise players that there are situations where they should go down to get the foul. Other players try simulating a trip to kid the referee. A foul is usually punished if it affects the player in some way. The player's reaction often shows what is acceptable.

A study by Volkamer, in the early 1970s, reached a number of conclusions: losers foul more than winners; home teams foul less than away teams; fouls are more frequent when there is a slight difference in the score; there are fewer fouls in high-scoring matches; and lower-ranked teams commit more fouls, except where there is a marginal difference between the teams' rankings.

There is room for sophisticated analysis and historical analysis. Fouls were originally greeted by an apology, and free-kicks for fouls only entered the game in 1873–74. Looking at videos of matches from the 1950s, there seem fewer fouls then. On the other hand, some ex-players argue that the top-level game was at its nastiest in the 1960s, when the maximum wage had been removed and television was not yet scrutinising players' deeds. The 1968 European Cup Final had some cynical fouling on Best (Manchester United) and Eusebio (Benfica).

FOUL LANGUAGE See ABUSIVE LANGUAGE

FOUL THROW See THROW-IN

FOURTH OFFICIAL

During one professional match the fourth official spent most of his time sheltering from the wind at the head of the players' tunnel. He looked from one technical area to the other, like a driver at a busy crossroads, and occasionally appeased a coach's rage. He came to the touchline on a few occasions: to take a coin that the match referee had found on the pitch ('Is that my fee?'); to watch a player change his boots during an injury-break; to check the amount of stoppage-time; to hold up the stoppage-time board; and to oversee four second-half substitutions.

Fourth officials need a different skill-mix compared to the match referees, who jog a lot and are always involved, and assistants, who are essentially sprinters. Fourth officials have long gaps and then sudden involvement. At Stevenage one day the fourth official had to step in between two managers when one took exception to the other baiting a player (November 2004).

Fourth officials gradually evolved from reserve officials appointed for big games. They have specific duties: replacing a match official who is unable to continue (1991); assisting with any administrative duties required by the referee (1993); assisting with substitution procedures during the match (1993); supervising match-ball replacements (1993); checking players' equipment and informing an assistant referee of any equipment problems (1993); submitting a report on any misconduct missed by the other officials (1996); informing the referee of any untoward behaviour in the technical area (1999); informing the referee if the wrong player is cautioned (2000); and informing the referee if a player has been cautioned twice but not sent off (2000).

Some people think that the fourth official is the way forward – operating video equipment, constantly communicating with the referee through microphones, aiding with goalkeeper's positioning during a penalty shoot-out, etc. – but others point out that the proliferation of fourth officials in professional football means a dearth of much-needed experienced officials covering lower-league matches. There is also the question of whether the presence of a nearby official is provocative to managers.

The fourth official only assists the referee. The referee has the final decision on all matters connected with play. But the situation can change very quickly if the fourth official has to replace an injured referee during a match. That happened to Paul Durkin, who replaced the injured Dermot Gallagher during a France–Bulgaria match (June 1996).

CB Fry's Magazine (December 1905) referred to an incident where two players had been sent off in a match at Nottingham. The original offender had not been noticed by the referee, but several members of the FA Council spotted the offence and took action accordingly. A century later a fourth official saw Zidane (France) butt Materazzi (Italy) in the chest (June 2006).

FREE-KICK

Everton's Stan Bentham always enjoyed telling the story of the first time his wife Alwyn saw him play football. It was during World War II when Alwyn sat in the stand with a knowledgable friend.

'Alwyn, Alwyn,' the friend said, 'Everton's got a free-kick and Stan's going to take it.'

'He'll take anything free,' Alwyn replied.

A free-kick is exactly that – a *free* kick. It is the privilege of kicking at the ball without obstruction, and like snooker's free shot it comes after an opponent has transgressed the rules. The team breaking the law has no rights except not to be distracted by the referee.

A number of offences are punishable by direct free-kicks if the action is, in the referee's judgment, careless, reckless or with excessive force: kicking or attempting to kick an opponent; tripping or attempting to trip an opponent; jumping at an opponent; charging an opponent; striking or attempting to strike an opponent; and pushing an opponent. Direct free-kicks are also given against players who make contact with an opponent before touching the ball, hold an opponent, spit at an opponent, or deliberately handle the ball.

Indirect free-kicks are awarded for anything the referee considers to be dangerous play, offside, touching the ball twice before another player touches the ball after taking a restart (except for a dropped ball or if the ball goes out of play), impedance of an opponent's progress, failure to allow the goalkeeper to release the ball from his hands, or any offence which causes the referee to stop play and issue a caution or a sending-off. In addition, a number of goalkeeping offences merit an indirect free-kick – controlling the ball with the hands and not releasing it within six seconds, releasing the ball but handling it again before it has been touched by another player, or handling a backpass or touching it with the hands after receiving it straight from a team-mate's throw-in.

Free-kicks take place where the offence occurs. Gary Bollan (Livingstone) discovered that when he aimed a kick in the penalty-area at Jackie McNamara (Celtic) and conceded a penalty (even though the ball was downfield), and earned a red card (August 2001). For a short time in Sao Paulo (Brazil) they experimented with a white spray marking the site of free-kicks. The only sanctioned method, however, is for the referee to remember the spot. Sometimes a helpful assistant will stand in line with where the offence occurred. Footballers frequently advance the ball by a few yards at free-kicks, whereas golfers are pilloried if they replace their balls incorrectly.

A referee cannot give a free-kick if the offence occurs off the field of play. If, for instance, a winger pushes the ball past a defender and is clobbered while off the field, it cannot be a free-kick. The offender can still be disciplined.

Other than a free-kick for making a fair catch, there were no free-kicks in the laws until 1871–72, when it was deemed necessary to create a free-kick (confusingly called a penalty-kick) for handling the ball. In 1873–74, the free-kick punishment was extended to infringements of laws 6, 8 and 9. A player couldn't touch the ball twice from the free-kick (without another player touching the ball), and a goal couldn't be scored direct. The first direct free-kick was the twelve-yard penalty-kick (1891). Until 1903, all other free-kicks were *indirect*, meaning that a goal couldn't be scored 'unless the ball had been played or touched by a player other than the kicker before passing through goal'.

The laws cater for three types of free-kick – indirect, direct and the penalty-kick – but there are many other classifications. There are quick free-kicks and ceremonial free-kicks, disputed free-kicks, indirect free-kicks within ten yards of the opponents' goal (where the defending team can line up on their own goal-line between the posts), free-kicks inside the team's own penalty-area (when opponents must be at least ten yards away *and outside the penalty area*), and free-kicks necessarily delayed by a substitution, an injury, a caution or a sending-off. Each of these has a different procedure.

The most dramatic direct free-kicks are those within range of goal. About 10 per cent of direct free-kicks around the penalty area result in goals, but obviously this figure will vary with the level of skill.

'Five in the wall,' the goalkeeper yells. 'Stand on the ball, let the referee pull you back.'

'Five, he wants five,' a defender repeats.

'Right, right, to the right,' the goalkeeper shouts.

'Come on, Ref, get them back,' calls an attacker, as the referee starts to pace out ten yards. (Some referees pace backwards so they can keep their eye on the ball.)

'Wait for me,' says the referee, as he points to his whistle and concentrates on his pacing.

'You, too, Adam,' the goalkeeper shouts. 'Get in there.'

'Get back here, number two,' says the referee to the wall. 'And you, five.'

Finally, all is ready. The trouble is that it can take a minute to set it all up, and it makes you wonder which team is being punished. Newcastle won two twenty-yard free-kicks in quick succession at Chelsea (2005). Robert waited 65 seconds to take the first, and 55 seconds to hit the second. (This issue was raised at the 1987 IFAB meeting and there were suggestions of limiting the wall to a maximum of three players – nothing was done.)

These free-kicks are known to referees as ceremonial free-kicks. The taker wants the wall of defenders back the required distance, the referee ready, and the kick taken on the sound of the referee's whistle. In contrast is the quick free-kick, where the referee gives a signal (not necessarily a whistle) and the player is happy to take the kick quickly, even though opponents may not be the required distance from the ball.

Some referees only permit quick free-kicks in the team's own half. Others are happy for the kick to be taken quickly wherever it is, providing the ball is stationary, the kick is taken from the correct place and the referee has given a signal (a wave of the arm or 'OK').

A quick free-kick set up Manchester United's equaliser against Blackpool and changed the course of the 1948 FA Cup Final. A quick free-kick taken by Bobby Moore (England) set up an equaliser for Geoff Hurst against West Germany in the 1966 FIFA World Cup™ Final.

Attacking players may realise that a quick free-kick, while the opposition are arguing, can be beneficial. Defending players, recognising that a quick free-kick could catch them out, often stand near the ball, deliberately failing to retreat the required distance (a cautionable offence). This tactic came in during the 1960s.

Gordon Strachan (Leeds United) equalised at Stoke with a chipped free-kick while Stoke were still trying to organise their defensive wall (September 1989). The defending side does not have a right to a wall. Indeed, a free-kick should not benefit the team conceding it.

If a quick free-kick does not work out well, a team cannot go back and try a ceremonial free-kick instead. It is one or the other. Play continues if a quick free-kick is intercepted by an opponent who has not retreated the required distance. And play also continues if the player taking the quick free-kick wastes the ball with a bad pass.

Carlisle United scored a bizarre 89th-minute winner against Halifax Town in March 2005. Halifax goalkeeper Ian Dunbavin thought he had a free-kick so he wandered out of the penalty area holding the ball. Instead the referee gave a free-kick to Carlisle for Dunbavin handling the ball outside the area. The goalkeeper threw the ball down in disgust, Carlisle took the free-kick quickly, and Magno Vieira scored.

Within the space of a few seconds referees have to answer a lot of questions: Is it a free-kick? Direct or indirect? Where is it? Is the ball in the right place? Are the defenders ten yards away? Should I caution the defender who is standing on the ball? Should I caution the player conceding the free-kick? Should I caution the second defender who tries to stand on the ball? Who's taking the kick? Does he want a quick free-kick or a ceremonial one? Do I give a signal for a quick free-kick? Am I in the way if I stand here? How will I get out of the way? Should I pace out nine steps? What's the jostling in the wall? Is the ball still in the right place or has somebody moved it? Shall I whistle now? Has the ball gone in? Is my assistant signalling a goal?

Ceremonial kicks give rise to other problems. In the 1991 FA Cup Final, Glover (Nottingham Forest) stationed himself on the edge of a Tottenham Hotspur wall and pulled a defender out of position so that a free-kick from Pearce (Nottingham Forest) could go through a gap in the wall. Referees started watching for this. Sometimes it causes further delay if a referee has to talk to, or caution, an offender.

Ceremonial free-kicks can also be slowed down by encroachment problems. Four Chelsea players in the wall were cautioned for failing to retreat the required distance at Everton (October 1974), and a wall of seven Notts County players were cautioned *en bloc* against Manchester United (December 1983).

A team cannot score against itself directly from a direct free-kick. During stoppage-time in the second half of a Wimbledon–Millwall game, Wimbledon were awarded a direct free-kick just outside their own penalty area (December 1983). Wally Downes took the kick, and chipped the ball back to goalkeeper Dave Beasant. Unfortunately it went over Beasant's head and into the net. The referee erroneously gave a goal to Millwall, making the final score 4–3 to Wimbledon, whereas he should have awarded a corner-kick. There is a subtle rationale behind this. A team cannot score against itself from an indirect free-kick (e.g. offside) (1927). A team winning a *direct* free-kick does so because the opposition has committed a more serious offence (e.g. handling the ball). Therefore you cannot punish the team more severely when they are taking the direct free-kick as the whole idea is to *punish the opposition more severely*.

When the referee of the 1929 Scotland–England international gave an indirect free-kick to England six yards from the opposition goal, the Scotland players didn't know they could line up on their own goal-line, between the goalposts. They started ten yards behind the ball, encroached a little and somehow managed to block the shot after Wainscott (England) received the short pass.

An incident in a Spain–Argentina international highlighted the need for a special signal for indirect free-kicks (1952). The only goal of that game came as a result of an indirect free-kick awarded for dangerous play. An Argentinian chipped the free-kick towards goal. Had the Spanish goalkeeper been certain the kick was indirect, he could have stepped aside and let the ball go straight into the net (and the referee would have awarded a goal-kick). Instead he tried to punch the ball out to make sure. He mis-punched it, and a forward tapped it in.

In the early 1950s, Portsmouth chairman Vernon Stokes suggested a raised arm signal to indicate an indirect free-kick – one arm raised high in the air like a classroom swot who can answer a question. Referee Arthur Blythe took up the idea and it became commonplace (FIFA Referees' Committee 1953) and eventually part of the laws (1979). Referees had to keep their arm raised until another player had touched the ball or the ball went out of play (IFAB 1979).

Manchester United and Manchester City met in a two-legged League Cup semi-final in 1969. The winning goal came from an indirect free-kick. Not noticing the referee's raised arm, Francis Lee (City) shot for goal and goalkeeper Alex Stepney (United) instinctively tried to stop the ball. He only parried the shot and Summerbee (City) scored from the rebound.

In an England–Holland game, Stuart Pearce (England) curled in an indirect free-kick and the ball skidded through into the net without anybody touching it (June 1990). The same thing happened when Sasa Curcic (Bolton Wanderers) put an indirect free-kick straight into the Chelsea net (April 1996). In both cases the referee correctly awarded a goal-kick.

Goalkeeper Steve Mildenhall (Notts County) scored directly from a free-kick from his own half against Mansfield Town (August 2001). This was from a direct free-kick, but it is a reminder that referees always need to signal correctly for an indirect free-kick, even when the free-kick is a long way out.

If a player takes an indirect free-kick, the ball hits the crossbar and then hits another player and goes in then it is a goal. If a player kicks an indirect free-kick directly into his own team's goal without any player touching the ball, the decision is a corner-kick to the opposing team.

Free-kicks given on or near the goal-line were often difficult to take – the net restricted the goalkeeper's run-up. From 1978, free-kicks in the goal area could be taken from any point on the same side of the area as the offence occurred. In 1992 this was changed again, so that the defending team could take such kicks from anywhere in the goal area, thus making this consistent with the taking of goal-kicks.

Sheffield Wednesday's winning goal at Portsmouth came when Portsmouth had a free-kick in stoppage-time (April 2003). The referee told a Portsmouth player to move the ball back inside his own half. When the player kicked it back, his colleague played on as if the kick had been taken. Michael Reddy (Wednesday) charged the ball down and went on to score. The Portsmouth manager's reaction was to blame the referee for allowing play to continue. There are, however, coaching points that can be made to cover this circumstance. A player can roll the ball back to a colleague with the hands to show that the ball is still being positioned for the free-kick.

All free-kicks should be taken with the ball stationary. Sometimes players throw the ball forward with a backspin motion and it is difficult for the referee to tell whether the ball is stationary. Referees usually keep their eye on the ball. In the final of the 2006 African Nations Cup, two Egypt free-kicks were retaken because the ball was not stationary. When England met Uruguay, there was a dispute about one of the Uruguay goals (June 1954). The England players felt that a free-kick had been taken from the wrong place with the ball still moving.

The player taking the free-kick is not allowed to touch the ball again until another player has touched it or the ball has gone out of play. In the early 1970s, Cambridge United visited Portugal and played against Portimao on a sand pitch which saw the ball bouncing unpredictably. According to a Cambridge United programme (4 March 1972): 'All our players stood around and roared with laughter when John Collins, who was a big favourite with the crowd, placed his foot under the ball when taking a free-kick and lifted it over a wall of players only for the referee to award Portimao a free-kick on the grounds that John had kicked the ball twice.'

In a legendary incident, Willie Carr (Coventry) stood with the ball between his heels at a free-kick outside the Everton penalty area (October 1970). Carr jumped up and flicked the ball a few feet into the air. Ernie Hunt (Coventry) met the ball on the volley and struck it into the net. The match referee gave the goal, but it was considered unacceptable on a regular basis (IFAB 1971). As Carr had the ball wedged between both feet when he 'donkey-kicked' the ball into the air, he had touched the ball twice.

However, both these rulings were later changed. The Carr-Hunt donkey-kick and the Collins scoop kick are allowed.

FRIENDLY MATCHES

The laws of the game apply equally to friendly matches, and all matches must take place under the auspices of the relevant national association. Otherwise carded players could slip through the punishment net. The IFAB recommended a minimum one-match suspension for players dismissed in friendlies (IFAB 1987). Teams may, however, agree the number of substitutions, providing the referee is informed. Tape may be used if a crossbar breaks.

Some friendly matches are notoriously unfriendly. The Northern Ireland–Italy 'footbrawl friendly' was one of the roughest games ever played (December 1957). It was intended to be a FIFA World Cup™ qualifier but the appointed referee was stranded by fog in London. An Irish official deputised and the match was called 'a friendly'. It had bad tackles, running feuds and a sending-off, with Italian players being attacked by Irish supporters at the end.

Players have also been sent off in testimonial matches, and one between Arsenal and Barcelona broke out into a brawl after a poor challenge by Zenden (Barcelona) on Dixon (Arsenal) in May 2001. A Bournemouth–Southampton friendly was so fractious that the referee called all the players together (September 1939). A relatively high number of players (eighteen) were sent off in the first five months of the 1915–16 season, when the matches were all friendlies because of the war.

FULL-TIME See FULL-TIME WHISTLE

FULL-TIME REFEREES

The Professional Game Match Officials Limited (PGMOL) was formed in 2001 in order to provide officials for professional matches in England. This included forming an elite cadre of full-time referees. This was the culmination of years of debate about full-time referees at the top level. Those in favour stressed a number of points: (i) an improvement in fitness levels; (ii) more time to study tactics and decision-making; (iii) better pay; (iv) easier arrangements for disciplinary hearings; and (v) a career goal for all referees.

Opponents of full-time referees cited a number of issues: (i) the cost of full-time salaries; (ii) an enforced early retirement age (47 or 48); (iii) no guarantee that full-timers would make better decisions; and (iv) full-timers might be too willing to please people and keep in favour so as not to lose their jobs.

FULL-TIME WHISTLE

Sheffield Wednesday played Huddersfield Town in a 1930 FA Cup semi-final, and a crowd of nearly 70,000 watched the game. Huddersfield led 2–1, with time running out, when Wednesday's Jack Allen shot towards the Huddersfield goal. The referee blew his whistle for full-time while Allen was in the act of shooting. The ball found the net but no goal was allowed. The crowd and players were confused. Spectators had to buy a newspaper on the way home to check the score: Huddersfield Town 2 Sheffield Wednesday 1. Imagine leaving a semi-final and not knowing the result.

Sheffield Wednesday officials complained that the 1930 semi-final referee had played short time and one supporter with a stopwatch claimed that the second half had lasted only 43 minutes. But such arguments are irrelevant because the referee is the sole judge of time. The 1930 semi-final incident raised a debate that has often been resurrected: should referees stay clear of controversy when blowing the full-time whistle, or should they blow the moment the second-hand reaches 45 minutes?

After 86 minutes of a France–Argentina match, the referee blew his whistle for an infringement, but the crowd thought it was the final whistle (June 1930). Mounted police had to clear the field so that the outstanding four minutes could be played.

Incidents such as this eventually led to referees developing a special signal to denote full-time (three separate blasts on the whistle and pointing to the dressing-rooms).

There is one other good reason for timing the final whistle well. Lovick understates it beautifully in his early advice-book for referees: 'When blowing for full-time in a game when you have sensed there may be some hostility towards you (and this will happen occasionally to every referee) position yourself so that when you do blow for time you have the shortest possible route to the dressing-room.'

A referee at Maltby, Yorkshire, incurred the wrath of the fans (1952–53). Making sure he ended the game when he was next to the dressing-rooms, he made a swift escape. The linesman on the far side of the pitch was not so amused. Not only did he have trouble getting across the pitch, but the referee had locked the dressing-room to keep out irate fans.

Top-class referees prefer the ritual of blowing while in the centre-circle, waiting for assistants to sprint to them, getting support from security officers, and having close witnesses in case of attack! Occasionally assistants have sprinted towards the referee on the sound of 'the full-time whistle' only to discover that it is a free-kick.

A different kind of finale came when Liverpool entertained Manchester City in an FA Cup replay (February 1956). Manchester City were leading 2–1 when the ball reached John Evans (Liverpool), just inside his own half. The referee blew for full-time as Evans swept a long pass forward to his team-mate Billy Liddell. The players involved had not heard the whistle. The referee stood watching near the halfway line as Liddell shot for goal. The ball went into the net and Liddell turned to celebrate, only to find that other players were leaving the field. The game had ended before his goal. Even though the referee had blown the whistle at the halfway-line it had not staved off controversy.

In a 1978 World Cup match against Sweden, Brazil were awarded a stoppage-time corner-kick, which was delayed while the Polish linesman ensured the ball was inside the corner arc. Only seconds now remained. The referee, Clive Thomas, blew the final whistle when the ball had travelled about ten yards from the corner-kick. He turned and pointed to the tunnel. A roar from the crowd greeted a header from Zico (Brazil) going into the net. The referee did not allow a goal and the result was 1–1. Other examples include disallowed 'goals' by Gordon (Hull City in 1905), Tueart (Manchester City in 1977), Roberts (Crystal Palace in 1996), Gayle (Wimbledon in 1998), and Cahill (Australia in 2006), all of which affected the match result. Most referees would opt to blow up before a corner-kick was taken if there are only a few seconds remaining. Or they would wait until there was a definite outcome from the corner.

Denis Howell has written about a game early in his refereeing career, when the ball hit his watch and caused it to stop. He solved the problem by timing his game approximately by the one on the next pitch. But the referee of a Crystal Palace–Fulham match didn't have that option when his watch failed to restart after an injury break (October 1978). He guessed full-time from the stadium clock, but the two linesmen later agreed that there were still four minutes to play. The referee stopped the players from changing, and went back out to complete the match.

Referees usually carry two watches. They have strong views on what is the best watch on the market. One local referee always took his wife to matches because he got so involved that he lost track of time. She kept the watch.

In two situations, referees have little chance to sound the final whistle – after a golden goal and after the winning penalty in a shoot-out. Ten Newcastle Ladies players rushed from the centre-circle when their goalkeeper's save seemed to ensure a 5–4 shoot-out success against Liverpool Ladies, but the referee ordered a retake (February 2006). After much confusion, the shoot-out resumed, and Newcastle eventually lost 9–8.

The referee's jurisdiction continues after the final whistle – until he leaves the pitch. A referee was charged with failing to apply the laws properly when he neglected to red-card Gillespie (Sheffield United) at Reading (October 2005). The player had committed a sending-off offence after the full-time whistle and was still on the pitch.

Gg

GAMESMANSHIP

According to Stephen Potter in *The Theory and Practice of Gamesmanship*, the art of gamesmanship is to use dubious but technically legal tactics to win a game. Gamesmanship is usually against the spirit of the game but not against the rules.

The standard for soccer gamesmanship was set by Leeds United in the 1960s and 1970s. United players would have called it professionalism rather than gamesmanship. They used the laws to their own advantage.

To hear opponents, Leeds United players wasted time, tugged shirts and even pulled hair. United coaches encouraged players to take the ball into the corner to waste time when a lead needed defending. They would also kick the ball into the corner and get tight on the opposition rather than keep possession. They had referees assessed for individual tolerances.

The gamesmanship at Leeds United under manager Don Revie became such an obsession that some say it crossed the line between fairness and unfairness, sporting and unsporting behaviour. But players can be cautioned for unsporting behaviour – known as ungentlemanly conduct until 1997 – and lawmakers have worked hard to turn acts of gamesmanship into cautionable offences and infringements. On the other hand, coaches simply invent more ways to circumvent the laws.

GLASSES *See* EYESIGHT

GLOVES

Goalkeepers have always worn gloves but the style has changed over the years. In the 1940s it was hard to buy decent gloves. Everton goalkeeper Jimmy O'Neill got his from a policeman who did traffic point-duty. The gloves came to him full of holes but his wife Angela darned them. Other goalkeepers bought woollen gloves from the Army & Navy Stores, and their wives stitched leather on the knuckle to make punching the ball more comfortable. The laws have no limit on the size of gloves but referees would consider it unsporting if a goalie wore three-foot plastic ones for a penalty shoot-out.

Gloves for outfield players became popular in the 1960s and 1970s. Clyde Best (West Ham) wore gloves at Ipswich (November 1969). It is sensible practice for players with Raynaud's disease, who react strongly to cold conditions.

GOAL See METHOD OF SCORING

GOALKEEPERS

The laws on goalkeeping have two major narratives: (i) how goalkeepers have progressed from an Aunt Sally in the firing line to more of a protected species (especially in the goal area); and (ii) the constant appraisal of what to do to speed up the game when goalkeepers have the ball.

Goalkeepers were first mentioned in the Sheffield offside rule (1870) – 'The goalkeeper is that player on the defending side who, for the time being, is nearest his own goal' – and their special handling privileges were noted soon afterwards. The goalkeeper's role was clarified in 1882: 'No player shall carry, knock-on or handle the ball under any pretence whatever except in the case of the goalkeeper who shall be allowed to use his hands in defence of his goal, either by knocking-on or throwing, but not carrying the ball.'

Carrying was defined as taking more than two steps when holding the ball. This carrying restriction was to balance the fact that goalkeepers were allowed to roam upfield handling the ball. 'In defence of his goal' was considered to be anywhere in his own half (1887). In 1912, the goalkeeper's use of hands was confined to the penalty area.

In the 1880s goalkeepers had to be protected from onrushing opponents by team-mates. Goalkeepers were attacked when they *didn't* have the ball (especially at corner-kicks). They were often violently bundled over by one forward while another was shooting. Several goalkeepers were seriously injured as a result, so IFAB inserted a provision that goalkeepers could only be charged when they were 'in the act of playing the ball or obstructing an opponent'. 'Since this amendment was passed the lives of goalkeepers have been much less liable to forfeiture,' wrote Pa Jackson, the founder of the Corinthians, in the 1890s.

Contrary to Jackson's opinion, goalkeepers were still in danger, as indicated by a story in *Thomson's Weekly News* (1911–12):

> One of the Clapton players sent in a shot, and in clearing Mearns, the Barnsley goalkeeper, fell, but retained possession of the ball. In a moment Bevan was on top of him, and so prevented him getting the ball away. Soon there were at least sixteen players lying in the goalmouth, and this scramble lasted for about three minutes. Then one of the Clapton men went in

the goal and pulled the goalkeeper through by the legs. The referee allowed the goal.

The goalkeeper's plight can also be illustrated by Chelsea's 61st-minute goal in the 1915 FA Cup semi-final against Everton: 'McNeil centred, Mitchell ran out to catch the ball. But before he could relieve himself [of the ball], Thomson charged him and the ball fell on the ground. Croal gained possession without trouble and quickly shot it on the ground in an oblique direction into the net.'

The matter of goalkeeper safety came to a head in the 1930s. The whole of Scotland was shocked by the death of Celtic's 22-year-old international John Thomson, who received a fatal head injury when diving at the feet of Sam English (Rangers) in September 1931. English's knee caught Thomson's head as he followed through from the shot. The goalkeeper died that evening without ever recovering consciousness. Over 30,000 people attended the funeral of the young man, who was known as the Prince of Goalkeepers.

Then came another fatality. The Chelsea–Sunderland game was by all accounts a rough one (February 1936). Goalkeeper Jimmy Thorpe (Sunderland) received some heavy treatment, especially during one pro-tracted goalmouth scramble. Thorpe, a 22-year-old diabetic, died two days later. According to the *Sunderland Football Echo* (15 February 1936), it was 'painfully evident from the inquest on Jimmy Thorpe that but for the rough treatment that he was subjected to he most probably would have been alive today'. After the Thorpe tragedy, the FA included a new item in the *Instructions to Referees*: 'It is not permissible for a player to kick or attempt to kick the ball when the goalkeeper is in possession, i.e. when he is holding the ball. The use of the foot amounts to ungentlemanly conduct and should be dealt with by the referee accordingly.'

Charging the goalkeeper could only take place outside the goal area (1901), but that left plenty of room elsewhere in the penalty area. Whereas continental players disliked shoulder-charging, British fans expected centre-forwards to charge goalkeepers in the 1940s and 1950s. If goalkeepers caught the ball, they faced the prospect of being knocked towards the net as soon as they touched the floor with their feet. Keepers started to protect themselves by coming out with their knees up. It was a moot point whether this was dangerous play.

A nasty incident in the 1957 FA Cup Final restarted the debate about shoulder-charging goalkeepers. The game was spoiled in the sixth minute. Peter McParland (Aston Villa) headed towards goal and followed up when goalkeeper Ray Wood (Manchester United) caught the ball. McParland was at top speed when his shoulder hit Wood's face as the goalkeeper turned into his opponent. Both players went flying, and Wood suffered a fractured cheekbone. McParland was booed throughout the rest of the game, but he scored two goals in Villa's 2–1 win.

A bad challenge on a goalkeeper can lead to all sorts of retribution and uproar. During the 1968 League Cup Final, McLintock (Arsenal) charged into goalkeeper Sprake (Leeds United) with his shoulder when Sprake was in the air. A mêlée of a dozen players erupted, one of the ugliest scenes in a domestic final.

A similar incident took place at Cardiff when Rafferty (Carlisle) miscued a close-range shot (April 1977). The ball spun off the goalkeeper, hit a defender on the line and broke free in the goal area. About ten players converged on the loose ball, and Latham (Carlisle) accidentally kicked the goalkeeper. A mass brawl broke out. Players split into well-matched pairs, with Robin Friday (Cardiff) looking as though he could have been a contender.

In the 1998 FIFA World Cup™, Argentina were drawing 2–2 with England when Campbell (England) headed in a left-wing cross. However, the referee awarded a free-kick for a foul by Shearer (England), who knocked the Argentina goalkeeper while he was in the air and still inside his goal area. This is the sort of protection goalkeepers should receive, as the law clearly states that a goalkeeper can only be charged if they have feet on the ground outside the goal area, and the charge must be shoulder-to-shoulder. *Any* collision with a goalkeeper in the goal area will probably be interpreted as careless and unfair (if the referee sees it). The theory is that it is tempting fate to allow any player to tip a goalkeeper's elbow or turn a goalkeeper's hip (even accidentally).

The law has come a long way from the days when goalkeepers were knocked from pillar to goalpost, but there are still huge problems. Everybody has a different interpretation of the law. The British culture is still full of legendary stories of Nat Lofthouse and Trevor Ford knocking goalkeepers into the net in the 1950s. Now, however, goalkeepers are protected, for three main reasons: (i) the obvious danger of injury, as with Trautmann, Wood and Gregg in successive FA Cup Finals in the 1950s; (ii) to prevent attackers from deliberately knocking a goalkeeper's arm when every cross comes in; and (iii) to deter major flashpoints.

The second major problem to bug lawmakers over the years is ensuring that goalkeepers do not hold on to the ball indefinitely. Goalkeeper safety is paramount but quick release is also important. In the 1940s and 1950s, goalkeepers had to release the ball quickly in case they were charged. When goalkeepers felt safer they held on to the ball for longer. Goalkeepers could grab the ball and hold on to it like they were clutching a baby in a tornado, waiting for the penalty-area crowd to clear before hoofing the ball into the wasteland of the sky. The seconds ticked away.

Until 1931, 'carrying' was defined as taking more than two steps while holding the ball or bouncing it on the hand. From 1931 goalkeepers were allowed four steps instead of two. When Luton played Brentford, goalkeeper Bernard Streten (Luton) took four steps, scraped the ball along the ground and moved on (1951–52). He grounded the ball but did not bounce it, so the referee penalised him for 'carrying'. On snow-covered pitches, however, a gentleman's agreement allowed goalkeepers to *touch* the ball on the ground rather than bounce it.

In 1967, it was decreed that goalkeepers *had to* release the ball after taking four steps. They were now rolling the ball across the penalty area. Even when they took more than four steps, they were rarely punished. There had to be some leeway because goalkeepers often caught the ball when they were running and their momentum carried them through the first few steps. Four steps eventually became ten or twelve. It was a surprise when Ray Clemence (Liverpool) was penalised for breaking the four-step rule (November 1976).

A player could stand in front of a goalkeeper or even move from side to side. If an attacker raised a foot when a goalkeeper was about to kick the ball, it was labelled dangerous play. When Gordon Banks (England) tossed the ball high in the air to kick it upfield, George Best (Northern Ireland) put his foot up, flicked the ball past Banks and tapped it into the net (May 1971). Best was penalised.

Goalkeepers were allowed to take four steps before releasing the ball until a Scottish FA proposal was accepted (IFAB 1983). The modification was that goalkeepers couldn't release the ball from their hands and then touch it again with their hands before another player had played the ball (1983). The wording of this clause was still being clarified two years later. Basically, if a goalkeeper caught the ball and rolled it across the penalty area, the goalkeeper must then kick it from the ground. A goalkeeper who released the ball in this way could be fairly tackled like any other player. In a match in 1995, goalkeeper Andy Collett (Bristol Rovers) collected the ball. Meanwhile, George Parrish (Brighton) had hidden behind the goalkeeper after a goalmouth incident, staying just on the field, on the line by the post, waiting as the goalkeeper surveyed the upfield scene. When the goalkeeper rolled the ball out, Parrish sprinted forward, tackled the goalkeeper, won the ball, and tapped it into the empty net for a goal.

In March 1989, goalkeeper Andy Dibble (Manchester City) caught a cross from the Nottingham Forest right wing. A City defender and Gary Crosby (Nottingham Forest) had gone in behind Dibble in a futile attempt to reach the cross. Dibble held the ball up in the palm of his right hand as a prelude to throwing the ball up and kicking clear. Crosby came from behind him, headed the ball from Dibble's hand, and tapped the ball into the net. The goal was given. Heading a ball when it was resting on a goalkeeper's palm was not regarded as dangerous play, but the law was later clarified to prevent this.

From 1991, goalkeepers were no longer allowed to pat the ball forward with their hands to get around the four-step rule. Intentionally parrying the ball was thus redefined as having possession of the ball. The only exception was when, in the opinion of the referee, the ball had rebounded accidentally from the goalkeeper's hand during the making of a save.

This 'goalkeeper in possession' item was constantly on the agenda during the 1990s, even after the backpass law was introduced (1992). It eventually became an offence to control the ball with the hands for more than six seconds before releasing it (1998).

It was deemed to be an indirect free-kick if a player prevented the goalkeeper from releasing the ball from his hands (1998). Thierry Henry (Arsenal) set about testing this new law. He toed the ball away from goalkeeper Brad Friedel (Blackburn Rovers) as the goalkeeper was kicking out of his hands, and the referee gave the inevitable indirect free-kick as Henry tapped the ball into the net (March 2004). Henry tried again against Wolves, flicking the ball away as goalkeeper Oakes went to kick the ball left-footed, and again the referee gave a free-kick (January 2005). Henry looked very skilful but parks players could be lethal.

Attackers should not run in front of the goalkeeper, stand in front, or attempt to play the ball until the ball has been properly released into play. Throwing up and kicking the ball is considered to be one action which happens while the ball is still in the goalkeeper's possession. But the ball is back in play when it is rolling along the ground. Goalkeepers have found another way of wasting time by dribbling the ball for as long as they want, until an attacker runs towards them. Also, as with the number of steps, there is a point where six seconds becomes nine or ten, and most referees wouldn't punish this unless it was a violation of the spirit of the law. Lastuvka (Shakhtar Donetsk) was penalised for holding on to the ball for thirteen seconds at Celtic (November 2004). Petrov took the indirect free-kick, just inside the penalty area, and Thompson (Celtic) scored.

Teams must designate a goalkeeper, and referees must be notified of a change of goalkeeper during the match (1901). This offence is now punished by an *indirect* free-kick (and caution for the new goalkeeper), because it is seen as an illegal change of goalkeeper rather than an illegal handball. In 1901, however, the punishment was a direct free-kick. Bury won the 1903 FA Cup Final by a record 6–0 score, but it could easily have been seven. Opponents Derby County changed their goalkeeper twice during the match and forgot to notify the referee on the second occasion. The referee admitted after the match that he should have given a penalty when the new goalkeeper handled the ball. It became easier to show a change of goalkeeper when goalkeepers began to wear distinctive coloured jerseys (1909). But the referee still had to be informed.

Sometimes several replacements have been made in the same game, and there are instances of the same player scoring against three different goalkeepers, for instance Chris Pike (Hereford) against Colchester United (October 1993). East Stirling gained lots of experience of changing goal-keepers when they played Albion Rovers in May 2003. Starting goalkeeper Chris Todd was injured after seven minutes. In the 53rd minute, replacement goalkeeper Scott Findlay was sent off for a professional foul. His deputy, Graham McLaren, was sent off when he brought down an Albion player for a penalty after 63 minutes. Kevin McCann, the fourth goalkeeper, saved the penalty and stayed in goal until the end of the match. East Stirling lost 3–1.

In a 1996 play-off final, Leicester City changed their goalkeeper towards the end of extra-time, thinking the replacement would fare better in a penalty shoot-out. Then Leicester scored in stoppage-time to win the game.

Goalkeeping is the only position mentioned in the laws. Since 1913, goalkeepers have been treated like any other player when they are outside the penalty area (except that they aren't forced to leave the field after receiving treatment). If a goalkeeper handles the ball outside the area, and the referee feels the goalkeeper is denying an obvious goalscoring opportunity, then the goalkeeper should be sent off.

Sorensen (Aston Villa) handled the ball outside the penalty-area as Bellamy (Newcastle United) attempted to play the ball past him (August 2004). The referee applied the same principles to the punishment as he would if an outfield player was involved. He awarded a direct free-kick for handling the ball, and then assessed whether Sorensen had denied an obvious goal-scoring opportunity. In this case the referee cautioned the player rather than sending him off because, in his opinion, there were two covering defenders.

Some goalkeepers have excelled as attackers, and there are even cases of two goalkeepers scoring in the same match. Goalkeepers are allowed to take penalty-kicks. Ernie Scattergood (Derby County) scored three out of three penalties for Derby County (1913–14), and took them for Bradford Park Avenue (1921–22) until goalkeeper Willis Walker (South Shields) saved one.

Goalkeepers often fancy themselves as good penalty-takers because they kick a lot of stationary balls (e.g. goal-kicks) and have faced plenty of penalties themselves. Arthur Birch (Chesterfield) and Fred Craig (Plymouth Argyle) each scored five penalties in the 1920s, and Alex Stepney (Manchester United) heralded a new era by converting two penalties in 1973–74. In Yugoslavia, in 1980–81, goalkeeper Dragan Pantelic (Radnicki Nis) scored a hat-trick of penalties in a match against NK Zagreb. Pantelic also saved a penalty himself, and Radnicki won 4–0.

It's fine until the goalkeeper misses a penalty and faces an undignified pitch-length sprint to resume normal duties. Burton Town beat Hednesford

15–0 in a Birmingham League match, and it might have been sixteen had Town goalkeeper Boam not had his last-minute penalty saved (January 1925). Charlton Athletic goalkeeper Sam Bartram found some pace after missing a penalty against Birmingham (1945–46). Coventry City full-back and penalty-taker Roy Kirk, deputising in goal for the injured Jim Sanders, came up to take one against Aldershot (1958). Kirk shot over the bar, but the crowd held on to the ball to stop Aldershot taking a quick goal-kick.

Charlie Williams (Manchester City) scored a goal against Sunderland from a goal-kick (1900). In those days a full-back had to take a goal-kick by lifting the ball into the goalkeeper's hands. Williams caught the ball and then kicked it from his hands. For most of football's history, goals direct from goal-kicks have been outlawed, but the law changed in 1997.

In August 1967, during the Charity Shield game at Old Trafford, Pat Jennings (Tottenham Hotspur) kicked the ball out of his hands. The ball bounced near the Manchester United penalty area, flew over the head of United goalkeeper Alex Stepney and dropped in the net. Even the referee appeared to hesitate before awarding a goal. A number of other League goalkeepers have scored in open play.

Goalkeepers are allowed to throw the ball into the opposition net from their own penalty area, but they are more likely to throw the ball into their own net. Gary Sprake (Leeds United) went to throw the ball right-handed to his left-back Willie Bell at Liverpool (December 1967). On seeing Bell marked, Sprake checked his throw only for the ball to go behind him into his own net. The Liverpool fans later serenaded Sprake with the words of Des O'Connor's contemporary hit 'Careless Hands'. Many other goalkeepers have scored own-goals with the hands. John Lukic (Leeds United) fisted the ball into his own net at Rangers (October 1993).

More common in recent years is the sight of a goalkeeper coming up for a stoppage-time corner-kick. Jimmy Glass (Carlisle United) saved his team from relegation with a stoppage-time winner against Plymouth Argyle (May 1999). One of his team-mates saw Glass's red jersey and thought it was a fan on the pitch.

GOALPOSTS

Goalposts are essential items. No goalposts, no match. A fixture between Bridgeport and Collin Glen (Northern Ireland) was postponed because of an absence of goalposts (August 1967), a Cup tie between Chester and Plymouth was abandoned when no suitable replacement could be found for a broken goalpost (September 1981), and there was a real problem for Hartlepools United when bailiffs took their goalposts (1985).

The greatest concern about goalposts is safety. During the 1990s on average one child a year was killed by a falling goalpost in Britain. Such tragedies happen around the world. A three-year-old girl died in New South Wales, Australia, when a steel goalpost fell on top of her (2003), and a twelve-year-old boy died of major head injuries when a goalpost toppled onto him in California (April 2004).

To minimise such danger, national associations have launched campaigns to set new standards for goalpost safety. When goalposts around the UK were tested in 2001–02, 22 per cent of junior goals failed stability tests. In June 2005, the Football Foundation announced a £4 million grant to replace unsafe and broken UK goalposts. All goalposts should be tested by an approved organisation, and wooden goals and home-made posts are not recommended. In 1994, the laws noted that any portable goals must be anchored securely to the ground. The cliché 'moving the goalposts' has sinister implications.

Goalposts were originally two inches square. The maximum width is now five inches (1895). The 1863 Cambridge rules had posts with nothing in between – no tape, no crossbar. The posts were as upright as the wind permitted.

After Crewe Alexandra had protested against the height of the crossbars at the Swifts' ground (December 1887), the FA restricted protests to before the kick-off. According to Jackson, 'This [incident], known as the "two-foot rule" episode, did much to disgust amateurs with the [FA Cup] competition, and to encourage the resolution among amateur clubs, since become general, to leave the Cup to professionals.' A similar incident occurred in the Scottish Cup, when Dumbarton Athletic protested that the Helensburgh goalposts were too high (1885).

A Central Alliance Cup second replay (Ashbourne Town versus Linby Colliery Reserves) was postponed because the goalposts were not standard equipment (January 1966). There should be no shapes other than those mentioned in the laws – square, rectangular, round or elliptical – and materials are limited to wood or metal or other approved substances. Octagonal goalposts, or square with chamfered edges, are not allowed (IFAB 1966). In 1988 it was stated clearly that goalposts must be white (after a club had asked if theirs could be yellow).

Hearts protested that one set of goalposts was three inches higher than the other at Real Mallorca's Luis Sitjar Stadium (October 1998). The game went ahead. Hearts drew 1–1 but lost 2–1 on aggregate.

It pays to have recourse to spare goalposts. When one broke during a cup tie between Wolves and Bournemouth, there was a delay of seven minutes while the damage was repaired (January 1957). But a broken goalpost delayed play for 45 minutes at Lincoln City before the last four minutes could be played against Brentford (August 1970). And Real Madrid had to replace a broken goalpost just before the start of a UEFA Champions League semi-final (April 1998).

If the ball hits a goalpost and rebounds into the field, the ball is still in play. Goalposts shouldn't play any part in the game but occasionally players use them as levers when jumping for the ball at a corner-kick. The player should be cautioned.

GOALSCORERS

'We never bothered about who got the goals,' said John Goodall, who played for Preston North End's 1888–89 double-winning team. 'They belonged to the side – not the man. Nobody offered gold watches or grand pianos for goals then. Newspapers did not publish lists of goalscorers. We had no jealousy.'

The lawmakers take the same stance as Goodall – it doesn't matter who scores as long as it is done fairly. But sometimes referees are asked their opinion on who scored the goal. One example was England's first goal against Wales, when Lampard's long-range shot deflected into the net off Owen (October 2004).

Bookmakers often offer odds on the first scorer, and sometimes a golden boot or sponsorship money rests on goalscoring. Bob Latchford (Everton) won a £10,000 prize offered by a national newspaper for the first player to score thirty goals in the top division (1977–78), and a Cheshire butcher promised the scorers of any Northwich Victoria goals against Watford a three-month supply of steak (January 1977). At some professional games it's easy to identify the goalscorer. He's the one receiving a caution for removing his shirt.

GOAL AREA

Originally there was a line six yards from the goal-line to aid the detection of encroachment when players were taking goal-kicks. When the goal area was first marked, it consisted of two semicircles of six-yard radius, centred on each goalpost. These two layouts overlapped between 1891 and 1902.

In 1902 a remarkable change took place. The semicircles and the penalty line were replaced and a new rectangular goal-box established. Starting from points six yards from each goalpost, lines were marked at right angles six yards into the field of play and then joined with a line parallel to the goal-line, thus constructing the recognisable box seen today, twenty yards across the pitch, six yards deep. This box was termed the goal area. Its measurements are based on the six-yard encroachment rule that was in place in 1902. Even when the encroachment distance was changed to ten yards in 1913, the goal area remained unaffected.

Free-kicks for offences within the goal area by the attacking side may be taken from any place in the goal area (since 1992), and the same became true of goal-kicks (1993). The goal area is also a protected space for goalkeepers, who cannot be charged while inside it. Also, they cannot be impeded. In a practice match at Leeds in the late 1960s, Jack Charlton stood under the crossbar and the left-footed Eddie Gray curled in a right-wing corner-kick so that the ball dropped just under the crossbar. Charlton just stood in the way and a tactic was born. The offence of impeding a goalkeeper makes it difficult for players to imitate Charlton legally.

GOAL-KICKS

During a game in the late 1940s, goalkeeper Reg Allen (Queen's Park Rangers) took a goal-kick but miskicked the ball towards a Plymouth Argyle forward on the edge of the penalty area. Allen followed up and took a second kick at the ball, which was still in the penalty area. The players expected an indirect free-kick against Allen for playing the ball twice. However, the ball had to go outside the penalty area before it was 'in play', so the referee ordered the goal-kick to be retaken (FIFA Referees' Committee 1947).

When defenders understood this rule, they realised that, if attackers threatened, they could step inside the penalty area and play the ball back to the goalkeeper before it came into play. There was no punishment and the kick would be retaken. Short goal-kicks also caused problems for referees and linesmen, who had to check that the ball had gone outside the penalty area. But the introduction of the backpass clause cut down on short goal-kicks (1992).

Manchester City full-back Bert Read once explained the way goal-kicks had been taken until 1936. Read was describing how City goalkeeper Charlie Williams scored from a correctly taken goal-kick at Sunderland (April 1900): 'I picked up the ball, placed it, and then just lifted it with my toe into Charlie Williams' hands. He drove it plumb down the centre of the field. It bounced and bounced, each time, so it seemed, gaining speed. Porteous and Gow, the Sunderland backs, were taken by surprise. They got in each other's way and the ball sailed towards Doig, the famous Scottish international goalkeeper. He seemed to have it covered, but a sudden gust of wind swung the ball off his fingertips into the net.'

The goal-kick probably originated in 1866, when the defending side kicked out (except after a goal) from within six yards of the goalposts. The opposition were not allowed to approach within six yards of the ball. In 1913 the distance of opponents from the ball was increased to ten yards. Later, opponents were required also to stay 'outside the penalty area' until a goal-kick had been taken (1948).

The commonplace technique of flicking the ball into a goalkeeper's hands lasted until an IFAB decision in 1936: 'It is not permissible for the goalkeeper to receive the ball into his hands from a goal-kick by another player in order that he may thereafter kick it into play; the ball must be kicked direct from the goal area into play, and if not kicked beyond the penalty area the kick shall be retaken.' This rule was extended to include free-kicks inside the penalty area (1937). One of the big questions at the time was whether goalkeepers or full-backs would take this new form of goal-kick.

The goal-kick law was changed in 1992 to permit goalkeepers to take goal-kicks from either side rather than the side on which the ball went out of play. This was intended to save some time. However, it meant that some goalkeepers then deliberately went to the farthest side in order to waste time. Referees issue a caution if they sense time-wasting.

The lawmakers have considered every eventuality. If a player kicks the ball over the goal-line before it has cleared the penalty area, the goal-kick is retaken. If the goalkeeper kicks the ball out of the penalty area from a goal-kick and the ball hits the referee and goes into the net, the referee should award a corner-kick (and learn how to anticipate the play).

Similarly, if the ball goes out of the area and the wind blows it back into the net then it should also be a corner-kick. Although the law was changed to allow a goal to be scored directly from a goal-kick in 1997, this applied only to the team taking the kick.

If a goalkeeper takes a goal-kick, the ball goes outside the penalty area, the wind blows it back and the goalkeeper knocks the ball into the net, then an indirect free-kick should be awarded against the goalkeeper for playing the ball twice before an opponent has touched the ball. But if it were a team-mate touching the ball into his own net, it would be a goal. These sort of events occur more often in matches involving children.

GOAL-LINE

The two goal-lines, sometimes called by-lines, run across the width of the pitch, through the goalposts, at ninety degrees to the touchlines. They define the shorter sides of the rectangle, and the maximum width of the lines is five inches.

GOAL-LINE TECHNOLOGY

Referees are the sole judge of a goal, but it is occasionally difficult to tell whether the whole of the ball has crossed the goal-line and passed between the goalposts. Calls for separate goal-judges first arose in 1893 (before goal-nets were pervasive) but the idea of extra officials was considered unworkable. In 2005, however, at the FIFA under-seventeen World Championships, there were experiments with an electronic system using balls with embedded chips that could send a signal to the referee when the whole of the ball crossed the line. The idea was to provide the referee with instantaneous knowledge.

There have been four main types of problem over the years: (i) the goalkeeper, or a defender, clears the ball from near the goal-line; (ii) the ball hits the underside of the crossbar and bounces somewhere near the line; (iii) the ball bounces out after hitting the net, a stanchion or a wall at the back of the net; and (iv) the ball goes through a hole in the net.

Technology became a cause célèbre after a goal-line incident at Old Trafford (January 2005). In the last minute of the game, Pedro Mendes (Spurs) attempted a long-distance lob against goalkeeper Roy Carroll (Manchester United), who was about ten yards off his line. Carroll back-pedalled and tried to catch the ball on his chest. The ball squirmed away and dropped behind the goalkeeper, who turned to claw the ball away. Television replays suggested that the ball was more than a yard over the line when Carroll retrieved it. The referee was near the halfway-line, and the assistant referee had to sprint along the touchline from a position in line with the last defender (over thirty yards from goal). No goal was given.

That same season a goal was awarded to Liverpool when Luis Garcia's shot was hacked away by Chelsea's Gallas (May 2005). The incident was very complicated. Goalkeeper Cech (Chelsea) looked to have fouled Baros (Liverpool) and denied him a goalscoring opportunity but Luis Garcia set off for the loose ball. The advantage was played, Luis Garcia's shot was scrambled away, and the assistant flagged for the goal. Cech had no longer denied Liverpool an obvious goalscoring opportunity so he stayed on the field, but the television station covering the match was unable to offer any camera angles that were as good as the assistant's view. Various computer simulations later offered isolated frames that seemed to suggest the whole of the ball had not crossed the line. But all frames must be considered.

On most occasions, officials are in a good position to see. During a scramble in the Norway goal area, after a Scotland corner-kick, Iverson (Norway) kicked the ball off the goal-line when it was about a foot above the ground (October 2004). Replays showed that the whole of the ball was not over the line, but Scotland manager Berti Vogts, viewing from the halfway-line, was convinced that it was. His protests put him in trouble with the referee. Vogts had probably made the visual mistake that many people make; they can see the whole of the goal-line and they think it's all over (to borrow a phrase from Kenneth Wolstenholme), but the ball is actually in the air above the line. On the other hand, some officials are overly eager to award the goal, like the one at West Ham when goalkeeper Schwarzer (Middlesbrough) fumbled on the goal-line (October 2005).

The second category of dispute is perhaps the most dramatic, when the ball hits the crossbar and bounces down. A split second of action needs a split-second decision. When Notts County beat Sunderland 2–0 in an 1891 FA Cup semi-final replay, the referee awarded the first goal from his position on the halfway-line when the ball hit the underside of the crossbar and bounced down.

A legendary incident occurred at 2–2 in the 1966 FIFA World Cup™ Final. Hurst (England) turned and his shot hit the underside of the West Germany crossbar and bounced down. The Russian linesman confirmed the goal, even though he was some distance from the goal-line. On other occasions, when referees have called 'play on', technology has later shown that a goal should have been given. Examples from big matches include shots by Michel (Spain) against Brazil (June 1986), Munteanu (Romania) against Bulgaria (June 1996), and Howard (Chesterfield) against Middlesbrough (1997 FA Cup semi-final).

Stuart Pearce (England) hit the underside of France's crossbar with a long-range free-kick but the ball did not cross the line (June 1992). England manager Graham Taylor said he had looked to the touchline in the hope of seeing the 1966 Russian linesman.

Thirdly, there are those incidents where the ball goes in and out. In 1908, England drew 1–1 with Scotland. The England goal was scored by Windridge, who shot on the run with such force that the ball lifted the roof of the netting and then sprung back into play. The Scots continued playing but the referee awarded a goal. But West Brom were denied a crucial goal against Blackpool when the referee thought the ball had hit the crossbar but in fact it had boomeranged back from the goal-net (1908–09).

Some grounds have perimeter walls immediately behind goal-nets. If the nets have too much slack, the ball comes flying out off the wall. Disputed goals were not unknown at the Nest, an early home of Norwich City. Lumsden (Carlisle) took a penalty-kick at Canvey Island, and the ball hit the board at the back of the goal-net and rebounded into the penalty area (March 2005). After some confusion the referee gave a goal.

Huddersfield Town won 1–0 against Manchester City in 1938 after a shot from Alec Herd (Manchester City) came back off the stanchion and the referee thought the ball had hit the crossbar. Manchester City were relegated. The same happened to Aston Villa, relegated in 1969–70, the season they struck the stanchion against Leicester City. And Clive Allen (Crystal Palace) had cause for complaint when television pictures showed he had scored against Coventry City (September 1980).

The final type of goal-line incident is the one where it is uncertain if the ball has gone inside or outside the goal-frame. A shot by Alan Hudson (Chelsea) hit the stanchion outside the Ipswich net and went through the net, and the referee gave a goal despite Ipswich protests (September 1970). A year later there was a five-minute delay in the Crystal Palace–Nottingham Forest match. The referee seemed to award a goal when a shot from Steve Kember (Crystal Palace) hit the side-netting, but Kember admitted that the ball did not go in, and the referee changed his decision.

There have been numerous cases of a ball passing through a tear in the goal-net, especially during World War II when nets were substandard. This is why match officials check the state of the nets before the match. In the 1890s, goalkeepers sometimes collected the ball after a goal and swiftly placed it for a goal-kick. Sometimes they got away with it. And then came goal-nets.

GOAL-NETS

'How often prior to the invention of goal-nets has a referee been hoodwinked by the gesticulations of an overanxious forward, and allowed a goal for a shot a few inches over the bar?' asked 'Rob Roy', in the *1894 Athletic News Annual*, just over two years after the first use of goal-nets in Scotland. Rob Roy would also have been aware that John Auld (Scotland) appeared to have scored against Wales but the umpire ruled that the ball had gone the wrong side of the tape (April 1889).

Goal-nets were first used in public in Nottingham, as described by Jimmy Catton in *Wickets and Goals*:

> These nets were invented by Mr J A Brodie, engineer to the city of Liverpool, who was afterwards engaged by the Indian Government for the laying out of Delhi, the new capital of that part of the Empire. Mr Robert Lythgoe, of Liverpool, placed the idea before the Football Association, who used the nets in the North and South match of January 1891. This was on the Town ground, near Trent Bridge, and on a cold and frosty day. I can see the late Dr Morley, of Blackburn, smoking the inevitable cigar, and wearing the equally inevitable silk hat, walking out to inspect the novelty.

Tom Holley added to the story in the *Soccer Review* (4 September 1965):

> Brodie thought it up all right but he came from the fishing town of Bridport in Dorset. In 1890, when he was watching a match in which a dispute over a goal caused a near riot, this man with fishing interests suggested a net similar to those used at sea. Despite a lack of enthusiasm, the man from Bridport made them and they were first used a year later. The idea caught on like wildfire. For fourteen years his patent was held by W Edwards

and Son, a firm which in 1947 amalgamated to form Bridport Industries.

When goal-nets first arrived, some goalkeepers, forgetting they were there, ran full pelt into them when setting off to retrieve the ball. Safety is still the number-one concern, as a considerable number of children have died when goals have collapsed, and a referee once seriously injured a finger when checking a net. Most football associations have guidelines for the construction of goal-nets. There was a call in 1980 to outlaw iron brackets and curved iron tubes.

Borussia Mönchengladbach were punished for not having a replacement goal apparatus when a goal-net collapsed two minutes from the end of their 1971 match with Werder Bremen. Mönchengladbach forfeited the match, even though the score was 1–1 at the time. When Barnsley played Sunderland, a player pulled the netting off the woodwork while trying to prevent a goal (April 1999). Men with ladders came on to repair the net.

Towards the end of the Portugal–Greece EURO 2004™ Final, a spectator ran on to the pitch and threw a Barcelona flag at Luis Figo (Portugal). The fan then flung himself at a goal-net before being carried away by stewards. There was a further delay because the referee's assistant had to check the condition of the net.

If there are assistant referees, they will check the nets before the start of the game and then run to the centre-circle to rejoin the match referee. This is probably a second check to ensure nothing untoward has happened since the first pitch inspection. In local football, the nets may still be going up five minutes before kick-off, so the late check is crucial. Goal-nets were compulsory in the FA Cup from 1893, but not mentioned in the laws until 1938. Competition rules will dictate.

A referee should check that the nets are securely pinned to the ground, and that there are no holes big enough for a ball to pass through. There was a disturbance after the goal that gave West Brom a 1–0 FA Cup victory at Leeds City (1912). Home fans claimed that the ball had gone through a hole in the net and hundreds refused to leave the ground until Leeds City manager Scott Walford appealed to them to go home.

When Barnsley beat Colchester United 3–0 in an FA Cup match, there was an incident where the referee seemed to have awarded a goal to Barnsley (January 1952). The Colchester players protested that the ball had gone through the side-netting, so the referee went over to talk to a linesman. The referee then altered his decision. He awarded a goal-kick and the net was repaired.

The Burnley–Manchester City game on Christmas Day 1957 started a few minutes late because the referee insisted that the nets be repaired. They were frayed at the bottom and had what the referee described as 'holes in the holes'. Some referees carry string in their bag in case there is none immediately to hand.

The FA Council approved the use of goal-nets in February 1891 but could not make them compulsory until the costs were more favourable. They were quickly introduced into international matches (IFAB 1895). By then a Scottish Cup tie – Raith Rovers versus 5th King's Rifle Volunteers (1894–95) – had gone to a replay because the home team had failed to provide goal-nets. Raith won the first match 6–3 but lost the replay 4–3.

It took a long time before goal-nets were used universally. It was only in the 1960s and 1970s that arrangements for local games began to include the immortal instruction for home-team players: 'report early to put up the nets'.

The area bounded by the net and the goal-line is not technically in the field of play. A player would be sent off for punching a player on this patch but it is not a free-kick or a penalty-kick (even if the ball was in play).

GOAL SIZE

The size of the goal has been eight yards wide by eight feet high ever since Sheffield acceded to the London rules on this point (1877). Ten years earlier, the Sheffield laws stated that 'the goalposts were four yards apart, with a bar across them nine feet from the ground, and at each side of the goal there were other posts four yards beyond the goalposts, also with bars at nine feet from the ground, these being called rouge flags.'

The target is 192 square feet, as the measurements are taken from the internal edges of the goal-frame (1938). Some people think this target is too small. In the 1960s, the North American Soccer League proposed nine by three yards, and later the United States Soccer Federation were refused permission to experiment with a goal that added two feet to the width and six inches to the height (1974). The Americans thought that a larger goal might help to increase goalscoring, take some of the pressure off crucial refereeing decisions, satisfy spectators, and redress the balance between attack and defence. Traditionalists believe that the sport would lose a lot of its tension and excitement.

Other people have suggested using bigger goals in extra-time as a way of settling cup ties that need a definite outcome. All proposals to increase the size of the goal have been thrown out, but goal size can be adjusted downwards for younger players.

On the first day of the 1991–92 season, Coventry were at home to Manchester City. When the referee did his routine pitch inspection, he found that the two crossbars were several inches too low. The problem was fixed after the referee threatened to postpone the match if nothing was done. Most referees have a way of checking the crossbar height by using some combination of their height, an outstretched arm and an assistant's flag.

GOLDEN GOAL

After experiments in FIFA tournaments (1993–95), golden goals were used in major tournaments for a short period (1996–2004) as a method of deciding the winner of a match needing a definite outcome. If the scores were level after ninety minutes, two fifteen-minute halves of extra-time would be played. The team scoring the first goal (the golden goal) would win the match. Thousands of small-sided training matches have ended with 'the next goal's the winner'.

Germany won the EURO 1996™ Final 2–1, thanks to Bierhoff's golden goal against the Czech Republic. One major problem was that the game was ended by the goal and not the referee's whistle. When Germany scored that golden-goal winner, the assistant had his flag up. A German player was in an offside position (although probably not actively involved in play). Before the referee had talked to his assistant, the celebrations were under way. How could the referee deal with that?

It was 1–1 after ninety minutes of the France–Portugal EURO 2000™ semi-final. In the 117th minute, the referee awarded a controversial penalty to France when Xavier (Portugal) was adjudged to have handled a shot by Wiltord (France). Portugal players surrounded the referee. Nuno Gomes (Portugal) was sent off and Figo (Portugal) took off his shirt in disgust. Zidane (France) scored the golden goal from the penalty mark. France then won the final with another golden goal.

Spain thought they had beaten South Korea in the 2002 FIFA World Cup™ when Morientes headed in Joaquin's cross in the third minute of extra-time, but the referee gave a goal-kick. An assistant referee had flagged that the ball was out of play, even though replays suggested it was not. South Korea went on to win the match.

When Bristol City won 2–1 at Boston United in the LDV Vans Trophy, the winner came from a golden goal in the 112th minute (November 2002). The referee controversially gave a corner-kick to Bristol City and Coles headed in Tinnion's kick. Mark Angel (Boston) was sent off immediately afterwards.

Golden goals were first mentioned in the laws in 2001, but it was sudden-death for the golden goal three years later. The golden goal failed to open up play as people had hoped. It was unfair on those who needed to plan for the game's end (transport workers and police), and it put too much pressure on referees, players and spectators. Too much unrest followed the scoring of a golden goal. Grave disorder was never far away.

GRAVE DISORDER

A cup tie on the Wareham recreation ground in the 1880s was ended prematurely by a disputed goal. Angry spectators invaded the pitch and penned the referee in a tool-shed for an hour. The referee handed his money and gold watch over to a Hampshire FA official for safekeeping and then made a break for it, running several miles to the nearest railway station.

In Canada, in one big game in the 1920s, a referee disallowed a crucial goal and bedlam broke out. One spectator kicked the ball and about 700 people rushed on to the field. According to one report it was 'the signal for one of the greatest battles this side of Texas'. Women joined in and much hair-pulling ensued.

Referees were empowered to stop a match (temporarily or permanently) in the event of grave disorder, but they had no right to decide the match outcome (FIFA Referees' Committee 1939, IFAB 1956). The term 'grave disorder' disappeared from the laws during the 1997 rewrite. But referees still have the right to abandon a match if there is outside interference.

A new era of pitch invasions arrived in the 1970s, and one pivotal match was the FA Cup tie between Newcastle United and Nottingham Forest (March 1974). Between 300 and 500 spectators ran on, the game was suspended, players returned to the dressing-rooms, and the police took eight minutes to clear the pitch. Twenty-three people were taken to hospital and another 103 people treated on the pitch. Police made 39 arrests. When the teams resumed, the 54,000 crowd helped to create an intimidating atmosphere, and ten-man Newcastle came back from 3–1 down to win 4–3. The result was declared null and void, but Newcastle were given the chance to 'replay' (at Goodison Park) and eventually won the tie.

Spectators caused abandonments of several matches, including Napoli–Swindon Town (May 1970), Wisbech–Yarmouth (November 1973), Aston Villa–Rangers (October 1976), Ilkeston–Enfield (February 1983), and Ajax–Den Haag (March 1987), just to name a few. A Rangers fan was jailed for six months after the episode at Aston Villa.

GRIEVOUS BODILY HARM See ASSAULT

HAIRSTYLE

In 2004, the Nigerian FA instructed referees at their youth championships to clamp down on excessive hairstyles such as braids and dreadlocks. In the same year the Iran Football Federation banned ponytails, hair bands and sculpted beards. These were probably local rules to prevent the spread of Western culture, but there is the question of whether certain hairstyles could be dangerous or problematic. The Norway women's international Marit Fiane Christensen has worn her hair in ponytails long enough to conceal her shirt number.

HALF-TIME INTERVAL

When football first became organised, teams changed straight round at half-time. Then the laws called for an interval, which couldn't exceed five minutes, except by consent of the referee (1897).

In 1899, Jackson wrote: 'The present practice of leaving the field at half-time for a rub down and refreshments is an innovation which came from the north, and became established by professionals, who frequently take a rest of ten minutes or so before recommencing.'

An FA Council decision stipulated that players *had a right* to a half-time interval of five minutes (FA, 1906), but the interval could only exceed five minutes with the referee's consent and then only in 'exceptional circumstances' (FA, 1919). On many occasions, especially in local football, players have willingly foregone the half-time interval for fear that the game may not be completed otherwise. Even in the professional game there can be good reason for minimising the interval: the forecast of fog (Charlton–Wolves in 1930); or the likelihood of the pitch freezing (West Ham–Nottingham Forest in 1997). Conversely, the half-time interval was extended to twenty minutes when BVV Hertogenbosch played Exeter City because the referee agreed to the band conductor's request to play an encore (May 1951). Oxford United's last game of the 1993–94 season had an extended interval while emergency services treated a fatally ill spectator.

After World War II, the norm was a ten-minute break. A proposal for a fifteen-minute half-time interval was rejected at first (1980) and then accepted (1995). Players are allowed to leave the pitch at half-time, but they must stay on the field during the short interval between full-time and extra-time. Neville Southall (Everton) once stayed on the pitch at half-time, leaning against a goalpost, while his team-mates discussed their poor first-half display in the dressing-room. In local football, staying on the field at half-time is the norm.

In 2004 IFAB rejected a proposal to increase the maximum length of the half-time interval from fifteen to twenty minutes. The proposal had commercial merit. Clubs could sell more food and drink during the interval, and television companies could run more advertisements.

Players are still under the referee's control during the half-time interval, whether they are in the tunnel, on the pitch, or in the dressing-room (FIFA Referees' Committee 1932). Johann Cruyff (Holland) was shown the yellow card for dissent after the referee had blown for half-time during the 1974 FIFA World Cup™ Final, and Joey Barton (Manchester City) received a second caution during the interval at Spurs (February 2004).

HALF-TIME WHISTLE

As the referee blew for half-time in the 1889 England–Scotland international, Jimmy Oswald (Scotland) put the ball between the goalposts. The referee refused to allow the goal. Scotland changed round 2–0 down (rather than 2–1 down) but came back to win 3–2.

A similar event occurred during a Blackburn Rovers–Liverpool match (September 1896): 'The Rovers attacked from the right wing and then a second after the whistle had sounded for half-time netted the ball. The spectators at first were under the impression that it was a goal, but of course it was not so.'

Lawgivers like William Pickford decreed that the referee 'should blow his whistle for time or half-time at the exact moment, whether the ball is in play or not' (*Bournemouth Guardian*, 14 October 1893). Nowadays, most referees would try to skirt controversy. They try to end each half at a safe point in the play (when the action is in midfield rather than the penalty area), and they use a distinctive signal (e.g. two or three tweets of the whistle and pointing to the dressing-rooms) to show that this is not a routine free-kick. The half can be extended for a penalty-kick to be taken but the kick has to have a definite outcome – neither the penalty taker nor any other player can follow-up the kick if the keeper saves it or if it rebounds off the woodwork.

In the late 1960s, referee Gordon Hill disallowed a superb 'goal' by Francis Lee (Manchester City) on the stroke of half-time. Hill later said that he would have allowed play to continue for those extra few seconds had he not made the cardinal error of turning his back on play to blow the whistle.

Incidents in the last seconds of the first half are unlikely to be remembered as clearly as incidents at the end of the game. Whereas many people can recall referee Clive Thomas disallowing a Brazil goal a second after the whistle (1978 FIFA World Cup™), few recall Pelé (Brazil) netting on the stroke of half-time during the 1970 FIFA World Cup™ Final.

The referee is the sole judge of time. Periodically, the case for an off-the-pitch timekeeper is put forward by people who think it will take some of the pressure off the referee (especially with the complex issue of stoppage-time). The North American Soccer League had a short spell ending matches, rather ironically, with a starter's pistol. FIFA disapproved.

HALFWAY-LINE

The halfway-line ('a line running right across the field dividing it into two halves') was introduced in 1887 and made compulsory in 1902. The line ensured that players remained in their own half until the kick-off or place-kick had been taken, and it marked the area where goalkeepers could use their hands (until 1912).

The next use of the line came with a ruling that players could not be offside in their own half of the field (1907). The line also became important as the place where substitutes enter the field and players return after changing equipment.

HALFWAY-LINE FLAGS

Halfway-line flags were used in the 1890s, but they were not introduced to the laws, as optional extras, until 1908. (They could be placed one yard from the touchline and had to be not less than five feet high.) They are there to help the referee assess the position of the halfway-line from a distance.

HANDLING THE BALL

George Whitelaw, known as Whitelaw the Outlaw, was what old professionals called 'a real character'. One day in the 1960s, playing for Halifax Town, Whitelaw was cornered by a dogged defender. He stepped over the ball several times, shuffled back and forth, and then looked at the defender. Whitelaw picked up the ball and handed it to his marker as if it were an honorary degree certificate. If only all handball decisions were as comically easy as that one.

Until 1866, FA rules permitted a fair catch, and players were also allowed to control the ball with the hand in a way similar to hockey. 'It was permissible to pat the ball down with the hand,' said Jackson, 'although this was by the better players considered to be bad form.'

In 1876, there was still confusion over handling rules. When Nottingham Castle played Burton-on-Trent, all the Burton players handled whereas only the Nottingham goalkeeper handled the ball. Wrote the *Sporting Gazette*: 'We should hardly think that the Burton men find many to play against them on such terms.' When the Sheffield and London rules were combined in 1877, outfield players were not permitted to handle the ball.

In 1881, the referee was empowered to award a penalty goal for wilful handling of the ball if the ball would otherwise have passed through the goal. This rule lasted only one year. The main problem was that referees were at this time off-the-field and too far from the play.

In April 1896, Burton Wanderers were awarded a free-kick when a Burton Swifts player handled the ball. 'The ball was put through without a second player touching it,' wrote a local journalist, and as a result no goal was allowed. Until 1903 all free-kicks for handling were indirect. The only exception was the penalty-kick (from 1891).

From 1897 the law stipulated that handling was only illegal when it was *intentional*. This crucial point has stayed with us ever since. During EURO 2004™, the Croatia goalkeeper ran out to kick a poor backpass but the clearance hit Trezeguet (France) on his outstretched arm. The ball fell kindly, and Trezeguet scored. As the player had obviously not *deliberately* handled the ball, the goal was given.

Another interesting incident came when Alan Shearer (Newcastle) jumped at the far post to head a left-wing cross towards the Aston Villa goal (April 2005). The ball was going towards the net until it hit defender Jlloyd Samuel (Villa), jumping with his back to Shearer, on the back of the arm. The referee played on. A *Match of the Day* pundit thought that it should have been a penalty, but any player with his back to the ball cannot possibly handle deliberately.

Another television pundit, discussing an incident in the Southampton–Manchester United match (August 2003), suggested that players should keep their hands at shoulder-height when blocking a shot. That means that a player chesting the ball is clearly not using an arm. Having arms overhead risks some referees giving handball – a Chile player was penalised against Italy (June 1998) – but penalties have been given when players have arms outstretched at their side too. Players have to put their arms somewhere.

It became commonplace to talk about 'ball to hand' (supposedly unintentional and unavoidable) as distinct from 'hand to ball' (supposedly intentional and avoidable). A United States shot hit a Germany player on the goal-line (June 2002). The incident denied a certain goal but the defender knew nothing about the ball until it hit him. No penalty was given. But 'ball to hand' and 'hand to ball' are not always good guides. A player can be bringing a hand towards the ball as part of another action (e.g. running). In other cases the hand can be going away from the ball but the handling can be intentional. Referees quickly weigh up a series of questions: Did the player move a hand or arm intending to handle the ball? Did the player deliberately leave the hand there? Was it an instinctive movement? Did the playing surface or a deflection contribute? Was the ball hit so hard from such a close distance that the player had no time to react?

From 1982, it was a sending-off offence to deny a certain goal by handling the ball. Whereas a flying goal-line punch by defender John Greig (Rangers) was punished only by Connelly (Celtic) scoring the penalty-kick (Scottish Cup Final 1973), it was an automatic sending-off when Kanchelskis (Manchester United) handled on the line against Aston Villa (1994 League Cup Final). Diego Figueredo (Paraguay) was sent off for a second caution after 'deliberately handling the ball' when attempting to score against Argentina (2004 Olympic Final).

Some people see an inconsistency here. A defender must be sent off for deliberately handling the ball to deny a goalscoring opportunity, but a striker is only cautioned for trying to punch the ball towards goal. An example of the latter was Michael Owen (England) against Azerbaijan (March 2005). A better example was Argentina's infamous first goal against England in the 1986 FIFA World Cup™. Hodge (England) miscued a clearance high in the air towards his own goal. Goalkeeper Shilton (England) came to punch the ball away with his right hand as Maradona (Argentina) jumped and knocked the ball forward with his left hand. Neither the referee nor the nearest assistant saw Maradona handling the ball. In a post-match interview, Maradona referred to the 'hand of God'. The referee should have seen the situation as odd – a diminutive Maradona jumping above a world-class goalkeeper.

'I blame the referee, I don't blame the players,' England manager Bobby Robson said years later. 'Players will try some things, saying they're legitimate. But this was a blatant handball. I don't think for a moment that Maradona thought he would ever get away with it. It's up to the referee, and the linesman, who was in a good position, to see that. That is their job. How they didn't see that, I don't know.'

But referees do miss things and, being honest people, they can only give a free-kick for handball when they *see* a player intentionally handle the ball. It is possible for the referee to be unsighted (and the players know this). Mr A T Randle, a referee from Coventry, kept notes on his games. He described a typical handling incident, from the game between Watford and Exeter (January 1911): 'Exeter netted about twelve minutes from time but the goal was not allowed as Bell handled the ball. Linesman J McKenzie was well up and in a line so I consulted him and he was positive that the ball had been handled. I accepted his decision. I was well up but the player was immediately in front of me and so obstructed my view.'

When Scotland met Wales at Anfield in a crucial World Cup qualifier, the turning point – Scotland's first goal in a 2–0 victory – came when the referee awarded a penalty (October 1977). A hand went up to knock away a cross, but later analysis showed that the hand probably belonged to Joe Jordan (Scotland) rather than a Welsh defender.

There is another type of mistake – when the referee thinks a player has handled the ball but it has touched another part of the player's body. It is often difficult for the referee to assess exactly where on the body the ball has been played, especially when it is on the far side of the player. Everton fans still talk about an incident late in the 1977 FA Cup semi-final against Liverpool when a left-wing cross was turned in by Bryan Hamilton's hip and the referee thought Hamilton had handled.

Handling is defined as playing the ball with the hand or the arm (up to the shoulder). The ball is handled if it is intentionally played with the hand, lower arm, elbow or upper arm (but not the collarbone or shoulder bone). Matthew Taylor (Portsmouth) played a cross from Prutton (Southampton) with his upper right-hand body, and the assistant referee immediately flagged for a penalty-kick (January 2005). At full-time two television pundits agreed that it was Taylor's shoulder rather than his arm. The next two pundits thought it was the upper arm. All that mattered was that the referee, agreeing with his assistant, had given a penalty-kick. As goalkeeper Peter Shilton said, years after the Maradona incident, 'I started running after the referee, and one or two of the other players did, but you just learn over the years that it's not going to do any good anyway.'

From 1912, goalkeepers were restricted to handling the ball inside the penalty area. Outside this area, the goalkeeper has to be treated as just another player. Linesmen have traditionally sprinted to the edge of the penalty area to check whether the goalkeeper handles outside the area. Barthez (Manchester United) clearly handled a ball outside the penalty area in the match between Real Madrid and Manchester United (April 2003). However, the incident took place beyond his right-hand side of the area. With the referee's assistants running right wings, and the referee's position in accordance, there was little chance that this could be spotted.

The biggest dilemma comes when a player handles the ball under a misapprehension. Burton Thistle were leading Stapenhill Comrades 2–1 with six minutes to play in a cup tie (April 1924). Burton were attacking when a Stapenhill player picked up the ball in his own penalty area believing it to be out of play. The referee gave a penalty, and a fiasco followed. The Comrades stormed off the field in disgust.

In a number of circumstances a legitimate goal can be scored even though the ball has been handled: a goalkeeper fists the ball into his own net; a defender handles the ball but the referee plays the advantage and the attacking team scores; or a goalkeeper throws the ball into the net (at either end).

HANDSHAKES

The referee and assistant referees will shake hands with the two captains during the pre-match ritual. In big tournaments, every player shakes hands with every opponent. In 2003, a similar post-match ritual was suggested, to provide a suitable cooling-down period (which might benefit post-match interviews). There was some debate about whether players might conduct retaliatory offences if they stayed on the field longer and the idea was shelved.

Handshakes at the end of a match are a remnant of a sporting age when team captains would call for three cheers for the opposition. Referees get half a dozen handshakes if they are lucky, but more likely they will be surrounded by stewards for protection. Stanley Matthews used to shake hands with referees and linesmen, and thank them for giving up their Saturday afternoons. Later, it became more likely for players to say, 'Hope you have a car crash on your way home.'

At the end of one local league match, a player offered his hand to an opponent but then followed through with a punch. An Arsenal fan faked to shake hands with Djbril Cisse (Liverpool) only to pull his hand away, put his thumb on his nose and wiggle his fingers (October 2005). Cisse hit the fan and was cautioned for common assault.

HEADGUARDS See PROTECTORS

HITTING A PERSON See STRIKING A PERSON

HOLDING

According to Tommy Tynan in *Tommy: A Life at the Factory*, managers teach players unlawful techniques 'like holding off people with your arms'.

A lot of holding is done away from the ball. In top-class football, where the marking is tighter, players often hold opponents as a corner-kick is being taken, letting go when the ball becomes active. Very few holding incidents are as blatant as that at Liverpool (October 1898). Allan (Liverpool) charged Sheffield United goalkeeper Foulke in the goalmouth. The big goalkeeper lost his temper, grabbed Allan illegally and turned the Liverpool player upside-down. The outcome was a penalty kick.

IFAB has often debated whether holding is use of the hands or arms, or whether it is a wider concept. Players can hold opponents with a foot up an opponent's shorts or their teeth in a shirt. Some people think that football has as many holds as wrestling. A half-nelson would be a sending-off offence.

All holding is provocative. Players may instinctively retaliate by flinging an elbow or a hand in an attempt to escape the restriction, and that may be all the referee sees.

Shirt-holding (or shirt-tugging) first occurred in the nineteenth century. It was one of the impacts of professionalism. Players started wearing their shirts inside their shorts because opponents were grabbing shirt bottoms. In the modern era, a new trend towards shirt-holding was noticed during the 1994 FIFA World Cup™, and coaches began studying basketball defence. By 1998 shirt-holding had become more disruptive. Defenders were being coached to hold and block opponents when the ball was played into the penalty area from a set piece. FIFA flagged the issue in 2001 and there was a high-profile decision in the Ireland–Spain match (June 2002). The referee gave a last-minute penalty when Hierro (Spain) held the shirt of Quinn (Ireland) as the ball came across from a corner-kick. In fact, Quinn's shirt was nearly over his head. Hierro was cautioned, and Ireland scored the penalty to take the game to extra-time.

Other decisions have been critical. Hamann (Germany) might have been held by Ronaldo (Brazil) when he lost the ball seconds before the first goal of the 2002 FIFA World Cup™ Final. In the 90th minute of the Portugal–England EURO 2004™ quarter-final, with the score 1–1, Sol Campbell (England) hit the crossbar with a header and then followed up to head the ball into the net, but the referee awarded a free-kick against John Terry (England), who was using his left arm to hold down goalkeeper Ricardo (Portugal).

HOME SIDE

Home clubs provide the match-balls, and may also be responsible for paying the referee (depending on the competition rules). Top-level hosts organise the policing and stewarding. Premier League home clubs are responsible for sending a VHS video recording of the match to the referee and the League.

In some cases, the police will determine whether it is safe to use the registered home ground. When Telford United drew Leeds United in the FA Cup, the match was played at West Brom's ground (January 1987).

Traditionally, the home club has had some power in fixing kick-off time, but there are procedures for communicating such times with referees, the league and other clubs. The home club also has to provide accommodation for the officials in accordance with the competition rules. Officials are not required to provide anything in return, especially on the pitch. Otherwise they are known as homers.

HOMER

Referees are called 'homers' if they appear to favour the home side, supposedly swayed to do so by the presence of home supporters or the size of the home club. During a match in the 1950s, Len Shackleton (Sunderland) consistently called the referee 'Mr Khayyam'. At the end of the match, when the referee asked him what all the 'Mr Khayyam' was about, Shackleton explained that he thought the referee had the same first name – Omar.

Home ground is considered to be an advantage, and statistics show that home teams generally score more goals than away teams. It is not necessarily refereeing that produces this. Home sides are favoured with a more generally supportive crowd, a familiar environment and less travelling to matches. What may seem like home bias, in terms of refereeing decisions and the issuing of cards, may be down to home teams attacking more and exerting more pressure. More penalties are awarded to home teams than away teams, but again this may be what one would expect if home teams spend a disproportionate amount of time in the opposition penalty area.

During a match between Manchester United and Newcastle United, Alan Shearer (Newcastle) intercepted a backpass and tried to go past goalkeeper Tim Howard (Manchester United) when his leg was clipped (January 2004). The referee did not award a penalty but video replays showed that he could easily have done so. That incident provoked a discussion about whether Manchester United, at Old Trafford, had had fewer penalties awarded against them than would be expected. In fact, there had been only three awards between December 1993, when Fox scored for Norwich City, and the Shearer incident over ten years later.

Arsenal manager Arsène Wenger was in trouble with authorities after contesting the referee's decision to give a penalty-kick to Manchester United, saying that it was to be expected from a referee who had given eight penalty-kicks to United in the previous eight matches he had refereed at Old Trafford (October 2004).

Alan Nevill, Nigel Balmer and Mark Williams have researched the 'homer' issue. They found that referees watching a videotape with the sound turned down awarded 15.5 per cent fewer fouls to the home team than referees watching with the volume up and the crowd noise apparent. But the more experienced the referee, the more balanced they were.

George Best has summed up the players' definition of the homer: 'It's human nature, isn't it, if you're a referee? If you go to Leeds and you've got forty thousand people screaming at you, or you go to Liverpool or Old

Trafford, you're going to go with the flow. That's what used to happen, and it still does to a certain degree. Referees are going to make decisions that the home fans want to know about.'

There is another meaning of 'homer' – the referee who likes to get home safely after the match.

Ii

IDENTIFICATION

Referees must be able to identify players: to report misconduct (cautions and sendings-off); as a memory aid during a prolonged mêlée ('red two and blue six started it'); and as a means of communication ('back two more yards, ten').

Players were originally identified by their individual caps and socks rather than numbered shirts. When Wanderers played Queen's Park in 1875, Hubert Heron (Wanderers) had 'grey stockings and an orange, violet and black cap'. Shirts still had no numbers in the 1930 FIFA World Cup™, when the wrong Peru player was sent off against Romania.

There have been plenty of cases of mistaken identity as regards cautions and sendings-off. The referee of a VfB Stuttgart–Cologne UEFA Cup tie was confused by the brothers Karl-Heinz Forster and Bernd Forster (1980–81). He cautioned Bernd instead of Karl-Heinz. Karl-Heinz had already been cautioned, so he stayed on the pitch when he should have been sent off.

Danny Wallace (Southampton) was cautioned instead of Jimmy Case (Southampton) at Newcastle (December 1985) and, as Wallace had already been properly cautioned earlier, he was sent off for a second caution. Although his second caution was later rescinded, it meant that Southampton wrongly played with ten men. But the referee's decision was final and the result stood.

It is hard to imagine two players more physically dissimilar than the diminutive black Wallace and the stocky white Case, but there have been other comic confusions – Gemmill (Scotland) instead of Gray against Czechoslovakia (October 1976), Johnson (Norwich) for Prior at West Ham (1994–95), Humphries (Raith Rovers) for Dennis at Motherwell (1996), Neuville (Germany) for Jeremies against the United States (2002), and Parker (Newcastle) for Carr against Sunderland (October 2005). When Hasselbaink (Chelsea) was sent off against Spurs, his red card was later rescinded and the real culprit, Melchiot, was banned for three matches (January 2002). FA guidelines allow an appeal on the grounds of incorrect identification (providing the real culprit is named).

In professional football, a fourth official can now bring attention to a case of mistaken identity. In grass-roots football, however, the number on a player's shirt may differ from that on his shorts! As the writer J B Priestley noted, every team should include a redhead so that at least one player can be identified.

IFAB *See* INTERNATIONAL FOOTBALL ASSOCIATION BOARD

IMPEDANCE

The concept of impedance first entered the laws as late as 1951, when obstruction was more clearly defined as an indirect free-kick offence. Obstruction meant intentionally running between opponent and ball or interposing the body so as to form an obstacle to an opponent. This also included an outstretched arm, dancing from side to side, deliberately stepping in front of a striker to shield a goalkeeper, blocking a player who was running into position, or shepherding the ball out for a goal-kick.

Obstruction was reconstructed as impedance in 1995. An indirect free-kick should be awarded against any player who, in the referee's opinion, is impeding the progress of an opponent. It is when a player who has no intention of playing the ball deliberately forms a block between the opponent and the ball. Or, alternatively, impedance is punished when the ball is not within the player's playing distance and the player is imposing the body so as to form an obstacle to the opponent.

Impeding the goalkeeper also includes stationing several players around the goalkeeper or a player deliberately blocking a goalkeeper's route to the ball. Goalkeepers are well protected now. It is also a foul to impede goalkeepers when they are clearly holding the ball.

All this is where there is no contact between players. If there is contact, the offence would be holding, pushing or any number of offences meriting a direct free-kick. Some people find the assessment of impedance as tricky as that of offside, especially as it often happens away from the ball. On lots of occasions during a game, players will naturally come between opponents and the ball but they are not intentionally baulking an opponent.

There is a narrow line between legally shielding the ball (or screening the ball) and illegally pushing, obstructing or impeding an opponent. The ball needs to be in a player's possession within playing distance (about two paces) for it to be legally shielded from an opponent. Otherwise the opponent is being impeded. Similarly, players are shielding the ball unfairly if they extend their arms to prevent the opponent getting around them.

The most common shielding situation is when an attacker chases a ball towards the goal-line and a defender comes across and shepherds the ball out of play for a goal-kick. Most referees side with the defending player because (i) the jostling often goes both ways, and (ii) defenders have become very good at disguising the fact that they may have no intention of playing the ball.

If the referee decides that the defender is not playing the ball (i.e. the ball is not within playing range) an indirect free-kick should be awarded for impeding an opponent. If the defender holds off the attacker with an arm or a leg, then it should be a direct free-kick.

In EURO 1996™, Turkyilmaz (Switzerland) got to the England by-line, crossed low and Grassi somehow hit the crossbar from minimal distance. The ball rebounded invitingly for a Swiss player but the referee ran across him and the chance was gone. Impedance doesn't include obstruction by the referee.

IN PLAY

The ball is first in play when it is kicked and moved forward at a place-kick (providing there is no infringement). Thereafter the ball is in play until the referee stops the game or the whole of the ball goes over the touchline or goal-line.

The ball comes back into play in different ways at different restarts. For goal-kicks it is when the whole of the ball crosses the penalty-area line. For corner-kicks, penalty-kicks, free-kicks and kick-offs, it is when the correctly placed ball is kicked and moved. (Between 1887 and 1997 the ball had to travel its circumference to be in play.) A throw-in is in play when it comes back over the line and has been correctly thrown. And so on.

Whether the ball is 'in play' or 'out of play' is critical because offences will be treated differently. Free-kicks or penalty-kicks cannot be awarded if the ball is out of play, although offenders can still be cautioned or sent off.

INDIRECT FREE-KICK See FREE-KICK

INELIGIBLE PLAYERS See ELIGIBILITY

INJURY

A player was knocked out during a lower-division game and the referee stopped play. The physiotherapist, summoned by the referee, brought the player round slowly, and assessed the player's consciousness with the usual questions: 'Where are you? What's the score?'

'I'm at Wembley,' the player replied. 'We're 2–0 up against Brazil and I've got them both.'

This is footballers' humour, but it also shows the referee's difficulty in distinguishing between two injury categories (serious and slight) that require different procedures. All head injuries are potentially serious. Any player who is knocked out should go to hospital immediately. The *FA Handbook* even lists local neurosurgeons.

Injured players should be quickly removed from the pitch and the game resumed (IFAB 1914). In 1924, the IFAB made a key decision: 'If in the opinion of the referee a player has been seriously injured the game shall be stopped, the player at once removed from the field of play, and the game resumed. If a player is slightly injured then the game shall not be stopped until the ball has ceased to be in play.'

Play must be stopped immediately for head injuries, rib and chest injuries, neck injuries, bad cuts, and serious leg injuries (fractures and knee ligaments). If a player lies still it is a sure sign that the injury could be serious, and a player's health and safety is far more important than a football game. Help must be called for immediately, and play can be restarted with a dropped ball. The referee will have made a mental note of the position of the ball as there could be a considerable delay before the game is restarted.

Serious injuries can be really serious. Bob Marshall (Leith Athletic) was knocked unconscious while scoring a goal and was brought back from the dead (1903–04). Goalkeeper Bernard Hall (Bristol Rovers) spent sixteen days in a coma after being injured against Middlesbrough (December 1966). Derek Dooley (Sheffield Wednesday) had to have his right leg amputated after gangrene infected a fracture (February 1953).

Physiotherapists have often acted quickly to help concussed players who have swallowed their tongue. In Kevin Moran's case, Manchester United physiotherapist Jim McGregor cleared Moran's air passage with the handle of his scissors.

In certain cases, the match has been terminated to prevent further discomfort. A Hope Valley League game between Bamford and Matlock United was abandoned after thirty minutes when a Matlock player received a severe leg injury and officials decided not to move him (December 1999). The other players left the field to seek shelter from the driving rain and after a delay of twenty minutes the referee abandoned the game. A further 25 minutes went by before the ambulance arrived.

The consideration given to injured players is perhaps best illustrated by the occasion when Andy Ducat (Aston Villa) broke his leg in stoppage-time at Manchester City (September 1912). Ducat had to be taken by horse-ambulance to Ancoats Hospital, but the referee wanted to make sure that the departing crowd didn't interfere with the vehicle's slow progress so he delayed resuming the game. This kept the crowd in the stadium until the vehicle had safely completed its journey.

If the injury is not considered serious, the referee should wait until the ball goes out of play before assessing whether a player needs treatment. Players will often help the referee by kicking the ball out, but that does not mean the physiotherapist will necessarily be allowed on. A statement in the 1920s set the tone: 'A player who is injured during a match shall be at once removed outside the nearest goal-line or touchline and the game resumed.' Referees usually ask players if they require treatment (unless it is obvious). Then they would check to see if the player could walk to the touchline unaided. If not, the physio would be summoned by a wave of the hand.

These are situations where the referee cannot win. Players want referees to keep the game moving but they don't want to be disadvantaged by injuries. In the build-up to the only goal of the 1952 FA Cup Final, scored by George Robledo (Newcastle), Don Roper (Arsenal) collapsed with cramp. As Arsenal were already down to ten men, and had two others injured, they felt that the referee should have stopped the game to allow treatment for Roper, but the referee was adamant that the game should be stopped only for serious injuries. The referee is the sole judge of whether a player should be treated for injury.

Thame United played Barton Rovers in an ICIS Division One game (March 1996). As Thame prepared to take a free-kick near the corner of the Barton penalty area, Barton players drew the referee's attention to an injured player on the halfway-line. Shouts of 'Ref, Ref,' are not always heard immediately on a noisy field. The referee blew his whistle for the free-kick to be taken, then saw the injured player and blew again to allow the physiotherapist on. When he turned back, Thame had the ball in the net. The player was treated and the free-kick retaken.

A new procedure for dealing with slight injuries was introduced in 1997. If a physiotherapist came on to treat a player it meant that the player must leave the field, either on foot or on a stretcher. A player is not automatically allowed on-field treatment. If they do have on-field treatment, they have to leave the field and cannot return until play has resumed (confirmed in the laws in 2002). Goalkeepers are the only exception. They are allowed to receive treatment and remain on the field because it would slow down the game too much to change goalkeepers twice for a minor injury. Players can be cautioned if they do not leave the field for treatment, i.e. do not comply with the procedure. Obviously it must be recognised that it will take a skilled physiotherapist anything from twenty to fifty seconds to assess the damage, and serious cases can take far longer.

The procedure was introduced to keep the game flowing. It was also to stop players feigning injury in order to win a free-kick, give team-mates a chance to recover, or quieten the crowd. It had become commonplace for a team 1–0 ahead, with a couple of minutes to play, to have a player go down injured, then make a substitution, all designed to take the impetus away from opponents.

While the new procedure helped the flow of the game, there was much criticism of the statutory requirement for an injured player to leave the field and not return until play had restarted. When the ball is back in play, players must return to the field from the touchline and not the goal-line. When the ball is out of play they can return to the field from either the touchline or the goal-line. The player has to wait for a signal from the referee, and all the other requisites for entering the field of play apply.

One problem was that an injured player could be punished. Rotherham United won 2–1 at York City with a stoppage-time winner scored when Barry Conlon (York City) was off the field (February 2000). Having received treatment on the field for a head injury, Conlon then had to leave the field and could return only when the ball was back in play. By then Rotherham had scored.

In 2001, the IFAB made it clear that referees should let players return to the field as soon as possible after treatment. Managers and coaches complain that a player can be well out of position when he comes back on to the pitch. On the other hand, it has caused many players to pull themselves to their feet and get on with the game without seeking treatment.

However, there was one incident waiting to happen, and it occurred with a comical sense of justice at Tranmere (October 2004). Ryan Taylor (Tranmere Rovers) was brought down in the penalty area by Curtis Davies (Luton Town). The referee gave a penalty-kick and the physiotherapist came to the side of the pitch as Taylor appeared to be injured. Taylor got to his feet and put the ball on the penalty-spot to take the kick but the referee ruled that he had to leave the field for treatment. Iain Hume (Tranmere), deputising for Taylor as penalty-taker, saw his kick saved, but the referee ruled that goalkeeper Dino Seremet (Luton) had moved off his line. Taylor came back on to the pitch and volunteered for the retake. His kick was saved, too, but he knocked in the rebound. The whole sequence of events took about five minutes and the match ended 1–1.

Players need to have a safe journey off the field. Referees will usually allow the stretcher to take the most direct route to the dressing-room, but there have been cases of stretcher-bearers slipping on wet turf and tossing a player on to the pitch.

A new procedure for dealing with bleeding injuries was also introduced (1997). A player bleeding from a wound now had to leave the field for treatment, and could not return to the field until the referee was satisfied that the bleeding has stopped. Most sports have introduced rules like this to protect players from the possible spread of infectious diseases, and a shirt-change is ordered if there is blood on the shirt. In Australian Rules football, a player took advantage of this rule to smear blood on an opponent's shirt, forcing the opponent to leave the field too. The offender was suspended for a match.

Before this rule, players would be bleeding through bandages, or dabbing blood with a sponge as they played. An example was Terry Butcher (England) who cut his head in an aerial challenge against Sweden (September 1989).

Butcher's head was stitched at half-time but he ended the match with his white shirt stained crimson. Faint-hearted television viewers pined for their old black-and-white sets.

Hasselbaink (Middlesbrough) suffered a badly cut head against Chelsea (September 2004). He was off the field for ten minutes while the cut was stitched, and he returned to the field with a clean shirt. After half-time the referee asked Hasselbaink to change his second shirt as that also had blood on it. Hasselbaink then wore another clean shirt with the name 'EHIOGU' on the back.

Players have always kicked the ball out of play to allow a team-mate to receive treatment. After the 1986 FIFA World Cup™, however, there was an increasing tendency for *opponents* to kick the ball out of play to allow treatment. Team-mates of the injured player reciprocated this gesture by conceding possession to the opposition at the resultant restart (usually a throw-in). One beleaguered manager remarked that giving the ball to opponents came naturally to his players anyway.

Critics point out that these sportsmanlike actions happen too much (for trivial injuries like 'a twisted sock'), and others have been angered when opponents unexpectedly kept the ball at the restart. One such incident was Blackburn's last-minute equaliser against Arsenal at Highbury (April 1997). Sutton (Blackburn) chased a ball that was intended for the Arsenal defence after an injury had caused a stoppage in play. Winterburn (Arsenal) conceded a corner-kick and Blackburn scored to draw 1–1.

An incident in the Arsenal–Sheffield United FA Cup fifth-round tie created a precedent (January 1999). Lee Morris (Sheffield United) went down with cramp. A Sheffield United player kicked the ball out for a token Arsenal throw. When Parlour (Arsenal) threw the ball towards the United goalkeeper, Kanu (Arsenal) collected the ball, set off down the right wing and crossed for Overmars (Arsenal) to score. The laws of the game were not broken, the referee was correct to allow the goal, but Arsenal manager Arsène Wenger offered to replay the tie and the FA agreed. This was against FIFA regulations as replays are only allowed when referees err in their knowledge of the laws (a technical error). FIFA insisted that both clubs sign a declaration – mainly for legal reasons – that the winner of the rematch would go forward into the next round. In any event, the result from the first game would stand. In fact, both games finished 2–1 to Arsenal.

In February 2000, goalkeeper Dave Beasant (Nottingham Forest) tried to kick the ball out of play to allow treatment for a prone Wolves opponent (Lee Naylor). Beasant's kick was intercepted by Michael Branch (Wolves), who scored to give his team a 3–0 lead after 25 minutes. This led to angry scenes and touchline discussions. Should Forest be given a goal to cancel out the injustice, or would that be seen as cheating?

Then goals were contrived in a Millwall–Bournemouth reserve game (2001–02) and in a Yeovil Town–Plymouth Argyle cup tie (August 2004). In the latter, Graham Coughlin (Plymouth) received treatment for an injury. When play restarted, Lee Johnson (Yeovil) offered to concede possession by returning the ball to goalkeeper Luke McCormick (Plymouth). Johnson put his head down over the ball and kicked it nearly fifty yards towards goal, only to find that the goalkeeper had moved to the side. The ball sailed into the net, and the referee had to give Yeovil a goal. Players of both teams looked stunned, and Plymouth manager Bobby Williamson was furious. Yeovil manager Gary Johnson immediately went over to Williamson to say that his team would concede a goal. From the kick-off, Steve Crawford (Plymouth) was allowed to walk through the Yeovil defence and equalise. Gary Johnson later joked that it was some of the worst defending he'd ever seen from his players.

Referees can get injured too. If the ball knocks out the referee, and then a player legitimately puts the ball into the net, a goal can be given if the incident was seen by a neutral linesman (FIFA Referees' Committee 1938, IFAB 1954).

During a Plymouth–Middlesbrough match, the referee had to receive treatment from both trainers after being accidentally kicked in the face (October 1964). In the space of a month, in 1966, two referees were seriously injured during matches. One was knocked unconscious at Nottingham Forest, and the other tore an Achilles tendon at Oldham. In each case a linesman took over, and a volunteer ran the line. A referee was knocked unconscious during a Nottingham Forest–Wimbledon match (1990–91). The Forest goalkeeper kicked the ball from his hands and the ball struck the back of the referee's head. Some referees learn their lesson the hard way – *never turn your back on play*.

Other suggestions for dealing with injuries have not been implemented. One was the National American Soccer League experiment with making players sit out for a compulsory ten minutes after receiving off-the-field treatment for injuries. Another idea, in the days before substitutes, was to punish a player who injured an opponent in a foul tackle. If the opponent had to leave the field, it was argued that the player committing the foul should also leave the field for as long as the injured player. This suggestion was considered too impractical and too liable to abuse. A player could feign injury to get a better player off the field.

Players injured during the warm-up can be replaced, even if the team-sheet has already been submitted. This includes players who have been injured in the pre-match photo-shoot. Don't laugh. Players have fallen off benches and ricked their backs, and players have been tripped up by fun-loving team-mates after they leave their pose. They have also hit their heads on dressing-room ceilings, tripped over a bag, or dropped a liniment bottle on their foot.

Injuries have a huge effect on the game and need to be dealt with sensitively. At the professional level, large sums are tied up in insurance, and injuries limit players to eight-year careers on average. At the amateur level, a person's job may still be affected by injury, and players must be insured. The case of *Watson v British Board of Boxing* (2001) showed that organisations can be liable if they fail to provide adequate medical facilities.

INJURY-TIME See STOPPAGE-TIME

INSULTING LANGUAGE See ABUSIVE LANGUAGE

INTERFERING WITH PLAY See OFFSIDE

INTERNATIONAL FOOTBALL ASSOCIATION BOARD (IFAB)

The International Football Association Board (IFAB) was established on 6 December 1882 when representatives of the four British associations – England, Ireland, Scotland and Wales – met in Manchester under the chairmanship of Major Marindin. The laws of the game were standardised at that meeting.

IFAB has continued as the ultimate ruling body for the laws. It meets once a year to make law changes and agree decisions on how the laws should be enforced. IFAB traditionally met in June, but since 1993 the annual meeting has taken place in February or March.

The Fédération de Internationale Football Association (FIFA), founded in 1904, accepted IFAB and later joined forces (1913). FIFA representatives were included on IFAB, but the associations of the four UK countries have been allowed a disproportionate representation on the Board (in respect of their role in drafting the original laws). In 1960 there were ten members of IFAB – two from each of the four British Associations and two from FIFA – and it needed agreement from four-fifths to instigate a change in the laws. The number of FIFA representatives was later increased. The IFAB is now made up of four FIFA representatives plus one from each of four British associations – the Football Association (England), the Scottish FA, the FA of Wales and the Irish FA. It needs a three-quarters majority (six from eight) to uphold proposals. IFAB has overseen two major rewrites of the laws, one in 1937 for 1938, the other in 1996 for 1997.

Jj

JERSEYS See SHIRTS

JEWELLERY

Paulo Diogo (Servette) set up his team's third goal at Schaffhausen and then jumped on to the perimeter fence to celebrate with Servette fans (December 2004). As he jumped down, his wedding ring caught in the fence, tearing away the top two joints of his ring finger. The rest of his finger was later amputated at the hospital. To add insult to injury, Diogo was cautioned for overcelebrating.

Players are not allowed to wear jewellery unless it is unquestionably safe. Flat rings may be taped but everything else should be removed. This applies to rings, chains, bracelets and medallions. Medical bracelets are perhaps best secured by Velcro. Tooth braces are best padded. Even plastic wristbands supporting good causes may be dangerous.

Ring injuries like Diogo's could also occur when players climb over obstacles near local pitches in order to fetch a ball. If a finger is severed, the advice is to put the separated part in a sealed plastic bag and then pack the bag with another bag full of ice.

There was little checking of jewellery until the 1970s. Then came the introduction of pre-match checks. Dennis Alas (El Salvador) was cautioned after 26 minutes of a match against the United States (September 2004). The referee had noticed that Alas was wearing a necklace. It was nineteen-year-old Alas's second caution of the match so he was sent off.

JUMPING AT AN OPPONENT

'The two-footed tackler is committing a foul,' said Liverpool manager Bill Shankly in 1966. 'There is nothing more to be said about him.'

The two-footed tackler is really jumping at an opponent, and victims can be seriously injured. Zico (Brazil) missed a year with injury after Marcio Rossini threw himself at the player with his full weight (1985). Ken Aston, an experienced referee, described a challenge by John Fashanu (Wimbledon) on John O'Neill (Norwich City) as 'the clearest case I have ever seen of a player jumping at an opponent'. Fashanu ended O'Neill's career (December 1987).

A double-footed lunge by Kevin Gray (Huddersfield) on Gordon Watson

(Bradford City) caused a very serious injury and sparked a major court case (February 1997). Once Gray was airborne and 'totally focused on the ball' he could do nothing to adjust his trajectory when Watson nicked the ball away. Gray was cautioned by the referee but Jimmy Hill, who watched the video, described it as one of the worst tackles he had seen in almost fifty years of football. 'It offended against both the unwritten as well as the written code of the game,' Hill said, giving evidence at Leeds High Court.

On Boxing Day 1999, Richard Carpenter (Cardiff City) launched himself at Chris Casper (Reading), who heard his leg snap and felt the intense pain. Casper twisted one way and saw his foot flapping in the air. While the world celebrated the 'new millennium', Casper was in hospital with a broken tibia, broken fibula, damaged knee ligaments and damaged ankle ligaments. Carpenter was cautioned for the two-footed challenge, and Casper's later compensation claim was settled out of court.

When Steven Gerrard (Liverpool) jumped with two feet into Gary Naysmith (Everton), the incident was well publicised (December 2002). The referee missed the incident but Gerrard was banned for three matches on video evidence. One interpretation, in September 2003, was that players should be booked for a two-footed jump that takes the ball and sent off if they take the opponent and the ball. If they miss the ball and take out the opponent then they should be phoning their solicitor. A player may get away with a so-called two-footed tackle if it is done from a short distance away, say a foot or two, and the ball acts as a natural cushion.

Pat Van Den Hauwe was sent off in a home match with Luton (1989–90). His 'two-footed tackle' was waist-high at Iain Dowie (Luton). The sending-off was inevitable, even though there was little contact. Similarly, Seth Johnson (Derby) was sent off for an ugly two-footed lunge at Bradford's Stuart McCall (April 2001).

There are two other kinds of jumping at an opponent. When players turn their back on the ball and jump as an opponent goes to head it, a referee will give a free-kick. And jumping at an opponent with one foot leading and the other tucked up is also a dangerous foul.

KICK-INS

The early London rules opted for the throw-in, but Sheffield rules favoured the kick-in. When the two sets of rules were amalgamated, in 1877, the throw-in was adopted.

The kick-in periodically returns to the agenda. It was a matter for debate in the 1920s, and there was an experiment with kick-ins in 1946–47 as an attempt to stop players deliberately kicking the ball out. After trials in Tunis in the 1970s, Sir Stanley Rous said, 'The kick-ins were going back to the game's origins and had been discarded for good reasons, not least because a casually won throw-in should not give the same advantage as a free-kick awarded for a deliberate foul.'

Further experiments took place in the Diadora League (1994–95) and the Belgian Second Division (1994–97). The theory was that a defender's fear of kicking the ball out might add more finesse to their game and the ball would stay in play more. In the Diadora League, players were given the option of taking a throw-in or an indirect free-kick. They would almost always opt for the latter, indicating their choice to opponents by raising an arm, and that seemed to slow down the game. IFAB concluded that the kick-in offered the game no major improvements.

KICK-OFF

In most respects, the requirements for restarting a game with a kick-off are the same as for the place-kicks at the start of each half: the kicking side must be behind the ball at the moment of the actual kick-off; the signal must be given; the ball must be kicked forward (1886) or it is retaken (IFAB 1903); the ball must move (until 1997 the ball had to roll its full circumference before it was in play); the player taking the kick must not touch it a second time until a second player has touched it; and opponents must not approach within ten yards.

The only difference is in determining who kicks off, and instead of alternating the kick-off to start each half, the side that has conceded the goal restarts the match. In the early days of football, the side *scoring* the goal kicked off. Reverend Vidal (The Wanderers) once dribbled right through opponents to score three in succession (1870s). Now, the only time that the goalscoring side kicks off is when the half-time whistle goes immediately after the goal and the scoring side is down to take the second-half place-kick.

Athlone Town scored against Limerick just before half-time, and there was no time for Limerick to kick-off (August 1972). Athlone kicked off at the start of the second half and scored straight from the kick-off without Limerick touching the ball. Wycombe Wanderers also scored twice without a Peterborough player touching the ball (September 2000). The half-time whistle went immediately after Jamie Bates had scored from a free-kick, and Jermaine McSporran scored inside ten seconds of the second half.

A bizarre kick-off incident happened at Wimbledon in October 1984. Alan Cork put the home side ahead, and then Wimbledon scored again without touching the ball. After Portsmouth had kicked off, the ball was played back to Noel Blake, who put it past his own goalkeeper.

From 1997 a goal could be scored straight from the kick-off, whereas previously this had not been allowed. In January 1998, the *Daily Telegraph* recorded two instances of players scoring direct from a kick-off in local football. One was Steve Hill (White Hart) against Mayflower in the Hatfield Sunday League (December 1997).

KICKING AN OPPONENT

Deliberately kicking an opponent is punishable by a sending-off and a direct free-kick (if the ball was in play). Attempting to kick an opponent is considered to be the same as kicking an opponent. If an opponent jumps out of the way, it should not affect the referee's action. 'I never touched him, Ref,' is no excuse.

The referee has to distinguish between a genuine attempt to kick the ball and an intentional kick at an opponent. Eric Cantona (Manchester United) was sent off for aiming a kick at Richard Shaw (Crystal Palace) in January 1995. The ball was in play at the time but well away from the incident. When Terry Hurlock (Millwall) was sent off for kicking Iwan Roberts (Leicester), the ball was already dead (March 1994).

KICKING THE BALL AWAY See DELAYING A RESTART

KICKS FROM THE PENALTY MARK See PENALTY MARK SHOOT-OUT

KIT See EQUIPMENT

LI

LANGUAGE OF THE LAWS

Interpretations of the laws are as important as the laws themselves. According to the philosopher Wittgenstein, all that matters is the individual meanings we assign to words. The great paradox is that we need to abide by the rules but each rule sparks multiple meanings. Football is a world game and a word game.

Ambiguity exists in every avenue of the legalese: explanations from fans; media summaries; player and coach interpretations; competition rules; guidelines from national or regional football associations; decisions by the FIFA Referees' Committee; and, ultimately, decisions by the International Football Association Board (IFAB), followed by translations into other languages. Rattin (Argentina) has always contended that he was merely asking for an interpreter when he was sent off against England (July 1966).

IFAB has an editorial committee to look at specific word choice. Special care is needed because statements must be translated into many languages with consistency. In the 1930s, the continentals found the physical British game intimidating, especially sliding tackles and charging of the goalkeeper. The 1936 Berlin Olympics brought some quarrelsome games as soccer broke from its British insularity, and interpretation of the laws grew more varied after World War II. 'There was a lot of spitting, pushing off the ball, and deliberate obstruction,' said one English player about Czechoslovakia (1946), but Continentals complained about the physical play of Arsenal (against Spartak Moscow) and Chelsea (against Red Banner) shortly afterwards. A FIFA refereeing conference in London began the process of standardising the laws (1948).

Archaic language has been handed down. People talked of a 'bounce-up' many years after bounce-ups had been replaced by the dropped ball (1914). And players claimed 'Played on, Ref!' years after the offside law was rewritten, in 1978, to explain that an opponent couldn't suddenly turn an offside player into an onside one.

Football's linguistic heritage is an oral culture developed by British working-class males. It took IFAB until 1994 to recognise the growth of women's football, and then through an antiquated he-means-she technique: 'references to the male gender within the laws of the game . . . are for simplification and refer to both males and females'.

On the pitch, where words are used sparingly, the scope for ambiguity is enormous.

'Is it here, Ref?' the player shouts, placing the ball for a free-kick.

'Right,' the referee replies.

Does that mean to your right, to my right, or that the ball is already correctly placed?

In one game, a player clattered into an opponent.

'I went after the ball, Ref,' the offender pleaded.

'Yeah, you went *after* the ball,' the referee repeated. It was a late tackle.

LATE TACKLE

It's a moot point whether there can be a 'late tackle'. Terms like 'late attempt to tackle', 'late arrival' or 'foul' would probably be more apt. What most people call a late tackle is when a player puts in a foot *after* an opponent has played the ball. A second earlier and it might have been a fair tackle. Sometimes, though, the late challenge is so late that the ball is some distance away and the referee's eyes are following the ball. A good referee senses when a player is going to continue the challenge and watches for the outcome.

The referee of the 1966 England–France match missed a late tackle by Stiles (England) on Simon (France) because the ball was almost ten yards away, but the player was reported by a FIFA official off the pitch.

Steven Froggatt (Coventry City) hardly played again after being injured by Nicky Summerbee (Sunderland) in the eighth minute of a match (February 2000). The tackle was variously described as a 'late challenge', 'a high challenge' and a 'high lunge'. Froggatt's team-mate Gary McAllister described the tackle as 'very late and very bad' as Summerbee led 'with the sole of his boot'.

LEARNING THE LAWS

There is very little formal teaching of the laws of football, and virtually no widespread dissemination of the real meaning of the seventeen laws. Referees initially receive about twenty hours of basic training. Almost all of them are stunned by how little they previously knew.

Qualified coaches hear a brief lecture on the subject, but the laws do not appear on the A level Sports Studies syllabus or in the training for Community Sports Leaders. The classic annual, *The Laws of Association Football*, should be as accessible as *The Highway Code*, but it is rarely seen by players and fans, rarely discussed, and plays a strangely peripheral part in the lives of most football people. One former professional player, Tony Cascarino, writing in *The Times* (13 September 2004), said that in his nineteen years as a player he was 'never once handed a rulebook by a club, never took part in a training session that explained some regulations, and was never party to a meeting about the laws'.

Most supporters and players learn the laws informally – through family, peer group, team-mates, pub mates, commentators and so-called experts. They learn from the reactions of role models. Whatever others do on the pitch, it will set some kind of example. Sometimes people learn the laws as they would like them to be rather than as they actually are.

An example of how English people view the laws in different ways came after a EURO 2004™ quarter-final between Portugal and England. In the last minute of normal time, with the score 1–1, Hargreaves (England) was fouled on the left wing near the penalty area. From Beckham's free-kick Campbell (England) sent in a strong header that hit the crossbar. Campbell followed up to put the ball into the net with an unchallenged header. There were two extreme positions on this incident. The first was that of hard-line England fans who were so convinced that it should have been a legitimate goal that they sent thousands of e-mails and abusive phone calls – and death threats – to the referee, whose contact details were released by a tabloid newspaper. At the other extreme, most referees saw that Terry (England) had held goalkeeper Ricardo (Portugal) with an arm over the goalkeeper's shoulder, and most experienced referees would have routinely given a free-kick (if they had seen the incident and had had the courage).

In between these two extremes were a whole range of responses. Some fans changed their mind after seeing the foul for the first time on television replays. Others didn't understand that the referee had to use his opinion in matters of fact. A number of 'informed experts' disagreed with the referee. Clive Allen (ITV) was one who clearly saw the offence, but others were adamant that the referee had got it wrong, and some didn't seem to understand that it didn't matter that the ball was not within the goalkeeper's range when he was fouled.

A similar controversy occurred in the last moments of a FIFA World Cup™ play-off, when Hussain Ali (Bahrain) kicked the ball from goalkeeper Kelvin Jack (Trinidad & Tobago) as Jack threw the ball up to kick clear (November 2005). Hussain Ali netted but the referee correctly disallowed the goal. The players all swarmed around the referee, but this was a straightforward decision.

Rumours spread quickly among the football public. A spectator shouts an opinion on the match. Hairdressers tell you what they've heard from within the club. The media condenses an argument to a sound bite. A commentator makes an offhand remark. Someone says that the referee will be biased.

Some referees argue that an alternative set of football rules are being presented via personalities in the media (pundits, managers, journalists, commentators and players). The dissemination of real knowledge is further thwarted because referees are rarely allowed to talk publicly in detail about their decisions (only on matters of law). Whereas top-class referees mixed with professional players in the 1950s – they often trained together at their local club – there are now few places where referees and players interact informally. Indeed, referees need to maintain a healthy distance from players and officials in order to protect their dignity and neutrality.

There are many myths when it comes to the laws: the notion that a player can be sent off for dissent; the idea that a player going off the field after treatment for injury makes no sense; that it's not a foul if you don't make contact or the opponent is 'going nowhere'; that there's nothing wrong with challenging a goalkeeper; that 'I got the ball' or 'I was going for the ball' makes it fair; that you can give a penalty-kick for obstruction; that calling 'My ball' should be an automatic free-kick; and so on. All these are wrong assumptions.

The only real way to learn the laws is to read them and then watch how they are interpreted. There is no cut-and-dried description of a foul, only a slow, empirical understanding of what top-class referees will give. If you watch a high-level game, agree with ninety per cent of refereeing decisions, and accept them all, then you understand the laws.

LEAVING THE FIELD

There was a bizarre incident in Leyton's 3–1 win against West Ham (April 1912). Having let in two soft goals, West Ham goalkeeper Geggus was subjected to 'some uncharitable remarks' by the crowd behind the goal. The goalkeeper pulled off his gloves and ran to the little wicket gate that led to the dressing-room. It took club officials over a minute to persuade Geggus to return to the pitch.

It is a cautionable offence to leave the field without permission (1939). Sometimes you will see coaches or physiotherapists directing players back on to the pitch if they look like wandering off without permission. The deciding factor for the referee is whether the player deliberately steps off the pitch (and therefore needs permission) or involuntarily leaves the pitch (and therefore does not need permission). Players are allowed to leave the pitch briefly when celebrating a goal.

In a match in the 1950s, Bryan Douglas (Blackburn Rovers) slithered over the goal-line after crossing the ball. He hauled himself to his feet, dashed on to the pitch, intercepted a backpass from Bill Asprey (Stoke City) and scored a crucial goal. If players leave the field by their momentum, as part of the natural action, they are not considered to have purposely left the field (IFAB 1934).

In practice referees may apply common sense and allow some leeway. They may prefer to see a player suddenly dash off to be sick on the sidelines (like Festa of Middlesbrough in December 2000) rather than vomit on the pitch (like Beckham of England against Ecuador in June 2006). Referees will prefer the vomit to be off the field rather than on their diagonal path.

An IFAB decision (1934) stated that 'if a defender suddenly steps off the field to put a player offside, the referee should caution him and the player is still onside'. McGrath (Blackburn Rovers) claimed that he was off the pitch when Wolves scored in the 1960 FA Cup Final, but the referee would have none of it.

LECTURES ON THE PITCH

Referees use a number of approaches in order to rebuke players and retain order. They may shout at players while the game is in progress, talk quietly during stoppages, give individuals public warnings, administer cautions and sendings-off, and call the two captains together to plead for control.

One of the last resorts is the mass lecture. Twenty minutes from the end of a cup tie between Hull City and Leicester City, the referee called together all the players except the two goalkeepers (1924–25). Other examples include a general warning to all the players of Norwich City and Charlton Athletic (January 1929), a guest lecture on 'the need to calm down' for Leeds United and Burnley players (1964–65), and a public oration to the lads of Newcastle and Burnley after a spate of heavy tackling (September 1965).

One local referee's homily to 21 players followed a Cantona-style flying tackle that seriously injured an opponent (February 1995): 'Look, I can't stop that before it happens. I've sent him off and I'll send in a report. We're going to start again with no fouls, and if you don't have the right attitude I'll abandon the match.'

LENGTH OF MATCH See DURATION OF THE GAME

LINESMEN See ASSISTANT REFEREES

LIQUID INTAKE

Da Silva and Fernandez studied a sample of twelve referees in Brazil in the autumn months. They found that the referees suffered moderate dehydration (2.05 per cent of body weight), and argued that this could interfere with physical and mental performance. Assistant referees suffered less (1.05 per cent of body weight). Studies of players have shown a range of dehydration effects (1.70 per cent of bodyweight to 3.08 per cent) depending on weather conditions.

These matters came to a head when Jack Charlton's Republic of Ireland team played at noon in ninety-degree heat in the United States World Cup (June 1994). Ireland experimented with water bags but Houghton was cautioned for having a bag in his hand when the ball came to him (versus Norway). The idea of a drinks break (as in cricket) has been rejected (IFAB 2002).

FIFA actively encourages the intake of liquids during a match. However, players should abide by certain basic rules: liquids may only be drunk during stoppages in play; drinks must be in plastic bottles and handed to players at the sidelines; bottles mustn't be thrown on to the field of play; players should stand at the touchline or goal-line while drinking; the goalkeeper may keep a plastic bottle in the corner of the goal; plastic bottles may be placed on the pitch surround, about a yard away from the touchlines and goal-line; bottles or people handing over bottles should never interfere with an assistant referee's pathway.

LONDON RULES See ORIGINS OF THE LAWS

LYING ON THE BALL

Goalkeepers can be cautioned for lying on the ball too long. This counts as unsporting behaviour. Of course, there could be good reason if the goalkeeper is injured.

In most cases where the ball is trapped under a player, the referee will quickly blow the whistle and restart play with a dropped ball. This is because players may start kicking dangerously at the ball. In one Hellenic League match the ball was lodged under a prone player. The referee blew quickly for a dropped ball, just as the player on the ground shouted, 'F*****g hell, Ref, he's kicking me in the balls.'

When Joey Barton (Manchester City) kicked at a ball trapped under a Doncaster Rovers player, it provoked ugly scenes in a pre-season friendly (July 2004).

Mm

MANAGERS See TECHNICAL AREA

MARKINGS See PITCH MARKINGS

MÊLÉE

A mass brawl at Old Trafford led to Manchester United and Arsenal being fined £50,000 each (October 1990). The 21-man battle broke out when Nigel Winterburn and Anders Limpar (both Arsenal) simultaneously tackled Denis Irwin (Manchester United). Arsenal were deducted two points, Manchester United one. (The previous year Arsenal had been fined £20,000 for their part in a brawl against Norwich.)

Mêlées are usually sparked by existing feuds, bad tackles, severe injuries, challenges on goalkeepers, sendings-off, a trapped ball, and goals: Carlisle and Morecambe players fought over the ball as it lay in the net (January 2005); a brawl at Middlesbrough followed an accidental kick by Ferguson (Everton) on goalkeeper Schwarzer (Middlesbrough) (January 2005); a twenty-man scuffle broke out when Jim Magilton (Ipswich) was sent off for kicking Gavin Peacock (QPR) (October 1999); a 22-player rumpus was provoked when Sedgemore (Macclesfield) and Richardson (Lincoln City) committed sending-off offences (April 1998); two players were cautioned after Damien Johnson (Birmingham) kicked at a ball trapped under Gareth Barry (Aston Villa), leading to a mêlée (December 2004); and a mass brawl broke out at Leeds after a two-footed lunge by Bowyer (Leeds United) had connected with the chest of Tottenham's Clemence (February 2000). This all helps to explain why the third person into an ice-hockey fight is punished more severely than the first two.

One Lincoln City player and three Carlisle United players were sent off in a match at Lincoln (August 2002). Richie Foran (Carlisle) was later found guilty of threatening behaviour at Gainsborough Magistrates' Court, and Carlisle United chairman John Courtenay was sentenced to 150 hours community service for his part in the brawl.

Some referees step in between players – others step back and observe. Referees can identify the numbers and actions of the perpetrators and perhaps a couple of other players. They may need to repeat the numbers and actions to themselves until the mêlée has settled down and they can start taking notes. It took officials three minutes to discuss unruly scenes at Leeds when Gillingham visited (March 2005). Pandemonium followed a challenge by Darius Henderson (Gillingham) and retaliation by Michael Gray (Leeds United). Most of the players were involved, plus people from both technical areas, and a few stewards. It is always very hard for referees to work out who is trying to stir up trouble and who is trying to stop it. Henderson and Gray were sent off.

The referee's ultimate privilege is to abandon the match. That happened after 65 minutes of an Essex Senior Cup semi-final between Chelmsford City and Braintree Town (January 2006). An incident near the Chelmsford technical area sparked a free-for-all involving players and officials of both teams.

METHOD OF SCORING

Many people have a natural urge to kick something like a stone or a ball from one place to another. In the early days, villages defined the boundaries. Players tried to force the ball towards a hole in the ground, a running river, a space between trees, bushes or posts, a church door or the water wheel of a mill. As football became more organised the goal became more standardised (1886): 'A goal shall be won when the ball has passed between the goalposts under the bar, not being thrown, knocked on, nor carried by any one of the attacking side. The ball hitting the goal or boundary posts, or goal bar, and rebounding into play, is considered in play.'

Some refinements were made over the years: the whole of the ball needed to be over the goal-line; the phrase 'intentionally propelled by hand' replaced 'knocked on'; and it was recognised that goalkeepers in their own penalty area could propel the ball by hand for a legitimate goal, by throwing the ball into the opponent's goal, or, more likely, their own (1962).

A major rewrite of the laws produced an unfortunate ambiguity (1997): 'A goal is scored when the whole of the ball passes over the goal-line, between the goalposts and under the crossbar, provided that no infringement of the Laws of the Game has been committed previously by the team scoring the goal.' This presumably meant no infringement since the ball was last dead or out of play (not since the start of the game!).

When the ball looks as though it has gone over the goal-line, between the goalposts and under the crossbar, the referee's first response is to look towards the nearest assistant to see if there is no infringement. If the assistant is running back towards the halfway-line, giving a sign (e.g. a thumbs up), then the referee can signal the goal by pointing back to the centre mark, back-pedal a little to check how the reactions are going, then keep an eye on celebrations. The movements are usually quite considered until agreement is reached between assistant referee and referee.

The referee's decision is final.

'That was never a goal, Ref,' says a defender.

'Look in tonight's paper and you'll see that it was,' the referee replies.

If the referee thinks it is a goal, then it is. If the referee 'disallows' a goal, play can be resumed immediately. If some players are erroneously celebrating it is their problem.

Football's scoring system is very simple. One goal equals one goal. Your team does not get two points for goals scored from outside the penalty area. There are headed goals, back-heeled goals, chested goals, chinned goals, spectacular goals, lucky goals, dramatic goals, disputed goals, top-corner goals, bottom-corner goals, own-goals and disowned goals, but they all count the same – one goal. The only exception was a brief experiment in China in the late 1980s when headed goals counted double in an attempt to improve the heading skills of the nation's players. FIFA disapproved.

MINI-CORNERS

The mini-corner was rejected after experiments in the 1970s. The idea was for a kick to be either taken from where the penalty-area line meets the goal-line (if the ball went out between the goalpost and the penalty-area line) or taken from where the corner was conceded (if the ball crossed the goal-line between the corner-flag and the penalty-area line). Short corner-kicks were not really an advantage as a penalty area packed with players was too difficult to penetrate. And 'mini-corner' proved a better term than short corner (an oxymoron).

MINIMUM NUMBER OF PLAYERS See NUMBER OF PLAYERS

MINUTE'S TRIBUTE

The traditional mark of respect for a recent death is a minute's silence. It can commemorate the passing of a person of stature (Sir Winston Churchill in January 1965), a major tragedy like the Dunblane massacre (March 1996), or the death of loyal servants, such as Ted Bates of Southampton (December 2003).

Referees usually bring forward the other pre-match rituals – greeting the captains, tossing a coin, etc. – and they summon players of both sides to the circumference of the centre-circle (as explained to the players before the match and announced to spectators). When the players are standing on the centre-circle line, the referee blows the whistle and, a minute later, eyeing the watch surreptitiously, the referee blows again. In 1945, a minute's silence to commemorate the death of American president Franklin D Roosevelt was impeccably observed by 133,000 Scotland–England spectators.

When Queen Mary died, there was a more extended mark of respect (March 1953). At Exeter the players, wearing black armbands, lined up in front of the grandstand. The band played one verse of 'Abide with Me', and then came the minute's silence. Finally, the band played the National Anthem. The crowd had been asked to arrive early.

Most minute silences are observed impeccably. The only noise is that beyond the participants' control – background traffic, a nearby park-football game, the gurgle of a baby, birdsong, people entering through the turnstiles – and that can add to the poignancy of the minute. But sometimes spectators are disruptive. The referee at a Southampton–Portsmouth match blew the whistle after 25 seconds when faced with noisy Portsmouth fans (December 2003). Some Sunderland fans disrupted a silence for John Charles at Cardiff (February 2004). A silence to commemorate the first anniversary of the 9/11 disaster was disturbed by Celtic fans at Motherwell (September 2002). And Hearts banned a season-ticket holder for life when he interfered with a one-minute silence in honour of Princess Margaret (February 2002).

An alternative to the minute's silence is a minute's applause, which was used at Celtic to mark the twentieth anniversary of Jock Stein's death (September 2005) and in some of the tributes to George Best (November 2005). Football fans tend to appreciate through noise rather than silence, and it is less susceptible to disruption.

MISCONDUCT

Misconduct includes anything that is likely to need further action by the relevant football association's disciplinary committee – cautions, sendings-off, issues raised in the referee's report (e.g. late arrivals), incidents involving team officials, match officials or spectators, incidents noted by observers, or incidents investigated by video evidence. The relevant FA will then pass judgment with suspensions, fines, point deductions or other punishments.

In 2005 the laws were altered to clarify that referees can impose disciplinary sanctions from the moment they enter the field of play to the moment they leave the field after the final whistle. The FA had ruled that a referee was incorrect to caution and show the yellow card to Dean Windass (Bradford City) when Windass confronted him *off the pitch after the match* against Luton Town (October 2004). But Windass could be reported for misconduct.

At New Brighton, in the early 1970s, John Clarke (New Brighton) was cautioned. One spectator heckled Clarke, whose team were losing 3–0, and the player shouted back, 'I'll get you after the game.' At the final whistle, Clarke ran to the edge of the pitch, leapt over the barrier and chased the spectator.

If referees see such off-the-pitch incidents, they should report them. In 1975, all eleven players of an Irish team were reported for a pre-match chant in the dressing-room. A referee reported Howard Smart (Rhyl) after the player had made comments (and refused to apologise for them) in the car-park thirty minutes after the end of a Welsh Cup semi-final. Another referee reported Stoke City manager Tony Waddington for comments at Liverpool Street station following an Ipswich–Stoke match. And Jens Lehmann (Arsenal) was reported to UEFA and suspended for two matches for squirting water over match officials in the tunnel after playing against Bayern Munich (April 2005).

The FA first imposed penalties for breaches of the rules in 1871–72, but they were already in place in Sheffield. The referee has to submit a report informing the relevant authorities of any incidents requiring further consideration: name of player and number; club; nature of the offence and description of the incident; whether the player was cautioned or sent off; and the time and place of the offence.

The earliest FA officials were tough. 'People like Clegg were dictatorial,' was one manager's view. 'You'd have thought people were talking about God. If you sneezed at a referee, you'd get suspended, not only for life, but for the hereafter.' Willie Woodburn (Rangers) was indeed suspended *sine die* (indefinitely) by the Scottish FA after he head-butted a Stirling Albion player (1954). Woodburn had been banned for short periods on three previous occasions. Contrast this with Dave Caldwell, who was sent off five times in one season (1987–88) and yet continued his career. In 174 appearances for Mansfield Town, Caldwell received 36 cautions and 8 suspensions (1979 to 1985).

County FAs are given clear guidelines on punishments for every type of offence. The most serious offences listed in the *FA Handbook 2004–05* are those directed at match officials – common assault (182-day ban and £150), assault attempting or causing bodily harm (*sine die* suspension and £250 fine) and assault causing serious bodily harm (permanent suspension). A Scottish 'A' league player was banned from football for a year after threatening a referee during a match (2004). Players have also been suspended for playing unaffiliated football, which included Sunday football until the Sunday ban was lifted (1955).

National associations had to agree to recognise suspensions by other national associations, and they developed a procedure to cover players who changed clubs and moved across associations while an investigation was under way. Misconduct became the job of the national and regional associations rather than the competition organisers (1905). After *Enderby Town Football Club v the Football Association* (1971), players could have a lawyer present at an FA appeal hearing if a legal case was being argued. Said Lord Denning, 'If a court sees that a domestic tribunal is proposing to proceed in a manner contrary to natural justice, it can intervene to stop it.' The following year, Ernie Machin (Coventry City) successfully sued for damages relating to a three-week suspension after the FA disciplinary committee had been judged to have failed 'to conduct a hearing in accordance with the rules of natural justice'.

From the start of 2000–01, the use of video evidence became more formalised in the English professional game. Off-the-ball incidents missed by the match officials (e.g. elbowing, spitting and head-butting) could be shown to a three-member panel.

There is a major problem, however, with matches taken by an unofficial referee. Some replacement referees do not report offences.

MISSILES See OBJECTS ON THE PITCH

MISTAKEN IDENTITY See IDENTIFICATION

MODIFICATIONS TO THE LAWS

With the agreement of the relevant national association, the laws may be modified to suit players under sixteen, women, players with disabilities, and players over thirty-five. Possible changes include: the duration of the game; pitch size; the size, weight and material of the ball; goal size; and number and type of substitutions.

There have always been modifications for schoolchildren. In the 1907–08 English Shield semi-final, at a time when boys left school at fourteen, Oxford Boys' fourth goal against Woolwich Arsenal Boys was disputed. The ball came back off the eight-foot crossbar, whereas the boys were playing to a lower crossbar that had been nailed on to the goalposts.

In 1989, to standardise across the world, the wording was changed to allow modifications for those 'under sixteen' rather than 'players of school age'. As referees hold positions of responsibility in games involving children, they are required to undergo Criminal Records Bureau (CRB) checks, and the FA formed a special child-protection unit.

After Sir Stanley Rous had flagged the rise of the women's game (1971), IFAB agreed that certain laws could be modified for women's football.

'Ungentlemanly behaviour' was replaced by 'unladylike behaviour', and handling was allowed for protection purposes. A 1920s American coaching manual advised girls to cross their arms in front of their breasts for protection.

Until the early 1990s, top-level women's matches were forty minutes each way. Now the rules are usually the same as for men. Solveig Gulbrandsen (Norway) was cautioned for pulling her shirt over her head after scoring her first goal against Sweden (June 2005).

In the women's game there is less dissent, simulation, gamesmanship and time-wasting. As one top male referee said, after the 1994 FA Women's Cup Final, 'There was more chat-up than backchat.' But some things don't change. Women still shout 'Man on!' to warn team-mates.

According to FA regulations, boys and girls are allowed to play together up to the age of eleven, but must play separately from then on. The teenager Theresa Bennett lost a court case on appeal when she wanted to play in a boys' team (1978). When Sharon Broadbent appeared in a Huddersfield & District League game – Shelley v Holme Valley Academicals – a spectator complained because mixed football was not allowed for competitive adult matches (April 1992).

Modifications for over-35s were introduced in 1992, and the New England Over-the-Hill Soccer League allows unlimited substitutions. In 2001, IFAB agreed that the laws could be modified for 'players with disabilities'. This has confirmed new forms of football for amputees, blind players and cerebral-palsy sufferers.

MOONING See DROPPED SHORTS

MULTI-BALL SYSTEM

The ball is cleared on to the roof of the stand. It bounces once near the roof's apex and then disappears over the other side. The crowd lets out a mock cheer. The referee turns to the bench and draws matching semicircles with the fingertips of each hand. An official throws on a replacement ball and it is kicked across the pitch in a three-man relay, only for it to arrive just as the match-ball comes back from behind the stand. Then comes another delay as the replacement ball is returned. Nearly thirty seconds have passed.

The multi-ball system has been designed to quicken this process and keep the game moving. Any previously checked ball can be thrown on by an official ball boy. The multi-ball system can add several minutes to the action, but there are at least three potential problems: (i) it raises the chances of two (or even three) balls being on the pitch at the same time, and this has led to referees having to stop play; (ii) ball boys (usually supplied by the home team) have been seen to vary tactics depending on the score (or they delay giving the ball to the away team); and (iii) the ball boys have been seen to use towels to dry the ball for the home-team's long throw-in expert but not for the away team's. Sometimes, referees have curtailed the system partway through a game (e.g. games at Brighton and Tranmere in November 2001).

Occasionally a ball boy will throw a ball at an away-team player. What can referees do? They can stop the multi-ball system (but that may benefit a home team preserving a lead) or they can write a note in the match report, which may lead to possible disciplinary action.

Nn

NAMES ON SHIRTS *See* SHIRTS

NATIONAL ANTHEM

Players are called from the dressing-rooms early if anthems are to be played before the coin-tossing ritual. This may be competition anthems or national anthems (before internationals or special occasions). The England anthem has traditionally been played before FA Cup Finals, even though sometimes the English players are in a minority. Only a quarter of the players engaged in the 2005 final were English.

Most anthem segments last between 45 seconds and 65 seconds. Planning is needed because there have been some serious mistakes. When England played Spain in 1932, the new Spanish government had just changed the national anthem, and the orchestra conductor had to ask a spectator to whistle the tune. When Nigeria played Tunisia, the Algerian anthem was played instead of the Nigerian one (February 2004). And the Israeli public address system was not able to cope with a CD of the Croatian anthem, so the outcome was silence (February 2005). It helps if the two anthems are allocated a similar amount of time. Scotland players felt they were listening to Uruguay's anthem for fifteen minutes, before they lost 7–0 (June 1954).

Anthems are emotional and can raise the adrenaline levels. Bobby Robson, England manager from 1982 to 1990, has talked about feeling the hairs on the back of his neck bristle with pride as he stood in his England blazer before his first match against Denmark (September 1982). In contrast, England players were angry when told by the British ambassador to give the Fascist salute to the German national anthem (May 1938).

French Algerians booed the French national anthem before a France–Algeria international (October 2001), fans of Corsica-based Bastia booed the French national anthem before the 2002 French Cup Final, and China supporters gave a fiery reception to Japan's national anthem before the Asian Cup Final (August 2004). But the playing of the Tibetan national anthem was a tremendously moving occasion when Tibet played their first-ever international – against Greenland in Denmark (June 2001).

NETS *See* GOAL-NETS

NEUTRALITY

Football's passionate and emotional world generates bias and favour. It is almost axiomatic that everyone supports a club. Even when a person doesn't show any obvious club affiliation they can be accused of aligning themselves with one stance over another – England or Scotland, north or south, the passing game or long-ball tactics, players or referees, professionals or amateurs, Premiership or Conference, television or radio, big companies or small companies, etc. It is rare to find neutrality in football.

On the field, the referee is the symbol of impartiality. Referees are taught not only to *be* unbiased but to be *seen* to be unbiased. Referees shouldn't accept a lift in a team's coach or a player's car, in case they are accused of siding with one team. Their integrity must be maintained. When West Ham won at Sunderland, much was made of the referee going into the West Ham dressing-room and asking Teddy Sheringham to sign a copy of his autobiography (December 2004). The Sunderland manager was not questioning the referee's decisions, but was implying that it didn't look very good.

Off the field, close scrutiny shows how hard it is to find true neutrality. Celebrity journalists align themselves with particular teams, and there is the story of a broadsheet journalist who jumped out of his press-box seat and shouted 'Get in!' when his home-town team scored. At the 1978 FIFA World Cup™, Scottish reporters were called 'supporters with typewriters', and certain members of television teams are known associates of particular clubs. When objective people do exist – FA officials, referees, journalists, etc. – they are often relatively unappreciated and sometimes pilloried. At times individual interests need to be sacrificed for the good of the game.

The most obvious source of bias is the partiality of fans. In 1951, two American university teachers, Albert Hastorf and Hadley Cantril, made a classic study of the perceptions of two sets of supporters. They showed a film of a fractious Princeton–Dartmouth American football game to students at each college. On average, the Princeton fans thought the rule infractions should have been called 9.8 to 4.2 in favour of Princeton, whereas the Dartmouth fans felt it should have been 4.4 to 4.3 Dartmouth's way.

Hastorf and Cantril concluded that there was no such thing as a game existing in its own right. The game only exists through an individual's perceptions, and particular happenings have significances in terms of the individual's purpose. 'Out of all the occurrences going on in the environment, a person selects those that have some significance for him from his own egocentric position in the total matrix,' said Hastorf and Cantril. In other words, fans see the game they want to see.

Administrators must also be seen to be unbiased. Conspiracy theories abound. One states that Rangers and Celtic were deliberately kept apart in the

Scottish Cup draws between 1947 and 1989 because that was the desired Scottish Cup Final. Another theory states that the FA has never wanted a third-tier team in an FA Cup Final. They point to a number of refereeing decisions in FA Cup semi-finals involving teams from the third tier: two dubious free-kicks that enabled Sunderland to come from behind against Millwall (1937); a debatable West Brom penalty-kick and a Port Vale 'goal' disallowed for offside (1954); a late shot by Bottom (York City) which seemed to go over the line for a likely winner against Newcastle United (1955); and a shot by Howard (Chesterfield) which hit the underside of the crossbar and bounced over the Middlesbrough line (1997). All hypothetical, of course, but it all fuels the fear of bias.

It took a while for neutrality to be built into the laws. In 1880, Scotland and England still differed over offside and throw-in rules. At that year's international match, in Glasgow, the English FA instructed the England team not to take the field until the referee, a Scot, had agreed to accept the English laws. The Scots gave way but the referee seemed to forget about the agreement at times during the game. But the Scots were livid about two goals by Spikesley (England) at Richmond in 1893 when the referee was Mr J C Clegg, an FA official who had helped to select the England team.

'In international matches the referees shall be neutral,' ruled IFAB (1930), 'and the linesmen shall be officials registered as referees with a national association.' Two years later, amateur international matches between the four British associations were excluded from this ruling. In June 1950, IFAB decided that referees for international matches had to be from a neutral country unless otherwise agreed by the countries concerned.

Ray Wood was a Huddersfield Town goalkeeper in the 1950s, and his father Les was a League referee. The League kept them apart. The Football League later asked clubs not to insert the home towns of referees and linesmen in their programmes to avoid any accusations of bias (August 1986). In the 1950s, representatives of English clubs complained to the Football League secretary that they always had Welsh linesmen at games in Wales (e.g. at Cardiff, Swansea or Wrexham). The League secretary retorted with the fact that Welsh clubs always had English linesmen when they played in England. Touché.

The choice of referee should also be seen to be unbiased. In the 1966 FIFA World Cup™ quarter-finals, Argentina v England was refereed by a German, and Germany v Uruguay was refereed by an Englishman. In more recent tournaments, quarter-final referees are chosen from countries no longer in the competition. Referees are duty-bound to decline any match where there is a conflict of interest. In November 1993, a rumpus broke out over an FA Vase game between Newmarket and Harwich because the referee had played for Newmarket as a teenager 29 years earlier, and Stan Gate was replaced as referee of the Carlisle–Aldershot Conference play-off semi-final because he had had a short spell at Carlisle as a youngster (May 2005).

NOTEBOOK

Referees, assistant referees and fourth officials carry notebooks (or pieces of card) for recording goals, substitutions, cautions, sendings-off and which team kicked off. Senior assistants and fourth officials need this information because they may have to deputise for the referee later in the game. When cautioning a player, referees will note the player's name, the time of the incident, and perhaps a code to remember the offence (if they don't trust their memory).

Referees make sure that their notebook (or notebook equivalent) is protected from rain and theft, and from players like Mike Bagley, who once grabbed a notebook and ate the page with his name on. There are cases of referees cautioning a player, losing their piece of paper, and having to telephone the club secretary for the player's name.

NUMBER OF PLAYERS

At first, competing clubs agreed among themselves on the number in each team. Kent played Surrey in a twelve-a-side game (1868), and Crystal Palace (fourteen men) once played Barnes (nine men).

Jackson described the pick-up games at Queen's Park (Glasgow) in 1868: 'The teams in those days varied from eleven to twenty-two, according as the material was available, and it was no uncommon thing for the numbers to rise and fall considerably during the progress of a two-and-a-half hours' fight.'

Robert Folliard uncovered a hotchpotch of team sizes when he studied the friendly games of the 1870s – nine Wanderers against ten Harrow Chequers (October 1871), a fourteen-a-side game between Clapham Pilgrims and Leyton (October 1871), and nine against nine when Wanderers played Hampstead Heathens (January 1872). The teams tended to be smaller in poor weather.

Wednesday were beating Heeley 1–0 at half-time in one game, but it was discovered that Wednesday had fourteen players and Heeley only thirteen (January 1876). The clubs agreed to cancel the first half and start again. Heeley found another player and the two teams played fourteen-a-side for twenty minutes each way. When Wednesday played Heeley again, in the 1877 Sheffield Cup Final, it was a twelve-a-side match.

Wording about the number of players ('eleven players on each side') was included for the first time in the 1897 laws. This was later adapted to 'not

more than eleven players on each side' (1923). When Burnley hosted
Blackburn Rovers, the Rovers players were so cold and querulous that ten of
them walked off the field, leaving their goalkeeper, Herby Arthur, alone to
face the opposition (December 1891). The match was abandoned when
Arthur delayed taking a free-kick for offside.

Chesterfield beat Stockport County 8–1 after four visiting players missed
the train and their leading scorer broke a rib in the first half (April 1902).
Kilmarnock played with seven men at Port Glasgow Athletic after four
players (including the goalkeeper) missed a train connection and then
assumed the match would be postponed through snow and ice (January
1908). The kick-off was delayed for 25 minutes, and Port Glasgow Athletic
won 4–1.

As late as 1912, a match ended with five men on one team. This was
Grimsby Town versus Leicester Fosse on a day when rain and sleet lay in
puddles on the pitch. Ten minutes from the end six Fosse players left the field
complaining that they were ill. During the last ten minutes, Grimsby
sportingly did not try to add to their 4–0 lead.

Eventually, IFAB recommended a minimum number of seven players,
although competition organisers were given the final say (until seven was
written into the laws in 1949). Matches are abandoned if one team is reduced
to fewer than seven players. A Mid-Hertfordshire League match was
abandoned when the teams were reduced to six against five on a bitterly cold
day at Veralaneum (St Albans) (February 1961), and an international in
Morocco was stopped after 65 minutes when Ethiopia were left with six
players (October 1992). Having lost six of their squad during an airport
stopover in Italy, allegedly to defections, Ethiopia took to the field with two
goalkeepers in central defence and a forty-year-old coach in midfield.
Morocco led 4–0 at half-time and only nine Ethiopia players appeared after
the break. Three more left the field during the first twenty minutes of the
second period.

A cup tie between Ipswich Town and Millwall came close to being
abandoned in September 2000. Millwall were reduced to seven men through
two sendings-off, two injuries and having used all their permitted substitutes.
When another player was injured, the referee explained to Millwall officials
that they must keep a seventh player on the field or the match would end, so
Tim Cahill (Millwall) returned to the field. But a match between Sheffield
United and West Brom was abandoned after 82 minutes when Sheffield
United were reduced to six men (March 2002). United had lost five players –
three sent off and two injured – and had used all three substitutes. The FA let
the result of the match – 3–0 to West Brom – stand.

It is the referee's job to check the number of players on the field, especially
before the place-kicks at the start of each half. If referees discover after, say,

ten minutes, that one side has twelve players, the match can be stopped and restarted with the correct number.

NUMBERS ON SHIRTS *See* SHIRTS

Oo

OBJECTS ON THE PITCH

An old cartoon shows a man in a hospital bed with a dart in his head.

'Tell me, doctor,' says a concerned woman at the bedside, 'Will he ever referee again?'

Sometimes the joke hasn't been funny.

Before the match, referees check the pitch carefully for any objects that might be dangerous to players. During the match, however, all sorts of other items may arrive. The history of missile-throwing is a study of desirable objects in British society – leeks (at a 1944 Wales–England game), British Railways cutlery (at Doncaster in 1956), ball bearings (at Bristol City in 1966), cigarette lighters (at Norwich in 1982), hot dogs (at Oldham in 1999) and mobile phones (at Liverpool in 2005).

Coins have been a continuing presence, toilet rolls plagued goal-nets and pitches in the 1960s and 1970s, and balloons from pre-match festivities littered fields in the 1990s. A dustbin lid was thrown on to the Ilkeston Town pitch during a game but the club acted quickly and taped up all the dustbins (1996).

Assistant referees, goalkeepers and corner-takers are particularly vulnerable. A can hit linesman Colin Cartlich when Leeds United played West Brom (April 1971), and a mobile phone was tossed at an assistant at Queen's Park Rangers (March 1998). A bottle knocked out goalkeeper Pat Jennings (Tottenham Hotspur) at Everton (February 1975), and the same goalkeeper was hit by a dart at Nottingham Forest (December 1979). Gary McAllister (Leeds United) was hit by an object while preparing to take a corner-kick at Birmingham City (February 1996). When Chesterfield played Darlington, there were several stoppages while players cleared the goalmouth of toilet rolls (November 1965).

Under the Football (Offences) Act 1991, throwing an object towards the playing area (or towards other spectators) is an offence unless there is a lawful excuse (with the onus on the accused to prove it). CCTV cameras help prosecutions. A spate of missile-throwing incidents occurred during the 2001–02 season, including several at Tottenham. January 2002 was a particularly bad month: a referee at Cardiff was hit by a coin, a meat pie was thrown at an assistant referee during a Millwall–Birmingham match, Louis Saha (Fulham) faced a storm of coins at Wycombe, and when Robbie Winters (Aberdeen) was hit by an object thrown by a Rangers fan, the referee suspended the match for seventeen minutes while police in riot gear contained the crowd at Aberdeen.

When Luis Figo (Real Madrid) returned to his old club, Barcelona, and prepared to take a corner-kick, he was peppered with objects, including a whisky bottle, billiard balls and a stuffed pig's head (November 2002). The match was suspended for twelve minutes, and Barcelona were later fined.

McFadden (Everton) scored at Plymouth after beating three players and two balloons (January 2005), and an object on the pitch played a part in Derby County's second goal against Nottingham Forest (March 2004). Goalkeeper Barry Roche (Forest) was preparing to kick away a backpass when the ball bounced awkwardly off a discarded plastic coffee-cup. Roche sliced his clearance and Peschisolido scored.

Mateja Kezman (Chelsea) was struck by a bottle against West Ham United (October 2004), and goalkeeper Roy Carroll (Manchester United) was hit by a coin when a number of objects (including a mobile phone) were thrown on to the field at Everton. The referee helped to move Carroll upfield, out of range, and then asked the goalkeeper if he was happy to continue. The game carried on.

In some cases the game has been temporarily or permanently stopped. Each incident is handled according to the situation, and results have been overturned by the authorities. Peterborough were ordered to replay their cup tie with Kingstonian behind closed doors after they beat them 9–1 (December 1992). The Kingstonian goalkeeper went to hospital after having been struck by a coin with the score at 3–0. Peterborough won the rematch 1–0. A match at Borussia Mönchengladbach was replayed after an Inter Milan player was struck by a missile when his team were losing 7–0 (1972), and Celtic and Rapid Vienna were rematched in Manchester after Weinhoffer (Rapid Vienna) had gone down at Celtic Park as if he had been struck by a bottle, and Rapid had used all their substitutes (November 1984). The Burton Albion–Leicester City FA Cup game was replayed behind closed doors after Burton goalkeeper Paul Evans had been hit by a piece of wooden seating (January 1985).

In a match in Italy, the fans of Foggia and Bari were behind their own teams' goals in the first half (1999–2000). After half-time, however, both goalkeepers were in danger of being hit by missiles thrown by opposition fans. The referee solved the problem by asking the two captains if their players would be willing to change ends again, so that the teams would be playing the same way as they had in the first half. This was only possible because there was no wind, no sun, the pitch had no slope, and the captains were willing to co-operate.

When Grimsby Town played Oxford United, fans were given lots of small balls as presents before the match, but during the game spectators threw them back on to the pitch (October 2004). The home club announced that the match would have to be abandoned if the balls kept coming on.

Sometimes it is the players who throw objects. Jamie Carragher (Liverpool) was sent off for violent conduct at Arsenal after throwing a coin back at Arsenal fans (January 2002). A man in the tenth row suffered a cut head, and a female fan was taken away in distress. If a player throws an object at the ball (e.g. a shinguard), the object is considered an extension of the hand and the equivalent of handling the ball.

The referee's action will probably depend on the manner in which the object is thrown. It is probably all right for a player to gently toss a liquid container off the field, but throwing it at a person would be violent conduct. In the 1962–63 League Cup semi-final, Derek Dougan (Aston Villa) threw snowballs at Sunderland supporters who had given him some banter. The referee and the player were able to laugh it off. But if a player throws a stone at another player while the ball is in play, the offender should be sent off and the free-kick taken from where the offender threw the stone (IFAB 1967).

OBSTRUCTION See IMPEDANCE

OFFENSIVE LANGUAGE See ABUSIVE LANGUAGE

OFFSIDE

The offside law has many key points, but what matters is the composite whole of these points. Put together they form a complex algorithm. On the pitch, they present a visual difficulty. Some scientists argue that it is impossible for the human eye to decipher all the relevant factors simultaneously, especially as the ball changes direction nearly 2,000 times in a game. The offside law's interpretation requires fit assistant referees who can react to events that unfold in the blink of a miskick. The best we can hope for is an efficient approximation to offside. When all else fails, the referee's decision is final.

Stated simply, the key points of offside are as follows:

You can be offside if you are in front of the ball, if you have fewer than two defenders (the goalkeeper counts as a defender) between you and the opponents' goal-line, and you are gaining an advantage (or interfering with the play or an opponent) by being in that offside position.

You cannot be offside if you are behind the ball, if you are level with the second-last opponent, or if the ball is last played by an opponent (but you cannot be 'played onside' by an opponent if you were already in an offside position when the ball was last played by a team-mate).

You can be offside if the ball is played to you from a free-kick taken by your team, but you cannot be offside if you receive the ball directly from a goal-kick, corner-kick or throw-in, or if you are in your own half when the ball was played.

You cannot be offside if you are in an offside position but not interfering with play or seeking to gain an advantage.

All these things are assessed at the moment the ball is played by a member of your team.

Some people argue that the offside law shouldn't exist. 'I have often thought about the seventeen laws in the game of football,' said Danny Blanchflower (Tottenham Hotspur) in 1960, 'and the only one I can't find any reason for is the offside law.' Advocates of this position would point to field hockey, where the offside law was abolished in the 1990s. Removing the offside law would certainly take away a major source of controversy. On the other hand it may bring other controversies, in particular judging whether a forward is impeding the goalkeeper. 'No offside' experiments have proved unsuccessful, e.g. the Metropolitan League (1972–73).

Offside probably had its origins in Eton School's 'sneaking' law: 'A player was out of play if only three, or less than three, of the opposite side were before him and the ball behind him.' The term *offside* is from the military expression *off the strength*. A soldier *off the strength* is one not entitled to any pay, rations or privileges until he is placed back *on the strength* by another soldier. Offside, therefore, is short for *off the strength of his side*, meaning a player who has to be brought back into the action by a team-mate.

Offside is football's equivalent of 'loitering with intent'. In public schools, in the mid-1800s, being offside was regarded as unchivalrous and unsports-manlike. At Winchester there was a severe offside rule, whereby the ball had to go backwards, as in rugby. Generally there was some rule to counter sneaking or goal-hanging. The FA had a very strict interpretation of offside for its first three years (1863 to 1866) – any player in front of the ball. The rule was then altered to allow a player to be onside when at least three of his opponents were between him and their goal-line (1866–67).

The original Sheffield FA offside law read as follows: 'Any player between an opponent's goal and goalkeeper (unless he has followed the ball there) is offside and out of play. The goalkeeper is that player on the defending side who, for the time being, is nearest to his own goal.'

In the 1870s, the Sheffield offside law required *two* players goal-side of the attacker rather than the London FA's three. Sheffield conceded this point to London when the rules were standardised (February 1877). Forty-eight years later, in 1925, the offside law was changed back to the Sheffield interpretation – a minimum of two players goal-side rather than three.

In the meantime there were still rule differences. In Scotland, in the 1880s,

Queen's Park favoured the two-man offside rule. They would play the three-man rule if an English team was involved, but they saw it as something that slowed down the game and caused frequent interruptions. When Blackburn Rovers met Queen's Park in 1884 and 1885, there were disputes over the different offside interpretations in Scotland and England.

The administrators quickly found it better to state the exceptions to offside, and that was how it was done in guidance notes for referees (and later became so stated in the laws). In other words, a player in front of the ball is offside when it is played by one of his own team, except in a number of crucial circumstances, one of which was three defenders goal-side of the player.

This requirement – three defenders goal-side of the last attacker – ran into trouble around 1910 when Herbert Morley, a tall, bony full-back at Notts County, started the offside trap. He and his short, tubby partner, Jim Montgomery, discovered that they could strategically run upfield and trap opponents in offside positions rather than wait for opponents to stray. In those days the two full-backs were like central defenders, the half-backs marked wingers, and the centre-half was more of a roving midfield player. Billy McCracken and Frank Hudspeth, full-backs at Newcastle United, developed the offside-trap technique to near perfection, and others followed their example. There were forty free-kicks for offside alone in one Newcastle game at Everton.

The change in the law – from three defenders goal-side to two (1925) – largely stemmed from the appearance of offside traps around the country, but the Scottish FA had been pushing for this change since 1894. There had been experiments with other ideas, including a line restricting offsides to within forty yards of the opponents' goal. In 1925–26, forwards found that they were no longer trapped in a twenty-yard sector near the halfway-line. The change was made to prevent the game being spoiled by too many free-kicks, but one side-effect was a goalscoring increase. On the first day of the new law, Sheffield United scored eleven against Cardiff City, Manchester City hit eleven against Crystal Palace, and Aston Villa ten against Burnley. The goals-per-match average increased from 2.54 (1924–25) to 3.44 (1925–26).

It wasn't long before Billy McCracken, now manager of Hull City, developed a different kind of offside trap. Other managers resorted to trapping forwards, and it was a tactic that lasted until towards the end of the twentieth century (when adaptations to the law made the tactic more risky). When Wimbledon used such a strategy in their 1–0 defeat at Coventry, the home side were trapped offside 22 times (October 1986). A dance routine for male strippers, used in the film *The Full Monty*, mimicked the actions of four Arsenal defenders who synchronised the art of stepping forward and raising their right arms.

From 1990, players were no longer considered offside if they were *level* with the second-last opponent. But what is level? It meant that assistant referees were akin to old-time horse-racing judges, who had to decide the winner without a photo-finish camera. Even worse, the assistant referee was dealing with a moving finishing-line. In 2005, assistant referees were given a new guideline – the position of any part of the player's head, body or feet (the parts used to play football) would be the deciding factor, and not the player's arms.

It is important to remember that 'two defenders' usually (but not always) includes the goalkeeper as one defender. If the goalkeeper is absent, it has to be two other players. Logie (Arsenal) chipped the ball over goalkeeper McIntosh (Sheffield Wednesday), and McPherson (Arsenal), with a defender goal-side of him, headed into the net (1950). The referee at first awarded a goal, but the linesman's flag was up so he changed his mind. Even though there had been a defender on the goal-line, in front of McPherson, the player was still offside because the goalkeeper, usually the last defender, was behind McPherson.

Portsmouth have been involved in at least two incidents of this kind. One was during a play-off semi-final (1992–93). They lost the first leg 1–0, and were winning the second 1–0 when Oldfield (Leicester) diverted a long-range shot into the net. One defender was goal-side of Oldfield but the Portsmouth goalkeeper was not. Portsmouth players ran to the linesman but the goal stood. The assistant referee was much more alert when Higginbottom (Southampton) put the ball into the Portsmouth net from the edge of the goal area (January 2005). The goal was ruled out even though a Pompey defender was on the goal-line. Goalkeeper Chalkias was near the penalty spot after punching the ball to the edge of the penalty area.

One of the many confusing aspects of offside is the proviso that players cannot be offside if the ball was last played (i.e. touched, kicked or thrown) by an opponent (1880). This has caused many a misunderstanding as there are three possible interpretations: (i) players are not offside when they latch on to ill-judged backpasses and misdirected clearances by the defending team (true); (ii) attacking players are not offside if they are in an onside position when a colleague passes the ball but in an offside position when the ball touches a defender on the way through (true); (iii) a player is 'played onside' if the ball touches a defender, even if the player had been in an offside position when a colleague first played the ball (false).

In the 1902 FA Cup Final, Sheffield United led and Southampton scored a late equaliser. Edgar Chadwick (Southampton) broke clear and passed through to Harry Wood, who seemed in an offside position. But the linesman thought that the ball had grazed the shorts of a United defender, so he kept his flag down. The defender later denied that the ball had touched him, and many years later Chadwick concurred that it had been an offside goal.

There were campaigns to clarify this 'played on' issue, and eventually IFAB stated the meaning very clearly: if an attacker is in an offside position when a colleague plays the ball, the attacker is in an offside position per se (1978). Ideally, it needs a quick whistle from the referee, before the ball hits any defenders (providing, of course, none of the other exclusion factors are present).

In a 1997 Inter Milan–Juventus match, the referee initially awarded a goal when Ganz (Inter Milan) converted from an offside position. Ganz received the ball after a heading duel between a player from each team. The assistant referee kept his flag down, thinking the ball had come to Ganz off the head of the defender, so the referee signalled the goal and the assistant showed his agreement by running back towards the halfway-line. Players surrounded the assistant, and the referee went over to sort it out. When he heard the assistant say that the ball had come off the defender last (even though Ganz was in an offside position), the referee was in a quandary because he knew the ball had come off the attacker's head and on to Ganz. As play had not restarted the referee changed his decision to an indirect free-kick to Juventus for offside.

Perhaps the most confusing part of the offside law is the question of whether a player in an offside position is interfering with play, involved with active play, interfering with an opponent, or gaining an advantage. It is not an offence to be in an offside position per se; it is only an offence if the person in an offside position affects the play. Interpretation of this has changed enormously over the years. In April 1971, at the time of a controversial incident at Leeds, players were likely to be judged interfering with play if they were anywhere on the pitch. By 2003, when Roberto Carlos (Real Madrid) scored a goal with three colleagues in offside positions, there was a completely different interpretation. This is an astonishing thirty-year story.

FA Council guidelines made it clear that referees shouldn't award a free-kick simply for seeing a player in an offside position (1910). The player had to be interfering with an opponent or interfering with play. Players were given guidelines in 1922: 'When a player finds that he is in an offside position, it is his duty to keep clear of the play and neither interfere with nor inconvenience an opponent, nor make the pretence of doing so.'

Two years later, the IFAB ruled on this point: 'It is not a breach of the law to be in an offside position, but only when, in that position, he interferes with an opponent, or with the play. If a player who is in an offside position advances towards an opponent, or the ball, and in so doing causes the play to be affected, he should be penalised.'

When Arsenal drew 4–4 with Spurs, Bobby Smith (Spurs) was penalised for offside when he was standing under the crossbar on the other side of the goal from where the ball entered the net (February 1958). Goalkeepers of that era argued that a player in that position was interfering with play because you could see him out of the corner of your eye, and you had to be careful where you pushed the ball if you made a save. A player in an offside position was usually given offside. As a player said, 'If you are on the field and not interfering with play, why bother to get changed?'

Some referees agreed. Their interpretation of a player not interfering with play was one who had gone down injured near the corner-flag. When Frank Lord (Blackburn) hit a late long-range shot into the Rotherham net, a team-mate was given offside (December 1967). Tony Currie (Sheffield United) seemed to have volleyed a superb goal against Stoke City in 1972 but the flag went up for offside against David Staniforth. The same happened in the 1975 European Cup Final when a shot by Peter Lorimer (Leeds United) was ruled out because a team-mate was in an offside position. In a 1976 FA Cup semi-final, David Nish (Derby) deliberately chipped the ball over the Manchester United defenders as they pushed up to play the offside trap. Nish followed up himself and put the ball in the net. But offside was given against another Derby player. All these players felt very aggrieved.

'You can't give him offside, Ref,' shouts one fan. 'He's not interfering with play.'

'He hasn't interfered with play all season,' shouts his mate.

A defining incident came in the Leeds United–West Brom match (April 1971). Hunter (Leeds) tried to pass the ball on the left but Brown (West Brom) intercepted and knocked the ball into space on the West Brom right. Brown saw the linesman's flag go up, but the referee waved play on, ruling that Suggett, moving towards his own goal in an offside position, was not interfering with play. Also, Brown was taking the ball through on his own. He continued in the clear and played it across the goal for Astle to score. In this instance the linesman raised his flag and the referee overruled him, as he was entitled to do. However, the linesman was left out of position when the referee overruled him, and Leeds United players justifiably claimed that Astle was offside when he received Brown's pass. The blame went on the referee rather than Hunter. Other referees might (or might not) have viewed the incident differently, but there should have been no questioning of referee Tinkler's decision, and BBC commentator Barry Davies unwisely said, 'Leeds have every justification for going mad.'

This incident raised a number of issues:

Who should decide if a player is interfering with play – the referee or the linesman?

What happens if an assistant is caught out of position?

Is every player interfering with play or can a player be allowed to return from an offside position?

Slowly, however, more referees allowed players to be in offside positions. Liverpool and West Ham were drawing 0–0 with three minutes of extra-time remaining in a League Cup Final (March 1981). Lee (Liverpool) and Bonds (West Ham) went up for a cross and Lee went down injured in the centre of the goal area. The ball ran loose, and Kennedy (Liverpool) drove his shot over the prostrate Lee, who was in an offside position, and into the net. The linesman flagged but the referee overruled him. He didn't think a player lying down could be interfering with play or seeking to gain an advantage. On the other hand, defenders are always considered to be interfering with play, even if they are obviously injured. John Hendrie (Middlesbrough) was onside when he scored against Wimbledon because Roger Joseph (Wimbledon) was lying injured on the far side of the pitch (November 1992). The linesman raised his flag, saw Joseph, and put the flag down.

In 1983, IFAB agreed that FIFA's Technical Committee should make a major study of the offside law and decide whether it could become less stringent. After a disappointing 1990 FIFA World Cup™, it was seen as important to increase goalscoring opportunities.

Dowie (Southampton) scored a six-yard winner against Luton Town (March 1992). His team-mate Shearer was in an offside position virtually on the goal-line but was adjudged not to be interfering with play (a complete contrast to the Bobby Smith incident of 1958).

By 1995 it was clear that attacking players were more favoured. To be offside, a player had to be (in the referee's opinion) involved *in active play*. This could occur in three ways: (i) interfering with play (playing or touching the ball); (ii) interfering with an opponent (obstructing, deceiving or distracting an opponent), or (iii) gaining an advantage (playing a ball that rebounds off an opponent or the goal-frame).

On the first day of the new season, the impact of the new interpretation was felt. A long pass by Chris Coleman (Crystal Palace) caught his colleague George Ndah running back from an offside position. Opponents Barnsley stopped but Houghton (Crystal Palace) continued and crossed for Iain Dowie to score.

In a 2002–03 Champions League semi-final, Roberto Carlos (Real Madrid) scored against Juventus from near the corner of the penalty area. The goal was allowed even though three Real Madrid players were in offside positions on the edge of the goal area. The referee decided they were not placed directly between goalkeeper Buffon (Juventus) and Carlos. In other words, the goalkeeper's line of sight of the ball was not impeded, and therefore the players were not interfering with active play. Critics of this interpretation point out that the positioning of these players may still enter the goalkeeper's mind, but the spirit of the new interpretation was that the goal would still have been scored even if those players had not been in offside positions. This was a distinctly different interpretation from the Lorimer effort in 1975.

Professional players started looking for ways they could benefit from the new interpretations. Van Nistelrooy (Manchester United) scored a contentious goal against Southampton (January 2004). He was in an offside position when the ball was played in and cleared from the Southampton penalty area. The next time the ball was played in, Van Nistelrooy scored from an onside position. It became a big issue, especially when Bolton equalised against Leicester City from a free-kick (February 2004). Two players were deliberately stationed in offside positions, presumably to distract the defence, and then the kick was directed elsewhere. Assistants learned to hesitate slightly so they could take in the whole situation before raising (or not raising) a flag.

Immediately prior to EURO 2004™, the authorities clarified that 'involved in active play' meant interfering with play, interfering with an opponent or gaining an advantage. An example of a referee upholding this was when Van Nistelrooy (Holland) scored against the Czech Republic in a group match. When the ball was played out to Robben on the left wing, Van Nistelrooy was in an offside position (by about 25 yards) and was deemed not to be interfering with play or gaining an advantage. But Van Nistelrooy was then favourably placed to convert Robben's cross from an onside position. Coaches were left wondering how they could defend against such situations. Defenders criticised an offside law that left them unsure whether an opponent would be offside or not.

In an Olympic women's semi-final, USA's winning goal against Japan came from a free-kick in the 59th minute (2004). Mia Hamm took the kick, Japanese defenders moved up, and three Americans – Lilly, Foudy and Wambach – were in offside positions. But Boxx (USA) was onside. She had timed her run perfectly. Boxx collected the ball and crossed towards the three Americans who had been previously offside. One of them, Wambach, scored.

The interpretation of 'interfering with play' had changed a lot since events at Leeds United in 1971, and so had the way assistants approached their job. In the old days, a linesman would flag if a player was in an offside position and then the referee would decide whether the player was interfering with play. That then slowly changed so that the assistant referee would weigh up all the options. The new interpretation has made life very difficult for assistants, but their flag-waving has a rationale.

A player of the defending side cannot step off the pitch in an attempt to put an attacker offside. When Wolves scored their second goal in the 1960 FA Cup Final, Des Horne (Wolves) looked offside, but McGrath (Blackburn) had stepped behind the goal-line. Referee Kevin Howley pointed towards McGrath to show that the Blackburn player hadn't gone off the field as part of his momentum. He had deliberately stepped off the field of play (which is now a cautionable offence). McGrath followed the referee to the halfway-line in protest but Howley stuck to his decision.

Players cannot be offside if they are in their own half when the ball is played (1907). This is why there are optional flags at the halfway-line (1908). In one game in the early 1970s, Kevin Hector (Derby County) felt he was in his own half when he was played clear. Hector sportingly ran after the ball, jogged back with the ball, and then unsportingly plonked the ball down in his own half, to suggest that the free-kick should be taken from there. He was cautioned.

A player can be offside from a free-kick, but cannot be offside from other restarts – a throw-in (since 1921), a goal-kick, a corner-kick, or (since 1995) a penalty-kick (as players now have to stand behind the ball). There was a period from 1880 to 1921 when players could be offside from a throw-in, but 'no player can be out of play in the case of a corner-kick' (1881). (Sometimes a corner-kick taker is offside when receiving a return pass after a short corner.) Similarly, players receiving the ball from a goal-kick have always been exempt from offside. Unfortunately for goalkeeper Phil Parkes (Queen's Park Rangers) he had drop-kicked the ball out of his hands into the opposition's net when a free-kick for offside was given against a colleague.

Given the outcome of a Conference experiment of 'no offside from free-kicks' (1987–88), the law will not be so changed in the near future. According to A R Hall, in a letter to the *Daily Telegraph* (31 January 1994), 'The result included walls of forwards to unsight the goalkeeper, the defence pushed back to the goal-line. The goalkeeper was marked, and every free-kick blasted into the crowded goalmouth in the hope of a deflection.'

There have been many experiments to find a better offside law – offsides only in the last 18, 30 or 40 yards of the pitch, no offsides from goalkeeper's clearances, no offsides when the ball is *played* from the player's own half of the field, offsides only in the penalty area, and offsides only in the goal area. So far nothing has persuaded IFAB to alter Law 11 radically.

Distinguishing offside is very difficult for referees, even with the help of neutral assistants. One difficult part is defining when a player is interfering with play. The most difficult part for control is deciding who will look for what. The assistant referee is not always in the best position to decide whether an offside player is in direct line of a goalkeeper's sight. The most difficult part visually is deciding exactly where the line of the second defender is at exactly the same time as the ball is played.

In a paper in the *British Medical Journal* (December 2004), Dr Francisco Belda Maruenda argued that a person cannot assess the relative position of two defenders, two attackers and the ball *at the same time*. Maruenda, a specialist in family medicine, established this by applying the response times of the five types of eye movement to the speed of the players' movements. Maruenda's argument is worth further investigation but he takes no account of whether assistants improve with experience, or whether their vision can adapt. Nor does he produce any statistics on how accurate judgments of offside are. If only one in twenty is debatable, is that a reason for introducing video evidence for every one (as he suggests)?

Technology has its own contentious issues when it comes to judging marginal offside decisions. First, it is essential to find the exact frame (or half-frame) when the ball is being kicked or headed. Second, this needs to be precisely matched with the movement of the other players (given that a sprinting player may take a stride every one or two frames). Third, the camera needs to be directly in line with the second-last defender (or there is the complex geometrics of assessing the angle of the line). And fourth, most complex of all, there is the issue of placing the line in the correct position vis-à-vis the most forward relevant part of each attacking player's body, especially as certain key components (e.g. chest and knees) are often off the ground and forward of the natural ground-level line. Cameras really need to be at ground level and in line with the second-last defender to help.

Almost everyone has a false impression. Players, coaches and touchline spectators are all concentrating on other parts of the action when they assess offside issues. A highly controversial incident occurred during a Leeds–Arsenal match (April 1971). In injury-time, with the game goalless, a ball went through to Jack Charlton (Leeds), who scored at the second attempt. Charlton looked well offside. Incensed Arsenal players surrounded the referee, and Charlie George (Arsenal) was cautioned for booting the ball into the stand. Later, when the Arsenal players saw the slow-motion replay, they had to admit that one Arsenal player was slow to come out and Charlton was onside.

A free-kick given for offside is indirect. The referee signals the indirect free-kick with one arm aloft. The assistant, having put up the flag, stands still, indicating where the ball should be placed – by pointing the flag to the sky (to indicate the far side of the pitch), parallel to the ground (to indicate the middle of the pitch), or at the ground (for the near side).

'In line with the lino,' the referee says, or some such choice phrase.

Players and commentators often moan about a 'late flag', but it has become increasingly good practice for an assistant referee to wait to see if the player in an offside position is gaining an advantage. Mellgren (Norway) was in an offside position in the 2005 UEFA Women's Championship Final against Germany when the ball was played long and square some thirty yards behind her. Mellgren turned round and sprinted towards the touchline, and just caught the ball before it went out of play, only to find the assistant now considered her to have gained an advantage. A player can still be offside if the ball is played sideways or backwards, but it takes a few moments to assess all these things. A 'thoughtful flag' or 'considered flag' would be a better phrase than a 'late flag'.

Offside decisions have changed the course of football history on many occasions. But, to quote a referee: 'If you disallowed a goal for offside people would talk about it for three hours; if you allowed a goal that was offside they'd talk about it for ten years.' An example of a long-forgotten decision is when Holland and Belgium drew 0–0 in a qualifier for the 1974 FIFA World Cup™. Verheyen (Belgium) converted Van Himst's free-kick in the last minute only to have it incorrectly disallowed for offside. Belgium failed to qualify despite winning four and drawing two of their six matches with a goals record of 12–0. Holland went on to reach the 1974 FIFA World Cup™ Final.

ORIGINS OF THE LAWS

Football in the Middle Ages was an unruly festival of the kind preserved today with annual games in the Orkneys and Ashbourne. Wherever the ball went, the mob followed.

The written laws have their roots in the English public schools of the early 1800s. Boarding schools needed a sport like soccer to fill the boys' time, keep them active and maintain the school's values. This was the era of muscular Christianity, when a healthy body meant a healthy mind, and a healthy mind meant good discipline, self-control, perseverance, courage, manliness and teamwork.

Association football brought an esprit de corps that was well suited to the spirit of war. In terms of the value system, it was not far from Charterhouse to the Crimea, or from Uppingham to Afghanistan. Until the Boer War, wars were fought around gentlemanly principles and a certain morality. You learned to take knocks like a man and you didn't cheat. An army team, the Royal Engineers, were FA Cup finalists in four of the first seven seasons (1872 to 1878).

The rules of soccer differed from school to school. Sometimes the rules were designed to fit the particular environment – at Winchester, for example, six-a-side was very convenient for an enclosure 80yd by 25yd – but when boys arrived at university, equipped with different sets of rules, there was a need for standardisation. Embryonic clubs grew up at Cambridge in 1846 and 1848, but they did not survive for long (and neither have copies of the rules). There were further attempts to reduce the various school rules to one workable code, but it was not until 1863 that some consensus was achieved. John D Cartwright pleaded for uniformity, and Rev R Burn chaired a committee at Cambridge. The outcome was the Cambridge rules.

When the Football Association was formed in 1863, they had to resolve a number of rule issues. For instance, there were at least four ways of starting a game – a place-kick from halfway, a place-kick from quarter-distance, a throw-up in the centre, and rolling the ball down the centre between two lines. Other issues that needed resolving were the length and breadth of the ground, the width and height of posts, crossbar or tape, offside, what to do when the ball went over the boundary lines, hand-play, hacking, tripping, mauling, packs, rouges, running with the ball, the fair catch, how to settle disputes, boots, throwing the ball, knocking-on, etc. When the FA laws were finalised, without hand-play and hacking, on 8 December 1863, Blackheath left the association and took up rugby. Two games – soccer and rugger – were then spread around the world. In Canada, in the 1870s, it was a matter of chance whether rugby union or association football rules were used. It depended on ground conditions and the desires of the players at the time.

In Britain, rules were taken around the country by the clergy, school-teachers, and factory executives, all of whom looked for safe ways to promote Christianity and controlled aggression. Some places, like London and Sheffield, had a head start. A club had been formed in Sheffield by ex-Harrovians (1857), and like most landmark clubs it was hosting games between its members – Smokers versus Nonsmokers, Bachelors versus Married Men, A–L versus M–Z. In 1876 about 700 individuals were playing football in the Sheffield environment every Saturday, and copies of the rules had been sent to many countries, including China, India, New Zealand and Fiji.

There were also rule developments in Scotland. In 1867 the only club in Scotland was Queen's Park, but a handful of others formed in the next five years. Even in 1884 and 1885, however, when Queen's Park reached the FA Cup Final, there were still differing rules. In fact, that probably contributed to Queen's Park's defeat in 1884.

The London and Sheffield associations resolved their differences in April 1877. Sheffield-area members conceded to throw-ins, the three-player offside rule, the 8ft-high goal (rather than 9ft) and only eleven players in a team, while London accepted the crossbar (rather than tape), the corner-kick, and an indirect free-kick for handling the ball.

OUT OF PLAY

In 1966 a Football League observer found that during a ninety-minute match the ball was *out of play* for 38 minutes 13 seconds. A stopwatch on the 1984 Skol Cup Final – Rangers versus Dundee United – showed that the ball was *in play* for only 56 minutes 39 seconds.

The ball is dead when the referee has blown the whistle to stop play, or the ball has passed over the touchline or goal-line and the players are awaiting a restart. Typically the ball is out of play for nearly half a match and a lot of things can still happen during that time. When Crystal Palace met Everton,

Mel Blyth (Crystal Palace) was sent off for elbowing an Everton player in the face as he waited to defend a free-kick (November 1972). The incident took place in the penalty area, so Everton players appealed for a penalty-kick. However, the ball was dead.

The ball can be out of play, and so can a player. If a player is over the touchline (or the goal-line) and is tackled recklessly, it is not a free-kick. The laws do not allow for taking a free-kick from a position off the pitch. The offending player can still be cautioned, though.

When Preston won a penalty-kick at home to Burnley, the visitors' manager, Steve Cotterill, claimed that Eddie Lewis (Preston) was off the pitch when challenged by Lee Roche (February 2005). The referee decided otherwise.

OUTSIDE AGENTS

Hilary Kerr had a plan for when Queen of the South played Berwick Rangers in March 2002. The 22-year-old redhead went to watch her local team wearing black hot pants and a full-length zip-up coat. When play stopped for a free-kick, in the 71st minute, she took off the coat, climbed over a barrier and sprinted on to the field wearing only the hot pants. Chased by a steward, she ran diagonally across the midfield of Palmerston Park, her long red hair flowing behind her, passing several players who stood with their hands on their hips. The steward caught up with her at the far side of the pitch and covered her with a jacket.

In football parlance, Hilary Kerr was an outside agent, which is anything that enters the field of play without the permission of the referee and plays or misdirects the ball or otherwise interferes with the game. Outside agents are different from pre-existing conditions, such as trees. Outside agents include birds, bees, animals, streakers, spectators, ball boys, mascots, photographers and team officials.

If the ball is in play when an outside agent appears, the referee will most likely blow the whistle to stop play and then recommence with a dropped ball. The only exception (since 2005) is when the outside agent is a named substitute. Then the substitute's team concedes an indirect free-kick.

A 1989 Welsh Cup second-round match between Brecon Sports and Miskin Manor was interrupted by a swarm of bees. A goalkeeper in a game in Staffordshire was once put off his game by a confused jackdaw, which continually flapped around him and tried to settle on his head. In a game in Holland in the 1980s, a high kick from the Feyenoord goalkeeper hit a pigeon, which fell dead on to the field.

Referees should never work with animals. During the 1946 FA Cup Final, the referee stopped play as soon as he saw a dog on the field. John Oakes

(Charlton Athletic) made friends with the dog, stroked it and led it away by the collar; but Oakes had less luck with his opponent, Jack Stamps (Derby County), who scored two goals in Derby's 4–1 victory.

Jimmy Greaves (England) went down on his knees to tame and catch a dog during a match against Brazil (June 1962), and goalkeeper Gordon Banks (Leicester) dived and grabbed a dog by the body (January 1966). This is not to be recommended, even for international goalkeepers.

The most definitive dog incident came when Brentford goalkeeper Chic Brodie was seriously injured when playing against Colchester United (November 1970). A stray mutt ran full pelt into Brodie as he collected the ball, and Brodie suffered career-ending ligament damage to his left knee. The moral of this story is simple – referees should stop play as soon as they see a dog on the pitch, because dogs chase balls. Play restarts with a dropped ball.

There are plenty of other 'beware of the dog' tales. An Aldershot–Brentford match was stopped when a small dog grabbed a linesman's flag and ran off with it (October 1955). Tom Dimnock (Blackpool Nomads) had to be taken to hospital when he was bitten by an Alsatian after clearing the ball from the goal-line (December 1957). The start of a Bristol Rovers–Workington match was delayed for three minutes while officials rounded up a dog (November 1964). Jim McNichol (Torquay United) was bitten by a police dog during a vital game against Crewe Alexandra (May 1987). And a mongrel dashed on to the field and foiled a goalscoring opportunity by knocking the ball away from a Gwynfi striker in a game against Treowen (February 1998).

A dog once ran on to the pitch during a game involving twelve-year-olds. The dog annoyed one of the players by snapping at his heels when he had the ball, and the player reacted by kicking the dog. The dog's owner ran on to the pitch and started hitting the boy. A free-for-all followed, and the referee abandoned the match.

Other species have made guest appearances. A black cat raced down the wing at Hibernian (October 1999), a chicken was let out on to the Arsenal pitch (mid-1970s), a fox appeared during a Rangers–Celtic game (November 1996), a squirrel disturbed Arsenal and Villareal for ten minutes (April 2006), a Burton Albion player claimed he saw mice on the Old Trafford pitch (January 2006), and farm animals have occasionally strayed from nearby fields.

There are fewer excuses for people on the pitch. In the 1966 FA Cup Final, an Everton supporter, Eddie Cavanagh, ran on to Wembley after an Everton equaliser. The match was suspended for a few minutes as police chased him around the pitch.

A spectator ran on to the Leyton Orient pitch, picked up the ball and kicked it into the Hull City goal (January 1973). If a spectator comes on while the ball is in play, and tries and fails to stop the ball going into the net, a goal should be awarded if the incident hasn't interfered with any players (FIFA Referees' Committee 1951).

After mass invasions in the 1980s, there were suggestions of electric fences and birching offenders in front of a match-day crowd, but more civilised penalties were drafted in the Football (Offences) Act for England and Wales 1991. It became an offence for a person to enter the playing area, or any area to which spectators are not generally admitted (e.g. the technical area) without a lawful excuse (which had to be proved by the intruder). The Football (Offences and Disorder) Act 1999 covered the procedures for dealing with these offences. Some grounds have signs: 'It is a criminal offence to encroach on the pitch'.

A spectator received a five-month prison sentence after he went on to the Burnley pitch and threatened a Blackburn Rovers player (February 2005). In many leagues there are ground requirements designed to keep people back from the touchline, thus preventing more stories of spectators tripping wingers with umbrellas or putting corner-kick takers in arm-locks.

Streakers in England and Wales are liable to the same prosecutions as any other invading spectator. In addition they may be prosecuted for indecency or exhibitionism. When Dunstable Town played AFC Wimbledon, a naked streaker ran the length of the pitch and jumped into a goalkeeper's arms before being led off the pitch wearing only a pair of handcuffs (October 2004).

Another problem arises if players take matters into their own hands – it is a sending-off offence to kick or strike a spectator. The Barnet goalkeeper should possibly have been sent off when he kicked a streaker during a match against Torquay (May 2001). So might Ian Walker (Leicester) when he pushed away an abusive spectator during his team's 5–0 home defeat against Aston Villa (January 2004). The fan, who was banned for life, said he had no idea what he was doing. One moment he was in the crowd, the next he was approaching Walker, asking the question that was on the lips of all committed Leicester fans: 'What's happening?'

The most complex case occurred when a male streaker ran on to the Altrincham ground to interrupt a Unibond Cheshire Senior Cup Final (March 2004). It was a corner-kick to Witton Albion when the streaker appeared. He ran around the pitch for several seconds while the players watched. One of them, Brian Pritchard (Witton Albion), an off-duty policeman, tripped up the streaker and apprehended him. Pritchard was then sent off by the referee for violent conduct. The score was 0–0 at the time, and opponents Woodley Sports went on to win 2–1 in extra-time. Pritchard's appeal for wrongful dismissal was upheld by an FA disciplinary commission and the red card rescinded.

Spectators sometimes stop a ball from going out of play. The correct decision is a dropped ball at the point the spectator interferes, even if a spectator stops a certain goal by clearing from the goal-line. However, if a penalty-kick hits a spectator the kick should be retaken.

Ball boys and photographers have also interfered. In one professional match in the 1950s, a photographer was so close to the touchline that he kept the ball in play with his leg at one point of the match. And ball boys have collected the ball *on the pitch*. When Crystal Palace played Oldham Athletic, the ball spun back into play but the ball boy caught it anyway (December 2002), and at York City a ball boy picked up a ball that ran along the goal-line (January 2005). In these cases the referee blew his whistle and restarted with a dropped ball.

Perhaps the most disturbing case of outside influence came in Alicante, Spain (December 1924). The ball hit a live electric wire, which broke and fell on to the pitch. The player who attempted to remove the wire died through electrocution.

OVER THE LINE

The *whole* of the ball must be over the *whole* of the line before the ball is out of play or a goal is scored. On referees' courses, tutors usually set up an exercise asking their trainees to view a ball on the touchline from some distance infield.

'Tell me when it's over the line,' the tutor says, shifting the ball a little at a time.

Most budding referees call too soon. But they soon learn to judge the position of a rolling ball.

An early clause in the laws catered for the ball being out of play either on the ground or *in the air* (1888). 'Prior to this it was no uncommon occurrence from a corner-kick when the wind blew towards the field of play, to see the ball kicked fifteen or twenty yards behind the goal-line only to be blown back in front of goal before touching the ground,' said Jackson. Assistant referees now station themselves near the corner-flag at corner-kicks, to see if the ball swerves out of play while it is in the air. If it does, it is a goal-kick.

Much has been made of the need for technology to judge goal-line incidents between the goalposts (see the entry on goal-line technology) but there is an argument to say that judging the rest of the goal-line is just as important.

Controversial incidents swung two FIFA World Cup™ quarter-finals in extra-time – a disallowed goal by Morientes (Spain) against South Korea (June 2002) and Uruguay's winner against the Soviet Union (June 1970).

The first use of photographic evidence came after the 1932 FA Cup Final.

A Newcastle United player centred the ball from over the line, and a colleague scored against Arsenal. Photographs taken from along the goal-line caused this to be known as the 'Over-the-line Final'. History repeated itself in a match between the same two teams years later. Arsenal defenders thought that the ball was over the goal-line before goalkeeper Bob Wilson (Arsenal) touched it (January 1969). But the referee awarded a corner-kick and Newcastle scored in injury-time from the corner.

OVER-THE-TOP TACKLE

Professional footballers probably despise an over-the-top tackle more than any other kind of foul. The classic incident is where the victim kicks the ball as an opponent goes in with one foot over the ball, studs first, and catches the player's extended leg halfway up the shin. It is a potentially leg-breaking, knee-damaging tackle. It should be an automatic sending-off.

Early in the 1965 FA Cup Final, Bobby Collins (Leeds United) was well over the ball when he went into the thigh of Gerry Byrne (Liverpool), who suffered a broken collarbone in the collision. Collins himself was the victim a few months later when his thigh bone was broken by a high challenge from a Torino player.

After three minutes of an FA Cup replay, a lunge from Kevin Muscat (Wolves) seriously injured Matty Holmes (Charlton) in February 1998. Eleven Charlton players and 25 other witnesses were willing to testify that the tackle was 'over the top' but the case for damages was settled out of court. The fact that Muscat was not issued with a card added weight to the argument often advanced by players that referees could do more to recognise the worst kind of tackles.

Pp

PENALTY-AREA ARC

The penalty-area arc was added to the pitch markings in 1937. The arc is drawn at a ten-yard radius from the penalty mark and helps the judging of encroachment at penalty-kicks.

The encroachment distance at other free-kicks was increased from six to ten yards in 1913 but the penalty-kick was initially excluded from this change. In 1923, the FA noted that some teams unsportingly defended penalty-kicks by forming a solid ten-man phalanx on the edge of the area, thus restricting the run-up of the penalty-taker.

Even when the distance of players from the ball at penalty-kicks was increased to ten yards (1929), there was still a tendency for players to stand outside the penalty area but not far enough from the ball. Most penalty-takers took a short run, but some, like Eric Houghton (Aston Villa), needed a longer run-up. It was as hard getting people the correct distance from the ball for penalty-kicks then as it is now for free-kicks just outside the penalty area.

Herbert Chapman, the Arsenal manager, claimed to have seen the penalty arc in Europe as early as 1930. FA Council members saw the arc when the England team toured Switzerland and Italy (May 1933).

PENALTY AREA

The first concept of a penalty area arrived in 1891 when the penalty-kick was introduced. That penalty area encompassed the area bordered by the goal-line, the two touchlines and the penalty line, which ran across the whole width of the pitch, parallel to the goal-line twelve yards out. A short eighteen-yard line was introduced to assist the referee in encroachment decisions at penalty-kicks.

The term *penalty area* was first coined when radical changes were made to pitch markings (1902): 'Lines shall be marked eighteen yards from each goalpost at right angles to the goal-lines for a distance of eighteen yards and these shall be connected with each other by a line parallel to the goal-lines; the space within these lines shall be the penalty area.'

There has been some confusion over the years concerning whether the eighteen-yard measurements along the goal-line were from the inside or the outside of the goalposts. The laws eventually showed that the measurements were 'from the inside of the goalpost' (1997). The pitch markings are included in the penalty area, so the 44-yard total width includes the two five-inch lines.

The penalty area now serves a number of unconnected purposes: it represents an area where the goalkeepers are allowed to handle the ball; it is an area where direct free-kicks against the defending team must be upgraded to a penalty-kick; together with the penalty arc, it marks the encroachment boundary when a penalty-kick is about to be taken; it is an area opponents must avoid when a goal-kick or a defensive free-kick is being taken from within it; and it is an area that goal-kicks and defenders' free-kicks from within it must clear before the ball is in play again.

PENALTY GOAL

For the 1880–81 season, on the instigation of Mr J H Cofield of the Birmingham Association, the FA adopted a suggestion to give the referee power 'to award a goal in any case, where in his opinion, a score had been prevented through the wilful handling of the ball by one of the defending side'. This was withdrawn after a season's trial. It was felt that it gave the referee too much power, bearing in mind that the 1881 referee was making these judgments from a position off the field around the halfway-line.

PENALTY-KICK

The penalty-kick is one of football's most sensational and engaging rituals. It seems such a simple concept and so easy to replicate – one on one in the schoolyard – but it can be very complicated.

The penalty-kick is credited to William McCrum, a Milford Everton goalkeeper who worked in the family linen business in Armagh. McCrum persuaded the Irish FA to propose a 'penalty' law to IFAB (1890). The idea was turned down because a law recognising serious infringement within twelve yards of goal admitted the existence of ungentlemanly play. An event the following season changed their minds.

Notts County led Stoke 1–0 in the last seconds of an FA Cup quarter-final (February 1891). Then Hendry (Notts County) fisted out a Stoke shot with his goalkeeper beaten. Stoke were awarded an indirect free-kick, the maximum punishment of the day, and the ball was scrambled away. Notts County won 1–0 and eventually reached the FA Cup Final. Hendry's actions were obviously not in the spirit of the game.

In 1891 the English FA supported the Irish FA's penalty-kick idea, and the following law was introduced:

If any player shall intentionally trip or hold an opposing player, or deliberately handle the ball, within twelve yards of his own goal-line, the referee shall, on appeal, award the opposing side a penalty-kick, to be taken from any point twelve yards from the goal-line, under the following conditions: All players with the exception of the player taking the penalty-kick and the opposing goalkeeper (who shall not advance more than six yards from the goal-line) shall stand at least six yards from the ball.

A line (the penalty line) was drawn across the pitch twelve yards from goal.

The first official penalty-kick was scored by Alex McColl (Renton) at Leith. This was the first time that the rules allowed for a goal to be scored directly from any free-kick.

Some people remained staunch opponents of the new law. Pa Jackson argued that it permitted unsportsmanlike defenders to take part in the game. The organisers of the Arthur Dunn Cup, a competition for public-school old boys' teams, refused to adopt the penalty-kick (until rebuked by the FA). For many years the goalkeeper of one top amateur team, the Corinthians, would stand by his post to allow an easy goal from a penalty-kick. The true Corinthians felt that if one of their players was unsporting enough to concede a penalty then the team deserved to concede a goal. In 1937 the law was changed to ensure that the goalkeeper stood between the posts.

The penalty-kick process begins with an offence. In 1902, when the penalty area was introduced, a penalty could be given for any of seven intentional offences within the area: tripping; charging from behind; pushing; kicking; jumping at; holding an opponent; and handling the ball.

A hundred years later, a penalty-kick could be awarded for any of ten offences. Six of these are offences if the referee considers them to be done in a manner which is careless, reckless or using excessive force: kicking or attempting to kick an opponent; tripping or attempting to trip an opponent; jumping at an opponent; charging an opponent; striking or attempting to strike an opponent; and pushing an opponent. The other four offences are: making contact with an opponent before touching the ball in the act of tackling an opponent; holding an opponent; spitting at an opponent (if the spitter is inside the area); and deliberate handball (except for the defending goalkeeper).

China were awarded a penalty-kick against Iraq even though the ball was in the middle of the pitch (July 2004). Goalkeeper Ahmed Ali Jaber (Iraq) was seen head-butting a China player in the penalty area. The goalkeeper was sent off and play was delayed until Iraq had substituted a goalkeeper for an outfield player. A penalty-kick can be awarded irrespective of the position of the ball, if it is in play, at the time of the incident (IFAB 1924).

There should be no discrimination between offences on the halfway-line that merit a direct free-kick and those in the penalty area that result in a penalty, as shown by the penalty given when Frontzeck (Manchester City) threw an arm around Cantona (Manchester United) as the players went for a United corner-kick (February 1996). Some referees think that it needs to be a clear foul in the box as so much is at stake. Said one referee: 'I say to my assistants, "If you think it's a penalty-kick, don't flag. If you know it's a penalty, flag. If you have to think about it, it isn't." ' When awarding a penalty-kick, referees blow the whistle and point to the penalty mark.

Most penalty-kicks are scored. In 1931–32, 64.6 per cent of Football League penalties were converted. Two seasons later the success rate had increased to 72.2 per cent. Evans and Bellion, in *The Art of Refereeing*, work on a 94 per cent success rate in all classes of football.

The chance of a goal from a twenty-yard free-kick is much lower. One potentially contentious issue, therefore, is whether the foul is inside or outside the penalty area. In the last minute of extra-time, during the 1938 FA Cup Final, Alf Young (Huddersfield) brought down George Mutch (Preston) on the edge of the penalty area. Young always protested that the tackle had taken place outside the area and Mutch had rolled forward. Mutch scored from the penalty and Preston won 1–0.

In the 1978 League Cup Final replay, John O'Hare (Nottingham Forest) accelerated towards the penalty area, only to be brought down by Phil Thompson (Liverpool). The incident began outside the area and finished inside the area. The referee glanced towards his linesman, who stood with his flag across his chest to indicate he thought it was inside the area. John Robertson scored the only goal of the game from the kick.

In the 1994 FA Cup Final, Frank Sinclair (Chelsea) challenged Andrei Kanchelskis (Manchester United) outside the penalty area and the two players battled on until they were inside the area. When Kanchelskis went to ground, the referee gave a penalty-kick. People watching video evidence later 'agreed' that it should have been a free-kick outside the area, a penalty (after advantage had been played), a penalty (after no foul outside the area) or 'play on'.

When Brazil met Turkey in the group stages of the 2002 FIFA World Cup™, the referee saw Alpay (Turkey) holding Rivaldo (Brazil) as the two players approached the penalty area. The referee allowed the advantage and then Alpay held Rivaldo's shirt inside the penalty area as well. The referee gave a penalty-kick, from which the winning goal was scored.

Last-minute penalty-kick decisions are particularly troublesome because they will be remembered more than most. Participants are tired, concentration may wane, and all sorts of things can go wrong. A contentious penalty at the end of extra-time decided a cup-tie replay between Chelsea and Leicester City (February 1997). Video replays suggested that Johnsen

(Chelsea) had fallen to the ground after running into a Leicester defender who was trying to avoid him. Referees are usually aware that strikers will be looking for penalties late in a game.

Penalty-kicks provoke some of soccer's most heated moments, and that is particularly true of last-minute awards. Norwich City lost 4–3 at Arsenal after leading 2–0 (November 1989). Arsenal's injury-time penalty winner was the catalyst for some disgraceful scenes, as a result of which both clubs were heavily fined.

If a penalty-kick is awarded and stoppage-time is completed, time can be extended for the penalty-kick to be taken. This judgment came about after an incident two minutes from the end of a match at Aston Villa (1891–92). Stoke were a goal behind when they were awarded a penalty-kick. The Villa goalkeeper picked up the ball and kicked it out of the ground. While the ball was being returned, the referee blew his whistle to signal the end of the match, so the penalty-kick was never taken.

The half can be extended, but only until the penalty-kick incident is over. This is when the goalkeeper has made a clear save, when the ball rebounds from the woodwork or when the ball passes fully over the goal-line (even if via the goalkeeper, woodwork or a combination of the two) (FIFA Referees' Committee 1934, IFAB 1956). If the ball touches the goalkeeper before passing between the posts, when a penalty-kick is being taken at the expiry of time, a goal is scored (IFAB 1901). Another possible outcome was the shot hitting the post and immediately rebounding into the net off the goalkeeper. This is also considered to be a goal (IFAB 1987). The spirit of this clause is to allow a goal if the ball enters the net as a direct outcome of the kicker taking the shot.

At Easter 1960, Tottenham Hotspur were well placed to win the League. Playing at home against Manchester City, they were awarded a penalty-kick on the stroke of half-time. Time was added on for the kick to be taken. Cliff Jones shot and Manchester City goalkeeper Bert Trautmann dived to parry the ball. Jones followed up and put the rebound into the net, celebrating what he thought was a goal. But the referee had extended play solely for the taking of the penalty-kick. The first half had ended with Trautmann's save and no goal was allowed. Spurs lost 1–0 and missed the League Championship by two points.

Under normal penalty procedure, the referee's first question is, 'Who's taking the penalty?' Sometimes the players don't know themselves. Sheffield United entertained Walsall in the last match of the 1980–81 season. A draw would relegate Walsall, but a Walsall victory would relegate Sheffield United. Walsall led 1–0 when United were awarded a last-minute penalty-kick. United's normal penalty-taker did not want to take the kick. There was some discussion before Don Givens stepped up and missed the penalty.

On Boxing Day 1924, Nottingham Forest were a goal down to Bolton Wanderers when they were awarded a penalty. Their penalty-king, Harry Martin, had been carried off the field injured and no one else wanted to take the kick. Forest captain Bob Wallace sprinted to the dressing-room and Martin was carried back on to the field (this was in the days before substitutes). He could only take the kick from a standing position, but scored with his one good leg. Referees have to decide how long they can wait.

The match between Birmingham and Chelsea was a dire relegation struggle (April 1939). A Birmingham win would send Chelsea down. Anything else would send Birmingham down. When Birmingham were awarded a penalty, no player wanted the responsibility of taking the kick. Half a minute passed. Eventually Dearson emerged from the conference of players to take the kick and, inevitably, he shot over the crossbar. Birmingham drew 1–1 and were relegated.

Sometimes players fight to take the kick. It took ninety seconds for West Ham to take a penalty at Bradford City (February 2000). Lampard (West Ham) collected the ball expecting to take the kick. He placed the ball on the spot but Di Canio (West Ham) picked it up again and the two players argued. Lomas (West Ham) arrived with a third opinion. Eventually Di Canio prepared to take the kick but there was a further delay while the referee sorted out some jostling at the edge of the penalty area. Finally, Di Canio scored.

At Huddersfield, in 1958–59, one home-team player placed the ball on the spot and then another (Les Massie) came out of a ruck of players to score from the penalty. Goalkeeper Don Leeson (Barnsley) complained that he didn't know who was taking the kick. He had a point. From 1986, the written laws confirmed something that referees had known for a long time – the penalty-kick taker had to be *properly identified* to the referee and the goalkeeper. The referee can then tell the taker, 'Wait for my whistle.'

In 1926 Portsmouth's Willie Haines infuriated Reading players by placing the ball on the penalty spot and kicking it into the net without a preliminary run, taking the goalkeeper completely by surprise. A similar ploy was used by others, including a Cheltenham Town player, as described by the *Gloucestershire Echo* (7 October 1939): 'When a Hereford man handled and the Town were awarded a penalty-kick, Brain scored with the craftiest shot imaginable. He took no run, but half-turned as he stood over the ball and then whipped it hard into goal.' After World War II, the penalty-kick became a 'wait for the whistle' ceremonial kick with everyone out of the penalty area (IFAB 1956). Against Australia, Trevor Francis (England) scored from a penalty but had to retake it because the referee had not blown his whistle (June 1983). Francis put the retake over the crossbar.

A penalty-kick must be taken with the ball on the mark and stationary. This can be a problem on windy days. One dramatic penalty occurred in the

75th minute of the 1936 England–Scotland match at Wembley. England led 1–0 when Tommy Walker (Scotland) placed the ball on the mark and stepped back to take the kick. But the wind blew the ball away before Walker could take the penalty. He tried a second time but again the wind blew the ball off its mark. At the third attempt, Walker took a short run and shot the equaliser.

Football can replicate itself in strange ways. Sixty years after Walker's dilemma with the wind, another England–Scotland match was blighted by a similar problem. England led their EURO 1996™ group match 1–0 after 76 minutes when Scotland were awarded a penalty. As McAllister (Scotland) ran up to take the kick, the ball rolled slightly away from the spot. McAllister kicked the moving ball and goalkeeper Seaman (England) saved the kick. It was almost impossible for the referee to notice the movement.

One of the most difficult issues to assess is the matter of encroachment at a penalty-kick. Players are encroaching if they are inside the penalty area or penalty arc when the ball is kicked. The referee's decision will depend on the outcome of the kick, and which team's players are encroaching.

Bristol Rovers drew 0–0 with Fulham (September 1958). Jim Langley (Fulham) scored from a penalty but the referee ruled that a Fulham player had encroached before the kick had been taken. The kick had to be retaken and Langley hit the post. Had Langley missed his first kick, the referee would not have ordered the kick to be retaken. Had players from both sides been inside the area then it would have been retaken whatever the outcome of the kick. Had an attacking player encroached and the ball hit the post, an indirect free-kick would have been given against the attacking team (IFAB 1956).

Television replays began to suggest that encroachment was a low priority for referees in the mid-1990s. For instance, players of both teams were in the area when Parker (Leicester City) equalised in a play-off final against Crystal Palace (May 1996) and when McAllister (Scotland) missed against England in (June 1996).

In 1997 the law was changed so that players encroaching at a penalty need not be cautioned. The encroachment issue had returned to the agenda. Suker (Croatia) had to retake a penalty against Romania (June 1998). He scored with both attempts.

In 2003, IFAB pointed out that referees needed to be stricter on encroachment and goalkeepers moving off the line. Referees took this to heart, and Yakubu (Portsmouth) took a penalty three times against Norwich City (January 2005). Portsmouth players encroached when Yakubu scored with his first two attempts. He scored with the third, too. It was a throwback to the days of Ronnie Rooke (Arsenal), who had once slammed a right-footed penalty into the net only to be told to retake it. Rooke hit his second attempt left-footed into the other corner only to be told to retake it again. He turned to the referee in frustration: 'Look, Ref, throw the ball up and I'll head the next one in.'

Referees and their assistants probably pay more attention to the goalkeeper's position than encroachment. In the penalty-kick's early years (1891 to 1905), goalkeepers were allowed to advance up to six yards, to the edge of their goal area. Some goalkeepers rushed out so quickly that they looked like reaching the ball before the kicker. When 21-stone goalkeeper Willie Foulke came out to narrow the angle, he made the ground shake and the stadium darken. Foulke saved two penalties from the same player at Burton United one day, and the penalty-taker answered criticism by saying, 'Of course I shot straight at the goalkeeper, there was no room either side.'

Two Manchester City players, Billy Meredith and Tom Hynds, practised chipping the ball over a goalkeeper's head. At Lincoln, in a 1905 FA Cup match, Meredith 'simply put his foot under the ball, and lifted it over the head of Buist, who was absolutely helpless'. Later that year, the law was changed so that goalkeepers could not advance beyond the goal-line (1905).

In the 1922 FA Cup Final, Preston North End players were incensed at the award of a penalty-kick when Billy Smith (Huddersfield Town) was brought down on the edge of the penalty area. They thought the tackle was outside the area. Goalkeeper Jim Mitchell, facing Smith, 'jumped up, down and along his goal-line and even advanced from it like an excited monkey on a stick awaiting the offer of a bag of peanuts'. Smith scored anyway, and Huddersfield won 1–0. Mitchell's antics, and those of Cardiff City goalkeeper Tom Farquharson, who stood inside his goal and advanced to the goal-line as the penalty-taker stepped forward, were considered undignified.

In 1929, the law was amended so that goalkeepers had to stand on the line until the ball was kicked, and *stand* meant not moving their feet (IFAB 1930). This change introduced much controversy. It is difficult for a referee – or linesman – to have one eye on the ball and the other on a goalkeeper's feet while a penalty-kick is being taken. An unsuccessful penalty-kick was to be retaken if a goalkeeper moved his feet before the ball was kicked. (The rule was rescinded in 1997, after which goalkeepers could move their feet, but had to stay on the goal-line until the ball had been kicked.)

The referee and linesmen liaise before the kick-off to decide who watches the goalkeeper's feet and who watches for encroachments. Paul Crichton (Doncaster Rovers) saved the same penalty three times (September 1990). He saved the first two attempts, from O'Shaughnessy (Rochdale), but was ruled to have moved too soon each time. Goodison (Rochdale) took the third kick and Crichton saved again. There was no fourth attempt for Rochdale.

In the 1984 European Cup Final penalty shoot-out, Liverpool goalkeeper Bruce Grobbelaar distracted takers by wobbling his knees, waving his arms like a windmill and puffing out his cheeks, while all the time keeping his feet still. He even bit the goal-net to perfect the image of craziness. Conti (Roma) and Graziani (Roma) shot over the bar, and Liverpool won. But referees are advised to be particularly vigilant for 'instances of gamesmanship'. Twenty-one years after Grobbelaar's wobbly-knees act, another Liverpool goalkeeper, Jerzy Dudek, performed similar heroics in a UEFA Champions League Final shoot-out when he was, according to Grobbelaar, 'like a starfish with jelly legs' (May 2005).

A team can change its penalty-taker for a retake, as long as the referee and goalkeeper are informed. Some teams have to change their taker. Having opted to take a penalty against Charlton Athletic, Dixie McNeill (Wrexham) grew so frustrated by the opposition's delaying tactics that he kicked the ball into the crowd and was sent off for his second caution, so Vinter took the kick (January 1980). Alan Webber (Crescent) wrecked his cartilage when approaching the penalty spot during a 1973 Devon & Exeter League match.

In a game against Portsmouth, three Notts County players – Kevin Randall, Don Masson and Brian Stubbs – all missed the same penalty (September 1973). The kick had to be retaken twice and each time a different player opted to take it.

Similarly, it is possible to change goalkeepers. In 1912, Glossop goalkeeper Butler saved a Chelsea penalty but was deemed to have moved off his line before the ball was kicked. Butler protested so much that he was sent off. Another player took his place in goal.

After Manchester United had conceded a penalty to Leicester City, goalkeeper Fabien Barthez (United) leaned against a goalpost, his back to play, picking dirt off his boot (November 2001). The referee blew his whistle and Muzzy Izzet (Leicester) rolled the ball into the empty net. The referee awarded a retake as he hadn't seen that Barthez was not *between the posts* (as required by Law 14). Barthez walked the ball back to Izzet and then saved the retake. What is odd is that the 'between the posts' phrase had been introduced in 1937 to ensure that the true amateurs defended their goal, and here was Barthez being ultra-professional.

In the 1950s, Tommy Harmer (Tottenham Hotspur) once ran up to take a penalty-kick and, instead of kicking the ball, he put his foot over it. Having waited for the goalkeeper to commit himself, he gently tapped the ball in the other corner. Harmer's action was later outlawed. A player can be cautioned for unsporting behaviour for faking to take a kick at the ball and then putting the ball in the other corner. (The kick is retaken if the kicker scores.)

Penalty-takers must kick the ball forward (1896) and must approach the ball in a single fluid movement (IFAB 1981). This rules out a deliberate stop-start run-up, but allows a slight change of pace, or a shimmy, assuming that the player maintains forward momentum. Pelé (Santos) did a samba shuffle before beating Springett (Sheffield Wednesday) from the spot (October 1962).

Dani (Spain) came on as a half-time substitute against England (June 1980). He scored with a 48th-minute penalty but seemed to stop in his run-up. Four minutes later Spain were awarded a second penalty. Again Dani halted before scoring, but this time the referee ordered a retake, which was saved by England goalkeeper Clemence.

Henry (Arsenal) took a penalty-kick that had a severe stutter in the run-up against Panathinaikos (November 2004). He scored from the kick and the goal was allowed, possibly because the stutter was early in his run to the ball, but the issue was a source of contention.

In 1892 the law was changed to stop penalty-takers from kicking the ball twice before another player had touched the ball. Otherwise, players could dribble the ball towards goal from a penalty-kick. In 1901, the punishment of an indirect free-kick was introduced for two offences: if a player touched the ball twice without a second player playing the ball; and playing a penalty-kick backwards (i.e. passing it back to a team-mate). Previously a penalty was retaken if a player erred in such ways.

If the ball hits the crossbar or the goalpost and rebounds to the penalty-taker without the goalkeeper touching the ball, the taker cannot touch the ball again without conceding an indirect free-kick. Peter Reid (Manchester City) hit the post with a penalty at Leeds and instinctively knocked the ball into the net from the rebound (September 1991). The same fate befell Teddy Sheringham (Manchester United) at Spurs (August 1997). The decision was the same in both cases: no goal – indirect free-kick.

Zenden (Middlesbrough) appeared to kick the ball twice in the same kicking motion when taking a successful penalty against Bolton (March 2004). It would be hard for a referee to spot this. Indeed, one might expect it to be detrimental to the kicker. Similarly, Lampard (Chelsea) scored a double-touch penalty against Southampton (August 2004). Lampard slipped as he shot with his right foot. The ball clipped his left foot and went into the corner of the net with the goalkeeper going the wrong way. Again, this could only be noticed on television replays and from Lampard's post-match admission.

In the 1950s, Northern Ireland internationals like Peter Doherty and Danny Blanchflower realised that you could pass the ball from a penalty as long as it didn't go backwards. They practised the two-person penalty in training and charity matches. John Newman (Plymouth Argyle) twice brought this move to a competitive match. Against Aston Villa he took Wilf Carter's pass and scored (February 1961). Against Manchester City Newman took a penalty and rolled the ball diagonally forward (November 1964). His team-mate, Mike Trebilcock, followed up from outside the penalty area and scored, only just reaching the ball before goalkeeper Alan Ogley. This tactic is perfectly legal, providing the ball is kicked forward, and the player receiving the pass is not encroaching and is behind the ball when the penalty-kick is taken. (In Newman's day the ball also had to travel its circumference and the players did not have to be behind the ball. Until 1995, players could be offside from a penalty-kick, but the law was then changed so that players had to stand behind the penalty spot.)

Bryan Douglas (Blackburn Rovers) worked the same move with Mike Ferguson on a heavy pitch against Barrow (September 1966). Johan Cruyff (Ajax) played a short forward pass to Jesper Olsen, collecting the return to score against Helmond Sport (December 1982), and Rik Coppens and Andre Piters (Belgium) exchanged a similar one-two to score against Iceland (June 1957).

It didn't work quite so smoothly for Robert Pires and Thierry Henry (both Arsenal) in October 2005. Pires tried to roll the ball sideways but the ball barely moved, and in the confusion Henry was beaten to the ball by Mills (Manchester City). The referee gave an indirect free-kick on the penalty mark, thinking Pires had touched the ball twice. As Arsenal manager Arsène Wenger said afterwards, the experience should have vaccinated Pires against ever trying it again.

So many things can happen at a penalty-kick. As Stan Bowles (Queen's Park Rangers) came up to take one at Luton, another ball was thrown on the pitch by a spectator (August 1974). The shot from Bowles went into the net but the referee ordered the kick to be retaken. Fortunately Bowles scored the second time as well.

The match officials need to watch a number of spots: the edge of the penalty area when the ball is kicked; the penalty-taker's run-up; the ball; the goalkeeper's feet (and the ball); and the goal-line (in case the ball hits the crossbar and bounces down or the goalkeeper scrambles it away). It is a lot for two pairs of eyes.

At Birmingham, in the last match of the 1923–24 season, Len Davies (Cardiff City) was unfairly denied a chance to win the League Championship for his club. Ivan Sharpe described the incident in *Forty Years in Football*: 'As the ball was crossing the line, with the goalkeeper beaten, another defender turned goalkeeper and fisted it out. Davies failed with the penalty-kick, the result was a goalless draw, and the unfair fisting cost Cardiff the League Championship, because points being level, Huddersfield led on goal average reckoning by 1.818 to 1.794.'

Sharpe suggested a six-yard penalty-kick to eradicate this sort of injustice. Mr S M Williams, in a letter to *The Times* (6 February 1992), suggested two penalty spots – one at ten yards for offences that prevented probable goals, and one at fifteen yards for other offences. Others have suggested a penalty-kick from twelve or eighteen yards, depending on where the incident takes place and the likelihood of a team scoring. And some people advocate penalty-kicks for cynical professional fouls that take place anywhere on the pitch.

William McCrum certainly started something in 1890. No wonder there are plans to erect a memorial to him in Milford, Northern Ireland. His invention has travelled across the world.

PENALTY-KICK MARK See PENALTY MARK

PENALTY LINE

The penalty line (1891 to 1902) was succeeded by the penalty area. The penalty line was marked parallel to the goal-line and twelve yards out, and it stretched from touchline to touchline. A shorter line was often added, eighteen yards from goal, to help the referee determine if players were six yards from the ball, but the only concession in the laws was two eighteen-yard marks opposite the goalposts (1901).

When Aston Villa played Burton Swifts, Worrall was brought down between the twelve-yard line and the eighteen-yard line. The referee gave a penalty but at that time penalties were only supposed to be awarded if the offence was up to twelve yards out. The referee had mistaken one line for the other. Worrall missed the penalty, so justice was done.

The Scottish FA wanted a penalty-kick to be taken at the point on the twelve-yard line opposite to where the infringement took place, but their idea was not supported.

PENALTY MARK

The penalty spot was introduced in 1902, a by-product of the change in pitch markings that introduced the penalty area. The penalty mark (as it has been called since 1974) is twelve yards from the midpoint of the goal-line. If a mark is not visible, the referee should stride out the distance and place the ball accordingly. However, the referee of a Derby County–Manchester City match at Derby's notoriously muddy Baseball Ground was so uncertain about the distance that he called for groundsman Bob Smith to whitewash a fresh mark (April 1977).

PENALTY MARK SHOOT-OUTS

In 1970, IFAB decided that kicks from the penalty mark could determine the results of drawn cup ties if a definite outcome was needed. The term *penalty shoot-out* is not strictly correct. These are not penalty-kicks (as there is nothing to penalise) but *kicks from the penalty mark*.

The first tie in England decided in this way was the 1970 Watney Cup match between Hull City and Manchester United. The format was five kicks a team, followed by 'sudden-death' penalties if the scores were still level. The deciding penalty was missed by the Hull goalkeeper and United won the shoot-out 4–3. When the Football League introduced play-off competitions to determine promotion and relegation, in July 1986, penalty mark kicks were used to settle the venue for the third game between Walsall and Bristol City (May 1988). Walsall won 3–1 at Bristol City in the first leg, and Bristol City won 2–0 at Walsall. After the match, Walsall won a shoot-out 4–2 and therefore won the right to host the third match, which they won 4–0.

In European competition, Spartak Trnava beat Marseille 4–3 after both teams had won 2–0 at home (1970).

The shoot-out stakes grew and grew. Panenka (Czechoslovakia) won the 1976 European Championship Final by deliberately chipping his side's fifth kick past the falling West Germany goalkeeper, while Alan Kennedy (Liverpool) sent the Roma goalkeeper the wrong way to win the 1984 European Cup Final, and Roberto Baggio (Italy) shot over the crossbar to concede the 1994 FIFA World Cup™ Final to Brazil. Four European Cup Finals in eight years (1984 to 1991) were settled by shoot-outs, three out of four FIFA World Cup™ quarter-finals in 1986, and both the 1990 semi-finals. In 2004, all three Conference play-off matches were decided in this way.

After Red Star Belgrade had won the 1991 European Cup Final (5–3 from the penalty mark after a 0–0 draw), their coach Ljubomir Petrovic admitted that his team had defended *en masse* with the aim of taking the Final to a shoot-out. Red Star had shoot-out experience from drawn matches in the Yugoslav League.

These shoot-outs are wonderful drama, and people worldwide can understand the surface principles (unlike the offside law). Yet the procedure is elaborate. All the usual laws still apply. Kicks from the penalty mark are not part of the match itself but players can be cautioned and sent off. Bristol City goalkeeper Steve Phillips was cautioned for dissent during a shoot-out at Brentford (November 2004).

The referee decides which end of the ground will be used for the shoot-out. There are a number of considerations: the wishes of police and safety officials; the condition of the playing surface at each end; the location of the changing-rooms; the position of the sun; other weather conditions; and the position of supporters.

Birmingham City manager Trevor Francis ordered his players to leave the field at Preston following a dispute over which end a shoot-out should be taken (May 2001). Safety officials persuaded the referee that fans at the Bill Shankly end might surge forward if the shoot-out was held at the Town End. Francis was disappointed with the decision. Birmingham missed their first two kicks and lost the shoot-out 4–2.

Japan and Jordan drew their 2004 Asia Cup quarter-final after extra-time. Japan missed their first two kicks in the shoot-out and Jordan scored their first. Japan complained about the slippery pitch, and the referee moved the shoot-out to the other end. Jordan scored the first at the new end, to take a 2–0 lead in the shoot-out, but Japan eventually won 4–3 after a total of fourteen kicks. Jordan's coach claimed the move had disrupted his team's concentration, but the referee was perfectly within his rights. Similarly, the referee of a 2004 Portugal–England game was justified in not moving the shoot-out after complaints about the condition of the turf next to the penalty mark. Where there seems no obvious end, a referee may toss a coin to decide.

The next question concerns who can take part in the shoot-out – those who are members of the team at the full-time whistle, including injured players receiving treatment (1974). A goalkeeper injured during the shoot-out can be replaced by a named substitute, providing the team have not already used all their permitted substitutes (1974). If a player has been sent off during the match, then team numbers must be equalised (2000). The captain of the team with more players should give the referee the names and numbers of the players withdrawn. An equal number of players should remain on the pitch. Players receiving a second caution during a shoot-out should be sent off, and the number of players in the centre-circle should be equalled accordingly.

The 2006 Nationwide Conference North play-off ended 1-1 after extra-time. Droylsden had finished with ten men, Lynch having been sent off in the 38th minute, so Stafford Rangers were asked to reduce their centre-circle complement to ten. Lovatt (Stafford) reluctantly trudged to the technical area.

This process of equalising numbers is still a cause for concern. Some people think a sent-off player's kick should count as a miss but this could be a problematic way to end a game. The method of equalising numbers is fairer than the previous system, where the sent-off player's kick could be taken by any of the other players.

Peterborough United beat Blackpool 7–6 from the penalty mark after a 0–0 Watney Cup draw (July 1972). Don Heath (Peterborough) took his team's fourth kick but he had already been substituted. Peterborough manager Jim Iley said that he had checked with the referee before Heath's kick. The competition organisers upheld Blackpool's complaint but decided that the result should stand. It was clarified, however, that a substituted player should not take part in a shoot-out. Players coming on as substitutes can take part, providing they have come on before the final whistle. During the shoot-out itself, only an injured goalkeeper may be substituted. In that shoot-out at Peterborough, goalkeeper Wood (Blackpool) replaced Burridge (Blackpool) after the fourth kick. There was also a foretaste of possible problems ahead when Peterborough fans invaded the pitch after Drewery (Peterborough) had saved from Barton (Blackpool) at 4–4, even though the shoot-out hadn't ended. After a delay of several minutes, Darrell (Peterborough), who had come on for Heath, shot wide. And on it went.

In a 1996 Wembley play-off final, Leicester City substituted their second-choice goalkeeper, six-foot-seven Zeljko Kalac, for first-choice Kevin Poole a minute before the end of extra-time. They thought that the substitute would fare better in the seemingly inevitable shoot-out, but Claridge (Leicester) made it 2–1 in stoppage-time.

Having decided who is taking part, the match officials will ensure that the participants take up correct positions. All the players except those immediately engaged (the two goalkeepers and the player taking the current kick) must stay in the centre-circle. The goalkeepers will be in one of two positions, either on the goal-line between the posts (if defending a kick) or at the point where the penalty area meets the goal-line (when a team-mate is taking a kick). Before 1998, the onlooking goalkeeper stood at the corner of the penalty area eighteen yards from the goal-line.

Only the players involved in the shoot-out should be in the centre-circle. Substitutes and team officials must be off the field of play. Sometimes, with children's teams, a team official (or a parent) may be allowed to stay in the centre-circle with the players. An equal number of players should be in the centre-circle before a player walks forward to take the first kick.

It doesn't always work out how it should. When Sheffield United beat West Ham 3–1 in a shoot-out, a cameraman and another outsider were in the centre-circle when Liddell (Sheffield United) scored the winning kick (February 2005). When Liverpool and AC Milan took part in the 2005 UEFA Champions League Final shoot-out, the substituted Liverpool players (Kewell, Baros and Finnan) were in the centre-circle.

A compulsory coin-toss decides who starts. The captain winning the toss will decide which team should take the first kick. Until 2003 the team winning the toss was automatically allocated first kick.

The two goalkeepers walk with the referee to the appropriate goal. The one facing the first kick takes up position, and the first taker steps forward. Kicks are taken alternately. After five kicks each, the team with the most successes wins. If they are level they go on to sudden-death kicks. The shoot-out stops when it is mathematically impossible for one team to win. (Until 1972, both teams took all five penalties.)

The goalkeeper's position when facing a penalty-kick must adhere to customary penalty-kick procedure. There were three retakes in an LDV Vans Trophy shoot-out (November 2003). Simpson (Wycombe) scored with a retake, and Capaldi (Plymouth) scored with his third attempt.

Other goalkeepers have come under fire for trying to advance off the line in shoot-outs. Video evidence would point suspicion at Brazil goalkeeper Taffarel (1994 FIFA World Cup™ semi-final), USA goalkeeper Scurry (1999 Women's World Cup Final), AC Milan's Dida (2003 UEFA Champions League Final), Shrewsbury Town's Howie (2004 Vauxhall Conference play-off final), and Liverpool's Dudek (2005 UEFA Champions League Final). None of these vital saves was punished with a retake.

The referee has to blow the whistle before each penalty – a kick by Carragher (England) was retaken against Portugal (June 2006) – and the referee must keep track of the score. The 2002 Dominican All Nations tournament ended in chaos. The referee erroneously declared Harlem Bombers the winners even though they led by only one penalty after a total of eleven had been taken. The two teams resumed the shoot-out a week later.

Another legal technicality concerns the definition of a successful kick. One from Bellone (France) hit the Brazil crossbar and rebounded into the net off the goalkeeper (June 1986). It is a goal if the ball goes in as a result of the penalty-taker's shot (i.e. off the goal-frame or the goalkeeper, or a combination of the two) (IFAB 1987).

When Cameroon beat Nigeria 4–3 on penalties, one Nigerian miss, by Victor Ikpeda, struck the underside of the crossbar, bounced down and came out (February 2000). Video replays suggested that the ball actually went over the line. This sort of incident is worrying as it might promote uncertainty, especially if it is a possible match-winner.

If a shoot-out is not completed, the result should be decided by the toss of a coin. This may happen if the light fades, floodlights fail, or there is a safety issue. Shoot-outs can be protracted. England and Portugal spent half an hour taking thirty kicks after their European under-eighteen semi-final (July 1992). Portugal won the shoot-out 12–11.

Tossing a coin might have been a less painful way to decide a Derby Community Cup under-tens tie (January 1998). As it was, 66 penalties were taken. Mickleover Lightning Blue Sox scored with their 32nd and 33rd kicks to beat Chellaston Boys B 2–1. The two teams had drawn 1–1 after extra-time and the first sixty kicks were missed.

When Wycombe Wanderers and Oxford City met in an FA Cup first-round replay, the score was 1–1 after extra-time (November 1999). The shoot-out was postponed because a fire broke out and the Adams Park ground had to be evacuated. The match was replayed.

A first-round West Riding Premier Division League Cup match went to a 34-kick shoot-out (December 2001). Littletown and Storthes Hall drew 1–1 after extra-time. The shoot-out score was 17–17 – all the kicks had been scored – when the match was abandoned because of bad light. The ground had no floodlights and, even though car-owning spectators had switched on headlights and there was some peripheral street-lighting, it was too dark to continue.

An FA Cup tie between Tunbridge Wells and Littlehampton Town went to a forty-kick shoot-out which Tunbridge Wells won 16–15 (August 2005). There had been two penalties in normal time too. The match lasted three hours ten minutes, finishing at 10.55 p.m.

PENALTY SPOT See PENALTY MARK

PERSISTENT INFRINGEMENT

Persistent infringement of any of the laws of the game was classified as ungentlemanly conduct (1907) and then defined as a cautionable offence in its own right (1924). If football matches average 35.5 fouls, what would you expect each player to contribute to that total? If one player is responsible for three or four of these fouls in quick succession then that player is *persistently* infringing the laws of the game. A referee often demonstrates this to the crowd by pointing to where those fouls had taken place. Two fouls in quick succession may be enough for a caution. Four fouls over the whole ninety minutes may not be. Evans and Bellion, in *The Art of Refereeing*, suggest a benchmark of four fouls in one half or six in the match. A study of USA's Major League Soccer showed that only 4 per cent of cautions in 2001 were for persistent infringement.

Robbie Savage (Blackburn) was cautioned when he committed three fouls in the first seventeen minutes of a match against Bolton (January 2005). In a women's international against Denmark, Östberg (Sweden) was cautioned in the 31st minute (June 2005). It was only the fourth foul of the match but three of these had been by Östberg.

Persistent infringement can also mean persistent fouls against the same opponent. A player may be cautioned for a first foul if it is one of several against the same opponent. When Arsenal played at Manchester United, Reyes (Arsenal) was fouled several times in the first half, and Gary Neville and Phil Neville (both Manchester United) were cautioned for their part (October 2004).

PHOTOGRAPHY

When an important evening match kicks off, camera flashlights now flicker like fireflies in the night, but authorities used to frown on spectators using cameras. There were two reasons: the flashlights may disturb the players; and official photographers had special rights and privileges. Official photographers can occupy a place pitch-side providing they stay behind the photographers' line (FIFA Referees' Committee 1952).

A referee may insist that photographers keep far enough away so as not to risk injury to any of the players. Dennis Viollet (Manchester United) accidentally kicked a photographer on the head when chasing a ball to the goal-line (1958 FA Cup Final), photographers swarmed on to the pitch after Brazil's goals (1962 FIFA World Cup™ Final), and paparazzi invaded Wembley to take ghoulish close-ups of Whelan (Blackburn) being put on a stretcher (1960 FA Cup Final). Zoom lenses have helped photographers keep their distance. Any photographer on the pitch during play is treated as an outside agent.

Photographers are not allowed to hang cameras on the goal-net or corner-flags, but cameras can be put on goal-net stands. Photographers risk injury to themselves if they stand too close to the goal-nets. Television cameramen may patrol the touchline, but this can be dangerous if the momentum of players takes them off the pitch.

PHYSIOTHERAPISTS

Physiotherapists can only enter the field of play after they have received a signal from the referee (e.g. a wave of the arm). The FA Council deemed in 1900 only players and linesmen are allowed on to the field without the referee's permission. Football is not like rugby union, where players can be treated on the field as the game continues.

While awaiting a stoppage in play – a natural break for a slight injury or the referee's whistle for a serious injury – physiotherapists usually run round the pitch perimeter to give themselves the shortest route to the player. Then they assess the injury and report to the referee on which procedural options will be followed. All physiotherapists should be aware of injury protocols. Players' health and safety is paramount, and training courses are available for club officials.

Physiotherapists can be reported for misconduct but it is a moot point whether they can be sent from the technical area as they have a special role to fulfil, there may not be a replacement, and competition rules may demand a medical presence. At the top level, physiotherapists have received one-match bans and fines for using abusive language to players, officials or spectators.

Manchester United physiotherapist Jim McGregor was a star of the 1991 Rumbelows League Cup Final against Sheffield Wednesday. Goalkeeper Les Sealey flew into a rage when told that he should leave the field for attention to a leg wound, but McGregor calmed him down and bandaged the leg on the field. Sealey's outburst was one of the liveliest moments of the match, which Wednesday won 1–0. Had Sealey hit his physio, as seemed possible at one time, the referee would have sent him off.

PITCH CONDITIONS See PITCH INSPECTION

PITCH DIMENSIONS

At first the pitches were farmers' fields, or they fitted into the space each public school could spare. The original maximum pitch dimensions were 200yd long and 100yd wide (1863). A minimum length (100yd) and a minimum width (50yd) were set later (1878).

The basic measurements changed to a length of 100–130yd and a width of 50–100yd, and the boundary-lines were specified as technically forming part of the field (1897). Smaller pitches were allowed for schoolchildren (1938).

Certain competitions have more stringent rules. The Premier League conforms to the standard brought in for international football in 1897 – 110–120yd long and 70–80yd wide. During the 1966 FIFA World Cup™ finals, all pitches were 115yd by 75yd.

The field must be rectangular (1897). Baseball aficionados talk of 'the diamond', cricketers refer to 'the square', and boxers meet in 'the ring' (even though the days when spectators formed a ring around the fighters are long passed), but football people almost never use the term 'rectangle'. Maybe expressions like 'wait till we get them on our rectangle' and 'get the ball into the right-angle' will one day become vogue.

Technically, the area of a pitch can be anything from 5,000 to 13,000 square yards. Most pitches are around 1.6 acres, which, with the surrounding land, is (as clubs have discovered when moving to new stadiums) enough space for 87 flats and a private hospital (Oxford), a supermarket complex (Walsall) or a retail park (Huddersfield).

Arbroath beat Rangers 4–3 in the Scottish Cup (November 1884). 'At the close the Rangers took exception to the ground, alleging the measurement across was less than minimum width,' reported the *Glasgow Herald*. Indeed the width was two feet too short. A replay was ordered, which Rangers won 8–1.

Some competition organisers now force clubs to declare their pitch size at the start of the season. Rangers were accused of moving the touchlines to create a pitch of minimum width for the visit of Dynamo Kiev (September 1987). Rangers had lost 1–0 in Kiev, and Rangers manager Graeme Souness felt that his team could disrupt the opposition by being physical in the home leg. On the Tuesday afternoon the Kiev players trained on Ibrox Park when it was a normal-sized pitch, and on the Wednesday they came out for the match and found the touchlines much closer. Similar tactics were used by Bolton Wanderers, who once deliberately narrowed their playing area by ten yards to cramp the famous Preston North End winger Tom Finney, and Crystal Palace, when Malcolm Allison was the manager.

In 2003, Dr Alex Morton and Henry Stott of Warwick University found a very slight tendency towards fewer goals on larger pitches. Some referees believe that a smaller pitch can lead to more tackles and more refereeing decisions.

Peppard beat Oxford City 1–0 in an FA Vase match (October 1993). When the referee measured the pitch, at Palmer Park, Reading, before the game, he found that it was five yards short of the competition's minimum required width. He allowed the game to be played, but Oxford City appealed and were awarded the tie.

PITCH INSPECTION

'It's a fine piece of pasture,' said a Yeovil Town player at Maine Road before a cup tie against Manchester United in front of 81,000 people (February 1949). That was one of the more cursory pitch inspections. Referees have to be much more vigilant. They have to decide whether the pitch is fit for play, and they have to check for anything that may be dangerous to players. If it is the first match at a new arena, a pitch inspection may be a stadium inspection. If it is windy or foggy, a pitch inspection may be an air inspection.

'The referee shall have power to decide as to the fitness of ground in all matches,' said Football League rules (1901–02), 'and each club must take every precaution to keep its ground in a playing condition, and, if necessary, the home club may require the referee to visit the ground two hours before the advertised time of kick-off.'

Most pitch inspections take place in bad weather, but they can be needed in good weather. Reading's Elm Park pitch was once put out of action by a dose of weedkiller (August 1986). Several Liverpool matches were postponed because of a collapsed sewer under the Kop (August 1987). A crater caused the postponement of a Durham Cup tie at Tow Law Ironworks (October 2004). Floodwater damaged the terracing and left silt and ashes on Carlisle United's Brunton Park pitch (March 1968), and when more floods occurred, in 2005, the pitch had to be treated and disinfected.

The referee's prime concern, when judging the fitness of the pitch, must be the safety of players and spectators. 'When I turned up for the trial, I found that a bomb had been dropped on the pitch,' said one player about his first sight of Notts County (1941). 'The upshot was that I fell awkwardly in the loose earth which filled the crater . . . and bang went another cartilage.'

Referees must also ensure that there is no peripheral danger to players or spectators. The roof of the Ipswich Town grandstand was blown off by a gale (November 1911). The corrugated iron destroyed a number of nearby trees and brought down tramway cables. Fortunately, it didn't happen on a match-day and nobody was hurt. A similar issue arose at Oldham when safety officials had to pass the stand fit after the impact of high winds (January 2005). And Montrose–Stirling Albion was postponed when a floodlight pylon was blown down a few hours before an evening kick-off (September 1990).

A pitch is unfit if it is impossible for people to get there. When Derby County played at Chelsea, the roads were icy and a bus carrying Derby fans collided with a lorry near Loughborough (January 1947). Two men were killed, two seriously injured, and ten others hurt.

The postponement of a Southend United–Brentford match provoked a debate about improving arrangements for pitch inspections (December 1965). More responsibility was shifted to a senior referee based near the ground. These referees are often more familiar with the pitch or surroundings ('The fog always lifts in Grantham'), they can inspect it the day before, and can make several inspections in a short space of time. The authorities realised that the system should take into account the travelling time of players and fans, and procedures should be in place for contacting visiting teams and the media. The 1978–79 Scottish Cup tie between Inverness Thistle and Falkirk was postponed a record 29 times.

Some people have called for committee decisions involving the clubs, but some managers are not objective, especially if they have injured players they want to get fit or are already behind on fixtures. When the referee inspected the bone-hard Old Trafford pitch before a 1971 Manchester United–Middlesbrough FA Cup tie he received differing responses from Matt Busby ('This is impossible') and Stan Anderson ('It's not so bad, is it?'). The referee is the sole judge of pitch fitness, but they can seek advice from weather forecasters and ground managers.

Nottingham Forest versus Fulham was postponed forty minutes before the kick-off, bringing protests from supporters who had wasted a journey (April 1966). The referee had arrived 45 minutes before kick-off, as the League ruling called for referees to attend the ground two hours before kick-off only from November to February (inclusive). No one had expected snow in April.

Pitch inspections are guided by a number of factors: the chances of completing a match; the safety of players and spectators; the desire to achieve a reasonable level of play; and whether visibility is good enough. A decision to start a match does not mean it has to be completed.

A referee who is talked into playing a match may have to live with the consequences. Peter Reid (Bolton Wanderers) was seriously injured on New Year's Day 1980, as recalled by Everton opponent John Bailey: 'The game should never have been played because there was three inches of snow on the pitch at kick-off time. It got heavier and heavier. The story goes that somebody said, "You've got to start now because the crowd's in. If you abandon it now, before the game, there'll be a riot." So they kicked off. I felt the injury to Reidy that day was caused by the ground conditions. Our goalkeeper George Wood came sliding out and he caught Reidy and it was a terrible injury. The game was abandoned at half-time and Reidy had been injured and was out for a year. It was an absolute joke that day. You had to flick the ball up to kick it because the snow ended up five inches deep.'

If the pitch is passed fit, referees will still have their regular pitch inspection to make. They check the nets, make sure the corner-flags are there, pace out the pitch to ensure it conforms, look for illegal pitch markings, and check there is nothing on the pitch that may be dangerous to the players (e.g. cans, dog mess, glass, tufts of grass, nails, stones, etc.). One pitch in a coal-mining area was built on a tip, and a player broke his ankle when he kicked a bucket-handle buried just below the surface. Glass had to be cleared off the Coventry pitch when Newcastle were the visitors (October 1984). Dog faeces should be removed and sanded over if necessary, and areas of vomit should be made safe (FA 2005).

PITCH MARKINGS

Goalkeeper Andy Dibble (Barry Town) was scarred for life by pitch markings at Carmarthen Town's council-maintained ground (December 1998). The lines had been marked with hydrated lime. When Dibble made one save, he had a four-inch strip of flesh burned off from shoulder to hip and had to have skin grafts as a result. Thirty months later, Carmarthen Town Council was ordered to play £20,000 in damages. Hydrated lime should never be used on pitches.

Once more the safety of players is paramount. V-shaped ruts are banned, and the traditional material for lines has been whitewash, sometimes mixed with a dye to make for blue lines on snow-covered pitches. The *FA Handbook* lists guidelines.

Marking lines calls for some expertise. Experienced groundsmen will develop a canny method for marking the pitch without going over the same ground too much. One referee found that a groundsman had steered his marking machine around a cowpat right on the touchline.

Whereas a groundsman in the 1950s could take two or three hours to paint lines with a three-inch Turk's-head brush, modern equipment cuts that down to the time spent walking with a marking machine. Council's have standard charges for pitch markings, and it is not something that clubs can cut corners on.

Some pitches host other sports. The Causeway Stadium, home of Wycombe Wanderers, was marked out for the London Wasps rugby union club (from 2002). At times both sets of pitch markings were visible. It must be annoying for players who plan their dive for a penalty only to find that they've stumbled over the 22-metre rugby line. When Brentford ground-shared with the London Broncos rugby league team, the markings could look confusing at first sight (2002–05).

The Parc de Princes, Paris, had been used for rugby union before it hosted the 1981 European Cup Final between Liverpool and Real Madrid. During their pre-match preparations, the Liverpool players noticed that the ball bounced unusually high when it hit one of the lines. Sure enough, towards the end of the match, a ball bounced higher than expected off the penalty-area line and hit Phil Thompson (Liverpool) on the nose. His team-mates dissolved into fits of laughter.

The markings should be not more than five inches in width, and the lines belong to the areas they enclose (IFAB 1950). An offence by the defending team on the penalty-area line is a penalty-kick (providing that it merited a direct free-kick).

In 1863 there were no pitch markings, only four corner-posts. Then came the touchlines and goal-lines (early 1880s), corner arcs (1887), halfway-line (1887), centre-circle (1891), semicircles from the goalposts (1891) which were converted to goal areas (1902), penalty lines (1891) which were superseded by penalty areas (1902), penalty spot (1902), and penalty arcs (1937). There are also optional marks, eleven yards from a corner-flag, off the field of play, to help assess the encroachment distance at a corner-kick.

No additional pitch markings are allowed. In the 1920s, goalkeeper Harry Hibbs (Birmingham and England) regularly dug a mark with his heel across the goal area to give him a sense of the midpoint of his goal. This later became a cautionable offence, and Jim Barron (Oxford United) was one of the first goalkeepers to be so cautioned (in the 1960s). Goalkeepers now have to rely on the penalty mark for guidance.

PITCH SURROUNDS

'Once at Wimborne, by the river Stour in mid-winter, the ball landed on the other side. Arthur Kingsbury swam across and retrieved it and then went on with the play, shaking the wet off like a spaniel.'

William Pickford's early tale is comic but cautionary. Pitch surrounds can cause serious accidents. James Beaumont was killed when he jumped into a quarry at Walkley (December 1877). Ditmar Jacobs (Hamburg) was taken to hospital after being impaled on a pitch-side spike during the match against Werder Bremen (September 1989). And a nineteen-year-old player died during a game in Harrogate, North Yorkshire, when he tackled a player, slid into a fence and a metal spike pierced his temple (1990).

There should be nothing dangerous near the pitch. It is an obvious and yet often unheeded point, even at the highest level. Nedved (Czech Republic) hurt himself on a drinks container during EURO 2004™, Ljundberg (Arsenal) injured a knee on an advertising hoarding at Chelsea (August 2005), and Degeorgi (Austria) was substituted after colliding with a cameraman and an advertising board (June 1982).

Referees look at the pitch surrounds when making their pre-match check. The competition rules may stipulate specific boundary conditions, but local referees will also look out for badly parked bicycles and discarded shopping trolleys. Some nearby cricket squares are dangerously roped off with iron stakes.

At top-level grounds, players have suffered broken collarbones and head injuries on the surrounding walls and dugouts, and 'gravel rash' from being knocked on to the cindered track. An early Portland Bill ground was on a cliff edge. A pitch at Sturminster was on top of a hill and young boys were paid to fetch the ball when it rolled down it. At other places players have fallen out of trees trying to reach a match-ball, or they have been bogged down in nearby swamps. On one pitch at the Sheepmount, Carlisle, a wayward clearance could thread the ball through the trees and on to the electric railway line. Bedlington Terriers have netting to protect nearby homes.

PLACE-KICK

A properly taken place-kick starts the game. A second place-kick resumes the game after half-time. If extra-time is played, two more place-kicks will be needed. Referees will have an extra check list for place-kicks: the number of players on each team; that the assistants are in place and set to run in the desired direction; that the goalkeepers are ready; and that their finger is on the stopwatch ready to start, or restart, the match. At the start of the second half, when checking the number of players on the field, the referee needs to take into account any first-half sendings-off and possible substitutions. The side taking the first place-kick is determined by a toss rather than the concession of a goal (as with a kick-off).

The second half of a Liverpool–Tottenham Hotspur game started short of one linesman (January 1954). This sort of embarrassment is why referees look towards both assistants before a place-kick.

The game starts when the ball is in play from the place-kick (rather than from the referee's whistle). 'In play' now means travelling forward by any distance, whereas the ball had to travel its circumference (before 1997). The referee's control begins when the referee enters the field of play, but the application of laws starts when the game begins (IFAB, June 1936).

Captains were given the option of 'kick-off or choice of ends' (1879), which was later changed so that the team winning the toss had to decide which goal to attack and the other team took the kick-off (1997). The ball has to go forward (1887), and players have to stay in their own half of the field until the ball has moved.

If a place-kick is incorrectly taken, it must be retaken and the referee's watch not started until the kick has been correctly taken (IFAB 1903). Possible reasons are encroachment, a player straying into the opposition's half, or the ball played backwards. A player sent off for an infringement delaying the first place-kick cannot be replaced. This could apply to a player who receives two cautions for encroachment (FIFA Referees' Committee 1932) or one who repeatedly plays the ball backwards from a kick-off (FIFA Referees' Committee 1947). As the 1996 League Cup Final between Aston Villa and Leeds United was about to start, three Villa players passed the match-ball back and forth. Referees usually frown on this. Celebrity kick-offs are also discouraged.

Until 1997 a goal could not be scored directly from a place-kick, but quick goals had been scored by a player who receives a pass from the place-kick and then sends a shot from the centre-circle over the opposing goalkeeper's head. They include a five-second goal by Malcolm Macdonald (Newcastle United) at St Johnstone (July 1972) and a four-second one by Colin Cowperthwaite (Barrow) against Kettering (December 1979). These goals show how important it is for referees to check that the goalkeepers are ready for the kick-off, especially if the teams have changed ends after the toss. Referees usually look at each goalkeeper, and exchange a wave or a thumbs up.

The team taking the first place-kick then defends the place-kick at the start of the second half. Notts County are said to have kicked off in both halves against Chesterfield (October 1969), and Derby County started each half against Velez Mostar (December 1974). Normally the referee notes which team kicked off at the start of a match. Players are notorious for wandering up to the ball at the start of the second half to see if the referee notices that their team has already kicked off.

The second half of an Arsenal–Luton game started without goalkeeper Pat Jennings (Arsenal), who was talking to his manager in the tunnel (March 1983). The referee decided to restart the second half. Some referees thought it should be a dropped ball. Others said a referee should wait until the ball was out of play. But the referee should have the courtesy to check with the goalkeepers at a place-kick. If a goalkeeper is still celebrating with the crowd when a kick-off is taken, then that's the goalkeeper's fault.

After 1997 a goal could be scored straight from a place-kick or a kick-off. Ricardo Olivera (Rio Negro) scored one against Soriano in the Uruguayan League (December 1998).

It is essential for matches to start on time, especially on the last day of a league programme, otherwise collusion is a possibility. Television schedules and carefully orchestrated pre-match rituals mean that timing is critical. Nobody would now put up with the behaviour of the likes of Archie Goodall (Derby County), who caused the 1898 FA Cup Final to start late by wandering outside to sell tickets.

The 1953 FA Cup Final could have started twenty seconds early, but the referee knew his responsibility was to start exactly on time. He asked Ernie Taylor (Blackpool) to undo and retie his bootlace so that the place-kick could be taken at exactly three o'clock.

As J J Bentley said about the days before 1888 (when the Football League was formed): 'It was no uncommon thing to find a team, coolly strolling up to an opponents' ground an hour or an hour and a half late, and then with only a bare majority of recognised first-team players.' The rules of the new League stated that the twelve clubs had to support each other, play their best available teams, *and start on time*.

PLASTER CASTS See PROTECTORS

PLAYING TO THE WHISTLE

There is plenty of evidence to prove the advisability of the 'Play to the whistle' motto.

Joe Edelston (Hull City) picked up the ball thinking it had gone out for a goal-kick but the referee gave a penalty to Grimsby Town (November 1919). In a game between Charlton and Cardiff, Bassett (Cardiff) handled a centre and all the players stopped, expecting a penalty to be awarded (January 1938). Bassett flicked the ball back to his goalkeeper, who let the ball trickle into the net, probably thinking, 'Let the penalty-taker fetch it.' The referee didn't give a penalty. He gave a goal instead.

In the 1950s, Arthur Ellis refereed a Tranmere–Rochdale match that had an interesting incident. Midway through the second half, with Rochdale leading 1–0, a Tranmere player broke clear but was elbowed and pushed by a Rochdale defender. The linesman's flag went up but the referee allowed an advantage. The Tranmere player crossed the ball and a Rochdale defender caught the ball having seen the linesman's flag. Penalty.

Bolton's winning goal against Rotherham United was scored in the 86th minute by Garry Jones (November 1972). Rotherham goalkeeper Jim

McDonagh placed the ball for a goal-kick on the assumption that the ball had gone out of play but Jones ran up to put the ball into the net with the referee waving 'play on'. A swarm of Rotherham players surrounded the officials, but the goal stood and Rotherham were relegated at the end of the season.

POLICE

In the early 1900s, professional matches were policed by a small number of officers whose main function was protecting the referee from the crowd.

'Thank you very much,' said one referee, when he reached the railway station safely.

'It's quite all right, sir,' the policeman replied, 'We like to take care of the blind.'

Such policemen were known as 'supporters with truncheons'. One copper stepped on to the pitch to protest when the referee gave the visitors a dubious corner-kick.

'It's your job to prevent trouble,' his chief superintendent told him later.

'I thought it was my job to see that justice was done,' said the policeman.

Although operating on private land, at the request of the management, the police had their normal powers of arrest. Policemen were taught to amble around the ground's perimeter track without blocking the spectators' view. Occasionally one would be hit by the ball – a policeman had to receive treatment when he was hit in the face during a Charlton–Birmingham City match (March 1957) – and some officers were stationed in the crowd to watch for pickpockets. Hull City had a coat-slasher who chalked up twenty incidents without getting caught (1948–49).

The 1960s and 1970s brought more crowd trouble. Pitch invasions brought police on to the pitch and that usurped the referee's control. One definitive match was an FA Cup tie between Newcastle United and Nottingham Forest that was interrupted for eight minutes by a major pitch invasion (March 1974). The FA's decision to order a 'replay' was criticised by the barrister Edward Grayson, who felt the match should have been awarded to Nottingham Forest. There are two interesting points here: (i) the relative roles of the referee and the police in the decision to resume (or abandon) a match; and (ii) whether competition rules should stipulate the punishment for crowd intimidation.

Many other games were suspended or abandoned after pitch invasions in the 1970s and 1980s, when the police role was generally concerned with shepherding fans to railway stations, segregating crowds, and monitoring behaviour through CCTV cameras. Police have always generally accepted that the referee is in control. At times, however, they have stepped in.

At Colchester United in 1980, Sergeant Frank Ruggles stopped play for three minutes while he cautioned a visiting player for using bad language. The referee was surprised at this intervention but he had to stop the game or he could be seen as interfering with the course of justice. The only time a referee can send a policeman off the pitch is for a football matter. All eleven members of the Barnsley Borough Police team were ordered off during a game in 1967.

Police have occasionally stepped in to deal with provocative gestures, visiting the Wimbledon dressing-room after a match at Barnsley (December 1985), leading away Macclesfield Town mascot Roary the Lion during a game at Lincoln (April 1998), and asking Chelsea manager José Mourinho to leave the technical area during the Carling Cup Final (February 2005). Newport County manager Jimmy Scoular had to be restrained by police after two of his players were sent off at AFC Bournemouth (November 1976). Chris Hutchings (Chelsea) was fined £250 for threatening behaviour after an incident at the end of the game at Brighton (November 1983). Terry Butcher (Rangers) and Chris Woods (Rangers) were found guilty of disorderly conduct and breach of the peace following an incident in a game against Celtic (October 1987). Police interviewed Gary Brabin (Blackpool) after an incident in the tunnel that resulted in Jamie Bates (Brentford) being taken to hospital (September 1996). And Willy Gueret (Swansea) was issued with a police caution after a match at Bury (May 2005).

As William Paul wrote in the *Scotsman* (16 April 1988): 'The lines that mark out a football or rugby pitch are not invisible barriers to police jurisdiction. The laws that govern a game are not licences for players to go wild with impunity, nor are they intended to be. A reasonable risk of being hurt does not mean a deliberate assault should be tolerated.'

The police may intervene immediately after an incident if it happens on a local park, but they may hold back on a professional ground (for fear of more ructions or a spectator riot). When Kamara (Swindon) assaulted Melrose (Shrewsbury) as the players left the field, the incident was witnessed by police officers and missed by match officials (January 1988). The police charged Kamara with grievous bodily harm.

At other times the police have arrested wanted men. A Portuguese Third Division match between Cinfaes and Paredes was abandoned at half-time when the referee, Armando Portulez, was arrested and taken to a local police station. A team of Killingbeck policemen phoned colleagues at half-time when they realised that one of their opponents was a man wanted for failing to appear on a drunk and disorderly charge (2000). A Droylsden player was arrested at the ground before the game against Ashton United as he was the subject of an outstanding warrant for breaching a court order (November 2002).

POSTPONEMENT

Referees will take a number of factors into consideration when deciding whether a match should be played: Will conditions be dangerous for players? Will conditions endanger spectators? Will conditions make the game farcical? Will the referee and the assistants have a clear view of the pitch and the line markings?

Most postponements are caused by weather conditions, but some happen when one team has fewer than the minimum of players (seven). Whole teams can be absent for all sorts of reasons – a train breakdown (Bradford Park Avenue–Newcastle in 1945), a traffic jam (Newport County–Mansfield Town in 1973), a motorway blockage after a sixteen-vehicle pile-up (Bury–Shrewsbury Town in 2004), political protest (Chile–Soviet Union in 1973), and a players' strike announced 25 minutes before the match because wages hadn't been paid for nearly two months (Clacton Town–Leiston in 2005).

Competition rules usually have clear guidelines on epidemics. An influenza epidemic once caused the cancellation of four games in England and three in Scotland on the same Saturday (6 January 1973), and a smallpox epidemic did for a Middlesbrough–Thornaby match (March 1898). Three Portsmouth games were postponed through illness in a short time period – against Cambridge United (October 1983), Middlesbrough (November 1985) and at Stoke (March 1986). Clubs will need to liaise with the appropriate authorities in such circumstances. Failing to fulfil a fixture at Blackburn cost Middlesbrough three points and relegation (1996–97), and Spurs lost two points for cancelling a match at Coventry (October 1988). Spurs were also refused a postponement when eight players fell ill before their match at West Ham (May 2006). Exeter City failed to fulfil a fixture at Scunthorpe when they had only ten fit registered players (April 1974). Exeter were fined £5,000 and deducted two points.

Another frequent reason for postponement is the need to rearrange other games. This happens so often that it challenges why fixtures are called *fixtures*. Matches are often rejigged because of cup priorities or television requirements. Matches have also been postponed while the authorities are conducting an inquiry. The 2004–05 Unibond League play-offs were suspended while various organisations tried to work out who should be in the play-offs in the wake of Spennymoor United's withdrawal from the league.

Among the more bizarre reasons for postponement are cracked floodlights (at Bradford City in 1981), the inability of stadium staff to get through the snow to the all-weather pitch at Queen's Park Rangers (December 1981), a suspicious package in the Worksop Town car park (September 1997), the lack of a ball (1887 London Cup Final), and intelligence suggesting a safety threat to a Millwall–Iran match (July 2005). Postponements in the wake of tragedy include the Senegal–Zambia match after 25 members of the Zambia team were killed in the Gabon air disaster (April 1993), and several games after the Hillsborough disaster (April 1989). All matches were postponed immediately after the death of Queen Victoria (1901), and Shrewsbury's match against Mansfield was called off when Mansfield's goalkeeping coach, Peter Wilson, collapsed and died during the warm-up, and the players were in no fit state to continue (November 2005).

A Scottish Youth Cup tie between Nairn County and Brora Rangers was postponed because the referee was unhappy about all the dog mess on the pitch. Dog faeces are a source of infection for human toxicariasis, which can cause serious eye injury or blindness, particularly in children. There are about a hundred new cases in Britain every year.

A cup tie between Mansfield Town and Preston North End was postponed on two successive evenings, as a serious fire at a plastic factory near the Mansfield ground had spread toxic fumes around the area (August 2004). The postponements followed meetings of a safety advisory committee, which consisted of club representatives, the local authority, the police and the fire department.

A flock of geese landed on Porthmadog's ground and hacked away in the penalty area to cause the postponement of a reserve match with Llangefni (October 2004). Scarecrows were brought in so that the pitch could be repaired. There is no truth in the rumour that one scarecrow kept his place for the re-arranged fixture.

All postponements have consequences. Sometimes angry fans demand refunds or travelling expenses. Swindon's match at Chesterfield was called off an hour after the advertised starting time when electricians failed to repair a floodlight problem (March 1987). The game was rearranged for the following day, admission free, but that did not suit everybody.

POSTS *See* GOALPOSTS

PRE-EXISTING CONDITIONS

Trees are close to the touchline at certain grounds. The ball may go out of play, hit a branch and come back into play (which calls for play to be restarted by a throw-in, corner-kick or goal-kick) or the ball may hit a branch that overhangs the pitch (which calls for a dropped ball). In the latter case the referee is not required to climb into the tree and drop the ball from there. Under the branch will do fine. A dropped ball was the decision when a clearance from goalkeeper Paul Robinson (England) hit a suspended video cube during the match against Paraguay (June 2006).

PRESSURE OF BALL See BALL

PROFESSIONAL FOUL

Pa Jackson, a true amateur, defines the professional foul as well as anyone in his 1899 book:

> From about 1889 nearly all the alterations in the laws, or in the rules of the Association, were due to the legalisation of professionalism. An intentional and persistent breach of the laws by an amateur would have led to the boycott of the offender. With the professional this was not so. He had to win somehow, if possible, and he carefully weighed the chances whether the penalty would be more disadvantageous to his side than the play which his infringement of the laws would prevent, and acted accordingly. This being so, more stringent laws were devised, and the penalties for certain offences increased.

This included stricter rules for cautions and sendings-off, and smoother misconduct procedures.

In the 1912 FA Cup Final replay, Tufnell (Barnsley) ran from the halfway-line to score the winning goal. Pennington (West Brom) resisted the opportunity to foul Tufnell on the journey. Similarly, Albert Stubbins (Liverpool) scored a Championship-winning goal at Wolves when his marker, Stan Cullis, could easily have committed a professional foul by pulling his jersey a long way from goal.

But times changed. By the end of the 1960s, professional footballers were assessing the benefits of preventing a possible goal against the punishment. Spectators witnessed defenders making rugby tackles as forwards broke clear. Defenders tried to foul strikers before they reached the penalty area.

Some high-profile professional fouls occurred – Pejic (Stoke) on Garland (Chelsea) (1973 League Cup Final), McFarland (England) on Lato (Poland) (October 1973), and Thompson (Liverpool) on O'Hare (Nottingham Forest) (1978 League Cup Final replay). Tom Stoppard wrote a play called *Professional Foul,* which won the television critics' award for best play (1977), and IFAB began searching for solutions (1979). What brought the professional foul to the top of the agenda was a foul by Willie Young (Arsenal) on seventeen-year-old Paul Allen (West Ham) as Allen was just about to break into the penalty area, which only brought a caution (1980 FA Cup Final). The Norway FA wrote to FIFA to say that 'serious foul play' must surely include the case of a player who intentionally fouls an opponent who has a clear run to goal. Others suggested a penalty-kick for a professional foul, no matter where the foul took place.

In July 1982 the Football League instructed referees to send off players if they committed professional fouls. This instruction produced a record 229 sendings-off in League matches (1982–83), an increase of 56 per cent on the previous season. The professional foul also included handling the ball. Colin Todd (Nottingham Forest) was sent off for handling the ball against Manchester United (October 1982). In the 1985 FA Cup Final, Moran (Manchester United) was sent off for tripping Reid (Everton) about forty yards from goal. Reid would have had a clear run on goal but many observers were shocked, as Moran was the first player ever sent off in an FA Cup Final.

Instructions on dealing with the professional foul changed a lot as authorities tried to take a stance while not alienating players and clubs. A number of arguments came to the fore. Some people argued that players shouldn't be sent off as it spoiled the game as a contest (ten against eleven). Others felt that a sending-off was poor punishment as the saving of a goal was more important than playing with ten against eleven. Indeed, Manchester United's ten men went on to score the winning goal in the 1985 FA Cup Final.

In 1990 there was a change in the law: 'If in the opinion of the referee, a player who is moving towards his opponents' goal with an obvious opportunity to score a goal is intentionally and physically impeded by unlawful means, i.e. an offence punishable by a free-kick (or penalty-kick), thus denying the attacking play's team the aforesaid goalscoring opportunity, the offending player shall be sent off the field of play for serious foul play.'

Bruce (Manchester United) was an early culprit (September 1990), and there was much debate about the consistency of referees' decisions. Case (Southampton) was sent off for a trip on Bryan Robson (Manchester United) forty yards from goal, but goalkeeper Sealey (Manchester United) was not sent off for bringing down Rod Wallace (Southampton) in the same match (January 1991). There was an outcry when Tony Gale (West Ham) was sent off in the 26th minute of the 1991 FA Cup semi-final against Nottingham Forest. Gale's foul seemed innocuous but the circumstances meant that the referee could send him off. This one did spoil the balance of the match – Forest won 4–0.

In 1991 it was made clear that deliberate handball would be classed as a professional foul. A goalkeeper handling the ball or fouling an opponent outside the area would receive a red card if it *denied an obvious goalscoring opportunity*. The authorities were busy drafting criteria, but many people were baffled by the apparent inconsistency. Goalkeeper Bosnich (Aston Villa) was not sent off for bringing down Aldridge (Tranmere) and he stayed on to save three kicks in a shoot-out (February 1994). Walker (England) was not sent off for a clear foul on the runaway Overmars (Holland) (April 1993), and Ronald Koeman (Holland) was also spared after blatant shirt-tugging as Platt (England) approached the penalty area (October 1993). In other cases, players were sent off for bringing down opponents they couldn't have seen when first stretching out for the ball. And Rory Gleeson (Harlow Town) was distraught when he was sent off for conceding a debatable penalty in the sixteenth minute of a cup tie at Peterborough United (November 1991). Peterborough went 2–0 up from the spot and were 6–0 ahead at half-time.

Referees were eventually issued with a list of criteria for deciding what was a goalscoring opportunity: Is the attacker moving directly towards the goal? Are there fewer than two defenders between the offending defender and the goal? Is the ball close to, and in possession of, the attacker? Does the attacker have a reasonable shooting opportunity? Is the foul committed near enough to the goal to ensure a goalscoring opportunity?

All this did nothing to eliminate the professional foul. As John Giles said, in the 1990s, 'Now, I don't know any professional footballer who wouldn't have the instinct to pull down a player if he was going through.' Ole Gunnar Solskjaer (Manchester United) cynically brought down Rob Lee (Newcastle United) in a vital match (April 1998). As Mike Wright and Nabuyoshi Hirotsu point out, in the *Journal of the Operational Research Society* (March 2003), a professional foul can still benefit the team even if it doesn't benefit the individual player. They believe the rules need to be changed so that professional fouls punish the *team* by raising the probability of a goal (e.g. giving a penalty goal rather than a penalty-kick). The penalty goal is normally rejected because it puts too much responsibility on the referee and could create a provocative situation.

PROTECTORS

Footballers can wear lightweight covers to protect injuries in a manner that is safe for other players. Examples include the arm-casts fitted to Gary Lineker (England) in June 1986 and Freddie Ljungberg (Sweden) in June 2004. Paul Gascoigne (Lazio) wore a face-mask in 1993–94, Jeff Bryant (Wimbledon) protected a mouth injury with a gumshield against Halifax Town (August 1977), and Thickett (Sheffield United) allegedly played through the 1899 FA Cup Final with 46 yards of specially stiffened canvas protecting two broken ribs and a ruptured side.

Rene van der Kerkhof (Holland) played with a protector in the 1978 FIFA World Cup™:

> We got a penalty against Iran but I had fallen on my hand and broken it. I went to hospital and they wanted to put my hand in plaster. If I had had my hand in plaster then I could not have played any more. That day they sent by express-mail a special sort of plaster from Holland with which you can still play. The

next day the plaster arrived and they put it round my broken hand. Together with FIFA they decided I could play the match. For nearly seven weeks I walked around with this plaster.

I played five matches with this plaster and then there was an incident during the Final. The referee said that I couldn't play with my hand in plaster because Argentina's captain, Passarella, had pointed it out to him. The referee agreed with Passarella because he was pro-Argentina anyway. Ruud Krol, our captain, talked to him and made him understand that if I wasn't allowed to play, none of the Dutch team would play. Of course, they were very shocked and they argued for about ten to twelve minutes. Finally they decided that I had to have some tape to strengthen my plaster. I didn't understand why this was necessary because this tape made my hand very tight and it frustrated me. The referee felt my hand and realised that whether or not the tape was there, it didn't make a difference and I was allowed to play again. And all this hassle because we said that no one would play if one of our team wasn't allowed to play. Everybody agreed with this decision and we were one. Millions of people were watching us on television. Imagine if the Final had not continued. The situation was ridiculous – I had played five matches with my plaster and suddenly during the Final it was a problem. The whole situation definitely influenced my game, and also that of the others; we started the match with some hostility.

There is also a movement to provide children with head protectors, and Joy Fawcett (USA) set an example by wearing a headguard during major women's tournaments. Researchers at Glasgow University have warned professional footballers that heading the ball (even the modern footballs) may increase the likelihood of Alzheimer's Disease.

PROVOCATION See RETALIATION

PUNCHING See STRIKING A PERSON

PUNISHMENT See MISCONDUCT

PUSHING

Referees are continually making decisions about whether to punish a player for pushing an opponent. Rarely does a couple of minutes go by without players wanting a direct free-kick because they feel they have been inhibited from proceeding in their natural direction. But opponents believe they have a right to use their body strength to hold their position, whether jumping to head the ball, running into position, or dribbling with the ball.

The offence of pushing is as complicated as t'ai chi's 'push hands' discipline. Players can interact co-operatively, receiving precisely the same amount of force as they give out, or they can use the smallest amount of energy to topple the largest of people. Football contests work as long as players stay in their own space, but most players are single-minded about a challenge. As Ray Entwistle says, in *I'm not God . . . I'm Just a Referee*, players 'get so wrapped up in an incident that they tend to lose touch with reality'. They are so focused on getting the ball that they don't realise that they're fouling.

For a short time in the early 1860s, before the Sheffield rules were formalised, Sheffield players had to carry half-a-crown in each hand to prevent them pushing with the open palm. But pushing is more than hand pushing. It's also hip to hip, thigh to thigh, elbow in the side, etc. If a goalkeeper pushes with the ball while holding it inside the penalty area, the referee should award a penalty-kick (FIFA Referees' Committee 1952). Players are not allowed to push off from the goalpost and, unlike in rugby union line-outs, they shouldn't push off from a team-mate's shoulders to gain extra height.

Players push with their fronts and push with their backs. In *A Life at the Soccer Factory*, striker Tommy Tynan said, 'I do a lot of backing into defenders and I can get away with it the whole match long with some referees. Other referees penalise me every time.'

Strikers back into defenders in order to upset the defender's balance or win a free-kick. Sometimes both players topple over and it's difficult to tell whether a defender is pushing forward or the attacker is pushing back. The foul can go either way.

QUICK FREE-KICKS

Referees are encouraged to restart play as soon as possible. A quick free-kick is one that takes place virtually immediately. Opponents are not necessarily ten yards away, and a whistle is not essential. A word from the referee (or a gesture) is sufficient.

Ian Harte (Leeds United) scored from a quick free-kick when goalkeeper Seaman (Arsenal) was by a post organising his wall (August 2001). Beckham (Manchester United) did the same at Blackburn (August 2001), as did Hasselbaink (Chelsea) against West Ham (February 2002). The referee has no obligation to inform defenders that the kick is going to be taken quickly. The referee's only obligation is not to distract defenders.

Thierry Henry (Arsenal) scored from a quick free-kick at Aston Villa (January 2004). Henry asked the referee if he could take it, and the referee nodded his consent.

Henry also scored from a quick free-kick against Chelsea (December 2004).

'Do you want a wall?' the referee asked.

'Can I take it, please?' Henry said.

'Yes.'

Gudjohnsen (Chelsea) was only a yard or two from the ball when Henry clipped it through a gap into the net.

Quick free-kicks are nigh impossible when the referee has to issue a card, summon a physiotherapist or oversee a substitution. A referee at West Brom cautioned a home player for dissent and was still setting up the wall when Dunne (Manchester City) hit a screaming 22-yard free-kick into the net (January 2005). The referee, committed to a ceremonial free-kick, had to order a retake as he hadn't signalled with the whistle.

Rr

RACISM

Racism operates at a manifest level through words and chants (racial abuse) and at a latent level through more subtle forms of prejudice. In October 2004, the Commission for Racial Equality reported that non-white people were underrepresented in football's positions of authority.

In 2001, Gurnam Singh, a referee, won an industrial tribunal case against the FA after claiming that FA officials took exception to his racial background and 'wanted to get rid of him'. James Hussaney, a black trainee at Chester City, also won an industrial tribunal case – after his manager Kevin Ratcliffe had racially abused him (November 1997).

Any remark that is discriminatory by ethnic origin, colour, race, nationality, religion, sex, sexual orientation or disability is a sending-off offence, as recommended by the 1998 Football Task Force. Nenad Jestrovic (Anderlecht) was sent off for racially abusing Mohamed Sissoko (Liverpool) in November 2005, and Sinisa Mihajlovic (Lazio) was suspended for two matches after admitting that he had racially abused Patrick Vieira (Arsenal) in 2000. John Mackie (Reading) issued a public apology to Carl Asaba (Sheffield United) for comments made after a game (December 2002). Mackie was banned for three matches and fined £1,500. He also donated two weeks' wages to the 'Let's Kick Racism out of Football' Campaign, an organisation formed in 1993 to challenge racism and work for positive change. Their ten-point plan was later adopted by UEFA and Football Against Racism in Europe (FARE).

Racial abuse is against the law in Britain (and in many other countries), and indecent or racialist chanting is an offence under the Football (Offences) Act 1991. Crowd abuse was present when Albert Johanneson (Leeds United) was baited with chants mimicking those in the film *Zulu* (1964), and it became more noticeable when John Barnes (Liverpool) was showered with spit and bananas against Everton (October 1987).

Action has been taken in certain cases. In Hungary, a referee threatened to stop the match when Ujpest FC fans chanted anti-Jewish abuse at the MTK Budapest team (December 2005), and racist behaviour by Lazio fans during a match against AS Roma led to the club being banned from playing one game on their own ground (April 2001). Getafe (Spain) were fined €3,000 by their football federation after the referee reported that Samuel Eto'o (Barcelona) had been abused by the crowd (November 2005).

A number of incidents involving spectators have gone to court. Brian McPhee (Hamilton Academicals) was the victim in two separate incidents that culminated in an Albion Rovers fan and a Forfar Athletic fan being convicted of racial abuse. A St Johnstone supporter was fined £450 after racially abusing two Livingston players (October 2002). And a Blackburn fan was fined £1,000 and given a four-year ban from matches in England and Wales after he pleaded guilty to abusing Dwight Yorke (Birmingham City) during a match (November 2004).

If spectators or players become aware of racial abuse, the matter should be reported to the police or stewards (if they are present), and to any other people responsible – the club, the manager, and representatives of campaigns such as 'Let's Kick Racism out of Football'. Certain local authorities can expel convicted clubs from council pitches. Public gestures of support have also helped. Treviso players lined up with blackened faces as a supportive gesture for a victimised Nigerian colleague (June 2001), and an incident involving the abuse of Zoro (Messina) caused players to demonstrate against racist fans before a programme of Italian League matches (November 2005).

RAIN See WEATHER

RED CARDS See CARDS, SENDING-OFF

REFEREES

There is no simple way to categorise referees. It could be a grey-haired man in his seventies, slightly stooped, his legs working hard to reach the penalty area. Or a stocky man with muscular calves, his midlife crisis hovering, two pencils sticking out of the top of his sock. Or a fresh-faced young boy, his ruddy features concentrating earnestly as he studies the play. Or a woman dressed in a yellow shirt and black shorts, her long blonde hair bobbing safely in a ponytail as she lopes through the centre-circle. Or a vicar, in almost familiar black cloth with white collar, known for sending off players for offensive language. Or an athlete in his prime, running more than the players, his career in front of him.

The common thread is that they all aim to be well dressed, unbiased, decisive, autonomous, unambiguous in decision-making, and responsible. They know the laws of the game, they do their best to make consistent judgments in accordance with those laws, but they recognise that handling players is more important than understanding the laws. They have good powers of concentration. They cannot afford to switch off.

In March 2003, two academics, Nick Neave and Sandy Wolfson (Northumbria University) studied the psychological profile of senior referees who averaged twelve years of experience. They found that these referees were cool and confident with nerves of steel and a strong set of coping mechanisms. They were dedicated, committed people who took abuse in their stride and seldom acknowledged being in the wrong. The profile resembled those for police officers, politicians and military leaders. The referees tended to blame other people (for being biased or not knowing the laws) rather than themselves.

Referees have careers. The ladder originally had three rungs (1928 to 2001) but this was extended to ten categories (2001) – ranging from level 1 (national list) to level 9 (trainee referee) and level 10 (declared non-active referees). In addition, there are international-class FIFA referees.

Referees may be fulfilling lifelong ambitions, but most start by chance, sometimes when they are pressed into service after an injury has halted their playing career. They can gradually progress through the pyramid – from games watched by one man and his dog to the highest levels. They are promoted when assessors judge them capable of handling more pressure. At the top level they are very confident people. They know they have done it hundreds of times before.

Referees need to be fit enough to cover around six to nine miles per game, which is more than most of the players. According to Ron Boyles in the *Football League Review* (18 November 1967), pedometer experiments showed that a Football League referee covered about eight miles on average in a game, whereas a local referee would average more than ten miles. The higher the class of football, the more the referee could anticipate the play and the more linesmen could be trusted. Linesmen covered between four and five miles.

About a fifth of the referee's time is spent running backwards (to keep their eye on the ball), nearly a fifth sprinting or striding, almost half jogging, and the rest walking. The job also involves travelling to matches, writing match reports, and attending meetings and hearings.

Referees have an adage – give a wrong decision from nearby and players will accept it, but give a wrong decision from fifty yards away and there will be doubts. A referee near to the action can also diffuse arguments more quickly.

Referees have to be decisive. They make decisions every second of the match (if only where to stand). They often have to make several decisions simultaneously (like assessing the conditions for 'denying a goalscoring opportunity').

Refereeing involves a number of other duties to the game: good mental preparation and physical fitness; respect for players and team officials; being honest and impartial; declining matches when not mentally or physically fit, and informing the appropriate authorities accordingly; refraining from accepting offers of excessive hospitality; not tolerating inappropriate language; being a gatekeeper to the best interests of football; protecting the players; and not publicly criticising assistants or other match officials.

Depending on competition rules, referees arrive at a ground anything from half an hour to two hours before the designated kick-off time. They make sure that the pitch is not dangerous to the players. Premier League rules require that referees do a number of other tasks before the start of the match: receive the team-sheets (permitting amendments only if a named player is injured in the warm-up); check the ball; ensure the home club has a coloured ball available; choose a uniform that doesn't clash; ensure the players' kit complies with the rules; ensure the ball boys and stewards do not have kit that clashes; talk with assistants regarding flags and their position for patrol; and lead out the teams five minutes before the start.

Since 1991 registered referees in England have been covered by insurance for possible legal liabilities and third-party claims. The laws of the game document that match officials cannot be held responsible for injuries to players, officials or spectators, damage to property, or any loss suffered by individuals, clubs, companies that are down to the referee's decisions during the match (1995). Whether that would pass the scrutiny of a court of law is a moot point. In 2002, the Welsh Rugby Union admitted responsibility for a rugby referee's persistent failure to control scrums. A 29-year-old hooker, Richard Vowles, had suffered a broken back playing for a village team (January 1998). This case made all sports authorities aware of the possibilities of legal action, but the threshold of liability is high. Referees cannot be held responsible for errors of judgment or oversight.

Refereeing has come a long way from its origins. In the beginning there were two umpires (on the field). Then, when the umpires increasingly disagreed, came this third official called a referee. According to Lovick, 'He was usually an elderly gentleman in a tall hat and he was seated just outside the touchline near the halfway-line. Under this system, when the umpires failed to agree they walked to the touchline and *referred* the matter to him and he gave a decision which was final.'

The first official wording about the referee came in the 1871 FA Cup rules. The final matches had to have three *neutral* officials. If the two umpires disagreed, an appeal could be made to the referee 'whose decision shall be final'. This last phrase – *whose decision shall be final* – refers to all points of play (1893).

The referee was introduced gradually. In the 1871–72 FA Cup competition, two umpires sufficed until the final tie, and the first England–Scotland international relied on the two-umpire system and no referee (November 1872).

The referee was first mentioned in the laws in 1880–81. The referee's job was to keep a record of the game, act as timekeeper, and decide disputes between umpires. But the view from the halfway-line was not always perfect, and referees were often distracted by nearby spectators. John Weir has documented instances of post-match protests on the grounds that the referee had been drunk (*Association of Football Statisticians Report* No. 71). In 1886–87, Lugar Boswell and Dalry were asked to replay their second-round Scottish Cup tie. The referee was variously described as 'smeekit' and 'in a beastly state of intoxication'. He could remember little about the game when Dalry's protest was heard.

In 1889 referees were given additional powers – to stop a game when they considered the circumstances warranted it, to award free-kicks and send players off the field if they were guilty of ungentlemanly conduct (all without appeal). Referees continued to watch the game from outside the field of play, but they went on to the field to restart the game with a throw-up (from 1888).

On good days, referees did not have to make a decision in the whole match. On bad days, however, conferences between umpires and referee took up a lot of time. Finally, in 1891, the referee, complete with whistle and notebook, moved on to the field of play, and the umpires were moved to the touchline, where they became known as linesmen.

Referees were later given the power to make decisions without an appeal from the players (1896), and the referee's power came to include times when play had been temporarily suspended or the ball was out of play (1897).

Modern-day referees have inherited almost the same equipment check list as nineteenth-century officials – two watches (including stopwatch), two whistles, two pencils (pens can smudge in the rain), notepad (or scorecard), a coin, and the match-ball. A wallet of red and yellow cards is a more recent addition, and some change is practical if the referee is getting paid on the day.

In addition to these essential props, referees do their best to remember shirt, shorts, boots, socks, underwear, lucky charm, etc. They will carry a spare shirt in case of a colour clash, and make sure they have a choice of footwear for different ground conditions. They try to arrive on time, but sometimes have to change on the journey.

Derby County's match at Sunderland became known as 'the game of three halves' (September 1894). When the referee arrived at the ground, he found that the teams had already played one half, and Derby were trailing 3–0. The match official offered Derby the option of starting again or continuing. They started again and played two more halves, and Sunderland won 8–0 (11–0 in total). No referee has done this since, and it is not the correct procedure. A late-arriving match referee should take over the history of the game.

Competition organisers have procedures for replacing an incapacitated referee. A Unibond Division One match between Lincoln United and Workington was abandoned after 75 minutes when the referee was injured

(January 2004). The two teams argued about who should replace the missing official. But the game should have continued with only two officials, and Lincoln United were deemed guilty of not fulfilling a fixture.

The need for a replacement referee may arise through unavailability, injury, death, weather conditions or transport problems. More bizarre reasons include the need for the referee to return to his RAF station after two-and-a-half hours of the 1941 War Cup tie between Barnsley and Grimsby (when competition rules meant playing on until one team scored), and a referee being called away from a Bristol Rovers–Lincoln City match to attend a special Parliamentary sitting in the 1950s. A senior linesman took over at Everton when the referee was knocked out by the ball (August 1961), and a senior linesman handled the last forty minutes of a Rochdale–Newport match after the referee twisted his left knee and left the field on a stretcher (March 1967). A former League referee, watching the game, deputised on the line. When Manchester United played Sheffield Wednesday, a change of referee was necessary during the game and eight minutes of stoppage-time was played (April 1993).

The vacancy for a referee can arise at the last minute. When a referee was delayed by fog on his journey to a match between Exeter City and Bristol Rovers, a linesman took the whistle for the first twenty minutes while Exeter City reserve Jimmy McCambridge (ironically an ex-Bristol Rovers player) ran the line (December 1935).

The most curious absence of a referee came when Liverpool and Huddersfield Town played the first thirty seconds of the second half without the match official (March 1948). According to the *Liverpool Football Echo*:

> The second half had got nicely under way and the ball was travelling up towards the Liverpool goal, when the 22 players and the crowd suddenly discovered that there was something not quite right about this kind of football. The referee, far from not being on the field, had not even emerged from the subway! The roar of amusement which accompanied this false start was one of the most notable I've ever heard.

Footballers do like their pranks. The second half was restarted – by the referee.

Some referees accidentally get too involved. An early referee once headed the ball through the goalposts in a local match – he apologised but had to let the goal stand – and a referee 'scored' the only goal of a game between Barrow and Plymouth Argyle (November 1968). George McLean (Barrow) shot hard from the edge of the penalty area and the ball was going well wide. The referee jumped up to avoid the ball but caught it with his left ankle. The ball flew off in the direction of the goal and wrong-footed the Plymouth goalkeeper. The embarrassed referee pointed meekly to the centre-circle to confirm the goal. The ball is in play if it touches a referee who is inside the field of play. Referees are thus treated as if they were goalposts or corner-flags. This has proved a sensible decision. Had the referee been treated as an outside agent, defenders under pressure would probably try to belt the ball against the referee in an attempt to have the game stopped.

Sometimes the referee has more important touches than an off-form player. Cope (Manchester United) played a one-two with the referee in the 1958 FA Cup Final. The ball hit the referee four times during a Denmark–Holland European Championship semi-final (1992). A referee inadvertently started two Manchester United attacks against Middlesbrough when he was hit by the ball (May 1997). Another contributed to a goal when Bordeaux played AC Milan (1995–96). And one popped up on the Notts County goal-line to stop a shot from Carl Leaburn (Charlton), who scored from the rebound (November 1993).

When Sheffield United beat Bradford City 2–1, the first United goal came from an unusual incident (February 1998). Youds (Bradford City) hit a clearance from midfield but the ball struck the referee's head and bounced back towards the City goal. Gareth Taylor (United) calmly controlled the ball and scored. The referee looked crestfallen but the goal had to stand.

Similarly, the referee of a Reading–Norwich City match accidentally blocked a headed clearance from Dean Gordon (Reading) four minutes from time (April 2004). The rebound fell kindly for Philip Mulryne (Norwich), who scored the only goal of the game.

Referees need to anticipate the play. They need a good view of the action, they need to be close to the ball, and they need to keep out of the way. In an FA Cup semi-final, the referee collided with a Sheffield United player during the build-up to the Arsenal goal (April 2003).

Referees need some intuitive understanding of the way a football game unfolds. In his book *The Rules of the Game*, Pierluigi Collina stressed how important it is for a referee to study the tactics of teams. Collina believed that the more a referee understands a team's playing style and set-plays, the easier it will be to referee the game. This means watching teams, talking to other referees, checking the league tables, understanding the fixture's history, and working out which players might be special targets. Most referees would also argue, however, that each game must be treated on its own merits. All past history and prejudice against particular players should be left behind in the dressing-room.

Tactical knowledge also helps assistant referees to judge offsides. Some players dart back and forth, whereas others rely on bursts from midfield. It helps to know what the team is trying to achieve, and not be surprised by a sudden long ball in the tradition of Hoddle or Gerrard.

Patrick Berger (Portsmouth) scored one of the goals of the season at Charlton in August 2004. Unsworth (Portsmouth) took a free-kick on the left-side and unexpectedly played it quickly through to Berger, on the left-hand side of the pitch, about 25 yards from goal. Berger struck a superb left-foot shot which dipped into the postage-stamp corner of the goal. But the referee actually ran across the line of the ball. Had Berger's shot not been impossible to save, the referee may even have unsighted the goalkeeper. The referee had been taken unawares, perhaps expecting Unsworth to cross towards the far post.

In a match against Newcastle, Alonso (Liverpool) shaped to take a free-kick on the right-hand side of the penalty area. Instead of the obvious cross, he deceptively cut the ball back for Gerrard to shoot. The referee had to duck as he was in the line of Gerrard's shot, which went over the bar.

Not all refereeing interventions are accidental. Earls Colne Reserves led Wimpole 2000 by 18–1 after eighty minutes (December 2001). Wimpole had a rare attack and the ball came across the front of the goal. Brian Savill, a referee for eighteen years, intercepted the cross and hit a left-foot volley into the net. Then he signalled a goal for Wimpole. Earls Colne eventually won 20–2 and the referee faced a charge of bringing the game into disrepute.

This is a rare example of a referee's rebellion. Most referees are very professional. They would feel very insulted if anyone confused 'full-time' refereeing with 'professional' refereeing. The two are very different concepts. All referees are professional in the sense that they have undergone training, they receive remuneration for their services, and they are usually the sole decision-maker representing their professional association. They have an argot of their own (e.g. OFFINABUS for offensive, insulting or abusive language), and an objective fitness test, the Cooper Test, named after the author of *The Aerobics Way*. Referees also have a clear set of signals that have been developed to help players and spectators understand refereeing decisions – 'play is stopped' (sound of whistle), goal-kick (pointing to the corner of the goal area), corner-kick (pointing to the appropriate corner-flag), penalty-kick (pointing to the penalty mark), advantage (waving arms forward and calling 'play on, advantage'), indirect free-kick (raised arm), free-kick (pointing to the spot and indicating the direction of the kick), or full-time (three blasts of the whistle and pointing to the dressing-rooms).

In 1901–02, top-class referees were paid a guinea (£1.05) for a match up to eighty miles away and 31 shillings (£1.55) for one over eighty miles. According to Football League Rules (1901-02): 'any club paying a referee more than his just fee and railway fare, shall be deemed guilty of misconduct, and shall be dealt with as hereinbefore provided'. In the event of a postponement, a referee received half his fee plus expenses.

A number of payment-related issues may have a knock-on effect on the laws. There are set fees for each competition, but some clubs may try to increase the fee in return for special privileges. This may be through a substantial bribe or through bonhomie ('Keep the change, Ref'). The method of payment also needs to be considered. If home clubs are responsible for payment they may withhold the money if they are unhappy with the referee's performance. Alternatively, the competition organisers can pay the referee directly.

Fees need to be set at a level that attracts referees into the game and keeps them there. Most referees, however, do it for the love of football. Clive Thomas, who retired from refereeing in the early 1980s, felt that a referee's financial reward should have grown in parallel with that of professional players. In 1994 he was interviewed for the BBC *Kicking and Screaming* series:

> I think I was on something like £25 a match and they were starting to get their £500 and all that type of thing, which to me is a hell of a lot of money. Players have little respect for referees anyway, and the respect was diminishing when players' wages were going up like that. I saw a change in players' moods and their attitudes towards me. There's always been a separation with referees and players but it was going further apart.

On the local park, however, the referee is probably the only person on the pitch who is getting paid.

Traditionally about half of referees leave in the first couple of years after qualifying. The main reason they give is the abuse they receive from players, spectators or coaches.

The retention issue is not just a concern for refereeing organisations. Everybody needs to address it if football is to survive. If referees become extinct, so will the game. It is so hard to recruit and retain referees in some areas of the country that fifty per cent of matches start without a qualified referee, and clubs are having to provide their own. This can lead to biased decisions, excessive amounts of stoppage-time, unfiled misconduct reports, accusations and confrontations. After one Oxfordshire Invitational Youth League game in November 2004, the referee (an official of one team) traded punches with a spectator (the father of a player in the other team).

Referees are indispensable and yet they are rarely voted man of the match. They are more likely to be the subject of vitriol and ridicule. Some of the great referees of the past – John Lewis, Jack Howcroft, Kevin Howley, Jack Taylor, George Courtney, David Elleray – are hardly household names when compared with Billy Meredith, Stanley Matthews, George Best, Gary Lineker and David Beckham. Football history has not served referees as well as they have served football.

REFEREE'S REPORT

A referee's match report should include details of the score, teams, date, colours, substitutions, cautions, dismissals, misconduct, and any unusual matters – a delayed start, a team short-handed at the start of a match, a change of referee during the match, a team failing to provide a linesman, match officials' late arrivals, pitch inadequacies, substandard facilities, any colour change ordered, abandonment of the match, etc.

The report is submitted to the proper authority (e.g. national association, service association, local association, competition organiser) within a specific time period. Referees can be in trouble for not filing reports, not answering correspondence or missing disciplinary hearings. In 2002–03, Surrey FA received 10,220 misconduct reports on cautions and 2,476 on sendings-off. The average reporting time was 5.12 days.

Certain associations have e-mail systems and pre-printed forms to make the task easier for referees. The system of reporting and the time limit for sending in reports is left to competition organisers (1993).

Referees document cautions and sendings-off as briefly as possible – the player's name and initials (as given by the player and as they are on the team-sheet), the offence, when the offence occurred, whether the ball was in play, the referee's position, whether a player received medical treatment, and any later consequences of the incident (e.g. reactions of other players).

Other misconduct includes incidents involving the players before or after the match, or incidents involving coaches, physiotherapists or spectators. The police may ask to see a copy if there has been a serious incident.

Referees are also entrusted with the key task of recording the official score. 'Referees have been known to keep a tally on their shirt cuffs, do queer things with coins, putting one after another in certain pockets to represent the scoring,' said William Pickford, about the game's early days.

When Bolton played Notts County, the referee sent the wrong score to the Football League (October 1889). It was later corrected from 0–3 to 0–4. There are also instances of referees putting a goal down to the wrong team (2–2 instead of 3–1) and calling for extra-time to be played. Arbroath's victory at Stranraer was reported in newspapers as 5–1 but it was corrected to 4–1 when the referee pointed out that he had disallowed a late goal (March 1986).

Players are not always aware of the actual score. When Sheffield Wednesday played Wolverhampton Wanderers in the 1896 FA Cup Final, goalkeeper Tennant (Wolves) came off the field thinking his team had drawn 1–1 rather than lost 2–1. Wednesday's winner had passed Tennant, hit the crossbar, and bounced over the line and out. Seeing the ball in front of him when he came round from his leap, Tennant booted it upfield, and somehow failed to spot the kick-off.

When Australia beat American Samoa 31–0, the scoreboard operator erroneously showed the score at 32–0 and that had to be corrected later by the referee (April 2001). At Stoke, Liverpool were leading 7–0 when they were awarded a penalty (November 2000). As Fowler (Liverpool) placed the ball on the spot, the scoreboard changed to 'STOKE 0 LIVERPOOL 8'. It proved a correct prediction.

RESULT

Sometimes, in football, all that counts is the right result. Winning, drawing and losing were understood concepts from the off, but the matter wasn't added to the laws until 1923: 'A game shall be won by the team scoring the greater number of goals. If no goals have been scored, or the scores are equal at the end of the game, the game shall be drawn.' Cup competitions have rules for settling a drawn match that needs a definite outcome.

The biggest problem comes with determining the result of abandoned matches. They must be replayed unless competition rules specify otherwise. The score at the time of termination has occasionally been allowed to stand in exceptional circumstances. Newcastle's 3–2 lead at Walsall was accepted as a result because Walsall were blamed for the delayed start which eventually led to the abandonment after 78 minutes (December 1894). A 4–1 score in Middlesbrough's favour was considered a result because Oldham Athletic's Cook had caused the abandonment by refusing to leave the field after being sent off (April 1915). And Derby County's 1–0 lead against Fulham was allowed to stand because there were only 78 seconds to play (May 1983).

Authorities experimented with completing the abandoned match at another time. An FA Cup tie between Rotherham Swifts and Rotherham Town was twice abandoned – after 100 minutes with the score 0–0 and after 114 minutes with Town winning 2–1 (November 1889). The remaining six minutes were completed two weeks later. Two players were unavailable so each side played with ten men. Town scored again to win 3–1.

Similarly, when Sheffield Wednesday's home game with Aston Villa was abandoned after 79 minutes (November 1899), the remaining eleven minutes were played fifteen weeks later (March 1899). Any registered player was allowed to play, and the match was started by a place-kick rather than a dropped ball. Wednesday added another goal to win 4–1.

This procedure has been used more recently in other countries. Real Madrid and Osasuna played the remaining 47 minutes of their match three months after the first attempt had been abandoned (May 1989). Osasuna scored in February, and Hugo Sanchez (Real Madrid) equalised in May. The 1995 Spanish Cup Final was abandoned after 79 minutes when a storm broke out, so Valencia and Deportivo La Coruna returned to the stadium two days later to play the remaining eleven minutes.

These mini-matches were not considered a success by English authorities – they were hardly likely to draw big crowds – and the Football League adopted a different practice (1901–02): 'Any match not completed may be ordered to stand as a completed match, or replayed for the full period of ninety minutes as the Management Committee may direct.'

Replaying abandoned matches in full has sometimes seemed unfair. Ipswich Town led Aldershot 1–0 when their FA Cup tie was abandoned through fog, but they lost the replay 3–0 (November 1948). Lincoln City were losing 3–0 at home to Cardiff City when the game was abandoned (March 1958), but won the rematch 3–1 to avoid relegation (May 1958). Bury led 2–0 at Reading when a Cup tie was abandoned after 28 minutes, but lost the return 2–1 (November 1995).

Very occasionally a result will be overturned because of a technical error (a proven error in the referee's knowledge of the laws). Otherwise the referee's judgment has to be accepted. Of course, that doesn't stop managers from guessing what the result might have been.

Football results are such clear measures of success and failure. League tables are a form of continuous assessment, and Cup matches are the equivalent of one-off (or two-off) examinations. We are told that 'the league table never lies' and 'it evens itself out over 46 games'. Indeed, the league-table idea is so popular that it has been copied for schools, universities, and hospitals.

RETALIATION

Retaliation is often punished more heavily than provocation. Justin Edinburgh (Spurs) was sent off in the 1999 League Cup Final for reacting to a reckless foul by Robbie Savage (Leicester), and Garrincha (Brazil) was dismissed in the 1962 FIFA World Cup™ semi-final after responding to a series of fouls by Rojas (Chile). This may be partly because referees are more likely to see the second offence. The crowd in one part of the ground roars, the referee looks across and sees the retaliation.

Players know this. They will provoke opponents into reacting and maybe getting a second caution. Referees always have to try to punish the real culprit. In one notorious incident, Paul Davis (Arsenal) punched Glenn Cockerill (Southampton) and was caught on camera (September 1988). Davis later claimed that he had snapped because Cockerill had been overaggressive throughout the game, 'charging at me, using his elbow when he didn't need to, even stamping on me when I was on the floor' (*Guardian*, 17 September 2005).

Sometimes players need to be sent off for their own safety, as explained by a former professional who was interviewed for *Barnsley: A Study in Football: 1953–59*:

> We were playing Blackpool Reserves one day and the full-back hit me into a big heap. The next thing I knew was the trainer throwing a bucket of water over me and the referee standing there with his book out. 'Don't send him off, Ref,' said Chuckie. Then Skinner said to me softly, 'They'll carry him off.' The full-back stayed on the field and the next time he got the ball I heard the voices behind me: 'Let him come, let him come.' Chuckie hit him first and he was still travelling when Skinner hit him in the ribs. He was carried off.

RETURNING TO THE FIELD OF PLAY *See* ENTERING THE FIELD

ROUGE

N L Jackson described the rouge as it was in the 1867 Sheffield rules:

> The goalposts were four yards apart, with a bar across them nine feet from the ground, and at each side of the goal there were other posts four yards beyond the goal-posts, also with bars at nine feet from the ground, these being called 'rouge flags'. A goal was scored only by sending the ball between the central space, but if it passed between the goal and either of the side-posts (or rouge flags) a rouge was scored. In the event of no goals being scored, the match was decided by rouges, but a goal was far superior to any number of minor points.

Sheffield Wednesday won their first-ever match, at Dronfield, by one goal to four rouges (December 1867). The Sheffield rule-makers abolished rouges in 1868 and altered the goal-size so that goalposts were eight yards apart.

Ss

SCORING See METHOD OF SCORING

SECOND CAUTION See CAUTION, SENDING-OFF

SENDING-OFF

A sending-off is one of the most highly charged moments of football. This is when assaults on referees are most likely. When a Buckland player was sent off in a North Berkshire League match, he collected the dressing-room key and allegedly incited two youngsters to urinate on the referee's clothing (November 1999).

The disciplinary action of dismissing players from the field, so that they take no further part in the match, was first mentioned in the case of violent conduct (1880). Other offences were added: serious foul play; persistent misconduct after receiving a caution (1907); foul or abusive language (IFAB 1927), later known as offensive, insulting or abusive language (1997) and/or gestures (2000); spitting (1968); denying an obvious goalscoring opportunity (1990); and denying the team a goal or an obvious goalscoring opportunity by handling the ball (1990).

Dismissals were very rare in the early days. John Maddocks calculated that Manchester City had only 7 players sent off in the 74 years between 1892 and 1966. When Tom Cawley was sent off in error during a game between Sheffield Wednesday and Lincoln, the referee realised his mistake and called Cawley back but the player refused to return as a matter of principle (1888). When Tom Robertson (Queen's Park) was sent off against the Corinthians, the referee was surrounded by players of both sides, and the Queen's Park captain was eventually sent to fetch Robertson back (1892).

When sendings-off did occur, they were harshly punished. Frank Barson (Watford), sent off against Fulham (September 1928), was banned for the remainder of the season. Willie Woodburn (Rangers) received two lengthy bans before being suspended *sine die* after an incident in a League Cup match against Stirling Albion (1954). The ban was not lifted until 1957 (when Woodburn was 38 years old). In the 1950s, dismissals were seen as a disgrace. By the 1980s they were inconveniences.

A sending-off offence is a sending-off offence whether it occurs in the first minute of the match or the last. Giuseppe Lorenzo (Bologna) was sent off for striking an opponent after only ten seconds against Parma (December 1990). It may seem unfair for a team to lose a goalkeeper in the first minute of the match – as happened to Wrexham (1936), Crewe Alexandra (1994) and Sheffield Wednesday (2000) – when the same offence can cost the opposition a striker in the 89th minute. In the latter case, teams benefiting most are later opponents when the player is suspended.

In a Yorkshire Cup semi-final replay between Huddersfield Town and Bradford City, the referee sent off Robert Newton (Huddersfield) after thirty seconds for foul or abusive language (May 1976). One spectator, arriving two minutes late, took his seat, watched the game and, afterwards, puzzled, said to someone, 'What's the matter with Huddersfield, can't they afford eleven men?'

Teams can sometimes find it tough to make an extra man count. The ten-man opposition work harder to compensate for the sent-off player, and the eleven-man team can be frustrated by an inability to dominate the ten. After Motherwell had performed poorly against ten men in two successive matches, manager Terry Butcher wondered if his players were more likely to switch off against ten (November 2004).

While a nine-man team will most likely capitulate, a ten-man team can play above itself. Matlock Town player-manager Imre Varadi reflected on one such occasion after his team had drawn 3–3 (1995–96): 'Never before in my eighteen years in football have I been on a team leading 3–0 with six minutes left, playing against ten men, that hasn't won.' Other examples of ten-man heroics are Uruguay's 0–0 draw with Scotland after Battista (Uruguay) had been sent off in the first minute (June 1986), England's display against Argentina in the 1998 World Cup when they held the 2–2 scoreline for over an hour, and Turkey under-seventeens coming back from 3–0 down only to lose 4–3 to a last-minute Brazil goal (September 2005). Manchester United's 1985 FA Cup victory came after Moran (Manchester United) had missed the last 42 minutes. The opposing goalkeeper was Neville Southall (Everton): 'Once Kevin Moran got sent off, it worked for them rather than for us. We suddenly started to look tired.'

Three Amsterdam-based academics constructed a mathematical model to test the effect of a player being sent off in a game involving equally balanced teams (*Journal of the American Statistical Association*, 1994). Their assumptions could be challenged, but their results are still interesting. If a player was sent off in the first minute of a match, 65 per cent of matches would be won by the eleven-man team, 18 per cent by the ten-man team, and 17 per cent drawn. If a player was sent off in the last minute, 37.5 per cent would be won by the eleven-man team, 37.5 per cent by the ten-man team, and 25 per cent drawn. These two sets of figures gradually merge as the sending-off gets later and later in the game. However, the red card usually goes to the already weaker team. A sending-off may punish the individual, who can be suspended and may even lose a place in the team, but a professional foul may have a positive outcome for the team, in that it prevents an almost certain goal against.

In modern football, the referee signals the sending-off by holding up a red card, but there have been many ways to leave the field in the past. When Peter Lorimer (Leeds) was sent off at Oxford, during a break in the use of cards, the referee simply said 'Off' and pointed to the dressing-room (November 1984). Willie Duff (Charlton) walked immediately after hitting Dave Hickson. There are instances of referees dismissing unconscious players by informing team-mates ('When he comes round, tell him he's off, too'). And referee Tom 'Tiny' Wharton issued a second caution to the toothless John Hamilton (Hearts) by saying, 'The time has come, Mr Hamilton, for you to rejoin your false teeth.'

Nigel Pepper (Scunthorpe United) suffered a double leg fracture when challenging for the ball with Kidderminster's Paul Webb (August 2000). Then Pepper punched Webb while lying injured on the ground. Pepper was shown the red card as he was being put on to the stretcher. In situations like this, the red card makes it clear that no substitute will be allowed.

Players are under the referee's control for discipline from the moment the referee steps on the field, and that includes the period between full-time and extra-time. Guy Branston (Wycombe Wanderers) was sent off at Plymouth after an incident that took place between the full-time whistle and the start of extra-time (November 2003).

Players who have been sent off must return directly to the dressing-room, which can be a problem if the changing-rooms are locked. A dismissed player must leave the vicinity of the field of play (2001). They cannot watch from the sidelines or the technical area. But Kanchelskis (Manchester United), sent off for handling to save a certain Aston Villa goal, stayed behind the Wembley goal to watch the penalty-kick he had conceded in the 1994 League Cup Final.

Dismissed players cannot return to the pitch. In one of Stanley Rous's early matches as a referee, he sent off a player for kicking an opponent. It was the first time he had sent off a player and he wasn't certain of the procedure. During the interval club officials conned Rous into letting the player back on for the second half. It was a hard lesson for Rous, who had to explain himself to the Hertfordshire FA.

If two or more players have to be dismissed, most referees would deal with them one at a time (or the bell may sound for the next round of the fight). When Dave Hatton (Blackpool) and John Vincent (Middlesbrough) were sent off they resumed their fight in the dressing-room and had to be separated by ground staff (April 1972). The most striking example (literally) came when Derby County played Leeds United (November 1975). Norman Hunter (Leeds) and Francis Lee (Derby) had been at loggerheads throughout the game. Lee was accused of diving for a Derby penalty, and Hunter's reckless tackle on Lee led to a real scuffle. Among the punches was one from Hunter that split Lee's lip. The referee sent off both of them, and they had almost reached the touchline when their fight resumed. This time Lee dominated the flurry of blows.

Referees are required to wait a reasonable length of time for a sent-off player to leave the field. If a player refuses to depart, the match can be terminated. It took fifteen minutes for Michael Sulfaro (Lazio) to leave the field during an Anglo-Italian Cup match against Wolves, but the game continued (May 1970). In another match, Maltby were leading 1–0 when Armstrong (Armthorpe) was sent off with five minutes to play, and when the player returned to the field, the referee abandoned the match (April 2000).

Referee Arthur Ellis abandoned a friendly between Coventry City and San Lorenzo after 44 minutes when a dismissed San Lorenzo player refused to walk (January 1956). Jimmy Greaves (Barnet) caused an abandonment against Chelmsford when he refused to leave after complaining that he hadn't been shown the red card properly (November 1977).

A sending-off may threaten the future of a game in one other way – both teams need to have at least seven players on the pitch for the game to continue. There have been plenty of examples of teams being too depleted for the match to continue. All the Juventus Cross team were sent off at Waltham Abbey (December 1973), nineteen players were dismissed in the 1975 Chile–Uruguay international, six Ecuador players were sent off in Uruguay (1977), 22 players were sent off in an America–Guadalajara match in Mexico City (1986), and all the Gamonal side were given their marching orders against Toledo Imperial (1990).

At other times it has been a close-run thing. In the 1987–88 European Cup competition, Partizan Tirana (Albania) had four players sent off in the first leg against Benfica: the goalkeeper, sent off for kicking an opponent in the stomach, took six minutes to leave the pitch; two were sent off for spitting; and a fourth for throwing ice cubes at the referee. The referee played ten minutes of stoppage-time, Benfica won 4–0, and Partizan Tirana were disqualified from the competition.

The disciplinary code applies to substitutes who have not yet entered the game. Ian Banks (Barnsley) was sent off after 65 minutes of the game against Bournemouth (December 1989). Banks, sitting on the bench, used foul and abusive language to a linesman. Barnsley were permitted to keep eleven men on the field.

If a substitute enters the field without permission and socks an opponent, and then the opponent hits him back, the referee should send off both players. The injustice is that one team continues with ten men but the other continues with eleven (with a substitute short). Substitute Niall Quinn (Republic of Ireland) was sent off when he came off the bench to chase Garcia (Mexico) and remonstrate with the referee after a team-mate's dismissal (June 1996). Walter Boyd (Swansea) was sent off for using an elbow during the match against Darlington (November 1999). Boyd, a substitute, had just entered the field and play had yet to restart. Swansea continued with ten men.

Coaches and managers can be sent from the technical area. Gillingham player-manager Andy Hessenthaler, a substitute in the match at Cardiff, was sent from the dugout after forty minutes (September 2003). However, he was allowed to enter the field as a replacement for Spiller later in the match. He had clarified this with the referee before leaving the technical area. As a manager he had been ordered off, as a player he was unaffected.

Match officials have been known to send themselves off. When referee Andy Wain heard the Peterborough North End goalkeeper say, 'It's always the bloody same with you, Ref – we never get anything,' he hurled down his whistle, untucked his shirt and stood up to the goalkeeper (January 2005). Wain realised immediately that his action was unprofessional. He showed himself the red card and walked off without arguing with himself. Wain was banned for 35 days by the Northants FA.

One referee met with an embarrassing incident in a match between Bury North End and Redfern Athletic (1963–64). Having forgotten to bring his watch, the referee borrowed one from a player. During the game, however, the referee had cause to send off the same player, who asked for his watch back before leaving the pitch.

SERIOUS FOUL PLAY

Serious foul play is a sending-off offence. The major difference between serious foul play and violent conduct (also a sending-off offence) is that serious foul play takes place while the ball is in play and players are seemingly contesting for the ball, whereas an offence is categorised as violent conduct if the violence is away from the ball or the ball is dead. After serious foul play, the game is usually resumed with a free-kick for the serious foul.

Serious foul play means using excessive force – an over-the-top tackle, jumping at an opponent (the so-called two-footed tackle), a bad tackle from behind, deliberately stamping on a player, a rugby tackle, deliberately elbowing a player, deliberately kicking or hitting a player, or any tackle from the front or the side that endangers the safety of an opponent. Jeff Hopkins (Fulham) was sent off for a tackle that broke the leg of Huddersfield's David Burke (March 1985), and Henry Hughton was dismissed when Gerry Ryan (Brighton) suffered a leg fracture (April 1985).

A referee will assess a number of things – the degree of malice, the intent, the speed of the challenge, and the chances of a player winning the ball. Roy Keane (Manchester United) was sent off for stamping on goalkeeper Baia (Porto) three minutes from the end of the match (February 2004). The goalkeeper dived to collect the ball and Keane followed through. The referee felt that he could have avoided the goalkeeper, who always looked like winning the ball. Play was resumed with a free-kick.

Some actions can be either serious foul play or violent conduct: Mido (Spurs) was sent off for serious foul play when he elbowed Del Horno (Chelsea) with excessive force while jumping towards the ball (August 2005); but Solano (Aston Villa) was sent off for violent conduct for elbowing Hughes (Portsmouth) as the referee had already blown to give Villa a free-kick *against* Hughes for shirt-tugging (August 2005).

Attempt is treated in the same way as actuality. In January 2006 a two-footed lunge by Ronaldo (Manchester United) was punished with a red card even though there was no contact with Cole (Manchester City).

SHEFFIELD RULES See ORIGINS OF THE LAWS

SHIELDING THE BALL See IMPEDANCE

SHINGUARDS

Shinguards, introduced in 1874, were first mentioned in the laws in 1880. The first pads were worn on the outside of socks. Charlie Bambridge (Swifts) was recovering from a broken leg but was determined to play in a county cup final (1880s). He took to the field wearing a very large and prominent white shinguard outside one sock. His opponents happily hacked at the shinguard, only to discover later that Bambridge had deliberately put the pad on his sound leg.

There was controversy in the 1960s when shinguards were jettisoned by some players. Dougan (Blackburn) discarded his in the 1960 FA Cup Final, Corso (Inter Milan) rolled his socks down at the start of the 1967 European Cup Final, and Gemmell (Celtic) was padless when he smacked in the equaliser in the same match. George Best (Manchester United) had his socks rolled down when he rounded goalkeeper Henrique (Benfica) to put United 2–1 up in the 1968 European Cup Final. Other shinguard-free stars included Mario Kempes (Argentina), Marius Trésor (France) and Michel Platini (France).

Eventually, when IFAB were concerned about the AIDS epidemic and substandard footwear with dangerous studs, the wearing of shinpads was made compulsory (March 1988), and players without shinguards could be ordered from the field and not allowed to return until they were properly dressed (1992). Also, socks need to be visible as teams must be distinguishable by their colours.

Shinpads must be made of suitable material and should offer ample protection (1990). One travelling Bolton Wanderers team might have failed this test in the 1940s. The trainer had forgotten to pack the team's shinpads, so he bought 22 paperback novels from the railway-station bookstall at Middlesbrough.

SHIRT-HOLDING See HOLDING

SHIRTS

The first indication of a uniform was a small badge tied around the arm of Queen's Park players in the late 1860s. This was followed by reversible cowls (blue and red).

Jackson documented the sartorial elegance of Darwen's 1879 team: 'One or two of the Darwen team wore long cloth trousers, with braces over a dark shirt. Nearly all of those who boasted knickerbockers had those useful articles made of old trousers cut down. The shirts were all sorts, and the two men who wore "sweaters" were evidently the "Brummels" of the team.'

Not long afterwards, teams were wearing shirts of a uniform colour. As late as 1909, however, a goalkeeper's jersey was the same colour as the rest of his team. Then, following a proposal from Grimsby Town, it was decided that goalkeepers should wear shirts of a distinctive colour (royal blue, scarlet or white) and that restriction (with royal green added in 1912) stayed until the 1970s. IFAB decided that international goalkeepers should wear yellow jerseys (1921).

Most club goalkeepers wore green. West Ham were one of many clubs who carelessly packed a green goalkeeping jersey for the trip to Plymouth Argyle, the only League team wearing green shirts (October 1936). Plymouth helpfully kept a stock of spares.

A player must wear a shirt. Moments before the end of Kevin Hector's last match for Derby County, against Watford, the referee blew for offside but some Derby fans rushed on to the pitch thinking the game was over (May 1982). One souvenir-hunter peeled off Hector's shirt, and the player had to find a replacement before the referee would continue.

The uniform can be a mix of long-sleeve shirts and short-sleeve shirts, providing all outfield players wear the same colours. In the 2002 FIFA World Cup™, Cameroon wore sleeveless shirts. Later it was confirmed that jerseys must have some sleeves (IFAB 2003). In the same tournament, Edmilson (Brazil) was told by the referee to change his ripped shirt. Not wanting to penalise the player, the referee allowed the player to change his shirt on the field, even though the rules usually required the player to leave the field. As it happened, it took Edmilson three attempts to get the new shirt (with its built-in undershirt) on to his body. One of those attempts ended with the shirt back to front.

Safety is another concern. The referee of a Stoke City–West Brom game told Gordon Banks to change his goalkeeping jersey at half-time because its design, with buttons at the neck, could be dangerous.

Referees appeared in distinctive colours in 1908–09. After World War I, referees commonly wore blazers or jackets – David Hammond (Heywood) always placed his jacket under an injured man – and as late as the 1960s the laws said that blazers or blouses should be worn for international matches. Black was a sensible colour for the background stars of the game. It only became a problem when top-level teams started to play in black or dark navy. Premiership referees shifted to green shirts with thin black stripes (1992–93), and soon afterwards one fan shouted 'You've never been so good since you went unleaded.' The Italian League then brought in an all-yellow kit for referees, and suddenly referees were more noticeable. Many football coaches would agree with the writer Borges, who said that yellow was the most distinctive colour.

The issue of numbering players' shirts was first raised in 1906 and resurfaced in the 1920s. The FA International Committee were against the idea on the grounds that it reduced footballers to the level of horses or greyhounds. Star players preferred to be recognised rather than be known as a number.

In 1928, Arsenal wore numbered shirts at Sheffield Wednesday, and Chelsea did likewise against Swansea. The decision was left to league authorities. Arsenal manager Herbert Chapman found that his reserve-team players could wear numbered shirts but not his first-teamers. After an experiment with numbered shirts in the 1933 FA Cup Final, when Everton wore one to eleven and Manchester City twelve to twenty-two (goalkeeper), the Football League rejected the idea on the grounds of cost and disruption to a team's colours (June 1933).

A German universities team visited England and stated in their preliminary letter that 'our team will be numbered to thirteen' (1936). Sir Stanley Rous asked the FA housekeeper to sew numbers on to the shirts of both teams. As it happened, there had been a mistranslation. The Germans had merely written that their party *numbered* thirteen. However, FA committee members found the numbered shirts helpful as they could identity players from the programme. The England international team wore numbered shirts for the first time against Scotland (April 1937), and numbered shirts became compulsory in the Football League at the start of the ill-fated 1939–40 season.

The laws do not insist on numbered shirts but competition rules may demand it. The original purpose of numbers was to allow spectators to identify players. Later, with an increase in cautions and sendings-off, it became beneficial to referees, who could identify players for misconduct reports. A referee can check the spelling of number-seven's name against the team-sheet. Sometimes it's not straightforward. The start of a Charlton Athletic–Everton match was delayed because Gritt (Charlton) and Peake (Charlton) both wore number-four shirts (December 1987). Denmark were fined because a player wore the wrong shirt against Spain in the 1988 European Championships.

In the late 1990s, spectators began to complain that some numbers were impossible to see from the sidelines. They included teams playing in red-and-white stripes with black numbers (Brentford, Sunderland and Exeter City), Queen's Park Rangers (red numbers on blue and white hoops) and Stockport County (blue numbers on a blue background). Premier League clubs wearing stripes were told to put numbers on a distinctive square (2005).

Names were added to shirts for the 1992 European Championships and the 1993–94 season in England. When Southampton scored a last-minute winner against Norwich City, the scorer took off his shirt, dropped it on the floor and ran off barechested to celebrate with fans (April 2005). The referee picked up the discarded shirt and noted what he needed for his misconduct report – '37 CAMARA'.

SHORT CORNERS *See* MINI-CORNERS

SHORTS

In the beginning players wore long trousers. A rule stipulated that knicker-bockers worn by players should be long enough to cover the knees (FA 1904). This propriety rule was relaxed the next year – knickerbockers merely had to reach the knee – and abolished altogether in 1907–08.

Until 1990, the laws did not explicitly state that shorts were compulsory, but it was always assumed that players would wear them. A Derby Welfare League match saw a goalkeeper playing in a pair of bathing trunks (December 1955). In a goalmouth scramble, an attacker got his studs caught in the goalkeeper's shorts and ripped them off. The ball was cleared to the touchline but the referee decided not to stop the game as it was not an injury. A centre came in and a goal was scored past the swimsuited keeper.

Shorts are now compulsory. A team's shorts should be of uniform design and colour, but teams can wear the same colour shorts as the opposition. Advertising on shorts is not allowed (2002). If thermal shorts are worn, they must be of the same main colour as the covering shorts (IFAB 1991, 1997). In practice, it is unlikely to find this rule enforced on local parks.

A major controversy began when Cameroon players wore a one-piece bodysuit (2004 African Nations Cup). This began a legal battle between FIFA and the manufacturer, eventually settled out of court (October 2005). Shorts and shirt must now be separate items (2006).

Players are allowed to wear tights as long as they do not detract from the team's colours. Keith Weller (Leicester City) wore sparkling white tights in the 1970s, and Ryan Giggs (Manchester United) wore black tights under black shorts against Manchester City (February 2005).

Tracksuit bottoms are permitted for goalkeepers but not outfield players. They were introduced in the 1960s for frosty conditions, and Gabor Kiraly (Crystal Palace) made them fashionable again in the early 2000s.

SHOULDER-CHARGING

'Coming at any player with thirteen stone six pounds, used right, I could make my presence felt,' said Eddie McMorran, who played centre-forward for Northern Ireland (1947 to 1957). 'In those days you could shoulder-charge goalkeepers and many a match was won by that. The British used the shoulder-charge, the Continentals used obstruction. I'd watch the goal-keeper. As soon as he had hold of the ball and his feet were on the ground, then he could be charged. Goalkeepers were put in the net. And they were challenged when bouncing the ball. It wasn't a waste of our energy.'

Shoulder-charging has changed from a revered skill to an alien concept. In the 1870s Charles Alcock (England) made Catherine wheels out of Scotland opponents. There was a time in the 1880s when five or six players would try to steamroller the goalkeeper whenever the ball was nearby. Modern goalkeepers can only be charged if they are outside the goal area with both feet on the ground and the ball in possession, and it must be shoulder-to-shoulder. Some referees now believe that a fair charge is almost impossible.

When mentioned in the FA draft laws of 1863, charging was 'attacking an adversary with the shoulder, chest or body, without using the hands or legs'. Originally, any part of the body between shoulder and hip (excluding hands and arms) could be applied to the same part of an opponent's body (avoiding the spine and breastbone) when the ball was within playing distance.

Charging from behind was prohibited in 1870 but it was restored seven years later (if players were facing their own goal) because players were shielding the ball by turning their backs on opponents. Players weren't allowed to leap at opponents when charging them (1879), and charging was permitted only when a player was wilfully impeding an opponent (1882).

Because of heavy charging in the early 1890s, goalkeepers were protected by team-mates in the way that American football quarterbacks are covered by colleagues. In 1893 the law was made easier (but not easy) for goalkeepers: 'The goalkeeper shall not be charged except when he be in the act of playing the ball or is obstructing an opponent.' Charging goalkeepers was then restricted to when they were holding the ball or deliberately obstructing an opponent outside the six-yard semicircle (1901). Violent or dangerous charging was outlawed in 1905. The punishment for an unfair charge was a direct free-kick (for holding or pushing) but the punishment for charging a player at the wrong time (when the ball was not in the opponent's possession) was an indirect free-kick.

Shoulder-charging was not common practice outside Britain – a charge by Ted Drake (England) on Italy's goalkeeper provoked ugly scenes in the 'Battle of Highbury' (November 1934) – but British fans continued to see it as an essential ingredient. In a Liverpool–Wolves match in the early 1950s, Liddell (Liverpool) was flattened by a shoulder-to-shoulder charge from Wright (Wolves) in the penalty area. There were shouts for a penalty-kick, but the referee waved play on. Liddell himself accepted it as a fair charge.

Hungary officials were furious when Reilly (Scotland) laid out their goalkeeper Farago at Hampden Park (1954), and two crucial FA Cup Final incidents (1957 and 1958) suggested that the critics had a point. In the 1958 Final, Bolton Wanderers led Manchester United 1–0 when, in the 55th minute, Dennis Stevens (Bolton) shot from a distance. United goalkeeper Harry Gregg pushed the ball up in the air. As the ball fell under the crossbar, Nat Lofthouse (Bolton) charged in clumsily and knocked Gregg and the ball over the line. Most referees then (and all referees today) would have penalised Lofthouse's challenge, but the 1958 FA Cup Final referee saw it differently (or didn't see it at all) and allowed the goal. Gregg recovered after four minutes of treatment.

SIGNALS *See* ASSISTANT REFEREES, REFEREES

SILVER GOAL

The silver goal was used for a short period in the early 2000s as a way of resolving drawn cup ties that needed a definite outcome. The teams played a full fifteen-minute first half of extra-time. If one team led at half-time of extra-time, they would be declared the winners. If the match was still drawn, the two teams would play the second half of extra-time in full. Greece beat the

Czech Republic in the EURO 2004™ semi-final with a goal by Dellas in the last minute of the first period of extra-time. There was no time to restart the match. That silver goal had the same impact as a golden goal.

SIMULATION

The word simulation was introduced to the laws in 1999 to cover a range of unsporting offences that involved acting skills – pretending there had been contact when there hadn't, exaggerating the impact of minimal contact, dragging a leg in order to ensure contact, or feigning injury. Referees were instructed to caution players who were deliberately trying to deceive the referee (2002).

In the 1960s, it was said affectionately of Davie Wilson (Rangers and Scotland) that he could be tripped on the halfway-line only to fall in the penalty area. Francis Lee (Manchester City) won so many penalties for himself in the early 1970s that he became known as the Chinese player Lee Won Pen. Trevor Francis (Birmingham City) was once cautioned for feigning injury against Sheffield United (February 1973). And the cry 'Give him an Oscar' was regularly heard at amateur games.

There was anger after a 1981 FA Cup semi-final, when the referee judged a last-minute tackle by Hoddle (Spurs) on Hibbitt (Wolves) to be a foul, and Willie Carr (Wolves) equalised from the penalty mark. Later, the referee recognised that the Wolves player had made the most of the tackle.

Diving became more of an issue in the 1990s. There were several examples towards the end of the 1992 European Championship Final, and one critical incident on the last day of the 1993–94 Premier League season, when Everton beat Wimbledon 3–2 to escape relegation. Everton were trailing 2–0 when Anders Limpar (Everton) fell in the penalty area. A penalty was given, but it looked as though the defender may have held back from the challenge.

Referees had always had the power to caution divers for ungentlemanly conduct or unsporting behaviour. In a vital EURO 2000™ qualifier, Zahovic (Slovenia) was cautioned for feigning injury in the Ukraine penalty area. Dean Windass (Aberdeen) was sent off for a second caution against Raith Rovers because the referee ruled that he had dived in the penalty area (March 1996).

Detecting simulation is a difficult task. Referees have to check whether attackers are in control of the ball, whether defenders are avoiding the player or not, and whether attackers are trying to stay on their feet. Players may even practise clipping their own heels. The new injury-treatment procedure (1997) was partly designed to curb players feigning injury in order to waste time or disrupt the flow of a game.

In a 2002 World Cup game, as Rivaldo (Brazil) waited to take a corner-kick, the ball was kicked at him by Hakan Unsal (Turkey). Rivaldo went down clutching his face, even though the ball had hit him on the thigh. The referee did not issue a caution but Rivaldo was later fined £4,500 on video evidence. In the same tournament, Neuville (Germany) was cautioned for seeking a penalty against South Korea.

Diouf (Bolton) won a penalty at Blackburn and was later condemned for diving in a way that the referee couldn't detect (January 2005). Bolton scored the penalty and won 1–0. Ronaldo (Manchester United) was cautioned for simulation in the first few minutes of the FA Cup semi-final against Newcastle United (April 2005).

Robert Pires (Arsenal) was criticised for appearing to fix his leg around a Portsmouth defender before going to ground and winning a penalty (September 2003), but the same player was cautioned for diving in stoppage-time against Valencia (March 2003). Television replays were inconclusive when Julia Arca (Sunderland) was cautioned for diving (and sent off for a second caution) against Wigan Athletic (December 2003).

SIMULTANEOUS OFFENCES

If a player commits two (or more) offences simultaneously, the referee should punish the more serious offence (IFAB 1935). For example, if a player takes a throw-in, runs after it and knocks it away from an opponent with his hand, the player commits two offences – handball (direct free-kick) and playing the ball twice from a throw-in without another player touching the ball (indirect free-kick). Handball is the more serious offence, so a direct free-kick is awarded.

SIN-BINS See TEMPORARY EXPULSIONS

SLOPE OF PITCH

Yeovil Town's old Huish Ground had a diagonal slope of nine feet (about 4 per cent). In the 1960s, Yeovil's wingers were told to keep crossing the ball as some goalkeepers would misjudge the flight and then fall over as they moved back. The club moved to new premises in 1990.

Pitch slope is not mentioned in the laws, but competitions may have a maximum-gradient rule. In the guidelines for artificial surfaces, the suggested slope requirement is less than 1 per cent. Oxford United's Manor Ground (1925 to 2001) had a seven-foot slope from goalmouth to goalmouth, Rotherham United's Millmoor was only slightly less steep, and Lye Meadow (Alvechurch) dropped five feet from goal to goal. Other famous slopes are now defunct, because the club has moved (The Nest at Norwich), gone bankrupt (Peel Park at Accrington Stanley) or the pitch has been levelled (Hibernian's Easter Road). The eight-foot slope at Barnet's Underhill Stadium has been difficult to deal with because the pitch composition and the setting made levelling the pitch a real uphill task.

SNOW See WEATHER

SOCKS

Socks are essential equipment for players. The colour of a team's socks must be registered with the competition organisers. The Football League first introduced that requirement in 1937.

An assistant referee once forced a team to change socks when he complained that Sheffield United's clashed with Coventry City's. Occasionally, in local football, one team has been asked to put tape around their socks in order to make the two sets of socks distinctive.

SPECTACLES See EYESIGHT

SPECTATORS See ABUSIVE LANGUAGE, ASSAULT, GRAVE DISORDER, OBJECTS ON THE PITCH, OUTSIDE AGENTS, TEMPORARY SUSPENSION OF PLAY, TERMINATING THE GAME

SPITTING AT A PERSON

An incident in a televised game eventually led to a law change. Crerand (Manchester United) and Dobing (Stoke City) tussled with each other, and the referee jumped in between them (May 1967). Then, out of the referee's sight, Crerand spat in the face of Tony Allen (Stoke). The referee cautioned Crerand and Dobing for the original offence, but he didn't see the spitting incident. BBC *Match of the Day* viewers complained when they saw the incident later that evening. Spitting at a person was classified as violent conduct (IFAB 1968), and made a sending-off offence in its own right (1980).

Some British people believe that spitting at opponents was pioneered by foreign players – Celtic players complained about Racing (Argentina) opponents after the 1967 World Championship – but there have been examples of British fallibility. Billy Bonds (West Ham) was sent off for spitting in the face of a Hull City player (October 1970).

The law was not to stop players spitting, which is a natural and regular act for reasons of salivation, but to prevent the violent and provocative action of spitting at other people. Sometimes it is difficult to tell the difference. Vinnie Jones (Wimbledon) was sent off against Spurs after an angry lunge at Darren Anderton (Spurs) resulted in a second caution (September 1996). There were allegations that Anderton had previously spat at Jones, and counter-suggestions that Anderton had been spitting normally when Jones walked into the line of saliva-fire.

When Patrick Vieira (Arsenal) was sent off against West Ham United for two cautions, he reacted by spitting at Neil Ruddock (West Ham) and swearing at a police officer in the tunnel (October 1999). The spitting action was missed by the referee but clearly shown on BBC *Match of the Day* film. Vieira was charged with misconduct, suspended for six matches and fined £45,000.

Mihajlovic (Lazio) was suspended for eight matches after television footage showed him spitting at Chelsea's Adrian Mutu (November 2003), and Totti (Italy) was banned for three games for 'gross unsporting conduct' after television replays showed him spitting in the face of Christian Poulsen (Denmark) at EURO 2004™. Similarly, El-Hadji Diouf (Bolton) was caught on camera spitting in the face of Arjan de Zeeuw (Portsmouth) (November 2004). Diouf was also fined £500 (plus costs) at Teesside Magistrates Court when he pleaded guilty to disorderly conduct after spitting at a fan at Middlesbrough (November 2005). Spitting at a spectator is also a sending-off offence.

In 1990, Rijkaard (Holland) was sent off for spitting at Rudi Völler (Germany) when the referee spotted an incident that went unnoticed by large sections of the crowd. And the referee of a friendly in Wydad Casablanca (Morocco) could not help but notice when Fabien Barthez (Marseilles) spat at him (February 2005). Barthez was banned for eight months by the French Football Federation. Spitting at a referee is a serious offence.

SPONSORSHIP See ADVERTISEMENTS

SPORTSMANSHIP See FAIR PLAY

START OF GAME See PLACE-KICK

STOPPAGE-TIME

Referees have the power to add time to the end of each half to allow for time wasted, or lost, through accident or other reason (IFAB 1906). Stoppage-time includes time lost for injuries, substitutions, cautions, sendings-off, strategic time-wasting and temporary suspensions of play.

The first half of a cup tie at Bristol City lasted slightly under 67 minutes when an injury to Lloyd Owusu (Brentford) caused a long delay while an ambulance came to the side of the pitch (August 2000). A sending-off and a number of injuries led to eight minutes of stoppage-time at the end of the first half of a USA–El Salvador international (September 2004). The second half of Liverpool–Chelsea had six minutes of stoppage-time for six substitutions and two pitch invasions by lone spectators (May 2005). The first half of Grimsby Town–Derby County was extended by about fifteen minutes after a delay caused by a serious head injury to Grimsby's Steve Livingstone (August 2002). And Barton Rovers versus Chatham Town was suspended for 45 minutes while an ambulance arrived to deal with a head injury to Barnes (Barton) in September 2005.

Stoppage-time can be a tense, controversial period with a disproportionate amount of goals. Manchester United featured in two sensational periods of stoppage-time in the 1990s. They scored in the sixth minute of added-time against Sheffield Wednesday (April 1993), and twice in two minutes of stoppage-time to beat Bayern Munich in the 1999 Champions League Final.

In the 1994 FA Vase Final, Taunton Town lead Diss Town 1–0 until nearly ten minutes of stoppage-time had been played. Then goalkeeper Kevin Maloy (Taunton) was adjudged to have fouled Stephen Miles (Diss), and Paul Gibbs scored from the penalty. Cramp and minor injuries on a wet surface accounted for so much stoppage-time. Diss won 2–1 after extra-time.

A Leicester–Arsenal match caused controversy when Leicester equalised during a lengthy period of stoppage-time (August 1997). Conversely, the Blackburn–Leeds match seemed to halt suddenly when spectators expected lengthy stoppage-time after an eventful match (September 1997). Eventually, after experiment, the major British leagues adopted an Italian system whereby the fourth official holds up a board showing the minimum number of minutes the referee would add on. However, the match referee is the person in charge of the full-time whistle. In local football, there are tales of club officials, deputising for an absent neutral referee, adding on twenty minutes of stoppage-time while their team equalises.

Time is not added on for that lost in organising restarts (providing there is no unnatural delay). An assistant referee can aid a referee by signalling when the half's 45 minutes are used up (usually by holding the free hand across the chest). Time can be added on for a penalty-kick to be taken, but there needs to be a definite outcome (as explained in the penalty-kick section).

Calculating stoppage-time is more of an art than a science. Referees use various methods. Some stop their watch and restart it when the interruption ends; others point out that this is a risky method if you forget to restart the watch. Most keep a separate watch for stoppage-time. Others keep the stoppage-time in their heads, using a rough-and-ready method (thirty seconds for a caution, etc.). And one eccentric referee, believing that he only got paid for ninety minutes, carried a watch with no stop.

STREAKERS See OUTSIDE AGENTS

STRIKING A PERSON

In a pre-season friendly, Gordon Dalziel (Raith Rovers) got between Graeme Hogg (Hearts) and Craig Levein (Hearts) and sent in a shot, which was saved (August 1994). Then something happened to bemuse the 2,172 crowd. The two team-mates, Hogg and Levein, argued with each other and started fighting. Punches were thrown and they were sent off. Hogg was shown the red card as he was being stretchered off with a broken nose. The Tynecastle club carried out a swift internal inquiry, punished the pair and issued a statement strongly condemning their conduct. Hogg and Levein were later banned for twelve weeks, and Levein was stripped of the captaincy.

Striking an opponent was added to the list of sending-off offences in 1914. It was soon made clear that the offence applied not only to hitting an opponent, but also hitting a spectator or hitting a team-mate. Striking can include punching, head-butting, elbowing, slapping, or anything where an arm is raised.

A sending-off for striking another person may have more far-reaching consequences. According to the *Leicester Mercury* (2 April 1992), a player who punched an opponent in a local Sunday League match was ordered to pay the opponent £415 compensation, as well as £200 costs and a £100 fine. The opponent's jaw was broken in two places.

Football history has so many one-on-one spats that there are enough incidents for a book on boxing. There are stories from the lightweight division (Keegan versus Bremner at Wembley in 1974), the middleweights (Venables versus Callaghan at Tottenham in 1967), and the heavyweights (Todd versus Collymore at Bolton in 1997). Sometimes the weights are mis-matched, like Wise (Leicester) against Vieira (Arsenal) in September 2001.

The stars are not immune. Lauren Blanc (France) was sent off for striking Slaven Bilic (Croatia) in July 1998, and Zinedine Zidane (Real Madrid) fourteen red cards included one in the 2006 FIFA World Cup™ Final.

The laws interpret *attempting* to do something as the same as *actually* doing it. Lee Hendrie (Aston Villa) was sent off for attempting to strike Danny Mills (Manchester City) (November 2004). There was no contact – Hendrie faked to head-butt Mills but withdrew his head – and several television experts seemed to think that a player should not be sent off if there was no contact. In fact, the simulation was enough to warrant the dismissal, especially when viewed from the referee's angle (over Hendrie's shoulder).

Striking a spectator is the same sending-off offence as striking a player. Goalkeeper Darren Clayton (Armitage) was sent off against Tamworth for retaliating after being punched by a spectator, and Armitage went on to lose 11–2 (January 1994). Charlie George (Arsenal) was lucky to escape a sending-off at Norwich when he thumped a photographer who wouldn't return the ball (September 1980). The photographer pressed charges against George, who was fined £400 and £40 costs after pleading guilty to threatening behaviour (December 1980).

Kicking (or throwing) the ball hard at a person (especially a referee) is also punishable by a red card. Lavin (Bristol City) was sent off for kicking the ball hard into Reading fans (August 1999), and Gary Neville (Manchester United) was sent off at Everton for half-volleying the ball at a spectator (April 2005).

Striking a team-mate is also a sending-off offence and an indirect free-kick is awarded to the opposing team if the ball was in play (FIFA Referees' Committee 1930). The precedent was Billy Smith and John Duffy (both Darlington Reserves) who were sent off for fighting at Halifax (1903).

Derek Hales and Mike Flanagan (both Charlton Athletic) were sent off five minutes from the end of an FA Cup tie against Maidstone United (January 1979). They had fought with each other after an argument over a pass from Flanagan that caught Hales offside.

Tom Rees and Tom Watson (both Grimsby Town) were sent off at Darlington for fighting each other in a Leyland Daf game (December 1990), but David Batty and Graeme Le Saux (both Blackburn Rovers) went unpunished when they traded punches after four minutes of a European Cup tie against Spartak Moscow (November 1995).

In a match against Halifax Town, Scott Morgan (Forest Green Rovers) was sent off for violent conduct after he had head-butted his own captain (September 2003). Widespread publicity came after a fight broke out between Lee Bowyer (Newcastle) and Kieron Dyer (Newcastle) when their team was losing 3–0 at home to Aston Villa (April 2005). The ball was in play in the 82nd minute when the two team-mates began scrapping. Both players were sent off, and play restarted with an indirect free-kick to Aston Villa.

STUDS *See* FOOTWEAR

SUBSTITUTES

There is no better example of the game's increasing complexity than the trend towards more and more substitutes. The English game resisted their introduction until 1965–66, when 770 substitutes were used in 2,028 Football League matches (0.33 per game). Compare this to 2002–03 when 1,776 substitutes were used in 380 Premiership matches (4.67 per game). This escalation brings a variety of issues for all concerned – warming-up procedures (in colours that do not clash), where to sit (on a bench in the technical area), guidelines for implementing a substitution, a code of discipline for substitutes, additional stoppages in play, tactical shifts which accompany a substitute's arrival, differing competition rules for numbers of substitutes, terminology to distinguish *players* from *substitutes*, and a whole sequence of 'What if?' questions. FIFA's *Question and Answer* booklet contains more than twenty items on substitutes.

A lot can go wrong. Herne Bay used four substitutes instead of the permitted three in an FA Cup tie against Farnham (September 1999). Scott Liddell arrived late at the ground and then came on for the second half without the substitution being recorded by the officials. When the fourth substitution was made, with ten minutes to play, the error was not spotted. Herne Bay won the game but had to replay it at Farnham. Games have also been replayed when a referee has knowingly let on a substitute whose name is not on the team-sheet.

Tranmere Rovers made an illegal substitution in stoppage-time after Clint Hill (Tranmere) had been sent off against Sunderland (January 2000). Rovers played the last thirty seconds with eleven men rather than ten. The referee was suspended for two months.

The first big-match substitution was probably when Wales played Scotland at Wrexham (April 1889). Shortly before kick-off the Welsh selectors sent for Sam Gillam (Wrexham) as their regular goalkeeper Trainer (Preston) was unavailable. In the meantime, Alf Pugh, a local village player, kept goal. After thirty minutes Gillam replaced Pugh.

Substitutes were used in certain games if both sides agreed. Discussion of more formal arrangements arose after an injury to Makepeace resulted in England playing with ten men for most of the international against Scotland (April 1906). Davies (Wales) was allowed to replace injured goalkeeper Roose for the second half of the international against England (March 1908).

Substitutes were first mentioned in the laws in 1923. The general custom was to allow two substitutes in friendly matches (including friendly internationals) if both teams agreed (IFAB 1932). One substitute was for the goalkeeper at any time in the match; the other was for an outfield player up to half-time. The substitute could not be replaced by the original player. Substitutes were not allowed in competitive matches.

The early substitutes were allowed to replace injured players only, and defining an *injury* was sometimes difficult. Officials for the Rest of Europe team tried to replace goalkeeper Zeman against England, but the referee refused to allow it because the player did not look injured (October 1953). A medical opinion at half-time forced the referee to allow the switch. A similar thing happened during the England–Hungary match (November 1953). When goalkeeper Grosics (Hungary) was replaced seven minutes from the end, the referee jiggled the player's arm until the goalkeeper's pain proved that he really was injured.

The hotter the climate, the more countries pushed for substitutes, whereas playing with ten men was part of the heroic nature of British football. There were legendary stories of players like goalkeeper Frank Moss (Arsenal), who dislocated a shoulder against Everton but returned to volley a goal from the left wing (May 1935). But players sometimes wrecked their careers by continuing for nuisance value.

There were calls for substitute goalkeepers after an injury to Moulson (Grimsby Town) spoiled an FA Cup semi-final (March 1939). The debate intensified when seven out of ten FA Cup Finals featured a ten-man team (1952 to 1961). IFAB rejected a proposal that an injured goalkeeper could be substituted in all games (1957). Finally, in 1959, IFAB allowed substitutions in competitive matches if the relevant national association or international association agreed.

In 1965, the Football League voted 39–10 for one substitute to replace an injured player. The responsibility of judging injury was left to the referee. In this first season of substitutes, a player might suddenly leave the field clutching a hamstring or claiming grogginess (perhaps because an opponent had been running rings around him). Out-of-form players were sometimes substituted because of a 'stomach upset'. Danny Blanchflower suggested that replaced players should be automatically banned from their team's next match.

A year later, in 1966, the English leagues permitted substitutions *for any reason* (tactical or injury). Substitutes were introduced to the FA Cup and League Cup in 1966, and to local football the following year. The Scottish FA and League followed this line, and substitute goalkeepers were allowed in home internationals. In June 1967 IFAB allowed two substitutes per team (for any reason), if the national association agreed, but the names of the substitutes had to be given to the referee in advance.

Injured players can be replaced right up to kick-off without it counting as a substitution. Blyth (Coventry) was injured in the kick-in (September 1979), Digweed (Brighton) was injured in a pre-match warm-up (September 1991), on-loan defender Overson (Shrewsbury) pulled a calf muscle before the kick-off against Rotherham United (October 1997), and Turner (Everton) replaced Wright at Chelsea (February 2006).

A Czechoslovakia substitute was sent off before he came on to the field against England (October 1975). The Czechs continued with eleven men and one fewer substitute. Other internationals to be dismissed from the bench include Katanec (Yugoslavia) against Argentina (1990), Felip (Spain) against Morocco (2000), and Caniggia (Argentina) against Sweden (2002).

What about the mind-set of substitutes? Some are calm and concentrative. Ole Gunnar Solskjaer, veteran of well over 100 substitute appearances for Manchester United, retained an excellent temperament on the bench, spending his time studying the game to see how he could take advantage of the opposition. Goalkeepers like Nigel Martyn (Leeds) and Kevin Poole (Bolton) spent a whole Premier League season on the bench (2002–03).

Some watching substitutes get riled. John Ritchie (Stoke) was sent off thirty seconds after coming on at Kaiserslautern (1972), Paul Hooks (Notts County) was dismissed three minutes after appearing as a substitute (August 1977), and Bobby Houston (Kilmarnock) was sent off before he touched the ball against Partick Thistle (November 1979). Houston, playing against his former club, came on in the 58th minute and was sent off within sixty seconds for lunges on Gibson and Whittaker.

Some substitutes may take a time to adjust to the game (physically and mentally) whereas others are magical. Joe Craig (Scotland) scored with his first touch in an international (April 1977). Jimmy Pearce (Spurs) crammed a full game's activity into ten minutes against Rapid Bucharest. He scored a goal, had one disallowed, and was then sent off (December 1971).

Another issue concerns the reactions of the substituted player. In the law's early days, some substituted players felt disgraced. Even the normally placid Roger Hunt (Liverpool) once threw his shirt at the dugout in anger after being replaced by Bobby Graham (March 1969). Other players stood their ground. After an incident in Brazil, when a player refused to leave the field, IFAB ruled that the referee had no authority to enforce the change (1980). No offence had been committed.

It was in Malaysia that Sir Stanley Rous first saw numbered placards held up to signify which player would be leaving the field. During a match at Reading, Exeter City manager Brian Godfrey held the substitute board upside down – nine instead of six – but he realised his error just in time and prevented the wrong substitution (October 1979).

Two substitutions were allowed in international football (from 1970) and in Scotland (1972–73), but some coaches adjusted slowly to the new thirteen-a-side game. In 27 England internationals between July 1970 and October 1973, manager Sir Alf Ramsey used only 9 of the 54 substitutes at his disposal.

In contrast, England manager Sven-Göran Eriksson made 177 substitutions in 20 friendly internationals (February 2001 to November 2004) after unlimited substitutions had been allowed in non-competitive matches, providing both teams agreed and the referee was informed (2000). On four occasions Eriksson made eleven changes in a game.

When the number was reduced (2004), a Fulham–Watford pre-season friendly was abandoned because the two team managers wanted to use more than the permitted six substitutes (July 2004). The managers pointed out that ninety minutes was asking too much of players in the summer heat. The limit on the number of substitutes in friendlies was lifted again in 2005.

In 1981, the laws confirmed that a substitute was under the referee's authority and jurisdiction whether called on to the field or not. Substitutes who entered the field without permission would be cautioned and removed from the pitch. The referee would restart the game with a dropped ball (later changed to an indirect free-kick to the opposition).

The wording of the law was tightened up to clarify that a substitution would be complete when the substitute entered the field of play (1986). A maximum of two from five substitutes was set in 1988, but competition organisers were allowed to set their rules within those constraints. In 1994, there was allowance for a third substitute who could be used as a substitute goalkeeper. The substitute goalkeeper could replace an outfield player if the starting goalkeeper had been sent off. This restriction on the third substitute was then lifted – clubs could choose whether or not they wanted a goalkeeper to be one of their named substitutes (1995).

When Wolves played Barnsley, Barnsley player-manager Danny Wilson was sent off in the 89th minute during a dispute over a penalty awarded to Wolves (April 1995). Wilson then arranged a substitution, which kept penalty-taker David Kelly waiting even longer. Kelly missed the eventual penalty, and the match was drawn 0–0.

It became the vogue for managers to arrange a stoppage-time substitution if their team was ahead. This was to take the momentum away from opponents who were pressing for an equaliser. Managers think they are clever if they take off the player farthest away from the dugouts, and even cleverer if they send a player to the far side of the pitch before replacing him.

At the highest level of the game, the board system was replaced with an electronic system (1996). The boards (known to some players as 'pop-up toasters') continued to be used lower down the pyramid. In local football, substitutions are gadget-free. Substitutes enter the field at the halfway-line during a natural stoppage in play. A player leaves the pitch and a substitute enters (after receiving a signal from the referee) (1973). Substitutes give their name to the referee, who makes a note. The substitution is complete when the game is restarted. Sometimes amateur substitutes appear with a convoluted explanation: 'We didn't have enough shirts, Ref, so I'm wearing this one.'

The general procedure at the top level is for the assistant referee to attract the referee's attention at a stoppage in play by placing a flag overhead and holding the flag with both hands (1982). The fourth official holds up a board with both numbers on after checking the substitute's footwear. The referee watches the two players pass and notes the numbers. As soon as substitutes enter the field they become players. This elaborate procedure was developed after a number of occasions where teams had twelve players on the field.

Even with substitutes, teams are sometimes caught short of a full complement. In a 1996 play-off final, Izzet (Leicester) was cautioned for a foul on Simon Rodger (Crystal Palace), who was left a virtual passenger. As Rodger had himself been the third Palace substitute to become a player, Palace were left with ten fit men. The same happened to West Germany when, having used both substitutes, Beckenbauer was injured by a bad tackle and forced to play extra-time against Italy with his arm in a sling in the semi-final of the 1970 FIFA World Cup™.

In 1996, the law noted that 'the rules of the competition shall state how many substitutes may be nominated, from three up to a maximum of seven'. This meant that the number of substitutes on the bench at international tournaments increased from five to seven; but only three could be used.

SUSPENSION OF PLAY *See* TEMPORARY SUSPENSION OF PLAY

SWEARING *See* ABUSIVE LANGUAGE

Tt

TACKLE FROM BEHIND

Martin Pringle (Grimsby Town) had his back to the Stockport County goal when he received the ball in the 52nd minute (February 2002). Challinor (Stockport) tackled from behind and Pringle's career ended with a double fracture of the leg. Challinor was cautioned, and substituted soon afterwards.

A tackle from behind is when a player risks going through part of an opponent in order to reach the ball. In this situation a player slides into the back of an opponent rather than allowing the opponent to turn. It is almost impossible to tackle properly through a player's legs, or round a player.

'I was going for the ball,' is not an excuse.

'I got the ball,' is rarely an excuse.

If a player makes contact with the man before the ball it is a foul. If the player makes contact with the man after playing the ball, it is probably a foul. Vieira (Arsenal) made some contact with the ball when challenging Park Ji-Sung (PSV Eindhoven) but it was still a tackle from behind (November 2004). Vieira was cautioned.

Many serious injuries have been caused by the tackle from behind. John Edgar (Gillingham) was not the same player after an incident at Norwich in the 1960s: 'I laid a ball off and a player wrapped his legs around me as I turned.'

Footballers are at their most vulnerable when turning. Against England, Jacques Simon (France) received a pass in his own half, facing his own goal, and played the ball to his left with his right foot (July 1966). After the ball had gone Stiles (England) slid in on a slippery pitch and caught Simon on the turn. Simon was carried off injured.

There have been periodic culls on the tackle from behind. It was permitted in the 1970 FIFA World Cup™ if the ball was played first, but it was a target in the so-called 'Ref's Revolution' (1971–72). Before the 1994 FIFA World Cup™, there was a ban on any tackle from behind and this perhaps contributed to one of the best goals of the tournament. Saeed Owairan (Saudi Arabia) went on a mazy run past five players and scored the only goal of the match against Belgium.

In 1998, referees issued red cards for every tackle from behind that endangered the safety of an opponent. A yellow card was issued for a reckless or careless tackle from behind, and a red card for one using excessive force. Sometimes a tackle from behind will be acceptable, but usually only when both players are standing up and the player behind pops a foot through to nick the ball without touching the opponent.

TAPE See CROSSBAR

TEAM-SHEETS See BEFORE THE MATCH

TECHNICAL AREA

Coaching from the touchline was banned until 1993. The authorities originally believed that the players had to be responsible for their own actions on the field. Referees had instructions to prevent any coaching from the sidelines.

'Stopping us shouting was a silly rule,' said one former manager. 'Everyone else on the ground could shout instructions but not the manager.'

In 1993 a technical area around a team's bench was created, one yard from the touchline, and a coach was allowed to call tactical instructions to players. Markings were recommended after their success in the 1994 FIFA World Cup™ (1995). The fourth official was given powers to inform the referee of any irresponsible behaviour in the technical area (1999), it was made clear that coaches should return to their bench after issuing pitch-side instructions (2000), and the word 'coach' was changed to 'team official' (2001). Competition rules may dictate the maximum number of officials allowed in the area and the number allowed on their feet at any one time. From 2005, cigarette smoking was banned from the technical area in UEFA competitions.

Before 1993, players would go to the touchline on some false pretext ('Just getting a new tie-up, Ref') in order to hear their coach's advice. Referees used to be just as subtle, trotting over to the bench with some distraction ('I've got something in my eye') while delivering their main message in an aside to the coach ('If I hear one more word of coaching from you, I'll report you'); so managers began to ask substitutes to relay instructions while they were warming up along the touchline.

Coaches and managers have always been expected to uphold the same behaviour guidelines as players – no offensive, insulting or abusive language, no dissent, etc. Before 1993, certain coaches, such as Malcolm Allison, were often banned from the touchline for coaching. Alex Ferguson (Aberdeen) was ordered from the dugout after a verbal clash with the referee during Aberdeen's 2–1 defeat at Dundee United (December 1985), Bristol City manager Terry Cooper was reported for entering the field of play when David Moyes (Bristol City) was sent off (September 1986), and Brian Clough

(Nottingham Forest) received a touchline ban for striking a spectator (1989).

Being on the sidelines can be a nervous, frustrating, hair-tearing experience for managers and coaches. During the week managers are 'The Boss' or 'The Gaffer', and suddenly they have conceded authority to the referee and are reliant on their players. Some team officials stand in the technical area with folded arms, but most work the area like a stage. They watch, wave and whistle, in between yelling instructions and simulating every kick. Some managers run miles without leaving the technical area.

In parks football, the technical area may not be marked out and the benches may be park benches. Referees have to use their judgment on what is acceptable. Occasionally coaches will support the referee ('Walk away, son') but more often they will be critical ('Think before you blow, Ref'). It is more difficult to send off a local team official but the referee has the recourse of abandoning the match if a team official refuses to leave the pitch surrounds (IFAB 1981).

At the top level, managers are regularly ordered from the touchline. The offence is usually abusing an official after a refereeing decision. When Berti Vogts (Scotland) was sent from the touchline at half-time against Norway, it was because he felt (erroneously) that the ball had been over the goal-line when a Norway defender cleared it (October 2004). Coaches are not shown a red card when sent from the touchline as red cards apply only to players and substitutes.

Managers have been sent from the technical area for other reasons – kicking a ball away (Alex Ferguson in 2003), going on to the pitch (John Gorman in 2003), kicking a bottle of water on to the field (Graeme Souness in 2004), throwing a bottle of water (Dennis Wise in 2005), abusing the rival manager (David Hodgson in 2005), and having an altercation with an opposing player (Mark Wright in 2003). In July 2000, the FA introduced new penalties for managers and players who abused match officials. Intimidation could result in a £250,000 fine and a two-point deduction.

The technical area is not a place for sent-off players to sit. When Diop (Fulham) was sent off at West Brom (September 2004), Fulham were in trouble with the authorities for failing to ensure that the player left the technical area as well as the pitch.

TECHNICAL ERROR

The referee is the autocrat of the game. The referee's opinion is final on points of fact and opinion. Matches can only be replayed if it can be proved that the referee has made a technical error (an error on a matter of law).

In 1947, a match in Burma between Post & Telecoms and Civil Suppliers ended 3–3. It included an incident whereby a Post & Telecoms player received a pass from a goal-kick. He waited until the ball was outside the penalty area and then inadvertently sent a backpass into his own net. The referee gave a corner-kick rather than the statutory goal. FIFA ordered a replay as this was an error in law. The referee obviously didn't know what the correct decision was.

When Bordeaux played Toulouse, there was a definitive incident in the 86th minute (December 1992). A Toulouse defender passed back to the goalkeeper, who picked up the ball two yards from his own goal-line. The referee awarded an indirect free-kick two yards from goal and Bordeaux scored. The correct decision should have been an indirect free-kick on the six-yard line. Toulouse protested and the match had to be replayed. It was an error on a point of law.

The result of a FIFA World Cup™ qualifier between Uzbekistan and Bahrain was declared null and void in September 2005. Uzbekistan scored from a penalty-kick but one of their players had encroached. The referee awarded Bahrain an indirect free-kick; the correct decision was a retake. The Uzbekistan captain protested that the decision was wrong, but the referee stuck to his decision. This was clearly a technical error and witnesses and video evidence could prove it.

On two occasions the German FA were reprimanded by FIFA for incorrectly replaying matches. In the Bundesliga, a referee awarded Bayern Munich a goal against Nuremberg when the ball had clearly hit the side-netting (April 1994). Bayern Munich won the match 2–1 but the German FA misguidedly ordered a replay (which Bayern won 5–0). On matters of judgment, the referee's decision is final. This was not a technical error.

The referee of a Leipzig–Chemnitz match issued a red card for a second caution to Werner (Leipzig) after 72 minutes (1996). Unfortunately Werner hadn't been previously cautioned. But this was a refereeing decision on a point of fact, not a technical error. The German FA erroneously ordered a replay, but they were fined by FIFA and the original result was reinstated.

A dog called Susie was credited with scoring a goal for Knave of Hearts (Chell Heath) against Newcastle Town (November 1985). Susie ran on to the pitch, jumped up and diverted a shot that was going wide. This called for a dropped ball but the referee awarded a goal. But if the referee hadn't seen Susie's leaping header, it wasn't a technical error. There is no truth in the rumour that Susie went on to play for Bristol Rovers, Bedlington Terriers and Barking.

Reading once threatened to take action over a referee's 'egregious blunders and sheer incompetence' in the 1–1 draw against Southend but they soon discovered that they had no case (December 1922). The main talking point was a late penalty-kick. Alonzo Poulton (Reading) shot straight at the Southend goalkeeper but somehow forced home the rebound. The referee initially gave a goal but then changed his decision to a dropped ball after talking to both linesmen. Reading had no case for overthrowing the result – this was *not* technical error – but the referee was removed from the list.

The referee's authority on points of judgment was confirmed by the High Court of Ireland after Carew Park had contested a disallowed goal in a cup match (February 1999). The High Court judge said that while he had sympathy for Carew Park's position, football clubs had to accept the referee's decision (right or wrong). The alternative was hopeless anarchy.

TECHNOLOGY

The main argument in favour of technology-based refereeing is simple – technology can be used to make sure a decision is correct.

The arguments against technology are many: (i) Use of video replays and off-the-pitch information would slow down the game and interrupt its essential flow; (ii) A standby system would be needed in case of equipment-failure; (iii) Referees could lose authority and suffer even more abuse if they are seen to be making decisions based on information gained from elsewhere; (iv) A system introduced at the highest level must also be applied (with more reason) to help inexperienced referees at, say, Surreal Madrid (in the Camden Sunday League) and Marlow Donkey (in the High Wycombe Sunday Combination); (v) The costs may be prohibitive to some clubs; (vi) It would shift even more power to technology experts and television pundits, who do not always fully understand the laws of the game and may have no refereeing experience; (vii) Technology companies and television companies have a vested interest in introducing technology and raising its importance; (viii) Referees may become so equipment-dependent that they lose their own decision-making skills; and (ix) A lot of technology-based evidence is inconclusive and contradictory so nothing would be gained anyway.

Referees offer another argument in favour of technology – camera evidence often supports their decisions. This point was made in 1953 when reporters initially criticised a referee over a penalty incident only to change their minds after seeing newsreel that had been filmed from the opposite side of the pitch. Another definitive incident occurred when Norway scored a controversial late penalty winner against Brazil (June 1998). Spectators saw nothing wrong. Television replays showed nothing wrong. Then a few days later, after much criticism of the referee, a documentary film crew discovered footage, amongst their rushes, which showed Baiano (Brazil) clearly fouling Flo (Norway).

Sir Stanley Rous gave his views on modern technology in his auto-biography: 'With the referee now being judged by impersonal gadgetry, he should in future have electronics to aid him as well as to analyse him. Ever since Geoff Hurst's disputed goal in extra-time proved decisive in our World Cup win over Germany in 1966 I have favoured the electronic recording of goals.'

Having first ruled out the idea of technology (1992), and turned down the French FA's request to experiment with a video system during a friendly international (April 1997), the IFAB announced that technology had improved enough for experiments with goal-line equipment (2005). The FIFA under-seventeen Championship was designated in the first instance. But goal-judging incidents are rare and it needs a large sample of events.

Technology has already been introduced to football. Referees have experimented with different methods of communicating with their assistants through microphone link-ups and buzzers operated by buttons on assistant's flags (from 1999), and authorities have used video evidence to assess misconduct that has gone unnoticed by the match referee. The question is whether technology would help referees to judge other matters as the game is in progress.

Football is a continuous game, and referees are encouraged to keep the game flowing and not blow for too many trivial offences. The tempo of a match is not suited to being stopped for a second opinion. That second opinion has to be instantaneous, otherwise players might cool down and need to warm up again to prevent muscle injuries. In a Scotland–Wales rugby union international, the video referee took more than a minute to assess one incident (March 2005).

Video technology has also proved fallible at times. In an ice-hockey match between Buffalo and Philadelphia, video evidence from two camera angles seemed to show that Philadelphia's John LeClair had scored a perfectly good goal (April 2000). Five minutes later, the goal-judge was told that another camera angle showed the puck going past the outside of the post and into the net through the smallest of undetected holes. It was too late to change the decision.

In 1995 IFAB clearly stated the limits of video evidence: 'The board expressed its strong disapproval with respect to two decisions taken in Germany and Turkey in the use of video evidence to overturn the result of a match. It emphasised that according to Law 5, the decision of the referee on points of fact in connection with play is final and it underlined that audio-visual evidence is to be used solely as additional proof only in disciplinary cases.'

For technology to gain further hold, the laws would have to be rewritten. It is fairly obvious that the sport could not easily accommodate an extra official (a fifth official?) who is studying video replays off the field of play. This would be similar to the set-up of the 1870s when an off-the-pitch referee decided disputes between the two umpires. One reason that system was curtailed was the delay caused by the referee conferring with the umpires. At least the fifth official could be protected from the pressure of the crowd. This video-referee could be shut away in a studio, not really aware of which team were at home, studying the same incident from different camera angles on 26 separate screens, trying to make a decision within moments. It would be a stressful job without much physical exercise.

Other suggestions include introducing an option for coaches to make one or two appeals in a game (as happens in some American sports). This would only slow down the game occasionally, and would therefore only be used for major decisions (e.g. penalty-kicks and over-the-line incidents). In 2000, John Williams (Leicester University) showed that the majority of fans were in favour of technology to be used for important offside decisions (67 per cent) and possible penalty-kick decisions (57 per cent), and others thought they should be used for goal-line decisions (41 per cent). Meanwhile, 28 per cent of fans thought that referees should make all decisions.

A 2005 survey by the *Independent* showed that 96 per cent of the top 92 managers favoured video evidence for goal-line decisions, 48 per cent for penalty calls, 36 per cent for on-pitch incidents the referees miss during the match, 30 per cent for reviewing refereeing decisions after the match, and 18 per cent for offside.

The presence of cameras has probably reduced on-the-pitch violence (or improved detection) in the same way that CCTV cameras have altered spectator violence.

Michael Robinson (Brighton) and Noel Blake (Birmingham) were disciplined after-the-fact in 1983, but the first major 'trial by television' followed a game between Arsenal and Southampton (September 1988). A blow from Paul Davis (Arsenal) resulted in Glen Cockerill (Southampton) suffering a broken jaw. Davis was not cautioned but he was later suspended for nine matches and fined £3,000 by the FA. In response, Arsenal manager George Graham banned television cameras from Highbury.

Technology has also reached certain top grounds in the form of giant screens that show action to spectators. There can be no shots of spectators, nothing that might distract players or match officials, no pictures of the trainer's bench or substitutes warming up, only live action or action replays of *positive* incidents – in short, nothing that may question the judgment of match officials. This is a reminder of a minute from the 1970 IFAB annual meeting: 'The Board deprecated the emphasis placed in television recordings and television comment which challenged the authority of the referee. It was agreed to request the television authorities to refrain from any slow-motion play-back which reflected, or might reflect, adversely, on any decision of the referee.'

TEMPORARY EXPULSIONS

Temporary expulsions are not permitted at any level of football. Any leagues using temporary exclusions (or so-called sin-bins) are under threat of disciplinary sanctions (2002, 2003).

Birmingham City manager Freddie Goodwin called for sin-bins, or 'coolers', after a fractious game against Newcastle United (December 1973), and sin-bins were discussed by the Professional Footballers' Association in the mid-1980s, and again in 1999. The idea is to send cautioned players off the field for a short period.

Advocates of sin-bins point out that punishment should be immediate. In a 2002 FIFA World Cup™ semi-final, Ballack (Germany) was cautioned for a deliberate foul. He received no other punishment, and scored the winning goal a few minutes later. Ballack missed the final as it was his second caution in the knock-out phase, but the beneficiaries of the punishment were Brazil (the other finalist) rather than semi-final opponents South Korea. Had the sin-bin rule been operating, Ballack would have been off the pitch rather than scoring.

A second argument in favour of sin-bins is that it may give a cautioned player some time to cool down. Had Beckham (England) been 'binned' against Austria, he wouldn't have been sent off two minutes later (October 2005).

Opponents of sin-bins cite several problems: (i) some climates are too cold to have players sitting around; (ii) the need for players to warm up again so that they do not injure themselves on their return; (iii) the time taken up in disputing sin-bin decisions and getting the player off the field; (iv) referees being distracted by making sure that expelled players return at the correct moment; and (v) the risk of teams being reduced below the minimum number of players (seven). Had cautioned players from Germany and Cameroon been sent to sin-bins, the teams would have been eight against seven for a time (June 2002). But you could argue that the later cautions might not have occurred had the remaining players been aware of the risk of abandonment.

TEMPORARY SUSPENSION OF PLAY

The key points regarding a temporary suspension of play were present in the laws in the 1890s: 'The referee shall have power to stop the game for such a time as he may think fit, whenever he may deem it necessary to do so.' If play is suspended, the players are still under the referee's control. Play resumes with a dropped ball if the temporary suspension came when the ball was in play.

Referees use stoppages sensibly, by obtaining a weather report or talking to key personnel about the issue that precipitated the stoppage. There is a limit to the time spent waiting, as the players will need to warm-up again and families of spectators may worry if fans do not return home at a stipulated time.

Everyone needs to be told that it is a *temporary* stoppage. Derby County manager George Jobey told his players to jump in the bath at Bolton after the referee brought the teams off while the fog cleared (December 1937). Derby were 2–0 down at the time, and the match was abandoned.

Bad weather is one reason for suspending play. The referee took Leeds United and Anderlecht players off for seventeen first-half minutes while the fog cleared (March 1975). When Portsmouth won 4–3 at Northampton, the referee suspended play during a ten-minute hailstorm (April 1902). A match between Notts County and Birmingham was suspended for over an hour due to a severe thunderstorm (September 1923). A Port Vale–Stockport County match was stopped for seven minutes when a violent hailstorm broke out (March 1967), and Port Vale and Southport players were taken off for five minutes to escape a snowstorm (November 1966). Many leagues have safety regulations for thunder and lightning.

Sometimes referees call for a temporary stoppage so that players can calm down. This happened when Everton played Leeds United (November 1964). Sandy Brown (Everton) had been sent off in the fourth minute for striking an opponent, and two players, Willie Bell (Leeds) and Derek Temple (Everton), had been carried off with serious injuries. The referee suspended play for ten minutes in an attempt to restore order. Similarly, the Leeds United–Valencia Fairs Cup tie was suspended for ten minutes after three players had been sent off (February 1966), and there was a ten-minute hiatus when Luton played Oldham (April 1981). Play was suspended for four minutes at Ibrox Park after Craig Paterson and Hugh Burns (both Rangers) were sent off against Aberdeen (September 1985), West Ham and Arsenal players went to the dressing-rooms (April 1987), and the referee of the Barnsley–Liverpool match ordered a five-minute cooling-off period (March 1998).

A more common reason for temporary suspension is the behaviour of spectators. Serious disturbances occurred at many matches in the 1890s, and a new era of soccer hooliganism arrived in the 1960s and 1970s. The referee took off the players of West Ham and Manchester United for eighteen minutes during their match (October 1975), crowd trouble stopped a match between Newcastle United and Manchester City for eight minutes (January 1977), and Arsenal–West Ham was held up for nearly twelve minutes because of fighting on the terraces (May 1982). Birmingham v Stoke was suspended after a last-minute pitch invasion, but the teams returned after twenty minutes to play the last 35 seconds in an empty ground (February 1992).

It was hoped that pitch invasions would disappear when a new law made them a criminal offence, but spectators and streakers continue to cause temporary stoppages. A bizarre five-minute delay occurred during the 2005 High Wycombe Sunday Challenge Cup Final. A fight broke out in the Causeway Stadium's main stand. The rumpus disturbed the players, a few of whom came to the touchline to yell instructions at the volunteer stewards and the unruly participants, most of whom were known to the players through local football. Roles were suddenly reversed. The spectators were suddenly the players, and the footballers the onlooking coaches ('Sort it out'). The referee had to remember to restart play with an indirect free-kick for offside.

Bomb alerts are an obvious reason for stopping play and taking stock. During the 1940 Battle of Britain, the Home Office ruled that play must stop whenever an air-raid alert was sounded. Charlton Athletic's home matches were regularly interrupted, and one match against Brentford had a 65-minute suspension (September 1940). On another occasion, shortly after the second half had begun, the game was stopped for 75 minutes. The referee went to restart the game but half the players were in the bath and the other half had already returned to their jobs.

A temporary stoppage was necessary in a Holland–Cyprus international after a projectile had exploded at the feet of the Cyprus goalkeeper, who had to be replaced by a substitute goalkeeper (October 1987). Holland were heavily fined and ordered to replay the game behind closed doors. The following month a gas canister was thrown on to the Hibernian pitch, causing an eighteen-minute delay to their match with Celtic (November 1987).

Play has also been suspended and restarted in the wake of some major incidents. A retaining wall collapsed twelve minutes from the end of the 1914 FA Cup replay between Sheffield Wednesday and Wolverhampton Wanderers and about 75 people were injured. The players were taken off the field and the Wolves goalkeeper fainted when he saw some of the injured laid out in the dressing-room. He was unable to take his place when the game resumed, some twenty minutes after the stoppage. Wolves played the remaining twelve minutes with ten men and lost 1–0. They lodged a protest, which was dismissed by the FA. The apocryphal story is that the goalkeeper fainted again when he was told about the FA's decision.

A fire alarm led to over 2,000 spectators being evacuated from Elm Park's Norfolk Road stand after 75 minutes of a Reading–Notts County match (October 1994). A smouldering pipe had set fire to a jacket under a pensioner's seat. Spectators were ordered on to the pitch and the stand was emptied inside five minutes. Play resumed after a seventeen-minute delay.

In the 75th minute of a match between Watford and Grimsby Town, a two-foot-wide hole appeared at the edge of the penalty area (December 1961). The referee stopped the game for ten minutes while a barrow-load of soil was brought to the pitch and the hole was repaired. Some players had left the pitch and had to be brought back hurriedly from the dressing-room. Matches have also been temporarily suspended so that out-of-control sprinkler systems can be fixed, floodlights restored to action, glass removed from the pitch, or subsidence cracks repaired. The referee will sometimes give permission for all the players to leave the pitch. In other cases, for short delays, the referee will expect the players to wait on the field. Players may need to warm up again. When play resumed after the fire alarm at Reading, Stuart Lovell (Reading) pulled a hamstring muscle (October 1994).

Other unusual reasons for stoppages have included molehills, and rabbits eating goal-nets. A match in Cornwall between St Columb and Pelynt was suspended when the referee asked for dog dirt to be cleared from the pitch (February 2003). An FA Cup tie between Bolton Wanderers and Arsenal was halted when a man buzzed the Burnden Park ground from a fan-powered parachute (January 1994). The referee and four Long Eaton Town players had to leave the pitch for treatment when they suffered the delayed effects of a pre-match gas escape (December 1964). And a referee called a fifteen-minute suspension at Folkestone Invicta as he felt threatened and abused by spectators during the match against Hampton & Richmond Borough (January 2005).

A piercing scream from nearby bushes stopped an Oxfordshire Senior League game between John Radcliffe and Marston Saints (March 1996). Spectators and players apprehended a man who was allegedly assaulting a young girl. According to the *Oxford Mail* (11 March 1996), 'Play continued after police arrived and took the suspect away.'

The *Surrey Advertiser* (9 March 2001) included a story about a match in Shalford Park, Guildford. After about fifteen minutes of a game on Pitch Five, a young girl became stuck in a boggy area nearby. An assistant referee went off to help the stuck girl and the referee called a temporary halt. The officials and spectators combined to pull the girl out of the swamp, after which play resumed.

In the sixteenth minute of a match against West Brom Reserves, Gordon Strachan (Coventry City Reserves) was sent off for foul and abusive language and refused to leave the pitch (August 1996). Two minutes passed, and then the referee took the players off the field. The referee met with the two managers and then restarted play after a total break of fourteen minutes (with Strachan left in the changing-room).

The referee ordered a fifteen-minute suspension in the match between Vitesse Arnhem and PSV Eindhoven because he was unhappy at the abuse he received from Arnhem fans following a 62nd-minute sending-off (November 2004). The home players appealed for calm from the fans, and the game was resumed. This wasn't a precedent. When Woolwich Arsenal played

Tottenham Hotspur, the referee stopped the match on account of the bad language of the crowd (April 1900). Referees have every right to turn a temporary stoppage into a terminated game.

TERMINATING THE GAME

The referee has sole power to terminate a match (1891), although at times the referee must heed the advice of police, safety officials or others. A match between Tranmere Rovers and Mansfield Town was abandoned at half-time because a fan had climbed on to a stand roof and refused to come down (April 2003). Police decided to vacate the ground. Policemen and the fire services went on to the roof and helped the spectator down.

Bad light often stops play. Kick-off times need to be chosen carefully at grounds without floodlights. The Crewe–New Brighton FA Cup tie was abandoned after 82 minutes as the referee had difficulty distinguishing between the players unless they were close by (December 1937). All cup ties should start suitably earlier than league games if there is the possibility of extra-time and a penalty shoot-out. When Hull City met Tottenham Hotspur, bad light ended play after ten minutes of extra-time (January 1907).

The arrival of floodlights solved some problems and created others. The Chelsea–Preston North End cup replay was abandoned after 75 minutes when a small fire put out the floodlights (January 1969), and Derby County's first competitive match at Pride Park was abandoned after the floodlights failed in the 56th minute (August 1997).

If a match is abandoned the referee must submit an explanatory report to the appropriate authority. The laws require the match to be replayed in full unless the competition organisers have made some other provision. Millwall led Thames Ironworks 2–0 in a Southern League match that was abandoned through fog after seventy minutes (December 1899). The remaining twenty minutes were played over four months later when the two teams met at Millwall for the return league match. But this was the last time this was done in England. A game cannot be switched to another pitch. The home team's insurance may not cover the switch, the pitch dimensions are probably different, and one team may be disadvantaged in some way.

Norwich City won 2–0 at Chelsea in a League Cup semi-final first leg (December 1972). The second leg, at Norwich, was played on a foggy night. Norwich took a 3–2 lead (5–2 on aggregate) and only six minutes remained when a blanket of fog came down. The referee took the players off and waited. The fog cleared a little so he took the players out again. But he could not see the touchlines from the centre of the pitch, so he had to abandon the match. Norwich won the replayed second leg 1–0 and progressed to the final (January 1973). Swindon Town weren't so lucky when their match against

Bradford City was abandoned after 73 minutes (January 1987). Swindon were 3–0 ahead, but the rematch finished 2–2.

Spectators, players and officials need to be properly informed about any termination of the game. Sometimes players have gone through the fog to inform spectators (and make up dramatic stories about the game the fans couldn't see). A Worksop Town goalkeeper was unaware that a match against Lincoln United had been abandoned until the news was announced over the public address system (1997–98). He just thought that Lincoln weren't attacking much. A similar event befell goalkeeper Richard Siddall (Stocksbridge Steel) in the fog against Witton Albion in the same season. The match was abandoned and so was he. When an England–Scotland under-23 international was terminated, the blizzard was so heavy that one linesman didn't know that the referee had abandoned the game (March 1970).

A cloudburst caused the termination of Leicester City versus Southampton after 23 minutes (October 1983). The Leicester pitch drained quickly but the referee could not change his mind once the termination decision had been made.

Police and transport workers may need time to prepare for vacating grounds at top-level stadiums, and clubs may have to prepare for a backlash. When Grimsby Town played Sunderland, the match was abandoned after only six minutes (December 1993). Spectators were outraged after paying to watch a whole game, but the club issued vouchers to travelling away fans.

Another very short match was Stoke City against Wolverhampton Wanderers (December 1894). This game took place in a blinding snowstorm, and was abandoned after four minutes (some sources say three). In the fourth minute of an FA Cup replay at Thornaby, Benn Thompson (Dunston Federation Brewery) broke a leg so badly that it wasn't safe to move him on to a stretcher (September 2005). By the time the ambulance arrived, forty minutes later, players of both teams were traumatised by the incident. The referee abandoned the match.

A cup tie between Nottingham Forest and Tottenham Hotspur was abandoned after fourteen minutes (February 1996). An unexpected blizzard made conditions hazardous and refereeing impossible; Spurs wore all white and were indistinguishable from the surroundings, and the assistant referees could not see across the pitch to assess offside. The players were taken off, and the referee sought a weather forecast before terminating the match. Jason Dozzell (Spurs) had been cautioned during the fourteen minutes. His manager, Gerry Francis, queried whether the caution had to stand. It did at the time, but the FIFA Disciplinary Code now states that cautions should be annulled if an abandoned match has to be replayed.

Referees should terminate any game where the weather causes additional danger. A cup tie between Northampton and Burton United was abandoned, but Burton had already lost Teddy Pears (broken arm) and Dick Gray (three broken ribs) (1901–02). Nearly a hundred years later, a referee abandoned the Worthington Cup tie between Manchester City and Ipswich Town after 23 minutes, shortly after he had seen two players slide dangerously into a hoarding (December 2000).

No ball, no more play. One of the first games Pat Partridge refereed was between West End and Synthonia B (March 1953). After 46 minutes, the ball struck a hawthorn hedge and burst. There was no other ball. Partridge had to abandon the match.

No referee, no more play. International referee Mervyn Griffiths took little satisfaction from his first-ever headline– 'Referee struck unconscious by ball'. He regained consciousness on the dressing-room table. That match had to be abandoned because the competition rules stated that there had to be a neutral referee.

A match between AS Roma and Dynamo Kiev was abandoned at half-time after the referee, Anders Frisk (Sweden), was struck on the head by an object thrown by a spectator (September 2004). Frisk, who had just sent off Mexes (Roma) for kicking Verpakovskis (Kiev), left the field with blood pouring from his head. A fourth official was available but he was unwilling to take over in the circumstances. Dynamo Kiev, 1–0 up at the time of the abandonment, were later awarded a 3–0 win, and Roma had to play their next two European games behind closed doors.

Major incidents have produced varied responses. A fence collapsed after 23 minutes of a match between Vasco de Gama (Brazil) and Sao Caetano (Brazil), and 159 people were injured (December 2000). The match was abandoned with no further play, but it took ninety minutes to make the decision. There was a period of uncertainty at Hillsborough while the impact of a disaster that resulted in 96 deaths was becoming understood (April 1989), but games at Nottingham Forest (August 1968) and Bradford City (May 1985) were swiftly abandoned when fires broke out. A match between Boreham Wood and Dagenham & Redbridge was abandoned after 88 minutes because of a medical emergency in the crowd (August 1996), and Maine Road versus Atherton Collieries was abandoned after 69 minutes when a player suffered a serious head injury (February 2005).

In 1940, Ken Aston was refereeing a match between RAF personnel and low-level attack gunners when he saw a German light bomber coming in to attack. Aston abandoned the match, ran to the nearby guns, put on a helmet and gas mask, and took to his gun while still wearing his referee's kit.

Spectators have stopped many games, including a friendly international between the Republic of Ireland and England (February 1995). A Milan derby was halted after 73 minutes (April 2005). Flares were thrown on to the pitch in the 71st minute, and one of them injured goalkeeper Dida (AC Milan). The referee took the players off and then tried to restart the match 25 minutes later. The flares began again so he abandoned the match.

A match between ADO Den Haag and PSV Eindhoven was stopped by the referee after eighty minutes because of spectators' abusive chanting (October 2004). Some of the abuse was racist, some of the chanting questioned the referee's integrity, and some was directed at a PSV player's girlfriend. The Dutch FA awarded PSV Eindhoven a win, and ruled that Den Haag should play two home matches behind closed doors.

Players can be as unruly as spectators. In 1957, Honduras led Cuba 2–0 with fifteen minutes to play when a mass fight flared up. All the players, including the reserves, were involved, and the referee abandoned the game. The Scotland–Austria international was abandoned after 79 minutes when the referee had had enough of the fouling (May 1963).

Another problem comes when a sent-off player refuses to leave the field. Middlesbrough were leading Oldham Athletic 4–1 when the referee sent off Billy Cook (Oldham) in the 55th minute (April 1915). Cook stayed on the pitch. The game was abandoned and Cook suspended for a year.

Denis Howell was refereeing a junior cup tie when he sent off the home-team captain. The player sat down on the pitch. Howell gave him one minute to leave. When the player stayed sitting, Howell abandoned the match. The major question behind such incidents is how long a referee should wait until abandoning the game. When LuaLua (Democratic Republic of Congo) was sent off against Tunisia, he took four minutes to leave the field but the match continued (January 2004). Referees often try to discuss the matter with the captain.

During a cup tie between two amateur teams, Barton United and Swan Sports, the referee sent off a Swan Sports player (November 1992). However, the player kicked the referee's notebook out of his hand and then knocked the referee over by kicking the ball at him. The referee abandoned the game, but the player continued the assault by throwing a halfway-line flag.

A game must be abandoned if one team has fewer than seven players (1949). Winsford United had two such matches terminated in two years – after five were sent off against New Mills (2003) and two sent off and three injured against Northallerton Town (2005). A match between Sheffield United and West Brom lasted until Sheffield United were reduced to six men in the 82nd minute (March 2002). Three United men were sent off – goalkeeper Tracey (handling outside the area) and substitutes Suffo (head-butting) and Santos (jumping at an opponent) – and two more had left the field injured. United had used all their available substitutes.

Walkings-off can be as big a problem as sendings-off. A London Professional Charity Fund appeal match (Crystal Palace versus Clapton Orient) was terminated when ten Orient players walked off, and

Czechoslovakia players walked out on the 1920 Olympic Games Final after a disputed second Belgium goal went in. AC Milan were banned from European competitions after walking off the pitch during a floodlight failure at Marseille (March 1991). Eight Dunstable Town players walked off in the 38th minute of an FA Cup tie at Staines Town (September 1989). The other three had already been sent off. All the players were fined, and Staines were awarded the tie.

Referees have found a multitude of other reasons for ending matches prematurely. When Appleby Frodingham met Lincoln Moorlands, the match was abandoned when a police dog ran on to the field, attacked several players, and grabbed an assistant referee's flag (October 2002). And a cup tie between Chester and Plymouth was abandoned when no replacement could be found for a broken goalpost (September 1981).

THROW-IN

Most throw-ins are routine but some can change games.

In the 1995 Anglo-Italian Cup Final, Andy Legg (Notts County) took a throw-in, and the ball passed through a crowded goalmouth into the net. The referee awarded a goal because he thought the ball had touched someone on its journey – a goal cannot be scored directly from a throw-in – but slow-motion film suggested that the ball had not been touched. The referee's decision is final.

One of Ian Hutchinson's long throw-ins helped Chelsea win the 1970 FA Cup Final replay. Charlton (Leeds) misheaded the throw, and Webb (Chelsea) bundled the ball into the net. Scientific experiments showed that Hutchinson had an extension of the spine and was double-jointed in both shoulders. This enabled him to perform a 'windmill action' with his arms revolving rather than popping out. But the BBC *Match of the Day* team's slow-motion footage showed that some of Hutchinson's longer efforts were foul throws as both feet were not always on the ground when the ball was released.

A game can also be changed by a sending-off provoked by a throw-in. Adrian Serioux (Millwall) was sent off when he threw the ball at Lee Cook (Queen's Park Rangers), who was standing the required one yard away (November 2004). The law was then changed so that opponents had to be at least two yards from the thrower until the ball was in play (2005). It is a cautionable offence to be closer (2006).

Albert Jarrett (Stevenage) was standing some distance away from Lee Protheroe (Gravesend) when Protheroe took a throw-in and deliberately hurled the ball hard at the back of Jarrett's head (April 2005). Jarrett retaliated and both players were sent off.

Shaun Smith (York City) was cautioned by the referee after spending seventeen seconds taking a throw-in in the 57th minute of a match against Scarborough (December 2004). It was Smith's second caution of the match so he was dismissed.

In football's earliest days, the first player to touch the ball over the boundary-line was allowed to restart the game with a one-handed throw at right-angles to the boundary-line (1870 London rules) or a kick in any direction (1870 Sheffield rules). Presumably this is why the boundary-line became known as the *touch*line.

The idea behind kick-ins was to punish the side kicking or heading the ball out. If the punishment was harsh enough, all the players would strive to keep the ball in play to prevent a throw-in. But kick-ins have never proved a deterrent, and experiments in the 1940s, 1970s and 1990s have all ended with the retention of the throw-in.

When the Sheffield and London rules were eventually unified (April 1877), the compromise was to accept London's *one-handed throw-in* but also accept Sheffield's *any direction* rule. The throw-in was taken by a player of the opposite side from that which last played the ball, and it was taken from where the ball went over the line. Another player had to touch the ball before the thrower could play it again.

There was, however, still inconsistency between the Scottish throw-in (at right angles to the touchline) and the English one (in any direction). This led to a dispute before the 1880 Scotland–England match. These throw-in inconsistencies were discussed at the first-ever IFAB meeting (December 1882). The difficulties were resolved by an entirely new system – a *two-handed* throw in any direction. This restrained the first generation of long-throw experts. William Gunn (Notts County), John Graham (Preston), Ted Corrie (Everton) and Hugh Wilson (Sunderland) had all been capable of throwing the ball one-handed from the touchline into the goalmouth.

Throwing distance was further restricted by a rule compelling the thrower to stand with part of both feet on the touchline (1895). The rule was changed so that the thrower's foot had to be outside the touchline (1925) or on or outside the touchline (1932), and a new generation of long-throwers was born. Spectators were startled by throws into the goal area by Sam Weaver (Newcastle) and Tom Gardner (Aston Villa). Immediately after World War II, Dave Russell (Sheffield Wednesday) and Cliff Holton (Arsenal) developed long throws after practising with medicine balls. In the 1960s, David Mackay (Spurs and Derby County) prepared for his version of a long throw by wiping his hands on his shirt. But players are not allowed to dry their hands on a conveniently placed towel.

The referee keeps a mental check list for what constitutes a foul throw. If the answer to any of these questions is 'No', the throw-in is awarded to the other team: Is part of each foot on the ground when the thrower releases the ball? Is part of each foot either on the touchline or behind the line (both heels on the line and toes over the line is acceptable)? Are both hands used with equal force? Does the thrower throw the ball from behind and over the head in a continuous motion? Is the ball thrown (rather than dropped)? Does the throw come from behind the head? Is the throw-in taken from the right place? Is the ball thrown without any spin? Is the player facing the field with some part of the body? Has there been no use of a purposefully placed towel to dry the ball?

A foul throw was originally punished by a free-kick. After protests from many clubs, this was changed so that the other team was awarded the throw-in (1931). More recently, a throw-in taken from the wrong position was labelled a foul throw, and the throw-in conceded to the opposition (1987). Previously it would be taken again from the right place. In 1982–83, the Football League treated time-wasting at throw-ins as the equivalent of a foul throw, but this was quickly stopped by IFAB.

Foul throws have been spotted at the highest level. The 1974 FIFA World Cup™ Final contained a foul throw when a Dutch player failed to take the ball properly over his head, and the 2004 women's under-nineteen World Championship had a foul throw in the Germany–China final.

A goalkeeper was allowed to pick up a team-mate's throw-in for the first five years of the backpass law (1992 to 1997) but after 1997 a throw-in counted as a backpass. If the ball brushes the goalkeeper's hand and goes into the net, the referee would probably award a goal rather than an indirect free-kick, i.e. the referee would apply the advantage clause. Players cannot be offside from a throw-in (1920).

An important addition to the throw-in protocol – 'a goal shall not be scored from a throw-in' – was added in 1898. Frank Boakas (Barnsley) took a long throw-in and goalkeeper Breen (Manchester United) deflected the ball into the net for a legitimate goal (January 1938). A confident goalkeeper could have let the ball go into the net and be rewarded with a goal-kick (provided the referee agreed that the ball hadn't been touched).

When Barnsley beat Huddersfield Town 3–1, Huddersfield equalised with a controversial goal (August 1996). The referee ruled that Andy Morrison (Huddersfield) had got his head to Tom Cowan's long throw, but furious Barnsley players claimed that the ball had gone straight in. Birmingham City's second goal against Aston Villa had a similar controversy (September 2002). Goalkeeper Enckelman (Villa) attempted to trap a throw-in only for the ball to roll under his foot and into the net. The referee decided to give the goal on the basis that the goalkeeper had touched the ball with his foot. Otherwise the decision would have been a corner kick as a Villa player had taken the throw.

During Bournemouth's famous 1958 FA Cup run, Ollie Norris (Bournemouth) developed an unorthodox tactic of jumping up in front of opponents when they were taking throw-ins. This tactic was later classed as ungentlemanly conduct (IFAB 1966). Members of the defending side are allowed to stand within two yards of the thrower but they are not allowed to jump up and down, and not permitted to gesticulate or make facial expressions. They must stand still.

If the ball hits two players at the same time and goes over the touchline, referees try to give a quick signal. Some referees consistently give that sort of decision to the defending team; others consistently give the throw to the attackers.

Throw-ins are so abundant that they need to be taken inside the first five seconds if possible. In the 1960s, it was estimated that first-class matches averaged 85 throw-ins. There may be fewer now, but so much will depend on the width of the pitch, tactics, standard of play and weather conditions (especially wind).

Somersault throws by Changez Khan (Stafford Rangers) and Steve Watson (Newcastle United) were confirmed as legitimate (FA 1990). Such acrobats usually do a handstand on the ball before completing the somersault and throwing the ball in. Obviously all the principles of a throw-in need to be adhered to.

Other players have throw-in techniques that may need closer scrutiny, in the manner that authorities study the bowling actions of certain cricketers. In EURO 2004™, Reiziger (Holland) demonstrated an unusual style whereby he twisted to the right but seemed to correct the motion just in time so that he delivered the ball as he was facing the pitch and brought the ball over his head rather than his right shoulder.

TIMEKEEPING See FULL-TIME WHISTLE, HALF-TIME WHISTLE

TIME-OUTS

Experiments with time-outs came in the 1995 Women's World Cup and the 1995 under-seventeen World Championship. A team was permitted one ninety-second time-out in each half. This device might have proved popular with television companies, who could show advertisements, but only a third of the time-outs were used. Opinions on the scheme were 'divergent' (IFAB 1996).

TIME-WASTING

Towards the end of a match in the early 1960s, Bertie Auld (Birmingham City) sauntered over to the wing to take a last-minute corner-kick with his team ahead by one goal. Auld placed the ball, stepped back several places, studied the penalty area, and then loped up and casually kicked the ball out of play for a throw-in a yard from the corner-flag. By the time everyone realised what had happened, valuable seconds had gone by.

Referees have the power to caution players for deliberate time-wasting activities such as this, and they can add on any obvious time wasted (and time taken up for the caution). But there are so many time-wasting techniques to look out for, and sometimes it is not clear what is legitimate and what is not.

Here are a few suspicious circumstances:

A player seems set to take a throw-in but hands over responsibility to another player.

A goalkeeper slowly walks twenty yards to place the ball in the farthest corner of the goal area before taking a goal-kick.

A player unnecessarily kicks the sole match-ball into another game two pitches away.

A player delays taking a free-kick or corner-kick – by walking slowly to collect the ball, deliberately placing it in the wrong place, or stopping to tie a bootlace, etc.

A player pretends he can't hear what the referee is saying.

A player kicks the ball towards the referee rather than leaving it at the touchline.

The referee is the sole judge of time, and an assiduous referee can add on a lot of time. When Preston North End played Aston Villa, five minutes were added to the game, and Preston scrambled a winner in the last few seconds (January 1969).

Certain actions are not officially time-wasting tactics but they are against the spirit of the game and could be considered gamesmanship. These include shielding the ball near the corner-flag (which usually leads to a confrontation and a free-kick), passing the ball around (almost as a mickey-taking exercise), and the goalkeeper dribbling the ball around the penalty area until an opposition striker runs towards him in a futile attempt to challenge. When Charlie George (Arsenal) celebrated his winning goal in the 1971 FA Cup Final – lying down on his back and raising his arms – it was partly to waste time. Excessive celebrations are big time-wasters.

TOSSING A COIN

The coin-tossing ritual has been used in at least seven ways: (i) to decide ends and possession at the first place-kick; (ii) to decide ends and possession at the start of extra-time; (iii) to decide who takes the first kick in a penalty shoot-out; (iv) (sometimes) to decide which end the shoot-out takes place; (v) as a way of deciding the match after a penalty shoot-out has been abandoned; (vi) (occasionally in the past) as a way to decide the venue for the next replay; and (vii) (also in the past) as a way of deciding matches drawn after extra-time.

By far the most common is the pre-match ritual. The first draft of the 1863 FA rules stated that the side winning the toss should commence the game, but this was changed before the final draft. The procedure adopted that year was for the winners of the toss to be offered the choice of goals. That way the team losing the toss kicked off. A revision was made in 1875, when the winner of the toss was given the option – kick-off or choice of goals. Eventually, the law was changed back – the team winning the toss now decides which goal to attack in the first half, and the other team takes the kick-off (1997). Very few legal clauses have been re-established 122 years later. The 1997 regulation reduced the number of decisions to be made, and very few captains had chosen to take the kick-off anyway. Ron Atkinson captained Oxford United more than 200 times at the old Manor Ground (1960 to 1971): 'It was always the ritual: we won the toss and we kicked up the hill first.'

The pre-match ritual usually begins with a loud blast of the whistle to summon the two captains. Then handshakes all round, and the referee notes the captains' numbers in case they need to be identified later.

All referees have a favoured procedure. They decide who tosses the coin (away-team captain, home-team captain, the referee), whether the coin is caught or allowed to fall, and who calls. The procedure is quickly explained to the captains and the toss is made.

From 1972–73, at professional games, the linesmen joined the referee in the centre-circle to meet the captains and witness the coin-toss. This can be especially useful if the referee has left the coin at home and needs to borrow one from a colleague. At amateur games, if a referee has forgotten a coin, one option is to pick up a piece of grass, put one hand behind the back, and ask a captain to guess 'Which hand?' One referee called together two captains – Roy McFarland (Derby County) and Leighton James (Swansea City) – only to discover that he had forgotten to bring a coin (March 1981). He had the idea of letting the oldest one choose but neither captain would admit to his age.

A referee may arrange for the coin to be tossed before the teams go on to the field. If, for example, one goalmouth is hard and the other is very soft (because the sun has only got to one end), goalkeepers like to choose footwear to suit where they will be.

If extra-time is needed, captains have to toss again. The procedure is the same as before the match. The toss-winning captain (or acting captain if the original one has been substituted) decides which way to play (1997). The other team has the kick-off for the first half of extra-time. This may be followed by more coin-tossing ceremonies if a penalty shoot-out is required.

In the past, certain competition rules stipulated that the venue for a second replay should be decided by the toss of a coin. Oxford United won the toss three times when they drew 1–1 in a League Cup tie at Manchester United – the pre-match toss, the toss before extra-time, and the toss for the second-replay venue (December 1983).

Tossing a coin (or disc) has helped to settle cup ties in the past. Liverpool and Cologne had their European Cup quarter-final decided in this way (March 1964). One side of the disc was red (Liverpool), the other white (Cologne). When the referee tossed the disc, it spun and landed on its end in the mud. He had to spin it again, and this time it came down in Liverpool's favour. This is one reason why most referees catch the coin rather than let it fall in the mud.

TOUCHLINE

The original FA definition of *touch* was 'that part of the field on either side of the ground which is beyond the line of flags'. The touchline was originally called the boundary line as it was marked by boundary flags. William McGregor casually referred to these flags when describing Aston Villa's play around 1880:

> Flags were put at intervals down the touchline in those days, and Andy [Hunter] had one of these placed at a certain distance from the goal-line. The understanding was that Eli [Davis] was not to pass that post; when he reached it he must centre. Andy was always waiting for the centre, which he knew would be placed with beautiful accuracy, and many a goal to the Villa resulted from that compact.

The more familiar touchline was introduced in the early 1880s. Flag-staffs with pointed tops were banned, and touchlines and goal-lines must not be marked by a V-shaped rut (IFAB 1902). The maximum width of all lines is five inches (1939).

TRAINING GAMES

When John Hartson fouled Eyal Berkovic on the West Ham training pitch, Berkovic reacted angrily at his club colleague, and Hartson kicked Berkovic in the face (October 1998). This story became public knowledge when an amateur cameraman sold film of the incident to a national newspaper.

Hartson was fined £10,000 by his club, and, four months later, fined £20,000 and banned for three matches by the FA. He was the first player in the history of the game to be fined by the FA for misconduct on a private training ground.

The West Ham contretemps raised questions about the discipline system behind closed doors. Professional players probably play more unofficial games than they play official matches in public. The control of these matches is a moot point. Coaches often change the rules for small-sided matches so that players are allowed a limited number of touches, or players may have free-kicks given against them so that they learn a lesson. Novy Kapaida has told of an Indian coach who organised 'weaker leg tournaments' where players could only kick and tackle with their weaker foot in order to improve two-footedness (*Soccer and Society*, 2001).

Practice matches are sometimes so unruly that clubs stop them. Competitive reserve-team players may have a point to prove, and coaches sometimes tell players to rough up others to get a reaction out of them. A training-ground fight broke out between two Leeds United players, Bobby Collins and Norman Hunter, a day or two before the 1965 FA Cup Final.

In one full-scale practice match – first team against reserves – the manager was playing for the first team and refereeing. He tackled an opponent and the ball ricocheted between them and went out for a throw-in.

'Our ball,' the manager said.

A reserve-team player beat the manager to the ball and threw it in.

'Stand still my team,' the manager shouted.

The reserves made a big show of passing the ball around and then celebrated elaborately after putting the ball into the undefended net.

'Right, you've had your fun,' the manager shouted. 'Now it's our throw-in.' He took the throw-in.

'Stand still my team,' shouted a player from the reserves.

The manager sent him off.

TRIPPING AN OPPONENT

Tripping can mean dancing. George Best (Manchester United) tripped through Northampton Town's defence to score six goals (February 1970), John Barnes (England) tripped past Brazil's defenders to score famously (June 1984), and Ryan Giggs (Manchester United) tripped through the Arsenal rearguard (April 1999). But tripping has another meaning. An opponent may stick out a foot or clip the dancing player's heel.

Tripping was banned in the 1863 FA laws, and the definition of tripping was 'throwing an adversary by use of the legs'. The words 'or attempting to throw' were later inserted after 'throwing' and the action had to be intentional to be an offence (1887). Stooping in front of an opponent was considered to be tripping (1893). Tripping is now punished if the action is careless, reckless, or uses excessive force.

A trip is a trip, whether it is done before or after getting the ball, near the ball or well away from it.

TROUBLE-SPOTS

Certain periods of a match require strict policing: the first ten minutes; the five minutes either side of half-time; and the last ten minutes. There can also be a crotchety period midway through the second half when the outcome of the match is becoming clearer.

The same rules apply in the first few seconds of a match as in the last. Machiavellian referees fear that overindulgence will lead to more infringements and punishment in the long run. They believe that those in authority should be courageous from the start, making an example of the ringleaders. Overwrought players may need calming down; vendettas may be in place; a player may be trying too hard to impress on his debut; or a manager may have pumped up his players ('Get your retaliation in first'). In the 1972 FA Cup Final, Peter Storey (Arsenal) made a bad tackle on Allan Clarke (Leeds United) in the first few seconds, Vinnie Jones (Wimbledon) targeted McMahon (Liverpool) in the first twenty seconds of the 1988 FA Cup Final, and Johnsen (Chelsea) was cautioned in the first minute of the 1994 FA Cup Final against Manchester United. Jimmy Smith (Newcastle) was sent off after 53 seconds of a 1973–74 Texaco Cup tie when a tackle on Tony Want (Birmingham City) left him with a double-fracture of the left leg. In February 1982 Gerry Gow marked his first three minutes in a Rotherham United shirt with a caution (for a foul on Derby County's Powell) *and* a sending-off (for the high-and-late foul that broke Emery's leg).

In the 1991 FA Cup Final, the hyperactive Paul Gascoigne (Tottenham Hotspur) injured Garry Parker (Nottingham Forest) with a bad challenge in the opening minutes. Referee Roger Milford later regretted not cautioning Gascoigne because the player was seriously injured in another wild challenge a few minutes later.

Towards the end of a match, as players get tired, bad passes creep into the game, and play may become more end-to-end and desperate. Referees may get tired, and yet they still have to make important last-minute decisions.

There is a wider context to all this. There may be an awkward point three-quarters of the way through a season, when league-table positions are looking more fixed and teams are desperate for points. In the same way as the police rate games for possible crowd trouble, so referees have an idea of the relative difficulty of each game. But there is still no telling which games might erupt.

One of the worst fouls in football history – goalkeeper Schumacher (West Germany) jumping feet-first at Battiston (France) – came out of the blue in a 1982 FIFA World Cup™ semi-final.

TUNNEL

A memorandum in the 1890s stated the ground rules for a players' tunnel: 'Clubs are expected to provide a private way for players and officials from playing-ground to dressing-room wherever this is practical.'

At certain grounds players ran the gauntlet. An example was Prenton Park, Tranmere, in the 1950s, where players made their way through the crowd along a series of alleys and long passageways. 'If you were a visitor, going up there, there was nothing to stop anyone clapping you over the ear-hole,' said Harold Bell, who played 595 league games for Tranmere Rovers. 'It could be anyone, so no one could be accused.'

There have been so many tunnel altercations between rival players that it is surprising that no one has introduced partitioned tunnels in high-level competition. Whenever players leave the pitch, for whatever reason, incidents can occur.

Most incidents occur at the end of a match, like those allegedly involving Port Vale and Portsmouth players (March 1979), and Sheffield United and West Bromwich Albion players after their tempestuous abandoned match (March 2002). Joe Cole (West Ham) was fined after a tunnel incident at Bolton (April 2003), Turkey and Switzerland players fought at the end of a vital match (November 2005), and rival players clashed in the tunnel after a match between Manchester United and Arsenal (October 2004). In the Manchester fracas, a cup of pea soup was allegedly thrown over manager Alex Ferguson (Manchester United). Punsters took advantage of the players' names to ask whether the soup was Campbell's or Heinze's.

Half-time incidents are not unknown. Turkey and England players had an altercation in the tunnel, and both Football Associations were fined (October 2003). Muscat (Millwall) and Kenny (Sheffield United) were sent off for violent conduct when the fourth official saw an incident in the tunnel during the half-time interval (December 2004). The decision was explained to the two managers, and the second half started with ten players on each side. Another referee with good tunnel vision was Andrew Sainsbury (Wiltshire), who sent off Phillips (Exeter) and Stuart (Grays Athletic) for a half-time fight (November 2005). He called the offenders back on to the pitch to show them the red card.

The matter of where the referee's authority begins and ends was clarified by the IFAB in 2005 – referees can impose disciplinary sanctions from the moment they enter the field of play to when they leave the pitch after the final whistle. Two Leeds United players (Kelly and Gregan) began a war of words on the pitch, screamed at each other down the tunnel at half-time (until police and stewards stepped in) and then disappeared in a fury into the dressing-room (February 2005). A referee can issue cards at each of these locations at half-time.

Increasingly, with certain competitions requiring teams to come out side-by-side, there are altercations in the tunnel before the match. There were threats issued before the start of the match between Manchester United and Arsenal (February 2005), while Celtic players took advantage of a pause in the tunnel before the 1967 European Cup Final to sing 'Sure it's a grand old team to play for' to their Inter Milan opponents.

Another volatile time for the tunnel police is after a sending-off. In the 1990s, Ken McKenna (Bangor City) tussled with spectators as he left the Aberystwyth Town field after being dismissed. Aberystwyth then built two gates to separate the crowd from the players. They became known as the McKenna Gates.

TWO BALLS ON THE PITCH

Derby County conceded a strange penalty at West Ham in December 1921. There were two balls on the field when Storer (Derby County) caught one in the penalty area. He claimed he was about to throw it off the field, and that the other one was the match-ball. The referee disagreed.

In a match between Hamilton Academicals and Albion Rovers, play went on for nearly a minute with two balls on the field. It was New Year's Day (1968) so the players were perhaps expecting to see two balls. The goalkeeper tried to throw one off the field but an opponent stopped it and dribbled past a defender. Meanwhile, the goalkeeper took a goal-kick to the other wing, and suddenly play was progressing down both wings.

The introduction of the multi-ball system has increased the chances of a two-ball game. Problems arise when players and ball boys are unsure of what the restart should be, or a ball is returned from an unexpected direction. If the ball is in play when the second ball appears, the correct decision is to stop the game and recommence with a dropped ball, but sometimes referees will do what they can to keep the game flowing if the second ball isn't interfering. During an Exeter–Manchester United match, the referee kicked a superfluous ball off the field while play continued (January 2005).

TWO-FOOTED TACKLE See JUMPING AT AN OPPONENT

TWO REFEREES

In the 1930s, some people felt that the standard of refereeing was declining as the pace of the game quickened, and the idea of two referees was proposed. Opponents of the idea argued that a weak referee would still be a weak referee and more use should be made of linesmen. The catch phrase was 'one referee is bad enough, never mind two'.

Experiments with two referees included a game between Wrexham and Everton (May 1932), an amateur international trial (January 1935), and the Football League's 9–6 win against West Brom (May 1935). The two-referee scheme was eventually abandoned as being too complex and costly, and there were fears that it would divide authority. Some of the criticism of refereeing was deflected by the introduction of the diagonal system of control, which enabled the referee to be closer to the play and the refereeing trio to work together as a team.

The idea of two referees returned to the agenda in the 1960s, and more trials were held. Advocates of the change argued that a new system would relieve the stamina pressures on referees and keep the referees away from the central area of the pitch. It would be more difficult for players to do things behind the referees' backs, two referees could be more involved in offside decisions, and bribery would be almost impossible if there were two to fund. Opponents argued that it would lead to a shortage of referees – two referees is a not a great idea for leagues where it is hard to recruit one per game – and some referees opposed the idea because they felt that one referee should have sole control.

The two-referee experiment received a setback when a Sampdoria–Bologna match was chosen as the first match in Italy to try it (October 1999). The match was abandoned after 55 minutes following crowd disturbances, in which the Bologna goalkeeper was pelted with bottles and fruit. Bologna, leading 1–0 at the time of the abandonment, were awarded the match, and Sampdoria were banned from using their ground for six home matches. In 2001, IFAB reviewed the results of recent two-referee experiments and the idea was quashed.

Uu

UMPIRES

Lovick tells us:

> At first a twelfth man was added to each side. He was armed with
> a long pole and was called an umpire. The method of control
> was that each umpire operated in his own half of the field. When
> an umpire spotted an infringement he raised his pole. Play then
> stopped and both umpires proceeded to the centre of the field
> where they discussed the infringement and decided upon the
> penalty to be imposed.

In the early 1870s, disputes were settled by rival captains. Umpires were first
mentioned in the laws in 1874. A referee was used in the 1872 FA Cup Final
and was first mentioned in the laws in 1881. He sat off the field of play, and
made decisions when the umpires disagreed.

Pickford (Bournemouth Rovers) described the set-up in the 1880s:

> Our 'stock' umpire was Walter Bevis, and he could be relied on
> to dispute any of the opposition goals! I have known games
> stopped while the teams argued … The spectators, particularly
> at Ringwood and Fordingbridge, sometimes joined in the
> disputes.

Not all umpires were as 'reliable' as Walter Bevis. Sunderland scored a goal
when a Blackburn player kicked the ball against his own umpire and it
rebounded into goal (November 1890).

In 1885, in the days when players had to appeal for all free-kicks, the FA's
instructions to umpires and referees included the following:

> In conclusion, umpires should bear in mind that it is entirely
> against the spirit of the rules to give any advice to or make any
> claim on behalf of either side, and should be careful to ascertain
> that it is a claim made by one of the players and not by a
> spectator. Also that they are bound to give a decision one way or
> the other when appealed to. In cases where an umpire is so
> placed as to be doubtful about a claim, he should decide in
> favour of the side appealed against, just as in cricket an umpire
> would give a similar appeal in favour of the batsman.

In 1891, the referee was moved on to the field of play, and the umpires moved to the touchlines. Umpires' poles became shorter and turned into more recognisable flags. Umpires became known as linesmen (1892–1996) and thereafter assistant referees.

UNGENTLEMANLY CONDUCT See UNSPORTING BEHAVIOUR

UNSPORTING BEHAVIOUR

The term unsporting behaviour entered the laws in 1997 as a direct replacement for 'ungentlemanly conduct'. The earliest laws, drafted in the English public schools, conformed to the upper-class ethos of humanism, gentlemanly conduct, manliness and Christian morality. From 1881, ungentlemanly conduct was a cautionable offence.

Ungentlemanly conduct meant using bad language, calling out misleading instructions to an opponent to put him off his play, making insulting gestures or insulting remarks, refusing to obey a referee's orders, kicking the ball away, leaving or entering the field of play without permission, etc. As Pickford wrote in 1906, 'It [ungentlemanly conduct] does not mean blowing his nose without a handkerchief.' If a referee stops play to caution a player, play is resumed with an indirect free-kick to the opposition (IFAB 1934, 1935).

In 1920, an army officer circulated his troops with a series of hints on good sportsmanship. His profile of the true sportsman included the following: he plays a clean game; he never argues with the referee; he does not swank when his own side scores; he does not shake hands with men of his own side when they score; he appreciates and applauds a piece of good work by his opponents; he does not make excuses and grumble when beaten, but is the first to congratulate his opponents; he is a gentleman of the first order.

Ungentlemanly conduct became a catch-all category for everything against the spirit of the game that wasn't covered by the other cautionable offences. When Crystal Palace drew 2–2 with Mansfield Town, Palace's late equaliser came from a penalty-kick (November 1962). The Mansfield team lined up to applaud ironically as the referee left the pitch. The referee responded by taking ten names as he passed. John Gregory (Derby County) was once cautioned for throwing a bucket of water over a player, local players have been cautioned for talking on mobile phones, and Paul Mariner (England) was cautioned for pushing a referee out of the way against Kuwait (June 1982).

The number of unsporting behaviours meriting a caution has grown enormously over the years. Here is a shortened list: intentional handball; deliberately handling the ball to prevent a goal but failing to prevent a goal (whereas actually preventing a goal is a sending-off offence); unfairly distracting an opponent who is taking a throw-in; verbally distracting an opponent during play or at a restart; dancing about or gesticulating in order to distract an opponent who is trying to restart play; kicking the ball away after a decision goes against the player's team; time-wasting; using any deliberate trick to get round the laws; making a bad tackle on an opponent; simulating injury or the effects of a tackle in order to win a penalty-kick; celebrating a goal in an unsporting manner; using a deliberate trick to get round the backpass law; shouting 'Leave it' or some such words to deceive an opponent; lying on the ball for too long as a goalkeeper; preventing a goalkeeper from releasing the ball back into play; climbing on an opponent's (or colleague's) back in order to gain height on a jump; deliberately obstructing an opponent; shirt-pulling; stepping off the field of play in an attempt to play an opponent offside; adopting an aggressive attitude; dangerous play; fouling a player; reckless play; pushing or pulling an opponent; and tripping an opponent.

Vv

VENUE See HOME SIDE

VIDEO EVIDENCE See MISCONDUCT, TECHNOLOGY

VIOLENT CONDUCT

Violent conduct is a sending-off offence. It is when a player (or substitute) is guilty of violent aggression towards another person when not contesting for the ball. If two players are contesting for the ball and there is excessive aggression, it is deemed *serious foul play*.

Violent conduct can occur on or off the field of play, and when the ball is in play or out of play. The list of specific offences is wide ranging. Nolberto Solano (Aston Villa) was dismissed for *elbowing* a Portsmouth player (August 2005). David Beckham (England) *kicked* Simeone (Argentina) (June 1998). Francis Lee (Manchester City) *attempted to kick* a Sheffield United player (December 1972). Matthew Elliott (Leicester) *struck* a West Ham player (December 2001). Paul Weller (Burnley) *attempted to strike* Millwall's Dennis Wise (February 2004). Gianluca Festa (Middlesbrough) was sent off for *spitting* at a Sunderland player (January 2002). Gary Neville (Manchester United) *head-butted* a Manchester City player (February 2004). Paolo di Canio (West Ham) *stamped* on a Chelsea opponent (January 2002). Alan Ball (England under-23) *threw the ball* at the referee against Austria (June 1965), and George Best (Northern Ireland) was sent off against Scotland for *throwing mud* at the referee (April 1970).

Violent conduct is a sending-off offence no matter who the victim is. John McGinley (Lincoln City) was dismissed for head-butting team-mate Paul Smith following an argument over a bad pass during an FA Trophy tie against Maidstone United (February 1988). Jean-Claud Lemoult (Paris St Germain) was dismissed for striking a spectator who had thrown the ball away when the player wanted to take a quick throw-in (March 1983). A Woodlands (Peterborough) player was red-carded when, after the final whistle had just sounded, he feigned to shake hands with the referee and then slapped his hand instead (February 2006). And Barrios (Uruguay) was sent off for attempting to trip a referee (against Scotland in September 1983).

If the ball was in play at the time of the violent-conduct offence, the match is restarted with a direct free-kick (or penalty-kick) where the offence took place. However, if the violent conduct was against non-opponents while the ball was in play (kicking a streaker or striking a team-mate), play resumes with an indirect free-kick to the opposition. If the offence took place outside the field of play, and the ball was still in play, then play is restarted with a dropped ball. If the ball was out of play before the violent conduct, then play should restart in the manner intended before the offence occurred.

WATER INTAKE *See* LIQUID INTAKE

WEATHER

Football is played in all sorts of conditions. The laws do not stipulate a suitable temperature range, but some competition organisers may (especially for children). In freezing conditions, referees should consider the player with the lowest tolerance: the *Western Mail* (9 November 1989) reported on how a goalkeeper was literally frozen to the spot; eight extremely cold players had to leave the East Tanfield pitch during an FA Amateur Cup tie (1947–48); and a teenage Wairarapa United player suffered severe hypothermia at Featherston (New Zealand) (April 2005). A famous referee, John Lewis, once criticised himself for playing on at Accrington on a bitterly cold day in the early 1900s: 'It was not until the goalkeeper collapsed and was carried off that I thought it necessary to stop play.'

Weather conditions affect players' behaviour. Players dislike windy conditions, they can be niggly on hard pitches, and on greasy pitches some awkward defenders are like elephants on a tub of lard. On hard pitches, referees need to be tough on players who are making a back for opponents. On soft pitches there may be more leeway given to sliding tackles, but the pitch surrounds must be safe.

Thunderstorms may call for a temporary suspension of play because open soccer fields are high risk. Most American soccer associations have guidelines for lightning storms. Play is usually suspended at the first sign of lightning, which may occur before rain begins. All participants and onlookers find sensible shelter – a metal vehicle with the windows shut, a substantial building, or bushes in *low* ground.

In April 1948, two players died when lightning struck the Command Central Ground, Aldershot, during an Army Cup Final replay. One survivor, Jack Flavell, later a Worcestershire and England cricketer, always left the cricket field at the slightest sign of thunder (even if he was in the middle of bowling an over).

Lightning hit a football ground at Gavle, Sweden (July 1994). A sixteen-year-old goalkeeper, Veronica Ronn, was hurled into the air. Her boots and shinguards were ripped to bits and set on fire. The player's heart stopped beating but a teacher administered heart massage and brought her back to life. It is safe to handle someone struck by lightning; they are not electrically charged. Ronn recovered in hospital (except for hearing loss and burn damage).

Even when the storm has cleared there may be danger. In 1996, the referee temporarily suspended a match in Illinois, USA, and then resumed play when the skies had cleared. Unfortunately a 'bolt from the blue' killed one of the young players. The advice is to wait a minimum of thirty minutes from the last observed lightning or sound of thunder before resuming play.

History holds plenty of other warnings: Tommy Allden (Highgate United) died after being hit by lightning during an FA Amateur Cup quarter-final with Enfield Town, four other players were struck and the match was abandoned (February 1967); Andrew Thompson of Brackley, Northants, died eight days after being struck by lightning during a match at Lydney, Gloucestershire (October 1981); and a fourteen-year-old girl was killed by a bolt of lightning while on the field at Fredericton, Maine, USA (July 2003).

More often there is rain without the lightning. Conditions for the 1920 FA Cup match between Bradford City and Portsmouth were more suited to water polo. When Bradford City equalised, after 63 minutes, the referee found it impossible to locate the centre-spot and he abandoned the game.

Otherwise, unlike cricket and tennis, rain does not stop play. No special privileges are accorded players during the rain. An umpire used an umbrella when Vale of Leven played Queen's Park (December 1876), the referee stopped the game to get a waterproof at Southampton St Mary's (September 1893), and Nelson players thought it hilarious when the referee at Santander left the field for a waterproof in May 1923. The legendary tale of Arrowsmith (Aston Villa) running down the wing with a brolly entered folklore in the 1890s. A player would probably be cautioned for that now.

Snowy pitches can be perfectly playable providing they are ice-free, the pitch markings are distinctive and coloured balls are used. Hugo Porfirio (West Ham) scored with an orange ball in a 1–1 draw at Wrexham (January 1997). West Ham manager Harry Redknapp claimed that the Portuguese Porfirio had never seen snow before.

Weather conditions should never be blatantly unfair. Derby Carriage & Wagon played a cup tie at Holbrook (1947). It was anybody's game until a second-half blizzard blew into the faces of the Carriage & Wagon players. There was soon twelve inches of snow at their end of the pitch, but only six inches at the other. Holbrook won 4–1.

Ipswich Town scored a first-half goal when the Norwich City goalkeeper slipped in a frozen goalmouth (January 1965). At half-time ground staff scattered salt over that penalty area. Norwich fans were not pleased, especially when their team lost 3–0.

Great Harwood met Lancaster Town on a sloping pitch in a gale-force wind (January 1933). Great Harwood went 5–0 up with the wind in their favour, but Lancaster pegged them back to 5–1 by half-time. Then the teams changed round and so did the match. With the wind behind them, Lancaster scored five and came back to win 6–5.

Referees have to ensure that conditions do not render the game farcical. They have the option of terminating wind-affected games if the ball is persistently blown away, if too much time is lost in ensuring the ball is stationary at restarts, or if the players cannot kick a goal-kick out of the penalty area. Arbroath versus Albion Rovers was abandoned at half-time because of severe winds (February 1997).

Gales have decided many a coastal match. An FA Cup tie between Blackpool and Huddersfield, played in a gale-force wind, was settled by a 55-yard freak goal scored by Blackpool's Tommy Garrett (January 1953), and Ray Reeves (Reading) scored from the halfway-line at Grimsby (April 1960). Colin Clarke (Oxford United) tells a good yarn about playing at Workington (April 1963):

> It was a 200-mile-an-hour gale-force wind sweeping straight down the pitch. We were with the wind first half and we virtually camped in their half, but we couldn't score for love or money. So we turned round for the second half. Jim Barron was in goal for us and Jim wasn't the best of kickers. He was barely clearing the penalty area in this gale-force wind, and we lined up ten men on the edge of the penalty area, trying to head it on. And he took one kick and it barely cleared the penalty area, and the wind sucked it back in again and it went for a corner. We managed to draw the game nil–nil.

Winds interrupted a game at Portsmouth, and matches at Torquay and Swindon were postponed on the same day (29 October 1989). It was a borderline decision to play the match between Carmarthen Town and Rhyl (March 2004). The ball was kicked one way and it went the other. Unsurprisingly the game finished goalless. One point to each team and one to nature.

Some referees believe that the criteria for judging foggy conditions should vary with the standard of football. If it is a major match with a big crowd, then spectators should be able to see from one end of the pitch to the other. In a local game, visibility from halfway-line to goal should be enough. But if players are capable of hitting sixty-yard passes to unmarked colleagues then they should be allowed this range of vision. Most importantly, a referee's assistant should be able to see across the full width of the pitch in order to judge offsides.

A referee abandoned a foggy game at Chelsea when Charlton Athletic were attacking (December 1937). Fifteen minutes later, a policeman told Charlton goalkeeper Sam Bartram that the game had finished. Bartram thought his team had been well on top. Referees should check that all the players have left the pitch, and spectators should be informed of the decision.

Fog disturbed a World War II game between Hibernian and Hearts at Easter Road, Edinburgh. Visibility was less than ten yards, but people were worried that terminating the game might give valuable intelligence to the German Luftwaffe. The spectators saw nothing, the players saw very little, radio commentators made up events hoping their fiction would be heard by the enemy, and Donaldson (Hearts) was on the field long after the final whistle, unaware that the game had ended.

When Bradford Park Avenue played Southend United, the match was terminated after only eight minutes (December 1961). There was fog at the start and fog at the end. The first half of a Hull City–Southampton FA Cup tie took place in very foggy conditions (January 1966). The referee could probably see but the spectators' vision was definitely impaired. The fog finally cleared and Hull won 1–0 with a late goal from Ken Houghton.

A match between Tranmere Rovers and Norwich City went ahead despite the fog (January 1997). The referee could see both goals from the centre spot, and linesmen could see each other across the pitch, but people in the stands couldn't see all the action and BBC Radio Five Live had to abandon its commentary.

Whereas cricket umpires have light meters and scoreboard lights to assist them in judging whether it is too dark to continue play, football referees rely on the naked eye. The last thirty minutes of a Charlton Athletic–Blackpool match were played in farcical conditions of semi-darkness (November 1929). The referee consulted a linesman but continued the game to the end.

Chesterfield played Tranmere Rovers on a Saturday evening in April 1967. The match finished at 8.10 p.m. on an overcast day and, according to the *Derby Football Telegraph*, 'there can be little dispute that during the closing minutes it *was* too dark to be playing football'. Chesterfield installed floodlights that summer.

It's not all doom and gloom though. In September 1906, Manchester City played Woolwich Arsenal in temperatures of over ninety degrees Fahrenheit. City ended the match with six players (including one invalid). When a televised match – Birmingham City against Crystal Palace – kicked off at 1 p.m., the players looked uncomfortable in the heat (August 1996). The 1977 League Cup Final was played on a sunny day, Aston Villa manager Ron Saunders commenting, 'Our lads froze out there, it must have been the heat.'

Occasionally the sun causes other problems. When Luton Town played Stoke City, the referee asked a boy to hide his bottle of orange juice as the glass was reflecting the sun into the players' eyes (February 1954).

Goalkeepers are allowed to wear hats to shield their eyes from the sun, and some referees have worn sunglasses, but Nat Lofthouse (Bolton) held his hand to his eyes when watching high balls in the 1958 FA Cup Final.

Early guidelines for captains suggested that toss-winners should kick with the wind and sun behind them in the first half, because conditions usually change by the second half. When floodlit games started in the 1950s, captains would win the toss and say, 'We'll kick with the moon at our backs.'

WHISTLE

Referees grow very attached to their whistles. In the 1960s, a referee near Darlington forgot his whistle. He drove home to get it and the game was delayed for 45 minutes.

Around 1870, a Birmingham toolmaker, J Hudson and Co, began to develop a reputation as a leading producer of whistles. An Acme City whistle was introduced for an FA Cup tie between Nottingham Forest and Sheffield (1878). Prior to this the two umpires had used poles, handkerchiefs and voices. Referees continued to use flags for certain forms of deaf football. Re-enactment games played without a whistle have shown how much the modern game relies on Hudson's invention.

Referees normally attach their match whistle to their wrist, and carry a spare whistle in a pocket of their shorts or shirt. They do not keep the whistle in their mouth for two reasons: (i) the few moments between raising the whistle from their wrist and blowing it gives referees a little thinking time; and (ii) referees know that a whistle tastes awful if a ball hits you in the face. A referee was knocked out during the match between West Ham United and Wolves (November 1970). Bobby Moore (West Ham) picked up the whistle and blew it to stop the game.

Manufacturers have developed whistles that vary in pitch and volume. Referees can confer so that they do not use the same type of whistle on adjacent pitches. And this makes it less likely that players will be distracted by a whistle in the crowd.

WHISTLE IN THE CROWD

During a match at Newcastle, goalkeeper Ray Middleton (Chesterfield) heard a whistle (September 1947). Thinking a free-kick had been given for offside, Middleton placed the ball and walked back. Jack Milburn (Newcastle) ran up and put the ball in the net, and the referee gave the goal.

A game at Highbury was into stoppage-time when a whistle was heard (December 1955). On hearing the sound, goalkeeper Sullivan (Arsenal) stooped into the net to collect his cap, his team-mate Dennis Evans (Arsenal) kicked the ball into his own net to celebrate his team's 4–0 win, and several players began to leave the field. But the referee signalled a goal – the whistle had been blown by a spectator. Arsenal beat Blackpool 4–1 instead.

A whistle-blower caused confusion during a Millwall–Kettering FA Cup tie (November 1964). Five minutes before the interval the referee warned that he would call off the match if the whistler continued. Later a youth was escorted from the terraces by a policeman. When similar incidents occurred at Luton (September 1966) and Stoke (October 1966), the referees reported the problem to police on the ground. Officers moved to the relevant area of the crowd.

A whistle in the crowd caused Len Bond (Bristol City) to hesitate, an incident which led to the first goal of a game Orient won 2–0 (February 1972), and referee Roger Kirkpatrick took Sheffield United and Manchester City players off the pitch for five minutes after interruptions from a renegade whistler (January 1975).

A dropped ball is the correct decision if the referee hears the rogue whistle and considers it outside interference (FIFA Referees' Committee, 1935). An off-the-pitch whistle caused Kuwait players to stop playing against France (June 1982). France attacked unchallenged and seemed to score a fourth goal, but after seven minutes of unruly scenes the referee disallowed the score and restarted play with a dropped ball. Kuwait were fined £6,000 by FIFA for their protests.

Tony Daley (Aston Villa) scored the first goal against Derby County after a whistle from the crowd had caused Derby defenders to hesitate (October 1986). Ten years later, goalkeeper Kevin Dearden (Brentford) heard a whistle, so he tossed the ball forward ready to take a free-kick. Marcus Browning (Bristol Rovers) came from behind him and tapped the ball into the net. A goal was given.

WIND *See* WEATHER

WOMEN FOOTBALLERS *See* MODIFICATIONS TO THE LAWS

WOMEN REFEREES

Female officials occasionally appeared in football's early days, but a shortage of referees led to the active recruitment of females after the 1975 Sex Discrimination Act. Pat Dunn became the first woman to referee a competitive men's match when she took a Dorset County Sunday League game (September 1976). Dunn had been refereeing women's games after passing her referee's examination in 1967.

Sonia Denoncourt (Canada) was the first female to be appointed as an international referee (in 1994), followed shortly afterwards by Linda Black (New Zealand). Denoncourt refereed top men's league matches in El Salvador (1996) and Brazil (1997). She also refereed the 2000 Olympic Games women's final and the 2003 FIFA Women's World Cup Final.

Gertrud Regus first ran the line in Germany's Bundesliga in 1993, Nicole Petignat (Switzerland) refereed a UEFA Cup tie between AJK Solna (Sweden) and Fylkir (Iceland) in August 2003, and Nelly Viennot was the assistant referee who spotted Matthew Elliott (Scotland) strike an opponent for a red card against the Faroe Islands (June 1999).

In the English full-time professional game, the pioneering woman referee was Wendy Toms, who was the fourth official at Bournemouth (March 1991) and ran the line at Torquay United (August 1994). In 1999, Wendy Toms and two female assistants officiated the Nationwide Conference match between Kidderminster Harriers and Nuneaton Borough. Toms also ran the line in the 2000 Worthington Cup Final between Leicester City and Tranmere Rovers.

More and more women referees came into the UK game – 1,100 in 2005 – and some won promotion. But there were still allegations of prejudice. In October 1995, Georgina Christoforou successfully won damages against the South East Counties League. Christoforou felt that the authorities had blocked her natural promotion to the league's list of assistant referees. An industrial tribunal agreed that she was being refused promotion because of her gender rather than her ability.

Albion Rovers manager Peter Hetherston was in trouble with authorities after being quoted in the *Sunday Sun* as saying that assistant referee Morag Pirie should 'be at home making the tea or dinner for her man who came in after he has been to the football' rather than raising her flag against his team at Montrose (November 2003). Pirie had already refereed in the Highland League.

WORLD GAME

Soccer is a world game with British roots. One of the sport's astonishing features is that it has reached so many people via a universal statement of rules. We can thank the administrators for this. As Rous and Ford say, in *A History of the Laws of Association Football*, the period immediately after World War II was spent scrutinising the laws so that they could be 'universally interpreted in a like manner under different conditions, in order to preserve the spirit of the game and of the laws'. In the 1982 FIFA World Cup™, there were 41 referees from 41 different countries.

Football has the power to heal wounds as well as open them. The players of North Korea and South Korea took the field holding hands when they met in a goalless friendly (September 2002), China played Japan in the 2004 Asian Cup Final, there was a Greek–Turkish clash between Anorthosis Famagusta (Cyprus) and Trabzonspor (Turkey) (July and August 2005), and East Germany and West Germany met in the 1974 FIFA World Cup™.

When Iran played USA, in June 1998, American president Bill Clinton greeted the game with a speech: 'The World Cup is beloved across our planet because it gives the chance for people from around the world to be judged not by the place they grew up, the colour of their skin or the way they choose to worship, but by their spirit, skill and strength. As we cheer today's game between American and Iranian athletes, I hope it will be another step towards ending the estrangement between our nations.'

Legal systems differ from society to society, but soccer's set of rules remain constant across societies. In *The Spirit of the Laws* (1748), Montesquieu wrote that laws should be so appropriate to a nation's people that it is very unlikely that the laws of one nation can suit another. Association football has proved Montesquieu wrong. Association football is a world game.

Yy

YELLOW CARDS *See* CARDS, CAUTION